Buddhism in Court

Buddhism in Court

Religion, Law, and Jurisdiction in China

CUILAN LIU

OXFORD
UNIVERSITY PRESS

OXFORD
UNIVERSITY PRESS

Oxford University Press is a department of the University of Oxford. It furthers the University's objective of excellence in research, scholarship, and education by publishing worldwide. Oxford is a registered trade mark of Oxford University Press in the UK and certain other countries.

Published in the United States of America by Oxford University Press
198 Madison Avenue, New York, NY 10016, United States of America.

Library of Congress Cataloging-in-Publication Data
Names: Liu, Cuilan, author.
Title: Buddhism in court : religion, law, and jurisdiction in China / Cuilan Liu.
Description: New York : Oxford University Press, 2024. |
Includes bibliographical references and index.
Identifiers: LCCN 2023056785 (print) | LCCN 2023056786 (ebook) |
ISBN 9780197663332 (hardback) | ISBN 9780197663356 (epub)
Subjects: LCSH: Buddhists—Legal status, laws, etc.—China. |
Buddhism and law—China. | Law—Buddhist influences.
Classification: LCC KNQ2688 .L58 2024 (print) | LCC KNQ2688 (ebook) |
DDC 342.5108/52943—dc23/eng/20231214
LC record available at https://lccn.loc.gov/2023056785
LC ebook record available at https://lccn.loc.gov/2023056786

DOI: 10.1093/oso/9780197663332.001.0001

Printed by Integrated Books International, United States of America

MIX
Paper
FSC FSC® C183721

For you, Tanya

Contents

Figures

Figures

Acknowledgments

It is not possible to complete a work of academic rigor without a lot of support. I have so many people to thank, particularly those who helped guide my research and shape my thoughts, ideas, and writing over the past several years. I thank Leonard W. J. van der Kuijp, my PhD advisor at Harvard University, for his rigorous academic training and unconditional support in all of my intellectual pursuits; he helped me become the researcher and writer I am today. I started working on this book after finishing my PhD in 2014, but its completion would not have been possible without Leonard's continued interest in and support of this project as a friend and colleague. I also want to thank him for having me and many of his students at his house on various holidays during my years at Harvard. I will never forget the many occasions when he drove one hour each way to pick us up from campus, bring us to his house, and then drop us off at home. There were many other teachers at Harvard who also influenced the way I research and write. I thank James Robson, Michael Witzel, Janet Gyatso, and Shigehisa Kuriyama for the many conversations we had on how to be attentive to textual details while maintaining a bird's-eye view of a book project as a whole.

Robin D. S. Yates, my supervisor during my Mellon Postdoctoral Fellowship at McGill University, inspired me to conceptualize the theme of this book. It was in his Chinese history graduate seminar where I decided to research the legal relationship between Buddhist religious law and Chinese state law examined in this book. I thank him for reading the many early drafts of various chapters. His comments as an expert on Chinese law were invaluable for improving this work.

The final version of this book significantly benefited from the expertise of Shayne Clarke, Carla Nappi, Teemu Ruskola, and Xin Wen at my book manuscript workshop in October 2022. I cannot thank them enough for reading through my manuscript page by page and spending a whole day asking questions and offering suggestions chapter by chapter. My longtime friend and colleague Shayne Clarke spent every minute during his stay at this workshop discussing and checking Buddhist monastic law texts with me, even during our meals. I thank my colleagues Clark Chilson and Kun Qian for generously moderating the workshop over the weekend. I also owe a debt to Thomas Mullaney for inspiring me to set up the manuscript workshop and offering advice on how to organize it.

The development of this book benefited from the many opportunities I had to share my research. I thank Phyllis Granoff for inviting me to give a lecture at

Yale in 2018; Wei Huo and Changhong Zhang for inviting me to give a lecture at the Institute for Tibetan Studies at Sichuan University in 2019; Jinhua Chen for inviting me to give a lecture for the International and Intensive Program on Buddhism and East Asian Religions at Mount Wutai, in China's Shanxi province, in 2019; Tsering Shakya and Jinhua Chen for inviting me to give a lecture for the Himalaya Program and the Tianzhu Network for the Study of Buddhist Cultures at the University of British Columbia, in 2019; Maria Doerfler and Travis Zadeh for inviting me to give a lecture in the 2020–2021 Archaia Ancient Societies Workshop lecture series at Yale; and Carmen Meinert and Lewis Doney for inviting me to give a lecture for the BuddhistRoad Project in January 2022. I thank Phyllis Granoff, Koichi Shinohara, Tsering Shakya, Jinhua Chen, Kate Crosby, Eric Greene, David Brick, Yudro Tsomo, Yanqing Zhang, and many others whose valuable questions and comments during these lectures helped me enhance the book.

In writing this book, I learned not to be shy about asking for help. I thank Huaiyu Chen, Jacob Dalton, Paul Groner, Ann Heirman, Mark McClish, Patrick Olivelle, Venerable Rongdao, Alexander von Rospatt, Benjamin Schonthal, Robert Sharf, Sasaki Shizuka, Vesna Wallace, and Venerable Xinchan for generously sharing their thoughts on my questions concerning Buddhist legal texts, Indian law, Chinese and Japanese legal texts, and Buddhist legal practices and traditions. This book's development also benefited from many conversations with Robert Barnett, Shuojun Chen, Lewis Doney, Brandon Dotson, Christoph Emmrich, Franz-Karl Ehrhard, Grace Fong, Rebecca R. French, Emanuela Garatti, Frances Garrett, Amanda Goodman, Jens-Uwe Hartman, Berthe Jansen, David Kamitsuka, Dukar Kyi, Christian Lammerts, Ina Luo, Petra Maurer, Michelle McCoy, Ruth Mostern, Mark Nathan, Ronald Po, Johanna Selles, Yangmo Tso, Leif E. Vaage, and Wanming Wang.

Many friends generously helped me at different stages in this book's journey. When I was preparing the book proposal in 2021, Nathan McGovern, Ruth Gamble, Asuka Sango, Yii-Jan Lin, Jack Mingda Tsai, and Harshita Mruthinti Kamath not only shared their wisdom as published authors but also read my book proposal and offered comments for revision. Over the years, my writing partners made the writing of this book much less isolating and much more enjoyable. Yii-Jan Lin and I met online weekly to report our writing progress, share our next writing goals, and offer each other intellectual and moral support during the last phases of our book writing marathons. My earlier days working on this book also benefited from meeting regularly for writing with Lang Chen and Claire Deng. I thank all of them for their company and friendship on this journey.

This book was built on access to primary materials. I thank Zhang Yuanlin and Sun Yue for assisting me in getting access to Mogao Cave 321 to examine the mural painting based on the *Ten Wheel Sūtra* during my research trip to the

Dunhuang Academy in June 2018. I thank Fumi Yao for sharing detailed critical comments on the story of the six-tusked elephant in the Sanskrit manuscript, while we were attending the Buddhism and Law conference at SUNY Buffalo in September 2019. I thank Macy Zhang, Haihui Zhang, Linda Tashbook, and Kelsang Lhamo for assisting me in obtaining the legal texts and case documents in Chinese, Tibetan, and English that were crucial for writing this book. I also want to thank two lawyers, Sanjeev Malhotra for sharing the writ petition for the Ayodhyā case that is discussed in Chapter 1 and Sun Shuning for sharing information on a lawsuit over the estate of a deceased monk, which is discussed in Chapter 7.

I am indebted to many professionals working in the publishing industry. I am grateful to my acquisition editor Cynthia Read for her confidence and enthusiasm in this book as this secured my contract with Oxford University Press (OUP) after the peer reviews. After her retirement, I was blessed to work with Theodore Calderara and Egle Zigaite for completing the full manuscript for production. Over the years, the editorial skills of James Thomas and Glenna Jenkins significantly enhanced the final presentation of this book. I thank Thomas Jacobi for his meticulous copyediting, and Cynthia Col for a wonderful job on creating the index. I thank OUP's anonymous reviewers, whose comments and suggestions helped me improve the book. Chapters 5 and 6 were revised from two articles I previously published in the *Journal of Chinese Religions* and the *Journal of Law and Religion*. I thank the journals and the publishers for their permission to reuse those materials in this book.

My research for this book was made possible through generous institutional support from Ludwig Maximilian University (LMU); McGill University; Emmanuel College at Victoria University (Toronto); and the University of Pittsburgh. Two postdoctoral fellowships at LMU and McGill helped me structure the project in its early stage. I thank Robin D. S. Yates and Brandon Dotson for their supervision during my postdoctoral fellowships. The Spooner Travel Grant from Victoria University and faculty research grants from Emmanuel College allowed me to conduct extensive research on the Chinese legal materials I sourced for this book. At the University of Pittsburgh, I received generous administrative and financial support from the Asian Studies Center (Evelyn and Thomas Rawski Faculty Research Grant), the Office of the Provost (The Pitt Arts and Humanities Microgrant), the Dietrich School of Arts and Sciences (Summer Term Research Stipend), and the Department of Religious Studies (research funds and fund for my manuscript workshop). I thank Provost Ann E. Cudd; Dean Kathleen Blee; Associate Dean Adam Leibovich; former Associate Dean Holger Hoock; my department chair, Adam Shear; director, Joseph Alter, and associate director, James Cook, at the Asian Studies Center for supporting my research and teaching at the University of Pittsburgh. My thanks also go to my wonderful colleagues Brock Bahler, Clark Chilson, Margarita Delgado Creamer, Haya Feig, Benjamin Davis Gordon, Daniel Heifetz, Paula M. Kane, Rachel Kranson, Hilla Nehushtan, and Marcela Perdomo for having made the twenty-sixth floor of the Cathedral of Learning a delightful place to be every day over the past four years. I look forward to all the years to come.

As a first-generation college student and university professor, I owe every bit of what I have achieved today to my mother, Nengzhi Zhang, and my father, Guoxiang Liu. My mother always fought for the impossible. She inspired me to reach for the unreachable, aiming higher. If time could be turned back, I would wish to have finished this book sooner so that I could have shared the joy of its publication with Mkhan po Grags pa 'od zer at So thob Monastery, Jing Wang, Judy Gay, and John Gay, before their departures from this world. I am sure they knew how grateful I was. I still am.

Abbreviations

T.	Takakusu Junjirō 高楠順次郎, and Watanabe Kaigyoku 渡邊海旭, eds. *Taishō shinshūdaizōkyō* 大正新修大藏經. 100 vols. Tokyo: Taishō issaikyō kankōkai 大正一切經刊行會, 1924–1932.
X.	Kawamura Kōshō 河村孝照, Nishi Yoshio 西義雄, Temaki Kōshirō 玉城康四郎, eds. *Shinsan Dai Nihon zoku Zōkyō* 卍新纂大日本續藏經. 90 vols. Tōkyō: Kokusho Kankōkai, 1975–1989.
Bka' 'gyur.	Dpe bsdur ma. 109 vol. Pe cin: Krung go'i bod rig pa'i dpe skrun khang, 2006–2009.
Bstan 'gyur.	Dpe bsdur ma. 120 vol. Pe cin: Krung go'i bod rig pa'i dpe skrun khang, 1994–2008.

Conventions

To make this book useful to scholars from other areas, I use English translations for Sanskrit, Pāli, Chinese, and Tibetan terms and text titles from primary sources. For instance, I use "offense of defeat" to refer to the category of offenses known as *pārājika* in Sanskrit in the Buddhist monastic law texts. In the endnotes, I occasionally cite the original spellings of some non-English terms for scholars who are interested in checking the primary sources.

Unless noted otherwise, I adopt Charles O. Hucker's translations for names of administrative units, offices, and official titles in premodern China. I also capitalize and not italicize the Chinese official titles and units. For instance, the Minister of Works (Sikong gong 司空公) and the Office for Overseeing Meritorious Works (Jianfu cao 監福曹).

I use the terms "defrock" and "disrobe" to distinguish carefully between two different situations. I use "defrock" to refer to the act of forcing an ordained Buddhist monk or nun to leave monastic life, as a punishment for committing an offense. I use "disrobe" to refer to a monk or nun voluntarily choosing to leave the monastic community, without having committed any offenses. I also translate different types of Chinese legal documents as code (*lü* 律), statute (*ling* 令), regulation (*ge* 格), ordinance (*shi* 式).

For romanization, I adopt Pinyin for Chinese and Wylie for Tibetan. For consistency, I use traditional Chinese characters for the Chinese terms, including those appearing in contemporary Chinese sources as simplified Chinese characters. I also italicize all titles of legal texts and laws in imperial and contemporary China. For instance, the *Law of Succession*, the *Statutes of the Tang*. I abbreviate Sanskrit as "Skt.," Pāli as "P.," Chinese as "Ch.," and Tibetan as "Tib.".

For dates in the Chinese texts, I use the Gregorian calendar to cite contemporary dates in modern and contemporary Chinese sources—for instance, "August 1, 2018." When citing premodern Chinese texts, I preserve the original Chinese dating system—for instance, "the second day of the fourth month of the fourteenth year of the Hongwu era (1381)."

When citing the Taishō canon, I provide the Taishō number, followed by the page, section (a, b, c), and line numbers. For instance, T1442: 630c11. When citing the Tibetan Buddhist canon, I provide the volume and page number of the modern printing of the Dpe bsdur ma versions of the Tibetan *Bka' 'gyur* and *Bstan 'gyur*.

Introduction

> I became a monk after I killed someone.[1]
>
> Lu Da, *The Water Margin*

One of the most beloved Buddhists in China was the fictional fourteenth-century murderer Lu Da 魯達, who avoided criminal prosecution by becoming an ordained Buddhist monk. The killing occurred accidentally when Lu sought justice for Jin Cuilian, a woman who was forced to be a concubine of a local butcher. This butcher, who already had a wife, had gone to Jin's father and offered a bride price in exchange for his daughter. He then took Jin home as his concubine, but he refused to pay her father. Jin lived in the butcher's house for some time. However, for some unknown reason, the butcher's senior wife expelled Jin from their home. The butcher then visited her father again, demanding that he return the bride price—which had never even been paid—and threatening to harm him if he failed to give the money. When this came to Lu Da's attention, he immediately arranged for Jin and her father to leave town safely. But when he went to discipline the butcher, Lu accidentally killed him.

While fleeing, Lu ran into Jin and her father in another town, where she had become the lover of a wealthy local man. The affluent man had previously purchased a blank ordination certificate (*dudie* 度牒) and had pledged to send a candidate to be ordained as a Buddhist monk on his behalf. In premodern China, legal ordination was impossible without such a certificate. The ordination certificate now enabled this man to protect Lu in return for having saved his lover, Jin. With the certificate, as well as some other gifts from the wealthy man, Lu went to the monastery known as the Mañjuśrī Temple on nearby Mount Wutai, where he was ordained as a Buddhist monk and acquired his religious name Zhishen 智深, meaning "profound wisdom." While staying at the monastery, Lu committed a series of misdeeds and was eventually asked to leave. Over the next few decades, he lived an outlaw's life but nevertheless died an accomplished Buddhist master. In this nineteenth-century Japanese portrait of him below (see Figure I.1), Lu appears with tattoos covering his entire body.

This fourteenth-century murderer-monk story is recounted in the classical Chinese novel *The Water Margin* (*Shuihu zhuan* 水滸傳). For centuries, this story has continued to nourish the Chinese imagination, in which Buddhist

Buddhism in Court. Cuilan Liu, Oxford University Press. © Oxford University Press 2024.
DOI: 10.1093/oso/9780197663332.003.0001

Fig. I.1 Utagawa Yoshiharu 歌川芳春 (1828–1888), *Tattooed Priest* (*Kaoshō Rochishin*), 1856, woodblock print, ink, and color on paper, accession number 00.1342, © Museum of Fine Arts, Boston

monasteries are perceived as sanctuaries for sheltering fugitives from state law.[2] Thus, in the popular mind, becoming an ordained Buddhist has long been seen as an automatic guarantee for offenders to be exempt from criminal prosecution. This notion is representative of a sustained Buddhist longing for multiple clerical legal privileges: clerical immunity from trials in the state court, clerical immunity from punishment, or reductions in punishment. Is this perception of clerical legal privileges an original Chinese invention? If not, where did it originate? In what cultural context did the idea of clerical legal privileges emerge? And why is the circulation and reception of this idea in Chinese Buddhism important to understand?

To address these questions, this book investigates the transnational interplay of Buddhist legal ideas between India and China, the ongoing negotiations over the jurisdictional boundary between religion and the state in China from the fourth century to the present, and the transplantation of the negotiated results, from theory to practice, in the operation of law in China over the same period. In situating this investigation in the context of China, this book accentuates Chinese Buddhists' engagement with these negotiations. It highlights the innovation involved in breaking the state-versus-monastic-court dichotomy and in reimagining a tripartite legal infrastructure by inserting a hybrid court as a buffer between the state and the Buddhist establishment. In China, this hybrid court was more than an abstract concept employed in theoretical negotiations of the jurisdictional boundary between the state and the Buddhist establishment. Indeed, the hybrid court has continued to play a role in the handling of clerical offenses in contemporary China.[3] By demonstrating this, this book uncovers Buddhists as active participants in Asia's legal universe. It thus illuminates the urgency of correcting the legal Orientalist view that lawlessness prevails in Buddhism and in China.

Sanctuary and Clerical Immunity

Demarcating jurisdictional boundaries has long been a central theme in legal negotiations between religion and the state around the globe. For centuries, religious and state leaders have attempted to draw intangible lines through debates over one concrete question: who has jurisdiction over clerical offenders? Those debates traveled along winding roads, resulting in arrangements that either expanded, restricted, or revoked the religious establishment's jurisdiction over its clerical members. To illustrate the Buddhist journey along those roads, I must borrow two well-established Christian terms: sanctuary and clerical immunity. Scholars have studied how the operation of these two institutions shaped the battle between the Christian church and the state over legal jurisdiction regarding clerics and religious. Similar practices also exist in Buddhism, a religion with an estimated 480 million plus adherents worldwide, or 7 percent of the world's population,[4] but these practices in Buddhism have hitherto rarely been discussed. In the subsequent chapters, I will apply these two terms to analyze parallel issues in Buddhism. In so doing, however, I am not suggesting that Christians and Buddhists had exchanges over the establishment and operation of these two institutions. Instead, I am using the vocabulary of these established frameworks from Christian contexts to unpack the Buddhist fight over clerical jurisdiction.

As early as the fourth century, Christian leaders regularly fought to adjust the jurisdictional boundary between church and state through these two institutions: sanctuary and clerical immunity. The institution of sanctuary recognizes certain Christian churches as safe places for fugitives, where law enforcement officials cannot execute the legal process.[5] As John H. Baker explains, the underlying theory is that "consecrated places should not be profaned by the use of force."[6] Baker also points out that, in practice, sanctuary Christian churches became safe havens for outlaws, where they could enjoy temporary immunity from criminal prosecution for up to forty days, after which the church would force them to choose between going to trial in the king's court or forfeiting their property and being exiled.

The institution of religious sanctuary had a broad and lasting impact on the relationship between church and state in Europe and North America. It emerged in the Roman Empire as early as the fourth century. Around 344 CE, the Roman emperors Constans I (c. 320–350; reign 333–350) and Constantius II (317–361; reign 337–361) convened a Catholic church council in Sardica (located in what is now Bulgaria),[7] where they recognized Christian churches as sanctuaries. In 392, Theodosius I (347–395; reign 379–395), another Roman emperor, codified the Christian church's sanctuary status in what later became known as the *Theodosian Code* (*Codex Theodosianus*).[8] By the end of the sixth century, church sanctuary also received legal recognition in England. In 597, in a legal code that was promulgated that year, King Ethelbert of Kent (c. 560–616) recognized authorized churches as having the authority to function as sanctuaries.[9] As a legal institution, church sanctuary in England came to an end in the seventeenth century, when the British Parliament abolished it in 1624; however, some churches continued to serve as sanctuaries into the late nineteenth century.[10] In the United States, activists and church leaders found new ways to reactivate the institution of sanctuary in the 1980s, when many immigrants faced legal action. This renewed interest in church sanctuaries in the United States began on March 24, 1982, when five churches in California and one in Arizona declared themselves sanctuaries in order to offer shelter to Central Americans threatened with deportation.[11]

The physical boundary of the church sanctuary expanded over time. Initially, sanctuary was limited to the interior of the church. Around 450 CE, the Roman emperor Theodosius II (401–450) enlarged the bounds of the sanctuary to cover "churchyard walls or precincts, including the bishop's house, cloisters, and cemeteries."[12] To claim sanctuary, a fugitive must physically reach the boundary of the recognized church by passing over its boundary markers (such as the stone markers located at Saint John of Beverley Church in Yorkshire, England) or by knocking on the church door (for example, with the sanctuary ring on the western side of the Notre-Dame Cathedral in Paris).

While church sanctuaries offered protection to lay Christians, ordained Christian ministers, and vowed Christian monks and nuns, they historically tended to shutter their doors to adherents of other religions and offenders of certain crimes. In the Roman Empire during the fourth century, "debtors, embezzlers of state funds, Jews, heretics, and apostates" were all excluded from the protection of the church sanctuaries.[13] At the beginning of the sixth century CE, in Constantinople, the Eastern Roman emperor Justinian I (482–565; reign 527–565) declared in the *Code of Justinian* that "public debtors, tax officials, murderers, rapists, and adulterers" were ineligible for protection under church sanctuary.[14] In England, King Henry VII (1457–1509; reign 1485–1509) and King Henry VIII (1491–1547; reign 1509–1547) decided to limit sanctuary operations. In 1530, fugitives no longer had the choice of exile (abjuration of the realm) but had to remain in the sanctuary until death. In 1534, traitors lost access to church sanctuary.[15] In 1540, felons lost access to church sanctuary.[16]

The second important institution, clerical immunity, exempted individual clerical offenders from prosecution and trial in the king's court but required them to stand trial in the ecclesiastical court.[17] In the Roman Empire, this practice dates to the fourth century. It was also relevant in England and, later, in America. In 314 CE, Emperor Constantine the Great (c. 272–337; reign 306–337) convened a meeting at Arles, in present-day southern France, which was attended by representatives of Christian bishops. At this meeting, Constantine recognized the legal right of Christian clergymen to be tried in a bishop's court rather than the king's court.[18] In England, the practice of clerical immunity reached the apex of its influence in the twelfth century. Thomas Becket (c. 1118–1170), the archbishop of Canterbury, repeatedly confronted King Henry II (1133–1189; reign 1154–1189) over the jurisdictional boundary between the church and state. The king claimed state jurisdiction over clerical crimes, while the archbishop insisted that clerics be prosecuted in the ecclesiastic court.[19] This battle over clerical immunity from secular jurisdiction challenged the existing tradition of allowing a clerical offender to be tried in the church court and then be punished in the king's court. This battle ended with Becket's assassination in 1170, which advanced the king's official recognition of the "benefit of clergy,"[20] a privilege that allowed clerical offenders to claim exemption from the jurisdiction of the king's court and, instead, request a trial in the ecclesiastic court. In a letter to Pope Alexander III (c. 1100–1181), dated in late 1175 or early 1176, King Henry II officially exempted Christian clerics facing criminal charges from being tried in the king's court.[21] The exemption known as the benefit of clergy underwent many reforms but remained in effect in the English legal system until 1827, when it was abolished by the *Criminal Law Act*.[22] In the seventeenth century, the benefit of clergy reached America, a destination of exile for English criminals who claimed this privilege.[23] By the early nineteenth century, most states in the US had abolished the benefit of clergy, with some exceptions, such as South Carolina, where it remained until 1869.[24]

Christians were neither the first nor the only ones who struggled over jurisdictional boundaries with the state. Centuries before the Arles meeting of 344 CE, Buddhists in ancient India were already carrying out a campaign calling for institutional and individual legal privileges. Here, I use the word "campaign" figuratively to describe the continuing Buddhist efforts to promote the idea that ordained Buddhist criminals should be treated differently from lay criminals for committing the same crimes. As I demonstrate in the subsequent chapters, these efforts range from presenting stories of Buddhist institutions acting as sanctuaries for lay fugitives in Buddhist monastic law texts, to tales of ordained Buddhist criminals receiving legal leniency in the Buddhist monastic law texts;[25] to discussions of the need to exempt ordained Buddhists, even those who had committed the most heinous crimes, from physical punishments in the Buddhist nonlegal texts;[26] to artists commissioned to paint murals in the Dunhuang caves, depicting stories in which even the wildest animal would avoid harming malicious hunters disguised as monks;[27] to eminent monks petitioning Chinese emperors to exempt ordained Buddhists from trial and torture in the state court.[28] Unlike what we see in a contemporary political campaign where an organized team plans and executes a series of connected events, this Buddhist campaign leaves traces of consistent but scattered efforts from Buddhists over a span of two millennia, across national boundaries and a variety of media.

In Indian Buddhism, fighting for these legal privileges was important due to Buddhists' deep suspicions over the trustworthiness of the state's legal system. In ancient India, religious practitioners often perceived court judges as easily corruptible. This perception cultivated a collective panic among Buddhists and Jains who feared being mistreated in the state court should they face litigation. Another source of this alarm was what Phyllis Granoff described as "a fear of inciting public disapproval," since many worried this would diminish the extent of the active support Buddhist monastics could expect from the lay community.[29] In Buddhism, this fear transformed into formal monastic rules trying to dissuade and prohibit ordained Buddhists from engaging with the state court either as plaintiffs or defendants.

In essence, Indian Buddhism operated under the assumption that its monastic members were under the jurisdiction of the state, as attested by the fact that there were rules in Buddhist monastic law requiring all the ordained to comply with the orders of state court judges. At the time, Indian Buddhists did not prioritize jurisdictional control over ordained Buddhists. Instead, they focused on seeking immunity for ordained Buddhist convicts who had committed crimes either before or after their ordination. To translate this into the established Christian vocabulary, the goals of this Buddhist campaign corresponded to the institutions of sanctuary and clerical immunity. The practice of ceasing to prosecute a fugitive who had joined a monastic order in the Buddhist context was identical to the practice of sheltering fugitives in church sanctuaries in the Christian context. This practice was also similar to the Christian institution of clerical immunity, which offered clerical offenders immunity from trial and punishment in the state court.

In China, however, Buddhists significantly adjusted the goals of their pursuit for clerical legal privileges. Buddhism reached China during the first century CE. By the fifth century, Chinese Buddhists had access to Chinese translations of complete sets of Indic Buddhist legal texts from the four major traditions of Mahāsāṃghika, Dharmaguptaka, Mahīśāsaka, and Sarvāstivāda and, at the beginning of the eighth century, from translations of the fifth tradition, Mūlasarvāstivāda. Unlike their Indian predecessors, who had perceived themselves as being under the jurisdiction of state court, Chinese Buddhists sought to expand the Buddhist establishment's jurisdiction. From as early as the fourth century, they pursued this goal through two divergent approaches in Chinese Buddhism, marking a significant strategic shift in what Buddhists prioritized and how they negotiated their jurisdictional boundary with the state. Through these two approaches, Buddhists in China fought for the Buddhist establishment's limited jurisdictional autonomy over its ordained members.

The first approach was to create a hybrid court to break the monastic-state dichotomy—an unprecedented approach to negotiating the jurisdictional boundary between Buddhism and the state. In this book, a hybrid court refers to a judicial office that was physically located within the state government. I refer to this office as a hybrid court because it followed a set of hybrid laws that had been established by consolidating the relevant rules from both state and Buddhist monastic law. In fourth-century China, the state and Buddhist establishments were equally aggressive in claiming jurisdiction over monastics who had broken state law. In practice, they contested, in vain, over whether to try ordained Buddhist offenders in the state court as lay people or in the monastic court. Eventually, they collaborated in creating a hybrid court to avoid making decisions over the trial venue.

In China, from the fourth century to the present, this hybrid court has had a lasting impact on Buddhism's legal relationship with the state. Initially, this court was primarily responsible for overseeing religious affairs, focusing on ordained Buddhists and Daoists. The earliest record of this judicial office dates to 396, but this judicial office was not named a hybrid court. Its first official name was the Office for Overseeing Meritorious Works (Jianfu cao 鑒福曹), and it successively changed to the Office for the Illumination of Mysteries (Zhaoxuan cao 昭玄曹), then to the Bureau for the Veneration of Mysteries (Chongxuan shu 崇玄署), and so on. As I will show in Chapters 6 and 7, even in the post-1949 People's Republic of China, when no office existed under any of these names, two new offices (the Buddhist Association of China and the State Administration of Religious Affairs) continued to function as third-party hybrid judicial offices to deal with cases of monastic offenders who could not immediately be handled internally within the Buddhist institution or prosecuted publicly in the state court.

If the creation of the hybrid court theoretically avoided jurisdictional conflicts, the second approach—which aimed to differentiate monastic offenses into categories of criminal or civil, light or heavy, internal or external—made this avoidance practical and feasible. The category of a monastic offender's case determined whether it was tried in the state, monastic, or hybrid court. In general, the state court assumed jurisdiction over criminal offenses. Among the remaining civil disputes, the state court also assumed jurisdiction over serious offenses (for example, certain felonies). Among light civil disputes, the state court could assume further jurisdiction over external cases involving litigants outside of the Buddhist monastic community. While the state still had the lion's share of jurisdiction over clerical offenses, the Buddhist establishment in China succeeded in gaining limited jurisdictional autonomy and shared control over the hybrid court. Through these achievements in imperial China, Chinese Buddhists significantly transformed the earlier campaign in Indian Buddhism, which acknowledged the state's jurisdiction over ordained Buddhists and focused on protection, into one that sought to secure greater jurisdictional autonomy over clerics in China.

Buddhism and Law

Scholarship on Buddhism and law revolved around three central questions: what is Buddhist law, how does Buddhism influence the state's legal culture, and how do state laws regulate Buddhist practice? This field has seen significant advancement over the past few decades. In 1995, Frank Reynolds highlighted the study of Buddhism and Buddhist law when he edited a special "Buddhism and Law" issue of the *Journal of the International Association of Buddhist Studies*. Over subsequent decades, scholars in this field published edited volumes, founded an academic journal, and organized multiple workshops to promote the study of Buddhism and law.[30]

Scholarly writings on Buddhism and law predate 1995, however. Research on Buddhist law by historians, anthropologists, and religious studies scholars has burgeoned over the past century. Based on their different disciplinary orientations, scholars prioritized a variety of research agendas, ranging from Buddhist monastic law itself, to its impact on our understanding of monastic life in early Buddhism, to the influence of Buddhist ideas on legal thought in countries other than India, to the regulation of Buddhism by state law. In recent years, scholars in the field have become increasingly interested in how Buddhist law and laws related to Buddhism operate in legal practice.

The earlier research focused on making the Buddhist monastic law texts (Skt. *vinaya*) accessible through translation, to overcome linguistic barriers. The Buddhist monastic law texts, containing disciplinary rules for ordained Buddhist practitioners, are the primary source for understanding the legal world of the Buddhists, but they are primarily preserved in Sanskrit, Pāli, Chinese, and Tibetan, making them less accessible to most scholars in the broader field of law and religion and those working on other aspects of Buddhism. Early scholars concentrated on editing and translating these texts. This led to the publication of facsimile editions of the Sanskrit version of the *Mūlasarvāstivāda Vinaya* manuscripts, which were excavated from Gilgit, Pakistan, in 1931, and were recently published in a high-resolution edition that includes color images.[31] This effort also produced edited volumes and English translations of the *Pāli Vinaya*. The first edition came from Hermann Oldenberg (1854–1920),[32] which Isaline Blew Horner (1896–1981) later had translated into English.[33] Over the past a few decades, many scholars have translated and analyzed other Buddhist monastic law texts preserved in Sanskrit, Chinese, and Tibetan.[34] In 2009, efforts in this area saw a particular revival following the launch of the 84000 initiative, where scholars were recruited and funded to translate Buddhist monastic law texts from Tibetan into English and Chinese.

These monastic law texts have also attracted scholars who are interested in understanding monastic life in early Indian Buddhism. Publications in this area significantly overturn popular perceptions about early Buddhist monastic life, offering archaeological, historical, and textual evidence that suggests a completely different image of the lives, or the ideals, of ordained Buddhist monks and nuns in ancient India.[35]

Newcomers to this field have turned their attention in a new direction: how Buddhist law and state law related to Buddhism operated in legal practice. One driving force behind this shift was an urgent need to overcome the existential crisis of Buddhism and law as a research subject. Just as Teemu Ruskola laments, in his book *Legal Orientalism,* how he needs to defend Chinese law, the subject of his study,[36] Rebecca R. French also deplores the lack of recognition of Buddhism as a legitimate subject of study in the field of law and religion, where she notes that Buddhism "will perhaps seem weak" due to its lack of a "divine revelation, a law code that applies to an entire society, [and] a centralized body for enforcement."[37]

Disciplinary Engagement

Tracking the Buddhist pursuit of clerical legal privileges in China engages longstanding dialogues in three fields: law and religion, Buddhist studies, and China studies. My decision to focus on the interaction between Buddhist religious law and state law is largely indebted to studies of law and religion, particularly works on the institutions of sanctuary churches and the benefit of clergy. In the early stages of this book project, when I was reading the classical Chinese novel the *Water Margin* and trying to make sense of the fantasy of becoming a Buddhist monk to avoid prosecution, I stumbled upon Leona Christine Gabel's 1969 book *Benefit of Clergy in England in the Later Middle Ages*. This book provided the vocabulary to articulate the Buddhist manifestation of clerical legal privileges, which had not yet been discussed in existing scholarship on Buddhism and law, Buddhist studies, or Asian studies. It led me to read about individual and institutional legal privileges that manifested as clerical immunity and sanctuary churches. These encounters with scholarship on law and religion inspired me to consider more nuanced questions for my book: How did the Buddhist pursuit of clerical legal privileges affect the jurisdictional boundary between religion and the state in China? How did that boundary shift over time in history? And to what extent was that boundary respected in the operation of state law?

Regarding the field of law and religion, this book, in turn, fills an important gap in understanding how religion and law interact outside Abrahamic religious traditions. Over the three decades since the study of law "recombined with the study of religion" in the US, in the 1980s and 1990s, American scholarship on law and religion has concentrated around ten themes.[38] As John Witte notes in his 2012 interim report "The Study of Law and Religion in the United States," law and religion intertwine across these diverse themes, ranging from legal aspects of religious freedom, human rights, and family life, to religious law's place in society, to the influence of religious ideas on lay legal culture, natural law, legal ethics, and legal professionals.[39] This rich body of scholarship is disproportionately represented by works on Christianity and, more recently, on Judaism and Islam. The Buddhist perspective has been seriously underrepresented.

This situation has improved significantly since 2012. *Buddhism in Court* will be the newest addition to a body of burgeoning work representing Buddhist perspectives. It offers an East Asian sample, showing the significant regional differences in how Buddhism and the state interact in the legal arena in Asia. In this, it maintains a dialogue with scholars working on Buddhism and law and supplements recent contributions to the literature on this subject as it relates to Southeast and Central Asia.[40] A major difference between East and Southeast Asia is that Southeast Asian Buddhists—as revealed in the work on Myanmar (formerly known as Burma until 1989), Thailand, and Sri Lanka—focused on the development of a full-fledged monastic court with monk judges, whereas Buddhists in China focused on collaborating with the state to form a tripartite legal infrastructure that included state, hybrid, and monastic courts.[41]

This book will engage scholars in Buddhist studies by challenging the conventional understanding of how an India-centric obsession with "scriptural authenticity" dominated Chinese Buddhism. This is exemplified in Jan Nattier's analysis of how Chinese Buddhists onerously fabricated the Sanskrit version of the *Heart Sūtra* to make it a genuine Buddhist text with an Indian origin.[42] *Buddhism in Court* breaks this convention by revealing that Buddhists in China were not limited to mimicking Indian ideas and practices. In the battle over the jurisdictional boundary with the state, Buddhists in China took the jurisdictional privileges found in Indian Buddhism as aspirations, but they also reimagined these ideas based on what privileges were achievable in the Chinese context. This study is in conversation, too, with earlier scholarly writings that debated whether Indian Buddhism conquered China or whether China Sinicized Indian Buddhism. Erik Zürcher brings this debate under the spotlight in his 1959 book *The Buddhist Conquest of China*. When discussing Chinese reactions to the introduction of Buddhism as an imported foreign religion, Zürcher argues that Buddhists in China were able to culturally transplant Indic Buddhist ideas into the Chinese context without influencing the "official" Chinese worldview.[43] This book offers the latest attestation of this Chinese talent for transplanting legal ideas from Indian Buddhism.

Buddhism in Court is thematically and methodologically distinct from existing Chinese-language books on Buddhism and law. Thematically, the books on this topic in Chinese focus on explaining how Buddhist thought affected the development of the legal culture in East Asia and the state's administration of Buddhism.[44] *Buddhism in Court* focuses instead on the dynamic interaction between the state and Buddhist monastic legal worlds. Methodologically, *Buddhism in Court* departs from the convention of confining an analysis of the relationship between Buddhism and law to a single dynasty. Existing works on Buddhism, law, and China largely follow the dominant trend of treating imperial and postimperial China as mutually exclusive. Except for general histories of China, works on imperial China focus almost entirely on single dynasties and do not extend beyond 1911, and works on modern and contemporary China uniformly address post-1911 or post-1949 China and are less likely to make connections with the imperial period. While promoting detailed examinations of historical issues, this convention perpetuates the idea of a supposed rupture between imperial and postimperial China—a rupture that is taken to be so insurmountable that the scholarship on China remains arbitrarily compartmentalized into imperial (before 1911), republican (1911–1949), and communist (post-1949) China. Inspired by the French historian Fernand Braudel's *longue durée* approach, studying a subject over a long duration, *Buddhism in Court* breaks through this compartmentalization by examining selected layers of the legal interaction between Buddhism and the state at different times over the last seventeen centuries. Exploring the past relationship between religion and law in imperial China will also enhance our understanding of its presence in modern and contemporary China. Along this line, *Buddhism in Court* illustrates how dynasty-centered approaches to the study of religion and law in China amplify the ruptures and obscure the lasting continuities that have endured in the transition from imperial to postimperial China and into the present.

Primary Texts and Textual Interpretation

Diverse primary sources, spanning several languages and genres over a millennium and a half, inform the research behind this book. To trace the origin of the Chinese pursuit of clerical legal privileges, we must unpack how Buddhists imagined their legal place in a lay society within Indian Buddhism. I rely on extant Buddhist monastic law texts that were transmitted from six traditions—the Mahāsāṃghika, Sarvāstivāda, Dharmaguptaka, Mahīśāsaka, Mūlasarvāstivāda, and Theravāda—and are now preserved in Sanskrit, Pāli, Chinese, and Tibetan. Unless otherwise specified, I use my own translations and interpretations of the Chinese and Tibetan materials and consult existing English translations of the Sanskrit and Pāli materials referenced. When working with these texts, I do not treat them as reflections of historical reality (what Buddhists did or experienced in ancient India) but, instead, focus on the legal cases they present and what they tell us about the legal privileges Buddhists might have longed for.

These Buddhist monastic law texts are the primary sources for the first four chapters, and I regularly cite them in the rest of the book. To understand these ancient Indian works, some consideration of the dating and nature of such Buddhist monastic law texts is required. Dating these Buddhist works is a challenge. The rules codified in these legal texts are traditionally attributed to the historical Buddha himself, who lived around the sixth and fifth centuries BCE. The present scholarly consensus holds that the body of the Buddhist monastic law literature we have today, in its different traditions, was first transmitted orally. Later, members of the Buddhist community established and compiled these legal materials collectively over hundreds of years. However, the oldest surviving primary Buddhist monastic law texts are two fragmentary manuscripts that were written in the Kharoṣṭhī script and date from the first and second centuries CE, while the earliest Pāli manuscripts were composed much later, in the eighth to ninth centuries CE.[45] These dating challenges make it difficult to pinpoint the exact time of the formation of these legal ideas in Indian Buddhism. This, in turn, prevents us from contextualizing the development of Buddhist ideas on clerical legal privileges within a specific social milieu to understand their formation, contemporary influences, and reception in the Indian society of the time. As such, my analysis of the Indian origins of the Chinese pursuit of clerical legal privileges builds on records of these legal ideas reflected in the Chinese translations of Buddhist monastic law text that had began circulating in China at the beginning of the fifth century, whereas their initial formation in India may date to a much earlier period.

It is also important to note that the cases in these Buddhist monastic law texts may not reflect how ordained Buddhists actually interacted with the state in India's legal arena. They nevertheless reveal an ideal of such interactions as perceived by the redactors of the Buddhist monastic law texts. Through translations of such Buddhist monastic law texts, that ideal subsequently traveled to East and Central Asia.

The nature of these primary sources thus presents two restraints in the writing of this book. First, difficulties in dating the Buddhist monastic law texts make it challenging to ascertain the exact time of the formation of this Buddhist fight for clerical legal privileges. Second, a fruitful future research direction that I have excluded from this book, due to its focus on China, would be to investigate the state's response to the Buddhist pursuit of clerical legal privileges in early India. Pursuing this direction requires access to textual, visual, and archaeological materials that illustrate the state's reaction or lack of reaction to these Buddhist legal ideas in early India.

Analyzing Chinese Buddhists' responses to Indian legal ideas led me to a wide variety of additional indigenous Chinese sources. They range from official histories, biographies, and religious accounts to law codes, religious communities' bylaws, and court documents. To understand how agreed-upon legal policies were respected in legal practice, I focus on cases involving ordained Buddhists in postimperial China, because these more recent cases often leave written materials that allow me to discuss the responses of the state legal system.[46]

To that end, I chose to study two types of cases: one concerning jurisprudential conflicts over the property of deceased Buddhists, dating between 1984 to 2020, and the other concerning the treatment of an ordained Buddhist who had been accused of sexual, financial, or administrative offenses in China in 2018. These cases led me to examine more recent judicial opinions, court communications, legislative decisions, administrative announcements, news reports, and unofficial documents that have circulated publicly on social media.

The Buddhist Legal World

To understand how Buddhists fought for clerical legal privileges, we must understand how Buddhists constructed their legal world. What kind of rules did they establish for monks and nuns? How did they establish them? When a violation was reported, what legal procedures did they follow to investigate, adjudicate, convict, and recommend punishment?

Buddhists constructed their legal world using cases. When introducing a rule, the Buddhist monastic law texts often cited a case that led to the Buddha establishing a rule to prohibit monks and nuns from committing the same offense in the future.[47] In general, one case was considered sufficient to make a rule. It was also common to form a preliminary rule, then introduce additional cases to amend the earlier rule, and then eventually present the final version of the rule. On rare occasions, a Buddhist monastic law text could introduce several cases before arranging for the Buddha to establish a rule.[48] After the final version of the rule was introduced, the text provided a word-by-word explanation of the terms in that rule. Finally, some texts included examples of how the Buddha would adjudicate certain cases where a rule was broken after it had already been put in place.[49]

Navigating the Buddhist legal world is a different experience for Buddhists who are at different levels of their training. The Buddhist monastic law texts contain rules primarily for ordained Buddhists, including novice monks (Skt. *śrāmaṇera*; Tib. *dge tshul*; Ch. *shami* 沙彌), novice nuns (Skt. *śrāmaṇerikā*; Tib. *dge tsul ma*; Ch. *shami ni* 沙彌尼), probationary nuns (Skt. *śikṣamāṇā*; Tib. *dge slob ma*; Ch. *shichamona* 式叉摩那/*xuechu nü* 學處女), fully ordained monks (Skt. *bhikṣu*; Tib. *dge slong*; Ch. *biqiu* 比丘), and fully ordained nuns (Skt. *bhikṣuṇī*; Tib. *dge slong ma*; Ch. *biqiu ni* 比丘尼).[50] Ordained Buddhists who committed the same offense could receive a different conviction according to Buddhist monastic law, depending on their level of training.

These offenses could be identified among seven major categories.[51] In the following, I will introduce the two that are most relevant for monks and nuns engaging in litigation. The first was the offense of defeat (Skt. *pārājika*; P. *pārājika*;

Tib. *pham pa*; Ch. *boluo shijia* 波羅市迦, *boluoyi* 波罗夷), which was the most serious transgression an ordained Buddhist could commit. Literally, it meant if a monk or nun committed this offense, they would completely ruin all of their religious training. There were four acts that could lead to an offense of defeat. These included having sex, killing a human being, taking what was not given (stealing), or lying about having supernatural powers.[52]

The punishment for committing an offense of defeat was the status of "not in communion" (Skt. *asaṃvāsa*; P. *asaṃvāsa;* Tib. *gnas pa mi bya*; Ch. *bu gongzhu* 不共住). Here, the offender would permanently lose privileges that allowed them to participate in certain communal activities that were open to monks and nuns in good standing. Various Buddhist legal traditions differ on what privileges the offenders would lose. In the *Pāli Vinaya*, communion is defined as monks and nuns having "one work, one rule, and equal training," and as such, one who is not "together with this is therefore called not in communion."[53] In the *Mūlasarvāstivāda Vinaya*, in the section discussing the second offense—taking what is not given—we find another explanation of these restrictions, through a detailed, word-for-word analysis of the term "not in communion." It reads as follows:[54]

> Not in communion means the offender cannot live together with the other monks. When having the fortnightly retreat,[55] the confessional ceremony [for monks to point out each other's wrongs],[56] the ecclesiastical proceeding with a single motion,[57] the ecclesiastical proceeding with a single motion and a proposition,[58] the ecclesiastical proceeding with one motion and three propositions,[59] and the ecclesiastical proceeding on the twelve kinds of persons,[60] they [the offenders] should not be appointed to participate. Therefore, it is called "not in communion."

The same *Mūlasarvāstivāda Vinaya*, in the section on the first offense of defeat—sex—mentions additional punishments that prohibit the offender from sharing certain foods.[61] There, the list includes an additional punishment that prohibits offenders from sharing "religious food" (*fashi* 法食) and "tasty food" (*weishi* 味食).[62] These may be referring to the spiritual food of the Buddha's teaching or actual edible food. The *Mahāsāṃghika Vinaya*, too, prohibits offenders from enjoying these two types of food.[63]

Thus, in the *Mūlasarvāstivāda Vinaya*, the punishment of "not in communion" entails prohibition from attending four major communal activities: the fortnightly retreat for reciting the monastic rules, the ecclesiastical proceedings for deciding monastic affairs, the confessional ceremony at the retreat at the end of the summer rainy season, and the right to enjoy both religious food and tasty food. The first three kinds of punishments are further confirmed in the *Mahīśāsaka Vinaya* and the *Sarvāstivāda Vinaya*.[64] The *Dharmaguptaka Vinaya* only forbids offenders from attending the fortnightly ritual and ecclesiastical proceedings.[65] Nevertheless, one who was convicted of the offense of defeat could still remain in the monastic community.[66]

Convicting a monk or a nun of the offense of defeat is a strenuous process. A legal procedure must be followed to adjudicate a reported accusation. During the adjudication, the monastic investigators must determine whether the accused had the intention of committing the alleged crime. For instance, in the case of a reported homicide, in the *Mahāsāṃghika Vinaya*, at the end of the section discussing the fourth offense of defeat—killing a human being—the rule notes that to convict a monk of this offense, a set of five conditions must be met.[67] First, the victim must be a human being. Second, the killer must have perceived the victim as a human being. Third, the killer must have employed methods or tools to commit the killing. Fourth, the killer must have had the intention to kill the victim. Fifth, the victim must have died. If any of the five conditions is not met, then the accused cannot be convicted of having killed a human being.

Even when all of the conditions were met, Buddhists still recognized a few circumstances in which an ordained Buddhist killer would not be convicted of the offense of defeat for having killed a human being: first, if the killer had committed the offense before the Buddha had established the rule against killing a human being,[68] and second, if the killer had committed the offense while being mentally ill. These exceptions are recognized in the *Pāli Vinaya*,[69] the *Mahīśāsaka Vinaya*,[70] the *Mahāsāṃghika Vinaya*,[71] the *Dharmaguptaka Vinaya*,[72] and the *Mūlasarvāstivāda Vinaya*.[73] They are absent, however, in the *Sarvāstivāda Vinaya*.[74]

The second relevant category, which is also the second most serious, is the probationary offense (Skt. *saṃghāvaśeṣa*; P. *saṅghādisesa*; Tib. *dge 'dun lhag ma*; Ch. *sengcan* 僧殘, *sengqie poshisha* 僧伽婆尸沙, *sengqie fashisha* 僧伽伐尸沙),[75] signifying that the offender's act had ruined almost all of their religious training but that they are still redeemable. The type of redemption differs for monk and nun offenders.[76] It also differs when an offender tries to conceal the offense. In the worst-case scenario, if a monk offender has concealed the offense and repeated the offense during their period of penance, then this offender has to go through three types of penance before becoming re-admittable to the monastic community.[77] First, for concealing the offense, the offender would receive a punishment of probation (Skt. *parivāsa*; Tib. *spo ba*; Ch. *biezhu* 別住, *boli posha* 波利婆沙;),[78] which requires the offender to live in separate living quarters away from where monks in good standing are living. Having completed this step, the offender must request a second penance to please oneself and the other ordained Buddhists (Skt. *mānatva*; P. *mānatta*; Tib. *mgu bar bya ba*; Ch. *monachui* 摩那埵), by performing various duties for six nights.[79] If the offender completes this step but commits the same or another probationary offense again without trying to conceal it, this offender can directly begin their penance without repeating the first phase of the penance (Ch. *manochui benri zhi* 摩那埵本日治).[80] Finally, the offender can ask to exit the penance period (Skt. *āvarhaṇa*; Tib. *dbyung ba*; Ch. *afu hena* 阿浮呵那, *chuzui* 出罪).[81] This final step required the offender to publicly confess their transgression in front of twenty monks in good standing.[82] If fewer than twenty such monks were present during the confession, the offender could not exit their penance. Once this last step was completed, the offender would become eligible to be restored to their earlier status in the monastic community.

The penance for a nun who committed a probationary offense was slightly different.[83] Regardless of whether the nun offender had tried to conceal the transgression, she would receive a *mānatva* punishment (to please oneself and one's fellow nuns) for "half a month."[84] After that, she could ask to exit the penance period by publicly confessing her transgressions in front of twenty monks and twenty nuns in good standing.

In practice, however, those having committed probationary offenses could avoid their penance in six circumstances. These circumstances include the times when the offenders are learned in the Buddha's teachings, are learned in Buddhist monastic law, are learned on the commentaries of the Buddha's teachings, are of great merit and virtue, are an elder or a leader of the assembly, or feel extremely embarrassed by what they have done.[85] In those circumstances, those who had committed a probationary offense could restore their purity by having an instant thought of not committing the same transgression again in the future.[86]

Apart from these primary categories of offenses, a monk or nun who engaged with the state court could also face two types of secondary offenses resulting from attempting to but failing to complete an act that would have constituted an offense listed in one of the primary categories. One secondary offense was a grave offense (St. *sthūlātyaya*; P. *thullaccaya*; Tib. *nyes byas sbom po*; Ch. *toulanzhe* 偷蘭遮, *toulan zui* 偷蘭罪, *suitu luodi* 窣吐羅底;). Monks and nuns could face being convicted of this offense if they had caused others to die but their act did not fulfill all the five conditions outlined above, for instance, when the monk or nun did not have the intention to kill but accidentally killed the victim, or the victim did not die. In our contemporary legal context, the first is comparable to involuntary or negligent manslaughter and the second to attempted murder. Apart from crimes of homicide, ten other acts would also lead to being convicted of a grave offense: eating human flesh, storing human flesh, shaving body hair, pouring drugs into the anus, stocking up human hair to make a robe, walking naked, stocking up on stone bowls, and damaging clothes, living quarters, or pagodas out of anger.[87] In other words, the Buddhist monastic law texts imposed the same punishment on monks or nuns who accidentally killed another person and those who walk naked or stocked up stone bowls. Furthermore, in the Buddhist legal context, an offender convicted of a grave offense only needed to confess before one monk or nun in good standing (*yu yiren qian chanhui* 於一人前懺悔).[88] Once the offenders became contrite for what they had done, that contrition would cleanse them of their offenses.

The other secondary category of transgression that monks and nuns who litigate in the state court could commit was a much lighter offense of "wrongdoing" (Skt: *duṣkṛta*; P. *dukkata*; Tib. *nyes byas*, *'gal tshabs can*; Ch. *tujiluo* 突吉羅, *ezuo* 惡作, *yuebini* 越比尼, *yuebini xinhui* 越比尼心悔;).[89] The only penance required of the offender of the wrongdoing was to "immediately confess the violation in their mind" and that alone would suffice to redeem the offender.[90] If the offender had committed the offense immediately before a fortnightly retreat was about to begin, then they were to remember the offense and immediately confess it, in the same private manner, immediately after the fortnightly retreat ended.

Chapter Overview

This book unfolds in two parts. Part I examines the Indian origins of the Buddhist campaign for clerical legal privileges. Part II discusses how Chinese Buddhists responded to and reimagined earlier Indian provisions that gave immunity to Buddhist clerics who had committed pre- or postordination offenses. I also examine lawsuits involving ordained Buddhists in China to see whether the proposed hybrid courts and their laws were honored in legal practice.

Chapter 1 discusses Indian Buddhists' perceptions of their general legal rights and duties as both plaintiffs and defendants. The monastic law texts preserved in the six extant traditions reveal an overall panic over facing litigation in the state court in Indian Buddhism. This panic resulted in strict rules that banned monks and nuns from initiating lawsuits against anyone—ordained Buddhists, lay Buddhists, and non-Buddhists alike—in the state court. It also attempted to deter lay people from suing ordained Buddhists in state court. Collectively, these measures aimed at minimizing ordained Buddhists' exposure to the state court. Yet, despite their fear of the courtroom and desire to stay away from it, when considering their legal obligations Indian Buddhists nevertheless considered themselves subjects of the lay legal system. This self-perception led to the promulgation of rules in Buddhist monastic law requiring ordained Buddhists to appear in the state court when summoned.

Chapters 2 and 3 examine two aspects of the initial efforts to fight for clerical legal privileges in Indian Buddhism: immunity from prosecution for pre- and postordination offenses. Indian Buddhists sought these privileges to deal with circumstances where litigation became inevitable for ordained Buddhists. The Indian solution was to seek clerical legal privileges to exempt ordained Buddhists from trial and punishment for their pre- or postordination crimes. Chapter 2 focuses on the pursuit of clerical legal privileges to exempt ordained Buddhists from prosecution for preordination crimes, as reflected in cases involving two types of charges against women: adultery and theft. In both types of cases, women facing execution on either of these charges received advice from local community members to seek ordination in Buddhist institutions to avoid the death penalty. Once ordained as Buddhist nuns, these women became exempt from prosecution, either through an existing law that protected ordained Buddhists unconditionally or through a king's arbitrary personal intervention to protect ordained Buddhists, even at the price of breaking laws on punishing adulterers and thieves. These cases reveal a Buddhist perception of their monastic institutions as sanctuaries where fugitives could expect legal protection once they became ordained monks or nuns.

Chapter 3 focuses on the pursuit of clerical legal privileges for postordination offenses in Buddhist monastic law texts. Indian Buddhists did not seek complete exemption from being tried in the state court. Instead, they asked for absolute immunity from penalty, even for the most heinous crimes. Numerous cases from Indian Buddhist monastic law texts demonstrate that ordained Buddhists could end up litigating against others in civil disputes or face trials in the state court for having committed criminal offenses. Indian Buddhists presented the idea that law enforcement should never, under any circumstances, pass judgments to punish convicted ordained Buddhists; they also added that those who dared impose punishment on ordained Buddhists—whether convicted or not—would suffer greatly.

Chapter 4 traces how Buddhists expanded this campaign to justify their pursuit of clerical legal privileges in nonlegal Buddhist texts. Contrary to Jan Nattier's view that Chinese translators added these justifications to the end of the Chinese translations of the Indian texts, this chapter shows that these justifications were not fabricated in China but actually originated in India. In these nonlegal texts, Indian Buddhists justified their pursuit of clerical legal privileges in three steps. First, they predicted that ordained Buddhist criminals would inevitably appear when Buddhism became corrupt. Next, they used withered orchids and dead oxen as metaphors to argue that ordained Buddhists would always be more valuable than ordinary lay people, just as a withered orchid is still more fragrant than other flowers and a dead ox is still more useful medicinally than other animals, since it can yield ox bezoar. Finally, they used stories of how animals and rulers refused to hurt ordained Buddhist criminals as an argument that present and future law enforcement should, to the same extent, unconditionally avoid punishing convicted Buddhist criminals.

Part II shifts to focus on Chinese Buddhists' engagement with this campaign for clerical legal privileges in Indian Buddhism. Securing clerical immunity from prosecution required that ordained Buddhists be treated as subjects who were beyond the jurisdiction of the state judicial system. How did Buddhists justify this demand? Chapter 5 focuses on the Chinese transformation of the Indian model of the Buddhist establishment's legal relationship with the state. In early Indian Buddhism, Buddhists approached their legal relationship with the state from two extremes: first, by attempting to avoid confrontation with the state court and, second, by seeking absolute exemption from penalty. In practice, neither option seemed feasible in the Chinese legal context. Buddhists in China thus began to reconsider these extreme approaches in a search for an indigenous solution to the continuing quest for jurisdictional autonomy. In this process, Chinese Buddhists abandoned both approaches. Instead, they reassessed the importance of jurisdiction and laws that were applicable to the Buddhist establishment and decided to focus on two new issues. First, who had jurisdiction over ordained Buddhists? Second, what laws should apply in a trial that is set in a suitable trial venue: state law, Buddhist monastic law, or something else? Through this reassessment, Chinese Buddhists collaborated with the state to create the hybrid courts and hybrid laws to deal with legal matters pertaining to religious entities in China.

Did these hybrid courts and laws ever function in legal practices in China? Chapters 6 and 7 explore cases to assess whether and to what extent jurisdictional arrangements between the Buddhist establishment and the state in premodern China were honored in the courtroom. All of these cases featured ordained Buddhists in post-1949 China. These cases show that, despite the lack of official recognition in the Chinese legal system, the tripartite jurisdictional infrastructure continues to be in play, shaping the contours of the legal interaction between the state and the Buddhist establishment.

Chapter 6 discusses how the early medieval hybrid court has continued to affect the practice of law in contemporary China. It unveils this impact by examining how law enforcement handled accusations against the Buddhist monk Xuecheng for having allegedly committed acts of sexual, financial, and administrative misconduct in 2018. This case study reveals the state's reluctance to interfere with the Buddhist establishment's jurisdiction. In 2018, at the time of these accusations, the accused had been the president of the Buddhist Association of China (Zhongguo fojiao xiehui 中國佛教協會) and the abbot of China's popular Longquan 龍泉 Monastery, which is situated in a Beijing suburb. The principal accusation was that the abbot had sexually abused and harassed Buddhist nuns in nunneries that are affiliated with his monastery. In dealing with these accusations against this Buddhist monk, the state had been unwilling to let law enforcement get involved right away. Instead, the State Administration of Religious Affairs (SARA) led a preliminary investigation into all of the accusations. At its conclusion, SARA did little more than provide commentary on the sexual harassment and assault charges. It found the accusation of sexual harassment credible but not the accusation of sexual assault. On the charges of financial and administrative misconduct, SARA recommended that state law enforcement carry out further formal investigations. The unfolding of the case and its investigation illustrate how the state followed a premodern convention by treating this monk's case as an internal case, as it primarily involved ordained Buddhists within the monastic community. For that reason, this case was not immediately and directly left to the monastery or law enforcement; instead, it was handed over to the hybrid third party (SARA) for preliminary investigation. The handling of this case also shows that, in contemporary China, even the Chinese government unwittingly follows a principle derived from imperial China for dealing with religious matters, all cases involving only internal religious members—except for serious felonies—are initially left to the equivalent of a third-party hybrid court and hybrid law to process.

In Chapter 6, I show how the SARA functions as a third-party agency when leading the investigation of criminal charges against an ordained Buddhist monk. In Chapter 7, I show how the Buddhist Association of China assumes the role of a third-party agency when mediating disputes involving monastic institutions, lay heirs, the judiciary, and the legislature. Examining lawsuits over the property of deceased Buddhist monks between 1980 and 2020, Chapter 7 demonstrates how the state is extremely unwilling to weaken the authority of either Buddhist religious law or state law when the two systems are in conflict.

The Epilogue invites us to consider the significance of this Buddhist campaign for clerical privileges beyond its temporal, geographical, and religious confines. Understanding this two-millennia-old campaign for clerical legal privileges sheds light on a living conundrum regarding the practice of concealing clerical crimes that are committed in Buddhist communities around the globe today. Given China's historical connections with the rest of Asia, the anatomy of Buddhists' engagement with this campaign in China provides a meaningful reference for understanding the messiness of a pan-Asia Buddhist approach—or even a lack thereof—to negotiating its legal relationship with the state. To show the full implications of unveiling this Buddhist pursuit of legal privileges, I compare it with the Christian pursuit of similar legal privileges to highlight both the similarities and the differences between them. Christians pursued the benefit of clergy and sanctuary status, in broad daylight, for their churches and clergy, seeking official legal recognition of these privileges in written law. Buddhists sought clerical legal privileges with equal determination but through subtler means. If the Christian campaign for clerical legal benefits was a publicly announced war against the state, the Buddhist one was a persistent whisper of wishes hinted at between the lines in Buddhist literary traditions.

PART I

INDIAN ORIGINS

1
The Litigation Ban

> If a Buddhist nun goes to the palace of the king or the court of a judge and sues, her act constitutes a probationary offense.[1]
>
> The Buddha, *Dharmaguptaka Vinaya*

In 631, the Chinese Buddhist monk Xuanzang (602–664) arrived in the city of Ayodhyā, which was located in today's Uttar Pradesh in northern India. Later, in his travelogue, Xuanzang noted that in Ayodhyā he had seen over one hundred Buddhist monasteries and over three thousand Buddhist monks but only about ten non-Buddhist temples and very few non-Buddhist practitioners.[2] Xuanzang could never have imagined that his description of the predominant Buddhist presence in Ayodhyā would appear in a 2019 Supreme Court of India judgment that closed a dispute involving Hindus, Muslims, and Buddhists.[3] This dispute centered on the religious nature of a 2.77-acre plot of land located in Ayodhyā. Hindus and Muslims had begun to fight over its ownership in the sixteenth century. In recent decades, Hindus have claimed the disputed land to be the birthplace of the Hindu deity Rāma and have fought to build a grand temple there. However, Muslims considered it their right to restore a mosque that had stood atop this land until its demolition on December 9, 1992.

On July 23, 2018, this land dispute became more complex when the Supreme Court of India permitted a lay Buddhist to join the lawsuit.[4] The Buddhist petitioner Vineet Kumar Maurya, a native of Ayodhyā, considered Buddhists to be the actual owners of the disputed land. But unlike his co-petitioners, Maurya was not interested in building a Buddhist monastery on this land. Instead, he merely requested that the Supreme Court declare the disputed area a sacred Buddhist site and acknowledge that its Buddhist past predates the Hindu and Muslim presences. Given the Supreme Court's earlier dismissal of similar petitions from other Buddhists, in 2003 and 2011,[5] Maurya's success in getting a hearing for this lawsuit was a monumental victory.

This victory, however, was short lived. On November 9, 2019, the Supreme Court closed the case, causing Maurya to lose more than just a lawsuit. Supporting the Buddhist claim were textual records and archaeological findings pointing to a possible historical Buddhist presence at Ayodhyā. In addition to Xuanzang's description in his travelogue, Maurya also cited additional

Buddhism in Court. Cuilan Liu, Oxford University Press. © Oxford University Press 2024.
DOI: 10.1093/oso/9780197663332.003.0002

archaeological findings to show Ayodhyā's possible link to Buddhism. Between 1862 and 2003, British and Indian archaeologists excavated the disputed site, and under the mosque's ruins, they found early layers of structures with Buddhist or Jain origins.[6] This evidence, however, failed to secure a favorable verdict for the Buddhist litigant. In their final judgment, the Supreme Court's five-judge bench cited arguments supporting the disputed land's "possible linkages to Buddhist or Jain traditions," but they still adjudicated in favor of the Hindu litigants.[7] The court judges gave the disputed land to the Hindus for a new temple; they gave the Muslims land elsewhere on which to rebuild their destroyed mosque. In the massive 1,045-page judgment, these judges treated the lawsuit as only a biparty dispute between the Hindus and the Muslims. To add insult to injury, they did not even mention Maurya's name or comment on his claim that the disputed site had a significant Buddhist presence predating those of the Hindus and Muslims.

The frustration and disappointment this lay Buddhist litigant experienced in the Supreme Court of India are representative of what the Buddhists in ancient India had sought to avoid. If the Buddhist monks in Ayodhyā in the seventh century CE had advised Maurya, they would probably have discouraged him from litigating against other coreligionists in the state court in the first place. Their source for this advice would have been the Buddhist distrust of the state court system reflected in Buddhist legal literature.

Buddhists in ancient India had reasons to be wary of the state court. In ancient India, three legal authorities can be present in the courtroom: the king, the chief judge, and other judges.[8] The king was obliged to hear cases every day,[9] but he could either hear these cases in person or appoint a chief judge to hear them as his deputy in his absence. Brahmins, however, dominated the actual operations of the state court. They were almost omnipresent, penetrating all three legal roles. Brahmins could act as judges. They were also given exclusive privilege to sit in as chief judge when the king was absent. The chief judge's authority was only second to the king's, and only learned Brahmins could function in this capacity on behalf of the king.[10]

Brahmin writers considered the Brahmin legal consultants indispensable in operating the court. They not only made it mandatory for a king to appoint a personal priest to accompany him during a trial, but also considered Brahmins alone to be suitable candidates for such a position. When a king entered the courtroom, the Brahmin personal priest and counselors "who [were] policy experts" would go along with him to hear a case.[11] The writer Gautama, in the late second century BCE, advises that when conflicting evidence causes difficulties in adjudicating a case, Brahmin priests who are learned in the Vedas should assist the king in reaching a decision.[12] He further advises the king to "appoint as his personal priest a Brahmin who is learned, born to a good family, eloquent, handsome, mature, and virtuous."[13]

Being a legal consultant, however, was not risk-free. The legal writer Vasiṣṭha from the first century BCE declares when the king adjudicates unjustly, it is necessary to punish both the king and his Brahmin legal consultant, as the consultant's role is to help the king arrive at a just decision.[14] If they let a guilty man go free, then the king would be ordered to fast for one day and the priest for three days. For punishing an innocent man, the king must fast for three days, and the priest must "perform an arduous penance."[15]

To augment their influence in the state court, the Brahmins furnished the state court with their legal ideas on its operations. The above-mentioned Gautama considers the Vedas to be the most important source for guiding courtroom procedure. In particular, he argues that the king's administration of justice "should be based on the Veda, the Legal Treatise, the Vedic Supplements, and the Purāṇa."[16] He notes that judges should only consult the laws of the local regions, castes, and families when they are not in conflict with the sacred Vedic scriptures.

The Brahmins and their fellow equals, who could be either warriors or merchants, further assumed exclusive authority over interpreting the law in the courtroom. The above-mentioned Gautama warns that if a king allows a laborer from the low-ranking Śūdra caste to interpret the law, then his realm will sink "like a cow in mud," and the entire kingdom will be stricken with famine and pestilence and quickly perish.[17]

The overwhelming Brahmanical influence made the state court and its legal proceedings foreign, intimidating, and suspect for Buddhists whose religion was the result of an attempt to break free from ideas that promote Brahmin supremacy. These concerns about the state court pervade Buddhist monastic law texts. Buddhist legal writers present numerous cases in their attempts to show how litigation in the state court could become a significant source of criticism against ordained Buddhist plaintiffs and damage the Buddhist clergy's relationship with the lay community on whom they depend. They also fear it could ruin the Buddhist clergy's collective image in disputes with non-Buddhist practitioners. Even when ordained Buddhists use litigation in the state court to secure ownership of disputed land—these writers warned—their victory can invite criticism from the laity and garner accusations of skillful theft.[18]

In ancient India, Buddhists were not the only ones with these suspicions. Jains, too, doubted the integrity of the state court,[19] for the same reasons that the Buddhists did. First, they both perceived the state court as corrupt because judicial officials could easily accept bribes in return for arriving at unjust verdicts.[20] Second, having ordained Buddhists or Jains file suits in the state court could have invited public criticism that would have hurt the viability of these people's religions, regardless of the outcome of the litigation.

The Buddhist solution to the problem is to prevent monks and nuns from appearing in the courtroom. They came up with two methods to reach this goal. They prohibited monks and nuns from voluntarily going to the court to sue others, whether lay or ordained Buddhists. Similarly, Buddhist legal writers also warned laypersons against suing monks and nuns in the court. When these prohibitions and warnings failed, Buddhists proposed involving lawmakers and judges who would bend the law to exempt monks and nuns from having to appear in the courtroom. This chapter focuses on the first method: preventing ordained Buddhists from litigating in the courtroom, whether as plaintiffs or as defendants. The following three chapters will discuss a new method: campaigning for clerical legal privileges to exempt ordained Buddhists from standing at trial for pre- or postordination crimes, evidence for which has been found in Buddhist legal and nonlegal literary traditions.

The Dreadful Courtroom

The stories of many wrongfully accused Buddhist monks who were dragged to the state court sufficiently illustrate how Buddhists perceived ancient Indian courtrooms as dreadful. One case recounts how a monk is framed and then taken to court. As the story goes, monk Upananda finds unattended valuables lying on the ground.[21] He has no idea that some children have laid those valuables on the ground and are intent on framing him, hiding and waiting for Upananda to pick them up. The moment he touches the items, the children immediately accuse him of theft and drag him to court. As he defends himself in the courtroom, Upananda recounts how he came upon those unattended articles on the roadside and assumed someone had left them there for reuse by someone else. This defense convinces the judges, who are devout lay Buddhists, to acquit him. Their reasoning is that, as a monk, Upananda would have been used to seeing alms set aside for monks to reuse at their leisure.

Upananda is not alone in being set up and victimized. In Buddhist monastic law texts, theft was a common charge that brought multiple other monks to court. For example, the *Dharmaguptaka Vinaya* recounts a case of a group of Buddhist monks who find a bag of gold and return it to its owner.[22] However, the ungrateful owner accuses these monks of stealing some of the gold and takes them to the state court. King Prasenajit presides over the trial, and when the owner's description does not match the actual weight of the gold, the king rules that the claimant is not the real owner of the lost gold and thus decides to confiscate it. In the *Sarvāstivāda Vinaya*, some monks pick up pig intestines they find lying on the ground and consequently face accusations of having stolen and slaughtered the pig.[23] As a result, they are summoned to show up in the state court. On another occasion, some laypeople drag some monks to court for theft simply because the monks are found traveling with thieves on their way from the kingdom of Vṛji to the city of Vaiśālī.[24]

Sometimes a monk is wrongly accused of committing the much more serious crime of murder. The *Sarvāstivāda Vinaya* describes a situation in which a monk who needs to make an outer robe goes to a cemetery, finds a corpse lying in a nearby trench, and removes the dead person's outer garment.[25] Later, the dead person's family members go in search of their missing relative. They go to the monastery and describe the man to this monk, inquiring whether he has seen him. The monk informs them that he saw a person who fit the description, but that he had found him lying dead in a trench. He then discloses that he had removed a garment from the body. The family members ask the monk to show them where the body is. When they arrive at the trench and see that their family member is, indeed, dead and that his outer garment has been removed, they become overwhelmed with grief and accuse the monk of murder. The monk denies the accusation but is unable to convince them of his innocence. In the end, the family of the deceased takes the monk to the state court. During the trial, the judge asks the monk if he had killed the said person. He replies, "I am an ordained Buddhist monk. How can I kill a person? If I had killed him, I would have taken all of his garments away."[26] The judge, whom the text describes as a wise lay Buddhist, decides to acquit the monk on the assumption that an ordained Buddhist would not kill a human being.

Many wrongly accused monks, although ultimately acquitted, did not manage to walk out of the courtroom unharmed. The *Mahāsāṃghika Vinaya* recounts a case of a monk who suffers from physical injuries and is tried in the state court for supposedly abducting a married woman.[27] According to the story, the woman is a victim of domestic violence and escapes from her husband. As she flees, she sees this monk walking along a public road and begs him to allow her to travel with him, likely out of safety concerns. The monk tells her that he considers her free to walk on that road and that she does not need his permission. The woman interprets the monk's reply as consent and follows him as she goes on her way. When the husband finds his wife traveling with the monk, he curses the monk, accuses him of seducing and abducting her, then beats him and drags him to the state court. The text presents the judge as a wise man. He keeps the monk and woman apart and interrogates them separately, three times. The judge observes how the monk and the woman react to each of his questions. Since their testimonies match, he concludes that the monk must be innocent. During the final round of interrogations, the judge notices the monk's injuries. Outraged at her violent husband, the woman tells the judge that he has beaten and harmed the monk. After ordering immediately medical care for the monk, the judge jails the husband and confiscates his wealth.

In most cases, monks who were falsely charged were eventually acquitted because the judges were either Buddhists or wise enough to discover the truth. Because these court judges acquitted these wrongfully accused monks, it remains unclear whether a convicted ordained Buddhist offender would have received a reduced penalty or no penalty at all. These trials of the falsely accused, however, are still illuminating. They show that when ordained Buddhists were charged with theft, murder, or abduction, their religious identities could not protect them from being interrogated in the state court.

Ban for Monks and Nuns

The perception of the state court as harsh was sufficient to motivate Buddhists to eliminate or at least minimize a monk or nun's contact with it in two ways. First, Buddhist legal writers drew up rules that banned ordained Buddhists from voluntarily initiating lawsuits against laypeople, be they householders (or the offspring or siblings of householders), slaves, workers, or even hermits. Second, they threatened laypeople with dire consequences if they sued monks and nuns in the state court and lost their cases. Buddhist legal writers justified these bans by presenting cases that showed how litigating in the state court inevitably damaged Buddhism, regardless of the outcome for these ordained Buddhists, either as plaintiffs or defendants. Contrary to earlier scholarly opinions, the ban on litigation in the state court was not exclusively for nuns.[28] Monks, too, as I will show below, were prohibited from litigating in the state court.

Buddhist legal writers used three cases to dramatize the dire consequences of litigation in the state court. One case concerns a dispute over a fence repair between some Buddhist nuns and some nuns of another religion; another case, in four versions, concerns a dispute over the ownership of a donated property between some Buddhist nuns and the lay donor's son; and the last case concerns monks attempting to seize land from laypeople through litigation. The first case appears in the *Mahāsāṃghika Vinaya*, in the section discussing the probationary offense of litigating in the state court.[29] The case begins with a dispute between some ordained Buddhists and their naked non-Buddhist nun neighbors over property damage. A fence between their two residences has collapsed from rain damage and the Buddhist nuns are demanding that their neighbors repair this fence. They agree but ask to wait to do the repairs until after the rain has stopped. The Buddhist nun Sthūlanandā demands that they immediately begin repairs because, without a fence, the Buddhist nuns can see these neighbors' naked bodies. When they refuse to comply, the Buddhist nuns sue them in the state court. The judge, a faithful Buddhist, summons the non-Buddhist neighbors, chastises them, and orders them to repair the fence immediately. He further threatens to increase the punishment if they fail to follow his order. The neighbors immediately begin to repair the fence while it is still raining. Unfortunately, since it is the summer rainy season, the newly built fence keeps collapsing. These non-Buddhist ascetics become frustrated and complain. Their complaint travels successively from the lay Buddhists to the other Buddhist nuns, to the senior nun Mahāprajāpatī, and finally to the Buddha himself. This complaint compels the Buddha to assemble all the nuns in the city of Śrāvastī and promulgate the following rule:[30]

> If a Buddhist nun argues with and litigates against another (*zhengsong xiangyan* 諍訟相言), whether they be laypersons or ordained religious practitioners, whether it is for a day or even for an instant, even if she argues with and litigates against workers in the field or with a Buddhist novice, at that instant her act immediately constitutes a probationary offense.[31]
>
> . . .
>
> If a Buddhist nun goes to the palace of the king (*wangjia* 王家) or the court of a judge (*duanshi guan* 斷事官) and sues, her act constitutes a probationary offense. If she only complains [without officially pressing a charge], her act constitutes a grave offense. If she goes to the house of a lay Buddhist householder and then complains [without officially pressing a charge], her act constitutes a light infringement of the Buddhist monastic rules [for which she must reflect on her action and confess it to another person].[32] If she complains only in her mind, her act constitutes a light infringement of the Buddhist monastic rules [for which she must repent of this thought alone].[33]
>
> If a Buddhist monk[34] goes to the palace of a king to complain, his act constitutes a light infringement of the Buddhist monastic rules [for which he must reflect on his action and confess it to another person]. If he complains only in his mind, his act constitutes a light infringement of the Buddhist monastic rules [for which he must repent of this thought alone].

With the promulgation of this rule, the Buddha prohibited monks and nuns from litigating in the state court, yet the offenses for litigating differed between the two. If a Buddhist nun sued someone in the palace of the king or in the court of a judge, she was committing a probationary offense requiring a formal meeting of the monastic community. But if a monk did the same, it was a much lighter offense that only required confessing to another person.

In the *Dharmaguptaka Vinaya*, *Mahīśāsaka Vinaya*, *Sarvāstivāda Vinaya*, and *Pāli Vinaya*, Buddhist legal writers presented the ban on litigation in four versions of a different case concerning disputes over donated properties, in the sections discussing probationary offenses. In each iteration of this case, a lay donor has directly or indirectly offered a residence to an individual nun or group of nuns. When the donor subsequently dies or regifts the residence, their heirs or the new recipient of the residence enter into a dispute with these Buddhist nuns. In the *Dharmaguptaka Vinaya*,[35] the dispute centers on a donated residence a Buddhist nun has received from the junior wife of King Prasenajit. Later, this nun abandons it after having had some awful—yet unexplained—experiences living there. When the Buddhist nun leaves her residence to travel, her donor then regifts the residence to a woman from a non-Buddhist religious group.[36] When the nun learns about the transfer, she immediately returns to evict the new occupant and successfully forces her out. However, the non-Buddhist woman decides to sue the Buddhist nun in the state court.

Before the trial, the Buddhist nun tries but fails to avoid appearing in the state court. When the order to appear arrives from the court, she initially refuses to comply because she recalls that "the Buddha has promulgated a rule prohibiting [ordained Buddhists] from going to the court of the judge to speak."[37] Some nuns report her to some monks, who then report the matter to the Buddha. This compels the Buddha to amend his earlier promulgation and to clarify that "from today onward, if summoned [by a judge to appear in court], one should go."[38] Following this revised rule, the nun then goes to court. In the courtroom, she appears to be legally incompetent. When the judge asks her to defend her case, she only preaches on the merits of making donations to ordained Buddhists but says nothing to defend herself as the rightful owner of the disputed residence. She fails to convince the judge, who then adjudicates in favor of the non-Buddhist woman.

This verdict shocks many. The Buddha immediately expresses his concerns. He comments that the first donation is lawful and the regifting is unlawful. He further notes that the nun is unskilled in articulating her case, and the judge is unskilled in adjudicating. King Prasenajit is also unhappy with the nun's performance in the court, the judge's adjudication, and the Buddha's comment on the matter. As a result, he punishes the judge by confiscating his wealth. The incident also prompts the Buddha to establish the following rule forbidding ordained Buddhists from litigating in the state court:[39]

> If a Buddhist nun goes to see the judge and charges a householder or the son of a householder, a slave, or a servant, by day or by night, during the time span of one thought, of one snap of the fingers, or of one moment, then this Buddhist nun commits a probationary offense immediately.[40]
>
> ...
>
> If a Buddhist nun charges someone, a householder or the son of a householder, a slave or a servant, by day or by night, during the time span of one thought,

> of one snap of the fingers, or of one moment, just like a female non-Buddhist religious practitioner (*fanzhi* 梵志), goes to see the judge and announces her matter, she commits a probationary offense when the judge handles and decides the case. If she says it orally without revealing the name [of the accused], her act constitutes a grave offense.
>
> If a Buddhist monk [does it], it is an offense of wrongdoing. For a probationary nun, a novice monk, or a novice nun, [doing so constitutes] an offense of wrongdoing. This is called "to commit."
>
> "Not to commit": she does not commit [an offense] if she has been summoned; if one wants her to report something; if she has been taken there by force; if she has been brought there tied up; if her life or her pure conduct is in danger; if she says it orally but does not press a charge with the judge.
>
> "Not to commit": [the act was done] before the rule was originally promulgated; the doer was mad, confused, or tormented by suffering.

Like in the *Mahāsāṃghika Vinaya*, this rule in the *Dharmaguptaka Vinaya* also prohibited both monks and nuns from litigating in the state court, but the consequences were different. When a nun sued another person in the state court, her act constituted a probationary offense. But when a monk did the same, it was considered only a much lighter offense of wrongdoing.

In the *Sarvāstivāda Vinaya*, the ban on litigation in the state court expanded to also prohibit nuns from verbally or physically assaulting the accused. In this version of the case, the donor first gives the disputed residence to some monks, who then gifts it to a group of nuns.[41] When the donor dies, one of his sons becomes the heir to the donated property. This son then goes to evict the nuns, but the nuns refuse to move out, arguing, "We did not get it from you. We got it from the monks. If the monks ask us to move out, we will move out. We will not follow your words."[42] The verbal dispute quickly advances to a physical fight when a physically strong nun named Sumukha,[43] who comes from a Brahmin family, argues aggressively with the sons. Unable to hold his anger, the donor's son beats the nun with his hand. The nun thus goes to see the officials (*guan* 官), accuses the donor's son of beating her, and tells the whole story. The officials then summon the donor's son to the court. Having confirmed the donor's son's crime, the officials check the law to see how to punish one who beats an ordained Buddhist. The law says the punishment is to mutilate the body part that is used in committing the crime.[44] Since the donor's son had used his right hand to beat the nun, that hand is mutilated. When lay Buddhists learn about what has happened in the courtroom, they criticize the nun for suing and causing the donor's son to lose his right hand. The criticism soon spreads around and reaches the Buddha and compels the Buddha to promulgate the following rule for the nuns:

> If a Buddhist nun goes to [see] the king or to the place of an official (*guanren* 官人), a Brahmin, or a lay Buddhist and pulls rank to accuse others, it immediately constitutes a probationary offense that is confessable.
>
> . . .
>
> If the nun shows anger and hatred, scolds, curses, and beats the accused in front of the judge while the judge is investigating, her act constitutes a probationary offense. If she scolds and curses the accused in front of other people, her act constitutes a grave offense. If she shows anger and curses privately or does not speak [it out], she does not commit an offense.[45]

While the articulation of this rule does not specifically discuss monks, its placement in the *Sarvāstivāda Vinaya* as the seventh nonidentical rule (*bugong jie* 不共戒),[46] in the section explaining the seventeen rules on probationary offenses for nuns, could suggest that this rule also applied to monks. In the context of the *Sarvāstivāda Vinaya*, a nonidentical rule referred to a rule that applied to both monks and nuns but led to convictions of different offenses. For instance, the Chinese translation of a commentary on the *Sarvāstivāda Vinaya* informs us that a nonidentical rule refers to a rule whose violation would lead to different convictions, depending on whether the offender was a monk or a nun.[47] For example, a monk who deliberately ejaculates would commit a probationary offense. But for a nun, ejaculating would be considered a light offense that required confessing before another ordained Buddhist.[48] Therefore, classifying the ban on litigation in the state court for nuns as a nonidentical rule could suggest that this rule was applicable to monks, but monk and nun offenders of this rule may have been convicted of different types of offenses. The difference in conviction was as attested in the rule from the *Dharmaguptaka Vinaya* explained above, where it specified that for initiating lawsuits in the state court, a nun would be committing a probationary offense, but a monk would be committing a much lighter offense of wrongdoing.[49]

Other versions of this case are found in the *Pāli Vinaya* and the *Mahīśāsaka Vinaya*, where the Buddha forbids nuns from litigating but does not mention monks in the subsequently established rule. In the *Pāli Vinaya*, a lay Buddhist donor offers a residence to a group of nuns.[50] After the nuns have sued the lay donor's son in the court, the judge imposes corporal punishment on the losing lay defendant. At the end of each round of the trial, the losing lay defendant reacts aggressively. And each time, the nun responds by taking him back to the state court. After the first trial, the lay defendant curses the plaintiff nun Thullanandā as a "strumpet" with a shaved head. The curse causes the nun to take him to court a second time, whereupon he receives an unspecified sentence. The defendant then changes his attack strategy. He donates another residence to some naked ascetic neighbors of the Buddhist nuns and incites these naked ascetics to badmouth these same Buddhist nuns. This plot of attack leads the Buddhist nuns to take the defendant to the state court once again, where as punishment the judge has him tied up. After laypeople criticize the nuns' involvement in the lawsuit, the Buddha lays the following rule:

> Whatever nun should be one who speaks in envy concerning a householder or a householder's sons [or brothers] or a slave or a workman or even a wanderer who is a recluse, that nun has fallen into a matter that is an offense at once, entailing a formal meeting of the order involving being sent away.
>
> . . .
>
> "One who speaks in envy" means: she is called a bringer of lawsuits.
>
> . . .
>
> If she thinks, "I will bring a lawsuit," or looks about for a companion or goes herself, there is an offense of wrongdoing. If she announces it to one [person], there is an offense of wrongdoing. If she announces it to a second, there is a grave offense. At the end of the lawsuit, there is an offense entailing a formal meeting of the order.
>
> . . .
>
> There is no offense if she goes being dragged along by people, if she asks for protection, if she explains without reference [to a particular person], if she is mad, if she is the first wrongdoer.[51]

The main part of the rule contains an expression of Buddhist nuns who "speak in envy of others"; the word-by-word commentary on this term clarifies that it is referring to nuns who initiate lawsuits in the state court. This rule specifies that a Buddhist nun who initiates a lawsuit in the state court will commit a probationary offense. If she announces her plan to start a lawsuit to one other person without formally filing the lawsuit, it is a light offense of wrongdoing. But if she announces her litigation plan to a second person, it is a grave offense.

In the *Mahīśāsaka Vinaya*, the donor first provides a residence to some monks, who then gift it to a group of nuns.[52] The nuns later receive a garden donated by a queen and consequently abandon their former residence, which has been gifted by said monks. When the confrontation starts, the nuns ask the lay donor's son to leave them the donated property. They warn him, "We are not giving up this land. Do not make us go see the official and report it. [If so,] you will have greater loss."[53] Here, they mean to sue him in the state court. When the lay donor's son refuses to cooperate, the nuns take him to court, where he suffers a greater loss. This provokes criticism from the lay Buddhists. After the Buddha becomes aware of this incident, he promulgates the following rule for the nuns:

> If a Buddhist nun goes to see the official and tells others [her complaint], that Buddhist nun immediately commits a confessable probationary offense. If a Buddhist nun is harassed and assaulted, she should tell her parents. If she has no parents, she should tell her relatives. If she has no relatives, she should tell [other] monks, nuns, lay Buddhist men, or lay Buddhist women. If a powerful Buddhist monk or nun refuses to offer help, it constitutes an offense of wrongdoing. When telling [other people], [the nun] should say, "That person harassed and assaulted me. Scold and admonish [that person] for me." [She] should not disclose [the details]. If she goes to tell the official, upon completing the round trip, she commits a probationary offense. When the probationary nun and novice nun [does it], it is an offense of wrongdoing.[54]

In the *Mūlasarvāstivāda Vinaya*, the ban on litigation in the state court for monks is introduced with a different case in the section discussing the offense of defeat concerning stealing, where monks are prohibited from acquiring land through litigation.[55] When discussing different kinds of theft of land, the text says the following:

> What is acquiring through litigation? If a monk goes to the court of the judge to dispute over land with laypeople, the monk will commit a grave offense if he loses to the laypeople. If the monk wins and the layperson's mind can't settle on the case, the monk will commit a grave offense. If that layperson's mind settles on the case, the value [of the disputed land] should be assessed and the monk will have committed an offense as explained above.[56] This is called "acquiring through litigation."[57]

Therefore, depending on how the lay litigant responded to the outcome of the dispute over land, the monk litigant could have either committed an offense of defeat for stealing or a grave offense for a failed attempt to steal.

In the *Mūlasarvāstivāda Vinaya*, Buddhist legal writers also present another case in which a nun threatens to sue laypeople in the court, but this case only leads the Buddha to forbid nuns from collecting debts. The case appears in the section discussing the probationary offense 11, seeking the estate of a deceased person through litigation in the state court.[58] In this case, a wealthy man becomes very sick and decides to donate his wealth to renunciants, Brahmins, poor people, orphans, and widows. At that time, nun Sthūlanandā arrives at that man's house on her way to beg for alms food. When she learns that he is giving away his wealth, she asks for a donation. Unfortunately, the man tells her that he has finished giving away everything and has nothing to offer to her. When Sthūlanandā complains that she will leave empty-handed, the man says he still has some debt notes that she can take. Sthūlanandā gladly accepts them and says she will collect the debts. Before she leaves, the man asks her to take whatever the debtors can offer and not to be too aggressive with them as they are poor people. Sthūlanandā promises to do so accordingly. After the man dies, Sthūlanandā seizes the debtor and threatens him, "If you don't pay me this, I will take you to the king's palace."[59] This later leads to criticism from laypeople, and eventually some monks report the matter to the Buddha. The Buddha thus establishes a rule prohibiting nuns from "seeking payment of debt notes."[60]

In the cases where Buddhist nuns win lawsuits, their victories often entail severe physical punishment for the lay defendants, who lose more than what is under dispute. These defendants face either additional financial or corporal punishment or other unnecessary hardships, ranging from the confiscation of their property to imprisonment or mutilation. The outcome of each of these trials triggers public scorn toward the litigating nuns due to the physical and financial suffering they have caused to the lay defendants. The hardships the losing defendants suffer from ultimately lead to public criticism of the entire Buddhist monastic community.

While winning a lawsuit could be damaging for Buddhism, losing a case in the courtroom was worse for a monk or nun litigant. This is because losing a case in the state court, as shown in the case of the Buddhist nun in the *Dharmaguptaka Vinaya*, exposed ordained Buddhists' legal incompetence in defending themselves and disgraced the monastic community. This loss further provoked repercussions against the entire community of ordained Buddhists. The confiscation of the judge's wealth led the Buddha to further restrict ordained Buddhists' legal rights in the lay legal system. It provoked the Buddha also to introduce new rules to prohibit ordained Buddhists from suing and causing laypeople to suffer as a result.

Deterring the Lay Litigants

A lone ban to stop monks and nuns from suing others did not suffice to help ordained Buddhists avoid appearing in the state court. Shielding these people required a further strategy to discourage laypeople from taking ordained Buddhist monks and nuns to court. One approach by the Buddhist legal writers was to emphasize the consequences of losing a case, noting that laypeople who sued monks and nuns could risk being charged with making false accusations.

One case in the *Dharmaguptaka Vinaya* shows how a layperson's failure to convict an ordained Buddhist could have resulted in a severe criminal charge of making a false accusation against that lay plaintiff.[61] The incident takes place on Vulture's Peak Mountain in the city of Rājagṛha, where a group of six nuns are found to have carelessly poured buckets of night soil outside the fence of their residence.[62] It happens on a day when a minister on his way to greet King Bimbisāra passes by the fence, and his clothes become soiled with excrement. He attempts to sue all of these nuns in the state court, in front of a judge. When a Brahmin friend learns of his plan, he strongly discourages the minister from suing the nuns in the state court, noting that if he fails to convict them, he might be charged with making a false accusation. The minister takes his friend's advice and gives up on his idea of pursuing the lawsuit. Instead, his Brahmin friend deals with the Buddhist nuns himself, privately. He goes to see them, informs them of the incident with the minister, inquires who the culprit is, and advises them to refrain from doing so again.

Sometimes threats could fail to work. Some laypeople may still have sued monks and nuns regardless of the possible outcomes. In these scenarios, Buddhist legal writers advised accused monks and nuns to answer to the judges in the state court. This advice is well demonstrated in the case in which the Buddhist nun tries but fails to avoid appearing in the state court when she is being sued in a dispute over the ownership of a donated residence. In general, the Buddhist position is that if an ordained Buddhist is being sued and a judge has subpoenaed them, then they are to report to the state court.

Because laypeople normally did not have access to the Buddhist monastic law texts, this strategy to illustrate the disastrous consequences of losing a case against a monk or nun in these cases may not have been effective in deterring laypeople from suing monks and nuns. This challenge made further campaigning in the non-legal Buddhist texts, as I will discuss in Chapter 4, an even more important step.

Approved Venues

All the extant Buddhist monastic law texts of all the six traditions banned nuns—and some also monks—from initiating lawsuits as plaintiffs in the state court. But monastic life was not immune from damage and abuse. So what legal recourses were available to monks and nuns when they suffered and needed legal help?

Buddhist legal writers recommended two solutions for the ordained Buddhist victims. First, matters should be kept in-house as much as possible. This is such a high priority that even victims of sexual abuse were to refrain from seeking justice in the state court. One of the best-known victims is the Buddhist nun

Uppalavaṇṇā.[63] Before she becomes a nun, she suffers betrayals in two marriages. In her first marriage, her husband and mother fornicate while she is still nursing her newborn daughter. She leaves that marriage and remarries but suffers adultery again. In her second marriage, her new husband secretly marries a woman who turns out to be her daughter from her previous marriage. These betrayals shatter Uppalavaṇṇā, who then decides to leave her worldly life and become a Buddhist nun. But her suffering does not end there. A Brahmin falls in love with her. One day when she is away begging for alms, the Brahmin enters her hut and hides under her bed. When she returns home and falls asleep, the Brahmin rapes her. Uppalavaṇṇā tells the other nuns of the rape. The other nuns inform the monks, who then relay the information to the Buddha. The Buddha only declares that Uppalavaṇṇā has not committed the offense of defeat because the sexual intercourse had occurred against her will. However, Buddhist legal writers do not arrange for the Buddha to have any discussion on what Uppalavaṇṇā, as the victim of a crime, should do with her rapist.

Nuns were not the only ones to have been exposed to the dangers of sexual crimes. In the *Pāli Vinaya*, Buddhist legal writers dealt with monk victims in the same way. In one case, the victim was a monk who was forced by a group of young people from the Lichavi community to have sex with fully ordained nuns, novice nuns, and other monks.[64] Again, Buddhist legal writers arrange for the Buddha to focus on determining whether these monks and nuns have committed any offenses through these acts of sexual intercourse, never mind the circumstances. These legal writers also provide no comment on any options for these monks and nuns to punish their perpetrators. The only option they offer to victims of sexual abuse can be found in the case in the *Mahīśāsaka Vinaya* discussed above, where Buddhist legal writers advise that these nuns should seek to resolve the matter internally and informally.[65] As precautions to reduce the risk of becoming victims of sexual assault, Buddhist legal writers prohibited nuns from traveling, crossing a river, or spending the night alone.[66]

The second recommendation is to negotiate with the perpetrator to have one's loss returned. In the *Mūlasarvāstivāda Vinaya*, Buddhist monks are given three options for retrieving their stolen possessions: preaching to persuade the thief to voluntarily return their possessions, buying them back from the thief at half price, or buying them back at the full price of the stolen item. Three cases in *Mūlasarvāstivāda Vinaya*, in the section containing miscellaneous disciplinary rules, illustrates this set of options.[67] In the first case, some thieves have stolen robes and alms bowls from some traveling monks. When the thieves try to sell them in the market, the monks recognize them and report the thieves to the market officials. In the end, the monks successfully retrieve their stolen alms bowls. When someone reports this to the Buddha, the Buddha declares that the monks should not have frightened those thieves, because the moment they successfully steal something, the thieves become the new owners of the stolen goods. In the second case, which takes place later, some other traveling monks are robbed. Remembering what the Buddha had said earlier, those monks abandon all the robes and alms bowls the robbers have touched. This time, the Buddha blames those monks for having abandoned the items the robbers have touched. He tells the monks that they should continue to use those robes and alms bowls until the robbers come to claim them as their own. In the third case, some other traveling monks are robbed again. These victim monks recognize the thieves when they see them trying to sell their stolen goods in the Jetavana garden. The monks take the thieves to the king's court.[68] In the court, the thieves are caned, chained, beaten with a stick, and tortured. When the Buddha learns of this, he advises the monks to try their best to get their bowls back because "alms bowls and religious robes are difficult to obtain,"[69] but he notes that they should not have taken the thieves to court. Instead, the Buddha recommends that the monks preach to the thieves and beg them to return the stolen bowls. If this fails, then the monks are to propose buying back these items at half price. If the thieves still refuse to return the stolen items, then the monks are to offer the full price.

Penalties and Exceptions

Despite the inconsistencies among the Buddhist monastic law texts of different traditions in the presence of rules explicitly banning monks from litigating in the court, the Buddhist ban on litigation was not purely symbolic. Buddhist legal writers outlined specific penalties for monks and nuns who failed to avoid litigating in the state court as plaintiffs. When a nun failed to adhere to this prohibition, she committed a probationary offense that required her to attend a formal meeting with her order, where her transgression would be discussed. If the offender was a Buddhist monk, the offense was considered a much lighter transgression of wrongdoing. In the *Dharmaguptaka Vinaya*, there is a case of a Buddhist monk who has a dispute with a layperson and reports it to the state court.[70] His report leads court officials to arrest that layperson, who eventually dies in jail. The Buddhist monk doubts that he has caused the layperson's death and committed an offense of defeat. He goes to see the Buddha. The Buddha declares that if he had no intention to kill that person, then his act would not entail an offense of defeat. Rather, he notes that in reporting the dispute to the official, the monk has only committed a light offense of wrongdoing.

Buddhist legal writers were sensitive to the complexities involved in the practice of law. They did not consider it a transgression when monks and nuns appeared in the state court for an emergency, or due to mental illness, or for nonpersonal reasons. In all Buddhist monastic law texts, except the

Mahāsāṃghika Vinaya and the *Mahīśāsaka Vinaya*, Buddhist legal writers excuse those who litigated in the state court before the Buddha had laid down the rule against it. They also excuse nuns who appeared in the state court because they faced life-threatening danger or the risk of sexual assault, were mentally ill, were taken there against their will, or were summoned by a judge.[71] Even in cases where there was no emergency, monks and nuns who litigated in the state court for compensation for losses to the Buddhist community, rather than for personal losses, were not guilty of this offense either.[72] It was also not an offense for an ordained Buddhist to accuse an offender privately, in a concealed place, or to file a complaint without revealing the identity of the accused, to avoid causing damage to them.[73]

Different Buddhist legal writers had various reasons for adopting lenient approaches to accommodating exceptions. Some gave special consideration to the recipient and the venue of the legal complaint. In the *Mahāsāṃghika Vinaya*,[74] the Buddhist legal writers determined that if a nun privately complained about a dispute, this was a light offense of wrongdoing. However, it was a grave offense if she complained at the home of lay Buddhist householders or in public. If she presented a complaint to a judge of the king's court, then this was a probationary offense. The *Sarvāstivāda Vinaya* takes a similar approach.[75] Only when a nun initiated a lawsuit in front of the king, an official, a Brahmin, or a lay Buddhist, or scolded or cursed her perpetrator in front of a lay judge did it constitute a probationary offense. If she scolded or cursed her perpetrator in front of other people, this was a grave offense; but there was no offense if she privately scolded or cursed her perpetrator or remained silent about it.

Sometimes Buddhist legal writers focused on the experiences of lay defendants in cases involving Buddhist monks or nuns.[76] At other times, they carefully calibrated the development of an offense in determining its weight, distinguishing between thoughts of initiating a lawsuit, attempts to file a lawsuit, and completion of a lawsuit. Such distinctions are clearly illustrated in the *Pāli Vinaya*.[77] For instance, it was a light offense of wrongdoing if a nun thought about taking someone to court, set out on a journey to the court with or without a companion, or made the dispute known to one person. On the other hand, it would have been a grave offense if a nun informed a second person of the dispute. If she formally lodged a lawsuit in the state court, her act would have constituted a probationary offense.

Conclusion

Vineet Kumar Maurya's initial success in securing a litigating role in the Ayodhyā dispute in the Supreme Court of India in 2018 constituted a victory for his fellow Buddhists who had failed to achieve the same goal before him. However, for his Buddhist predecessors from over two millennia ago, this short-lived success in the state court would have constituted a betrayal. By choosing to litigate as a Buddhist in the state court, Maurya had ignored core Buddhist advice. Deeply rooted in monastic law texts, this Buddhist advice discourages ordained Buddhists, as well as lay Buddhists, from litigating in the state court. On one hand, when Buddhist monks or nuns felt that their legal rights had been infringed, Buddhist legal writers forbade them from suing laypeople or fellow monastics. This advice could have reduced an ordained Buddhist's chance of appearing as a plaintiff in the state court. On the other hand, Buddhist legal writers also tried to discourage laypeople from suing ordained Buddhists in the state court, to reduce the likelihood of an ordained Buddhist having to appear as a defendant in the state court. Since laypeople were outside the jurisdiction of the Buddhist clergy, Buddhist legal writers required monks and nuns to report to the state court when laypeople insisted on suing them there.

The state court failed to appeal to Buddhists as a venue in which to seek justice, for several reasons. The predominant presence of Brahmins and their legal ideas in these courts made them untrustworthy to Buddhist litigants. Another reason is that litigating in the state court required familiarity with court procedures, access to legal professionals, and time and money to go through the court's process. For monks and nuns living on alms for their food as well as donated clothes and residences, litigating in the state court invited nothing but legal, financial, and ethical challenges. Finally, court trials could bring damage to Buddhist litigants whether they won or lost a case, because the matter could invite public criticism regardless of the verdict.

Outside these legal venues, Buddhists still disliked their Brahmin peers and perceived this dislike to be mutual. But life in a monastic institution was not a legal vacuum devoid of conflicts and disputes. The perception of mutual hostility between laypeople and monastics could have led to serious challenges for monks and nuns when they needed legal interventions to solve disputes but could not trust the state court. Despite these challenges, Indian Buddhists were still determined to restrict monastics from entering the legal world of lay society. In so doing, they had been hoping to protect monks and nuns from torture, injustice, and disgrace as a result of being involved in cases in the state court.

In building this invisible wall to separate the legal worlds of the laity and the ordained, Buddhists had by no means become less litigious. On the contrary, their distrust of the state court motivated them to explore alternative trial venues to meet the legal needs of monks and nuns. Within the Indian tradition, Buddhists strived to secure such a trial venue by promoting jurisdictional autonomy within the Buddhist monastic institution. Following the Buddhist exodus from India, Buddhists in Southeast and East Asia fought for alternative legal venues in different ways. In Southeast Asia, Buddhists persistently pursued more jurisdictional autonomy within the Buddhist monastic institution. As a result, Buddhists in Sri Lanka and Myanmar succeeded in establishing monastic courts for dealing with matters related to Buddhism or Buddhist practitioners.[78] In East Asia, as I will show in Chapter 5, Chinese Buddhists established a compromise in their pursuit of clerical jurisdictional autonomy, crafting a unique solution where they and the state shared jurisdiction over ordained Buddhists in a third venue beyond the state or monastic courts.

2
The Adulterous Wife's Sanctuary

> If I kill the newly ordained nun, following the law, it will tarnish Buddhism and earn me a bad reputation. If I release her, however, it will diminish the authority of the law.[1]
>
> King Prasenajit, *Mūlasarvāstivāda Vinaya*

The Indian king Aśoka (reign 264–238 BCE) was proud to be a Buddhist.[2] In approximately 254 BCE, two and a half years after converting, and while on the 256th day of a tour, he felt an urgency to proclaim his devotion to his newly adopted religion. To show his commitment, and to spread Buddhism widely so it would endure, he issued an edict elaborating his passion for Buddhism, sent officials to publicize this edict, and had it inscribed on rocks and stone pillars throughout India.[3] In 250 BCE, fourteen years after his coronation, King Aśoka paid to have a Buddhist stupa doubled in size.[4] Moreover, in 244 BCE, twenty years after his coronation, King Aśoka visited the Buddha's birthplace in Lumbini and offered tax relief to the people who lived in that village.[5]

King Aśoka also wanted to protect Buddhism from corruption and bad practices on the part of monastics. In one edict, he urged monks, nuns, and lay Buddhists to study and reflect on the Buddha's teachings, including his works on Buddhist monastic law.[6] In another edict, he prescribed defrocking monks and nuns who caused division within the Buddhist monastic community.[7] To facilitate the study of this edict, he ordered that one copy be deposited in the offices of local officials and one copy to be given to the lay Buddhists.

This Buddhist king's devotion to Buddhism and his legal authority in the courtroom made him the ideal supporter of Indian Buddhists who were pursuing clerical legal privileges. In the late third century BCE, the Brahmin legal writer Āpastamba had already perceived the king's presence in a courtroom as indispensable. He considered the presence of a blazing fire, water, and the king all as crucial when the court heard cases from litigants from both sides of a legal dispute.[8] Another essential role of the king was to mete out punishments to criminals. Moreover, in the state court where Brahmanical legal ideas dominated, kings held the highest authority.[9] In ancient India, there were different types of stationary and mobile courts. Some operated under the king's authorization,

Buddhism in Court. Cuilan Liu, Oxford University Press. © Oxford University Press 2024.
DOI: 10.1093/oso/9780197663332.003.0003

others operated with the king's signet present, and in others, the king presided. By the late second century BCE, the Indian legal writer Gautama presented the king as the specific person who could adjudicate cases.[10] The king's court was the highest court to hear and judge appeals. The king had the greatest legal authority to amend previous judgments and to issue final judgments.

Buddhists understood the king's place within India's legal system. They also knew they could rely on his intervention. This encouraged them to pursue two forms of clerical immunity: one to forgive the crimes that ordained Buddhists had committed prior to their ordination and the other to forgive those crimes that were committed after ordination. This chapter focuses on the fight for clerical immunity for offenses that were committed before ordination. Chapters 3 and 4 will discuss the fight for clerical immunity for offenses that occurred after ordination, as found in both legal and nonlegal Buddhist texts.

In the fight for clerical immunity over preordination offenses, a key step is to annul earlier convictions and recommendations for penalties for ordained fugitives. Kings' edicts were considered supreme among the laws in ancient India's four legal domains.[11] The kings themselves were thus considered the ideal candidates to annul these convictions. Buddhist legal writers note at least three ways kings could have effectively performed this role: they could have acted spontaneously to protect ordained Buddhists unconditionally, referred to an existing edict that had already been proclaimed, or broken existing laws to protect the monk or nun in question. These interventions were decisive in enabling a Buddhist institution to operate as a sanctuary where fugitive monastics could escape capital punishment.

The Buddhist pursuit of immunity profited from a fear of capital punishment. Women in ancient India feared being convicted of two crimes that call for this extreme punishment. One was adultery. In the third or early second century BCE, Indian legal professionals recommended punishing adulterous women by making them emaciated.[12] The punishment could be much more severe for male offenders: they could face castration. If a man in one of the three upper castes committed adultery with a lower-caste woman, he was only banished. However, a lower-caste man who committed adultery with an upper-caste woman faced capital punishment.

Punishment for committing adultery became even more severe later on. In the first century BCE, an adulterous woman would lose her ears and nose.[13] Then, depending on the castes of the man and woman involved in the adultery, an adulterous man could face the confiscation of all his property, be branded with an image of a headless body, be executed by burning over a straw fire, or be boiled in a vat. In the second century CE, punishing adulterous men and women became a public spectacle. The king could have a dog devour an unfaithful woman in a busy market and have the man burned to death on a hot iron bed or on a pile of stacked logs that had been set on fire.[14] Only Brahmins were immune from such severe punishment for adultery, receiving a symbolic death penalty through having his head shaved.

The other fear-inducing criminal penalty was for theft. Indian kings had a duty to protect people from theft. Because they retained the right to collect one-sixth of everyone's earnings and impose levies, taxes, and duties on their subjects,[15] the kings who discouraged thieves also protected an important source of their income. Further, a king who failed to stop a theft would be cursed by his people and told to "gather all the filth of the entire population."[16] This curse motivated Indian kings to impose severe penalties on thieves. These penalties ranged from fines to mutilation to capital punishment. For stealing more than one hundred units of gold, silver, or clothing of high value, the offender would face capital punishment. When the stolen goods were valued at less than fifty units of gold, silver, or clothing of high value, the thief would lose a hand. For stealing other types of less valuable goods, the thieves could have received penalties that varied from one to eleven times the value of the stolen goods. Other dreadful punishments included being burned while covered in a thin wrap, being thrown into deep water with a sandbag tied to the neck, having one's head burned, having one's ears or nose cut off, having one's urinary tract burned with a hot iron, and dismemberment.[17] The prospect of receiving these punishments instilled fear among people in ancient India, especially woman convicts. Conveniently, this fear provided fertile soil for Indian Buddhists to pursue clerical legal privileges.

To laypeople, this Buddhist fight was naturally appealing for its potential to shelter lay convicts from punishment for crimes they had committed before ordination, as long as they were willing to become Buddhist monks or nuns. When discussing unqualified nun candidates, Buddhist legal writers present many cases in which women thieves and wives accused of adultery successfully became ordained nuns to avoid the death penalty.[18] In these cases, bold thieves and habitual adulteresses who frequently sought sanctuary in nunneries became ideal examples of why it was so necessary and urgent for Buddhist institutions to be recognized as sanctuaries that could save lives.

Buddhist legal writers present the stories of women seeking ordination in the Buddhist monastic community as examples of a well-known and effective strategy used to avoid capital punishment. In each case examined below, the woman convicted of adultery receives a tip from other women in her extended family or community on how to seek ordination in a Buddhist institution, which they consider the only way to survive the court system. In other words, Buddhist legal writers present Buddhist institutions' ability to provide sanctuary as if this were common household knowledge throughout the lay communities.

The Guardian Kings

Buddhists across traditions in India perceived kings as the most reliable saviors for newly ordained nuns who were still haunted by their criminal pasts. Buddhist legal writers present these kings as taking all ordained Buddhists under their wings and using their authority to prevent these Buddhists from being executed with a death penalty.

The *Pāli Vinaya* recounts a case where an adulterous wife survives because King Prasenajit is willing to protect newly ordained nuns.[19] In the story, the woman is the wife of an unspecified Licchavi man who lives in the city of Vaiśālī. She engages in adultery but refuses to stop when her husband asks her. At an assembly of the Licchavi community, her husband asks for and obtains the community's consent to kill his adulterous wife. As soon as the woman learns of her husband's intention, she grabs some valuables from their home and flees. First, she seeks ordination in some non-Buddhist religious orders but fails. Next, she approaches some Buddhist nuns for ordination and fails again. In the end, she uses her valuables to bribe the Buddhist nun Thullanandā, who helps her become a nun. When her husband locates her in the city of Kosalā, which is in King Prasenajit's domain, he goes to see the king but does not mention that his wife's crime is adultery. Instead, he accuses her of stealing and requests the king's permission to punish her. As soon as the king learns that the wife has become an ordained Buddhist nun, he tells the husband that nothing can be done against the woman because of her newly acquired religious identity. The king's excuse is that the woman's self-enforced entrance into monastic life should serve as a punishment for her wrongdoing.

Adulterous wives were not the only ones to benefit from the kings' recognition of Buddhist institutions as sanctuaries. In the *Dharmaguptaka Vinaya*, Buddhist legal writers present a case to show King Bimbisāra's enthusiasm in saving a woman who is guilty of theft.[20] The rescue occurs while the Buddha is staying in Vaiśālī. As the story goes, the said woman steals the possessions of a group of Licchavi women and immediately becomes the target of killers who have been commissioned by the victims' husbands. The frightened woman flees Vaiśālī for the city of Rājagṛha, where she successfully becomes a Buddhist nun. Her hideout is soon exposed. The Licchavi husbands locate her among Buddhist nuns and approach King Bimbisāra in the kingdom of Magadha for assistance in arresting her. The king's search team finds the woman, now an ordained Buddhist nun. This revelation prompts King Bimbisāra to inform the Licchavi husbands that he cannot order the arrest of a thief who has become an ordained Buddhist nun.

Buddhists expected kings not only to turn down a stranger's request to prosecute nuns but also to do so when the request came from the king's own general.

One such case is recounted in the *Sarvāstivāda Vinaya*,[21] where King Prasenajit prioritizes saving a newly ordained Buddhist nun over keeping his promise to the woman's husband, a general, even though, as a reward for his service, the king had previously granted the general permission to kill his disobedient wife. As the story goes, this general had fought and won many battles for King Prasenajit. For his reward, he asks King Prasenajit to grant him permission to kill his disobedient wife with a knife made in the shape of a cow's tongue. King Prasenajit approves this request. The husband plans the killing for seven days later, but this is met with resistance. His wife's well-connected family finds out about the planned execution and mobilizes a rescue. At an intense moment during the mission, an unspecified Buddhist nun arrives and sees the distressed wife. Having learned what is about to happen to the wife, the nun agrees to take her away to live a monastic life. The nun immediately places a ceremonial robe on the wife and escorts her to a nunnery, where the wife is ordained. Back home, the husband and his aides finally locate the woman among the nuns. They try to take her by force, but the other nuns resist and protect the woman. An ignorant young warrior from the husband's team suggests cutting all of the Buddhist nuns "into two halves with the knife made in the shape of a cow's tongue."[22] A senior warrior objects to this violent plan. He insists on consulting King Prasenajit before taking any action because the king is known as the protector of all Buddhist nuns. Before the warriors see the king, some nuns report this matter to Queen Mallikā, who then informs King Prasenajit about the woman's case. In the end, the king employs some tactics to save the accused woman. When he meets with the warriors, who are now pressing for the execution of the woman, the king first asks the warriors to do him a favor, since he had previously permitted their general to kill his disobedient wife. The king asks them to forgive the woman because "that general's wife has now gone forth and, thus, is living a new life. She is no longer that wife."[23] The warriors agree to this.

In all three of the above-discussed cases, it is only through the king's mercy that these ordained Buddhists received immunity from being executed for convictions of preordination offenses. The king had been willing to adjudicate each of these ordained Buddhists' trials and to intervene on the nuns' behalf. In these cases, the king's intervention alone allowed Buddhist institutions to function as sanctuaries. But these case-by-case interventions from the king were not enough to transform the Buddhist institutions in question into dependable permanent sanctuaries.

An Existing Law

In the legal context presented in the *Mahīśāsaka Vinaya*, a fugitive has a much better chance of surviving than a fugitive in the other Buddhist legal texts.[24] In the *Mahīśāsaka Vinaya*, Buddhist legal writers have equipped King Prasenajit with an edict in which he has sworn to punish those who dare to harm ordained Buddhists. This edict provides the king with an excuse to save a widow who is accused of having committed adultery prior to her ordination.

According to the story, this widow comes from the Licchavi community and is indeed an innocent victim. Following her husband's death, the widow's younger brother-in-law repeatedly tries to marry her but fails. In the end, the brother-in-law decides to set a trap. He pretends to hold a memorial service for his dead brother and invites the widow to come to offer incense. When she arrives, the younger brother intoxicates her with alcohol and coerces her to have sex with him. Afterwards, he bruises her body and gashes it with deep scratches. When the widow wakes up and sees the bruises on her body, she suspects that her brother-in-law had intended to kill her. She flees to the city of Śrāvastī and successfully becomes an ordained Buddhist nun there. Meanwhile, the widow's brother-in-law has gone to court to file a suit against her, claiming that she is his wife and accusing her of adultery.

In this case, the nunnery alone is not sufficient to save the widow. The law enforcement officials from that court search for the widow in her original jurisdiction and soon learn of her whereabouts in the city of Śrāvastī. They contact King Prasenajit to request that she be extradited, and in return, they promise to extradite any future criminals who flee the king's jurisdiction. After consulting his ministers, the king learns that the wanted woman is residing in his kingdom but that she has already become an ordained Buddhist nun. The ministers also remind the king of a proclamation he has issued, where he declares, "If anyone dares to violate Buddhist monks or nuns, they will receive severe punishment."[25] Because of this proclamation, the ministers admit that they dare not arrest the woman as she is now an ordained Buddhist nun. The king then tells the law enforcement officials from the other kingdom that the woman they are pursuing has already received ordination and that they cannot prosecute her for crimes dating prior to her ordination.[26] As the story ends here, this text does not inform us how the law enforcement officials from the Licchavi community respond to the king's reply. What it does provide is an internal criticism that comes from within the Buddhist community. Buddhists criticize the king's decision not to prosecute the woman, saying, "If we let this crime go unpunished, this kind of practice will ruin our country."[27] The irony is that the woman they want to punish is indeed an innocent victim.

Instead of relying on the king's spontaneous intervention, the Buddhist legal writers of this text seek a more stable endorsement for the Buddhist institutions to function as sanctuaries. By presenting a law they claim was promulgated by the king, these Buddhist writers ensure that concerns about clerical immunity from accusations regarding preordination offenses are no longer decided on at the king's mercy; instead, clerical immunity becomes a legal right guaranteed by the king's law.

The King Who Broke the Law

The most arduous challenge in fighting for preordination clerical legal privileges can be found in the *Mūlasarvāstivāda Vinaya*, where King Prasenajit not only lacks an existing edict to justify his protection of a nun who has been charged with preordination crimes but also must deal with the laws he created that require him to severely punish adulterers.

Buddhist legal writers solve this problem by arranging for the king to break his own law and exempt ordained Buddhist offenders from being prosecuted for preordination crimes. In the Chinese and Tibetan translations of the *Mūlasarvāstivāda Vinaya*, King Prasenajit allows his preference for protecting ordained Buddhists to override his law that requires extreme punishment for adulterous women. In the Chinese translation,[28] where this case's development appears to be more logical than in its Tibetan translation, the wife of a general named Sword-Holder frequently engages in adultery while her husband is fighting on the battlefield. When her husband returns home and learns about her infidelities, he punishes her with a whipping. However, this physical punishment does not stop the wife from continuing her adulterous behavior. General Sword-Holder then goes to see King Prasenajit and successfully requests that he promulgate the following law: "If [a woman] has failed to observe the virtues of a woman and has insulted the law, then she should receive an extreme penalty."[29]

Another woman soon tests this law. She is the daughter of another general and has also been unfaithful to her husband. Before leaving for the battlefield, her husband requests that King Prasenajit have his wife executed, following the law on adultery. The woman sees the court judge and asks for a pardon, but the judge declines her request, adjudicates her case, and arrives at a judgment that states she is to be executed seven days later. During the waiting period, the woman stays at home and weeps incessantly. One day, the Buddhist nun Sthūlanandā appears at the woman's house while begging for alms. When Sthūlanandā learns of the woman's upcoming execution, she asks her, "Why don't you leave this secular life and become ordained?"[30] Sthūlanandā also promises to preside over her ordination. Upon hearing this, the woman pays homage to Sthūlanandā and says, "Venerable, please save my life."[31] Thus, Sthūlanandā ordains the woman as a Buddhist nun. When her husband learns of her ordination, he swears to kill her six days later.

Nun Sthūlanandā quickly realizes that if she is to keep the newly ordained woman safe, she will need help. She first sees her friends in a group of twelve nuns and introduces the newly ordained nun as a high-ranking official's daughter who has now converted to Buddhism.[32] The nuns in the group of twelve promise that they will protect her and deal with whomever comes to hurt her. Yet, the words of protection from a group of unarmed nuns do not seem reassuring enough.

Sthūlanandā then goes to see the senior nun Gautamī, but Gautamī considers the woman to be a person lacking in virtue and refuses to help. Next, Sthūlanandā goes to see Queen Mallikā. The queen also considers the woman as lacking in virtue and notes that she should not have been ordained. Yet, since she has been ordained, the queen feels the need to report this to King Prasenajit, thereby placing him in a dilemma. The king explains the difficulty: "If I follow the law and kill the newly ordained nun, it will tarnish Buddhism and earn me a bad reputation. However, if I release her, it will diminish the authority of the law."[33] The king shares his concerns with General Sword-Holder. But the general contests the king's views, noting, "The strict law was established and made known to all. So why would the king go against the law to forgive this woman?"[34] King Prasenajit arrives at an arbitrary justification when he states, "It is better to forgive this woman. The law applies to others."[35]

The version presented in the Tibetan translation of the *Mūlasarvāstivāda Vinaya* varies slightly.[36] Here, two soldiers go to fight on the battlefield, but their wives are at home playing games, singing songs, and developing intimate relationships with fornicators, prostitutes, and frauds. The two soldiers ask themselves, "If we can discipline rebellious hill people, why can't we discipline our wives? We certainly need to establish some law."[37] They swear they will punish their unfaithful wives by cutting their heads off and disposing of their bodies. Someone suggests they petition the king to establish this important law. The soldiers then go with their general to see the king. When the king hears about the matter, he concurs with the soldiers that what their wives have done is evil. The text does not explicitly state this, but given the context and the parallel story presented in the Chinese translation, we can reasonably assume that, after this meeting, the king had established a rule to punish adulterous wives.

Later, a general's daughter commits adultery and violates this law. Other women learn about her story and say to themselves, "If she broke the law but did not receive punishment, we will also break the law."[38] When the soldiers hear these words, they complain to the general. The general asks himself, "I got the law established. How can I allow my daughter to break it?"[39] He then chooses to publicly disown his daughter and tells the soldiers to kill her. When the soldiers catch her, the general's daughter begs for forgiveness. The soldiers consider that what she has done is unforgivable, but they nevertheless give her seven days to live. This woman weeps while she awaits her execution, and shortly thereafter, the Buddhist nun Sthūlanandā appears at her house. When the nun learns the cause of the woman's grief, she asks, "Don't you want to become ordained?"[40] She then ordains the woman and leads her to a nunnery, where she hides in the residence the nuns use for their summer retreat. The soldiers swear to find and kill the woman even if she has hidden in a cow's horn.

Unlike in the Chinese translation of the *Mūlasarvāstivāda Vinaya*, the newly ordained nun reaches out for help but her officiating nun Sthūlanandā does not comply. The frightened general's daughter then seeks refuge among a group of twelve nuns, who promise to defend her by using their black alms bowls to beat the soldiers. The general's daughter realizes that these nuns will be unable to protect her, so she seeks protection from the senior nun Gautamī and from Queen Mallikā. Unlike in the Chinese translation, in the Tibetan translation Queen Mallikā petitions King Prasenajit to protect the general's daughter, and the king agrees. Next, the king meets with the soldiers, telling them, "This villager, the general's daughter, has taken refuge with the Buddha, has taken refuge in the dharma, has taken refuge in the saṃgha, has taken refuge in me, and has taken refuge in you. Please do not kill her."[41] The soldiers ask the king, "Lord, why would you break the law [to pardon her]?"[42] The king replies, "Compared with whatever the violation is, it is better to protect the ordained. For this reason, let us release the Venerable."[43] The text does not elaborate on the soldiers' responses, but news about this case soon spreads throughout the Buddhist community and complaints soon reach the Buddha.

In the case presented in both translations, the general's daughter commits adultery in a kingdom where the king has already established laws that severely punish adulterers. Yet, the Buddhist legal writers still advocate for clerical legal privileges from the king at the cost of damaging the authority of the laws he had previously established.

A Different Perspective

Buddhist communities in India are diverse. Their memories differ on what disciplinary rules the Buddha had established for monks and nuns. Naturally, not all Buddhist legal writers are on board with the pursuit of clerical legal privileges. This lack of consensus is evident in the *Mahāsāṃghika Vinaya*, where its author presents three cases to explain why it is necessary to carefully discern candidates who have requested ordination. These three cases focus on threatening to punish Buddhist nuns who dare ordain criminals. They pay little attention to the fate of ordained fugitives, let alone suggesting ways to exempt them from punishment.

The guardian kings who intervened to protect newly ordained nuns are absent in all three cases in the *Mahāsāṃghika Vinaya*. In the first case,[44] a young widow from the city of Rājagṛha seeks ordination from a Buddhist nun as she wishes to resist her uncle-in-law's marriage proposal. After losing her husband, the widow clearly states her lack of interest in men, but her uncle nevertheless attempts to marry her by force. When she explains her trouble to the other women in her community, she is advised to leave and seek ordination from Buddhist nuns. She does exactly that and receives ordination from the Buddhist nun Kālī, in the city of Śrāvastī. However, the uncle-in-law does not give up on marrying the widow. After locating her among the nuns, he challenges Kālī for having ordained the widow. "I have not given my permission. How could you ordain my wife?"[45] Nun Kālī does not respond to his question but asks where he comes from. As soon as the man reveals that he is from Rājagṛha, Kālī accuses him of being a thief and a spy. She threatens to report him to the king and have him arrested and put in jail. The warning works and the uncle-in-law gives up and leaves. But the ending is far from a happy one. The Buddha scolds nun Kālī for illegally ordaining an unqualified woman. As for the ordained widow, Buddhist legal writers either ignore what ultimately happens to her or do not consider it relevant to inform their readers.

Likewise, the adulterous wife in the second case also lacks the king's protection. This wife is a habitual adulterer. She refuses to change her nefarious ways even after her husband asks her to stop and threatens to punish her. Her refusal eventually brings her to the state court, where her husband accuses her of adultery. In the court, her husband tells the judges, "My wife committed adultery with that person. I hope the judge will punish her for me, according to the law."[46] The judge convicts the wife. The law in her jurisdiction requires that adulterers be punished by public dismemberment. So, the judge adjudicates to have her dismembered seven days later, in front of members from both sides of her family. The convicted wife returns home and cries. Other women see her weeping and inquire about the cause of her grief. When they learn about her upcoming execution, scheduled to take place seven days hence, they ask her, "Do you want to save your life?"[47] The wife affirms her desire to live. Those women then tell her, "Go see the Buddhist nun Kālī in the city of Śrāvastī. Ask her to ordain you, and then you can survive."[48] In the subsequent days, the woman seizes an opportunity to flee when everybody in her community is drunk. She goes to see the nun Kālī and asks to become an ordained nun. Kālī asks the woman whether she has permission to be ordained. When the woman asks what constitutes a permission, Kālī explains that unmarried candidates need permission from their parents and married ones need permission from their husbands or uncles-in-law. The woman tells Kālī that since her entire family allows her to be dismembered in public, she considers their abandonment as evidence of their permission to let her be ordained. Therefore, Kālī ordains her. When the woman's former husband comes to look for her in the nuns' living quarters, Kālī confronts him. When the husband demands that his former wife be transferred to him, Kālī accuses him of being a thief who is also a foreigner who has come to spy on her country. She threatens to report him to the king and have him arrested and jailed. This tactic works and the husband leaves in fear. However, the fact this woman has been ordained upsets the lay community. When their criticism reaches the Buddha, the Buddha lays down a rule that prohibits the ordination of convicted women. As in the first case, the fate of the ordained woman remains unknown.

In the absence of a protective king, the first two women at least have their officiating nuns to protect them. In the third case, even aid from other nuns becomes a luxury.[49] In this last case, a woman convicted of adultery seeks ordination from Buddhist nuns. However, no nuns dare ordain the woman because the Buddha has already laid down a rule prohibiting nuns from ordaining criminals. The woman then turns to non-Buddhists and successfully joins them. When her husband learns that she has become a non-Buddhist, he decides to stop pursuing her punishment because he perceives her falling into a community of non-Buddhists as a sufficient punishment. While staying with those non-Buddhists, this woman becomes disturbed about their behavior. She sees them drinking fermented drinks, walking around naked, and being excessively greedy. These erratic behaviors compel her to reach out to the same Buddhist nuns as before, and she pleads with them to rescue her from the hell these non-Buddhists have created. However, the Buddhist nuns still dare not ordain her. Eventually, the woman goes to see nun Mahāprajāpatī, who subsequently reports the matter to the Buddha. Having heard that non-Buddhists have already ordained the woman, the Buddha amends his earlier promulgation and declares that convicted women who have fallen among non-Buddhists can be ordained as Buddhist nuns.

The lack of support for the Buddhist fight for clerical legal privileges in the *Mahāsāṃghika Vinaya* reveals a different perspective. It suggests that at least some Buddhist legal writers do not take it for granted that all kings in India would have considered preordination crimes forgivable. Of the three cases, only the woman in the third case receives a pardon, however informal, from her husband, who decides to stop pressing for her execution. The fate of the ordained women in the first two cases remains unknown. What remains equally ambiguous is how the Buddhist community and the state court would have prosecuted this adulteress. A fascinating revelation in the third case is that Buddhists consider those already convicted of crimes as unsuitable for ordination. Yet criminals who first subscribed to another religion, after having committed a crime, could later become eligible for ordination in the Buddhist community.

Conclusion

Buddhists are creative in the ways they fight for criminal immunity. In the spirit of explaining the letter of the law, Buddhist legal writers recount stories of adulterous wives and women thieves to illustrate their determination to maintain the integrity of the monastic community by keeping criminals out. What these cases more subtly demonstrate, instead, are Buddhist attempts to save lay convicts from the death penalty. While the subsequently established rule pledges to punish future monks and nuns who dare to help officiate lay convicts' entry into monastic life, the punishment is mild and difficult to impose.[50] The recommended punishment is only that accused officiants publicly confess in front of an assembly of resident monks and nuns, after which they can remain in the monastic community. Moreover, the officiants only face this punishment if the ordained fugitives are found guilty of a crime and sentenced by a judge, and if the conviction is reported to the king.[51] In the *Mahāsāṃghika Vinaya*, as we have seen, the Buddhist legal writers add a further caveat that helps Buddhist institutions rescue lay fugitives: an amendment from the Buddha stating that it is legitimate to ordain a lay fugitive who has joined a non-Buddhist religious group prior to their conversion to Buddhism. The Buddhist prohibition against ordaining criminals, thus, paradoxically has the effect of supporting the Buddhist institution's function as a sanctuary: when a monk or nun ordains a convict, the ordained convict still gets to remain ordained, and the officiating monk or nun receives a light sentence or no real punishment at all.

It is a risky business to operate Buddhist institutions as sanctuaries for fugitives. By accommodating criminals' entry into their institutions, Buddhists could have faced resentment, and their institutions' reputations could have been tarnished. In the *Dharmaguptaka Vinaya*, the Licchavi husbands harshly criticize the Buddhist nuns who ordained the woman who had stolen from their wives, stating, "The Buddhist nuns are shameless. They are also thieves. In public, they claimed that they knew the true dharma. But despite knowing that the thief had been sentenced to death and that her crimes were known by many, they still conferred on her full ordination as a nun. How could they follow the true dharma?"[52] In the *Mahīśāsaka Vinaya*, other Buddhists criticize King Bimbisāra, who refuses to extradite an ordained widow who has been falsely charged with adultery. They worry that the practice of not punishing people who have been convicted of such crimes will compromise the kingdom's governance.[53]

Buddhists do not take these risks in vain. The Buddhist institution of sanctuary could save lives. This outcome alone could have earned Buddhism more support in the lay community, appealing especially to laypeople from lower castes. The legal privilege of immunity or of a reduced penalty in place of capital punishment, as outlined in the *Dharmaśāstra* legal texts, is restricted to the Brahmins and members of the upper castes. This is not a privilege that one could earn but is permanently tied to one's status at birth. Because Buddhism is open to all eligible candidates and has no restrictions based on caste, granting ordained Buddhists clerical immunity from having committed preordination crimes creates a possibility for anyone, especially those from the lower castes, to seek refuge when they face capital punishment.

This creative approach is not flawless. The cases that advocate for such exemptions are both gendered and inconsistent. Women convicts appear as the sole sanctuary seekers. In the sections of the Buddhist monastic law texts that discuss candidates who are unsuitable for ordination, criminal men are not presented as potential fugitives. The absence of specific regulations on what to do with male convicts seeking ordination makes us wonder whether Indian Buddhists perceived ordination as a viable outlet for men who wished to avoid capital punishment. As shown above, this approach to sanctuary also lacks consistent support in Buddhist monastic laws from different traditions. We examined Buddhist monastic law texts from six extant traditions,[54] and at least one shows no interest in advocating for clerical legal privileges over preordination crimes.

This flawed approach still manages to be a hallmark in the Chinese imagination of the Buddhist legal world. Complete Chinese translations of these Buddhist monastic law texts became available to Buddhists in China as early as the fourth century. The stories of adulterous wives and women thieves are a likely source for the Chinese fantasy of Buddhist institutions as sanctuaries for criminals. This fantasy is so widespread that Chinese storytellers repeatedly use it as a trope in developing unconventional characters, such as the tattooed monk Lu Da presented in the introduction. Unlike the European kings who officially confirmed the legitimacy of clerical immunity for eligible Christian men and women, Chinese rulers never acknowledged the Buddhists' pursuit of clerical legal privileges. Their laws are devoid of rulings that excused ordained Buddhists for crimes they had committed before ordination. This lack of legal recognition does not cause the fantasy regarding Buddhist sanctuaries to wither. Instead, it continues to lure criminals in contemporary China to take their chances. Many criminals still try to seek ordination in small Buddhist monasteries in remote areas in rural China.[55] But unlike the legendary tattooed monk, these men often fail to escape being hunted by police, being arrested, and facing execution.

3

Buddhist Killers at Large

> I am a renunciant temporarily living in this kingdom. How can you say that you will kill me?[1]
>
> Monk Danika, *Sarvāstivāda Vinaya*

> I am an anointed king. How can I jail and kill a renunciant? Now, you can go back immediately to see the Buddha. The religious king himself will deal with you according to the law.[2]
>
> King of Rājagṛha, *Mahīśāsaka Vinaya*

Over two millennia ago, Buddhists were already wrestling with the controversy over abortion in ancient India. In the *Mūlasarvāstivāda Vinaya*, Buddhist legal writers present the case of a man who is facing a big crisis, when a family friend offers to help.[3] This man's brother has been away from home for a long time without any news. At some point, the man's sister-in-law (his absent brother's wife) proposes that he cohabitate with her. She threatens to leave the family if the man refuses to accept her proposal. Soon afterward, they start living together, the sister-in-law becomes pregnant, and the man regrets his decision to live with her. As a self-imposed punishment, he immediately leaves their home and becomes an ordained Buddhist monk. When a family friend with medical knowledge visits the newly ordained monk in his monastery and offers to find a drug to terminate the pregnancy, the monk remains silent. The family friend interprets this silence as passive agreement and arranges for his daughter to deliver the abortion drug to the new monk's sister-in-law. After the abortion completes, the sister-in-law reveals to her close girlfriends that the monk had procured an abortion drug for her. These women believe that the monk has done a despicable deed and begin to publicly disparage him.

The text seems to suggest that the social norm of the time considered it a crime to help a woman abort a fetus, or at least for a monk to offer such help. Yet the Buddhist legal writers do not arrange for the Buddha to punish the monk for his supposed role in the abortion. They see it as passive, in that the monk only silently consented to procuring the abortifacient. As such, they differentiate between monks who assist in abortions from ordinary laypeople who have been similarly involved in these cases.

Buddhism in Court. Cuilan Liu, Oxford University Press. © Oxford University Press 2024.
DOI: 10.1093/oso/9780197663332.003.0004

The presentation of this case in the *Mūlasarvāstivāda Vinaya*, as well as many other cases in which monks and nuns have caused others to die after the Buddha has officially established the rule against killing human beings, reveals that Buddhists have grown more ambitious and are more aggressively seeking clerical legal privileges. Besides protecting lay fugitives from capital punishment for having committed crimes before ordination, Buddhists further aspire to protect ordained Buddhists from capital punishment for committing postordination offenses. This expanded approach is necessary as it aims to promote monastic life as more than just a temporary refuge but a permanent one, to make it appealing to future converts.

Buddhists carry out this approach subtly. Rather than explicitly demanding jurisdictional autonomy, they unveil their pursuit of clerical legal privileges in the way they treat two types of clerical crimes: homicide and theft. When citing cases of monk and nun killers, Buddhist legal writers do not elaborate on the judgments these criminals faced, beyond a scolding from the Buddha. In all of the cases of homicide by monks and nuns—even those cases when the death occurs after the Buddha has established the monastic rule against killing human beings—no monk or nun is convicted. Based on the legal principles in the established rule against killing human beings, even if a monk or nun were convicted, their foreseeable punishment would be much lighter than what a lay murderer would receive. As I explained in "The Buddhist Legal World" section of the Introduction, convicted monk and nun killers would be able to continue living in the monastic community, only with a reduced status.

Buddhist legal writers equally downplay the seriousness of clerical theft. Even when the victim of the theft is a king, Buddhist legal writers consider it necessary to keep the culprit's interrogation private. In the text, Buddhist legal writers call for kings not to inflict punishment on monks who have been convicted of theft. To spare ordained Buddhists from conviction and corporal punishment, Buddhist legal writers warn judges and lay litigants against making judgments and filing complaints that could cause monks and nuns to suffer. As positive reinforcement, Buddhist legal writers further provide examples of how even animals refrain from hurting individuals who disguise themselves as ordained Buddhists, and they conclude with more general opposition to corporal punishment due to its intrinsically evil nature and the irreversible damage it could cause.

Buddhists did not fight for clerical privileges in isolation. Buddhist legal writers portray the historical Buddha as being attentive to the laws of the kings. As presented in the case of monk Danika, which will be discussed later in this chapter, the Buddha has been keen to learn the laws of the kingdom in which he dwells. In some versions of the Buddhist monastic law texts, after learning about Danika's crime, the Buddha wishes to understand the country's sentencing guidelines for theft and immediately consults a monk who has previously been the minister of justice in the king's court. When such a monk knowledgeable in these guidelines is not available, the Buddha sends another monk to interview Brahmins, lay Buddhists, and other people in the public market to obtain the information he requires. In one case, the Buddha is not shy about directly asking the kings for clarification on the punishments for theft.

Buddhists' attention to the legal world around them continues after the Buddha passes away. In the first century CE, in his biography of the Buddha, the Buddhist writer Aśvaghoṣa delivers an unusually positive presentation of some Brahmins.[4] At the time of the Buddha's birth, the omens accompanying his wondrous arrival worry his father, King Śuddhodana. To comfort the king, some Brahmins explain how Śukra and Bṛhaspati outperform their sage fathers, Brgu and Aṅgiras, in composing treatises on the royal law.[5] This reference to the legal writings of Brahmin sages indicates a broader Buddhist interest in and familiarity with the legal writings of their non-Buddhist religious peers.

By the sixth century CE, Buddhists who were fighting for clerical legal privileges for postordination crimes would have found support from another Brahmin author. When discussing the composition of the king's court of justice, the Brahmin writer Bṛhaspati (not the one mentioned above) recommends that "cultivators, artisans, artists, money-lenders, companies, dancers, persons wearing symbols of religious orders, and robbers should adjust their disputes according to the rules of their profession."[6] This line comes from the *Recollection of Bṛhaspati*, a Sanskrit legal text dating to the fifth or sixth century CE. It reflects a much broader interest in pursuing jurisdictional autonomy for many groups beyond the privileged Brahmin caste. What Bṛhaspati proposes would allow religious practitioners to receive trials within their religious communities but not in the king's court.[7] It is not impossible that this proposal might have given significant support for the Buddhist pursuit of postordination clerical legal privileges.

Buddhist Killers

Buddhist legal writers introduce the rule against the killing of human beings, whose violation constitutes an offense of defeat, with the case of a serial killer, Mṛgalaṇḍika, who has murdered sixty Buddhist monks.[8] The presentation of this case—as well as that of other homicide cases occurring after the Buddha's official establishment of this rule—reveals a Buddhist longing for clerical legal privileges in the state court. In all these cases of homicide, monks and nuns have either intentionally murdered or unintentionally caused others to die. The most serious punishment the Buddhist legal writers have arranged the Buddha to impose on them is a conviction of the offense of defeat, which primarily entails the convicted offender's loss of access to several communal activities reserved for monks and nuns in good standing.[9] In all these cases, comparable to murder and involuntary manslaughter in the contemporary US legal system, the Buddhist legal writers remain silent on whether further legal actions should be taken on monks and nuns who had directly or indirectly caused other human beings to die.

Despite having committed multiple homicides, the killer Mṛgalaṇḍika nevertheless receives neither trial nor punishment, neither in the state court nor within the Buddhist monastic community.[10] Mṛgalaṇḍika's religious identity remains ambiguous, with the Buddhist monastic law texts varying across different traditions. Mṛgalaṇḍika ranges from being a layperson of the lowest Caṇḍāla caste in the *Mahīśāsaka Vinaya*; to being a Brahmin in the *Sarvāstivāda Vinaya*, the *Mahāsāṃghika Vinaya*, and the *Mūlasarvāstivāda Vinaya*; to being merely a man named Migalaṇḍika, with no reference to any religious identity, in the *Pāli Vinaya*. My introduction of the story below is based on the version presented in the *Dharmaguptaka Vinaya*, where the killer is specified as having been a Buddhist monk.

As the story unfolds, we learn that the killings begin after some Buddhist monks, who had been meditating on the impurity of the human body, become disgusted by the appearance of their physical bodies and want to end their lives. One after another, they approach Mṛgalaṇḍika and beg him to kill them. Mṛgalaṇḍika agrees but struggles after killing the first monk. While washing blood off his knife at a riverbank, he has doubts about having killed an innocent monk. At that moment, a demon appears to be standing on the water in front of Mṛgalaṇḍika, assuring him that it was indeed an act of merit to kill that monk, because he helped a Buddhist monastic who had been unable to become enlightened on his own. Mṛgalaṇḍika then kills all the other monks at their request, totaling sixty victims. These killings lead to a significant reduction in the monastic population.

When the Buddha learns of Mṛgalaṇḍika's murders, he does not take any legal action against him. The possible justification could be that Mṛgalaṇḍika had killed those monks before the Buddha had officially established the rule prohibiting ordained Buddhists from killing human beings. This could explain the Buddha's treatment of him in the *Dharmaguptaka Vinaya*, where he is identified as an ordained Buddhist monk. Therefore, the Buddha neither prosecutes nor punishes Mṛgalaṇḍika. In the other versions of this case, since Mṛgalaṇḍika is presented not as a Buddhist monk but rather as an outsider of the Buddhist monastic community, the Buddha therefore has no jurisdictional authority him, making it impossible for him to take any legal actions against this killer.

When the Buddha learns of the crime, he only assembles the remaining monks and promulgates a rule prohibiting monks from committing or seeking assistance with suicide. The final version of this rule in the *Pāli Vinaya* reads as follows:

> Whatever monk should intentionally deprive a human being of life or should look about so as to be his knife-bringer, or should praise the beauty of death, or should incite [anyone] to death, saying, "Hullo there, my man—Of what use to you is this evil, difficult life? Death is better for you than life," or who should deliberately and purposefully in various ways praise the beauty of death or should incite [anyone] to death: he also is one who is defeated; he is not in communion.[11]

Despite the establishment of this rule, the Buddhist response to this homicide case still reveals a longing for clerical immunity from trials and punishment in the state court by keeping ordained Buddhist killers in the monastic community. According to this rule, any monk or nun who is to be convicted of the offense of defeat for killing another human being can still stay in the monastery under the penalty of "not in communion" status, which, as discussed earlier in the Introduction, only deprives the offender of the privilege of participating in certain communal activities. In other words, this rule offers future monks and nuns an opportunity to avoid trial and punishment in the state court, despite having directly or indirectly committed the crime of homicide, which is against the state law.

The experiences of other monks and nuns who caused laypeople to die, after the rule against the killing of human beings was already established and effective, confirm the feasibility of this opportunity, as shown in the *Pāli Vinaya*, the Chinese translation of the *Sarvāstivāda Vinaya*, and the *Mūlasarvāstivāda Vinaya* in Chinese and Tibetan translations.[12] In these cases, the Buddha acquits monks and nuns who have caused others to die—a crime comparable to involuntary manslaughter in US legal system today[13]—of the offense of defeat, due to the lack of intention to kill their victims. The Buddhist legal writers do not arrange for the Buddha to take any further legal actions against these monks and nuns, such as sending them to the state court for further trial under the state law. In the following paragraphs, I introduce two cases that demonstrate this Buddhist approach to dealing with monks and nuns who have caused others to die.

The first is a case comparable to involuntary manslaughter, where a simple-minded Buddhist nun Yuanman 圓滿 killed sixty thirsty thieves by giving them salty vinegar (*yancu* 鹽醋) to drink, after the Buddha had already established the rule.[14] The nun's crime begins with her attempt to save these thieves' lives. One day, she is accompanying some other nuns on a visit to a cemetery. At the same time, King Prasenajit of the kingdom of Magadha has mutilated the hands and feet of sixty thieves and has abandoned them in the same cemetery. Another unspecified person is also at the cemetery, who sees the miserable thieves and says, "If a kind-hearted person intended to end their suffering, that person could offer them salty vinegar to drink. After they die, they will be reborn and enjoy the fresh milk of their mothers."[15] On hearing this advice, Yuanman is determined to obtain salty vinegar to relieve them of their suffering. She finds some and offers it to all sixty thieves, who die immediately after drinking it. Yuanman returns to her nunnery late at night and invites other nuns to rejoice with her for having helped the suffering thieves be reborn to enjoy their mothers' milk. However, the other nuns point out that she has committed the most severe transgression: killing human beings. Yuanman then realizes what she has done and becomes contrite. She thinks, *Haven't I committed the offense of defeat?*[16] Her doubts over the possible offense of defeat shows that the prohibition against killing human beings has already been established and is in effect. Yuanman discloses her deed to other monks, who report it to the Buddha. The Buddha, however, declares that Yuanman has not committed a transgression.[17] He explains that only a "person who has intentionally caused the death of another would have committed an offense of defeat"[18] and thus failed to live up to their goal of pursuing the monastic life. In the Buddhist monastic legal system, this is the most serious transgression. The Buddha further elaborates that intentions can make a huge difference in evaluating an ordained Buddhist's role in a case where there has been a death. Specifically, he adds an amendment prohibiting nuns from offering salty vinegar to sick patients, but clarifies that it would not be a transgression if a nun offered salty vinegar to patients while thinking, *With this medicine, the patient will depart from this pain sooner.*[19] It would be an offense of defeat only if the patients died after the nun had offered them salty vinegar while thinking, *This medicine will suffice to end their lives.*[20]

In this case, the law that prohibits ordained Buddhists from killing human beings has already been established when Yuanman causes the sixty thieves to die. Yet the Buddhist legal writers still arrange for the Buddha to acquit her due to the lack of intent to kill. Moreover, they do not recommend further legal actions in the state court regarding this nun. What we can foresee in the future, based on this treatment of the nun Yuanman, is that even if convicted, other monks and nuns who cause others to die without the intention to kill the victim will at most be convicted of a grave offense that only requires the offender to confess in front of one other monk or nun.[21] What this means is that monks and nuns who committed crimes comparable to today's involuntary manslaughter would be able to continue living in their monastery after confessing their crimes to another person and, subsequently, avoid trial and punishment in the state court.

The killer nun Yuanman is not alone in receiving such a lenient treatment. In a second homicide case, also comparable to involuntary manslaughter in today's legal system, a Buddhist monk Kālodāyin, who has sat on and killed a newborn after the rule against killing was in effect, is similarly acquitted of the offense of defeat. Like Yuanman, Kālodāyin receives neither trial nor punishment in the state court. The case of Kālodāyin is found in the *Sarvāstivāda Vinaya* and the *Mūlasarvāstivāda Vinaya*, both of which introduce a rule that prohibits monks and nuns from sitting down on a seat without inspecting it first.[22] The death takes place during a time when the Buddha is staying in the Anāthapiṇḍada grove in the city of Śrāvastī. As the story goes, Kālodāyin has converted a Caṇḍāla woman to Buddhism. The woman offers him a donation, but Kālodāyin refuses to accept it. She then proposes to prepare a special seat for the monk, at her home, so he can sit on it to eat his alms meal. Kālodāyin accepts this arrangement. Later, the Caṇḍāla woman gives birth to a baby.[23] Her husband tells her to wrap the baby in new clothes and put the baby on Kālodāyin's special seat for a blessing. When Kālodāyin comes to eat his alms that day, he directly sits down on the seat as usual, without noticing the baby. When the mother screams and tells him of the baby on the seat, he immediately stands up, but it is too late: the baby is already dead. The mother weeps inconsolably, but Kālodāyin says to her, "Little sister, do not cry. Your child was destined to live a short life."[24] When the Buddha learns of the incident, he declares that Kālodāyin did not commit the offense of having killed a human being. The unspecified but implied justification is that he had no intent to kill the baby. At the end, the Buddha establishes a rule prohibiting monks from sitting down without first inspecting their seat. Overall, the presentation of these cases seems to indicate that after causing others to die, monks and nuns could expect to receive an internal discipline and not have to face any further trials or punishment in the state court.

The Monk Thief

Apart from homicide, theft is the other crime for which Buddhists seek to exempt clerical offenders from trial in the state court over postordination offenses.[25] This pursuit is reflected in the case of the Buddhist monk Danika whose act leads the Buddha to establish the rule prohibiting ordained Buddhists from taking what is not given (or stealing).[26] In this case, Buddhist legal writers arrange Danika to receive a private, not public, trial and also arrange for the king to avoid imposing any punishment on the monk thief. Furthermore, the Buddhist legal writers also depict the king transferring his jurisdiction over the monk offender to the Buddha. Because the offense of defeat for stealing had not yet been established at the time Danika committed the crime, it is not possible to convict him of the offense of defeat. But the fact that the Buddhist legal writers do not arrange for the king, who is both the victim and the maker of laws for use in the state court, to convict and punish Danika using the existing state law on stealing shows a Buddhist pursuit of clerical legal privileges for post-ordination crimes.

In this case, Danika decides to take timber from the king's warehouse without the king's explicit consent. Danika needs to steal because his dwelling has been destroyed several times and has no materials. As the story reveals, he first builds himself a grass hut, but shepherds and wood gatherers demolish it because they want the grass. He then rebuilds his hut in wood, but the shepherds and wood gatherers destroy it again. This pattern repeats several times, until Danika uses his skills as a potter's son to build a pretty brick hut. But then he also loses this dwelling after the Buddha considers it too ornate and orders other monks to demolish it. Subsequently, Danika decides to build a wooden hut and plans to fetch timber from King Ajātaśatru's storehouse, which is managed by Danika's friend. When Danika claims that King Ajātaśatru has promised him some wood and he has come to take some,[27] the storehouse manager says, "If the king has offered you the wood, he has done a great virtuous deed, and you can take the timber as you please. Yet all the lumber stored in this city is intended for King Ajātaśatru's use and is well guarded. They are intended for repairing damage to the city of Rājagṛha. They are kept for dealing with difficult situations."[28] Without having explicit approval from the storehouse manager, Danika nevertheless takes a piece of lumber, cuts it into shorter pieces, and carries it all away. Later, a city guard notices the missing lumber when patrolling the street and reports this to the storehouse manager. The manager then recalls his conversation with Danika and deduces that he might have taken the missing wood. When the city guard asks King Ajātaśatru if he had promised to give the lumber to Danika, the king cannot remember having made such a promise and summons both Danika and the storehouse manager to his palace.

Since the king is the victim in this case of stealing, Danika has to see the king in his palace for an interrogation. This does not suggest that that all cases of theft committed by ordained Buddhists would receive a trial in the king's palace. While Danika could not avoid a trial, Buddhist legal writers arrange for King Ajātaśatru to keep the trial as private as possible. In this case, King Ajātaśatru is the victim; he is also the lawgiver and ultimate adjudicator in all legal matters in his kingdom. Therefore, the king's palace becomes the natural choice of venue for Danika's trial. The versions of the case in the *Sarvāstivāda Vinaya* and the *Mūlasarvāstivāda Vinaya* provide details of King Ajātaśatru's extra efforts in arranging a private trial for this monk. Both texts portray King Ajātaśatru as having a clear plan to handle this interrogation discreetly. In the *Sarvāstivāda Vinaya*,[29] Danika and his friend, the storehouse manager, are about to arrive at the king's palace. When the king sees them approaching from afar, he orders the city guard to send the storehouse manager back to the storehouse and orders Danika to come alone. In the Chinese and Tibetan translations of the

Mūlasarvāstivāda Vinaya,[30] similarly, Danika tells his friend to see the king first and says that he will be there shortly, but when the manager and Danika arrive at the king's palace, the king tells the manager to wait outside, allowing only Danika to enter the palace.

The *Dharmaguptaka Vinaya*, *Pāli Vinaya*, *Mahīśāsaka Vinaya*, and *Mahāsāṃghika Vinaya*, however, are unclear as to whether the king intends to keep the trial private. In the *Mahīśāsaka Vinaya*,[31] the king first interrogates the manager friend who has arrived before Danika. In this case, while the king afterward interrogates Danika alone, it is unclear whether he had intended to do this. In the *Dharmaguptaka Vinaya* and *Pāli Vinaya*,[32] the friend arrives at the king's palace first and Danika comes later. Neither text clarifies whether the king questions the friend and Danika separately. In the *Mahāsāṃghika Vinaya*,[33] the friend is already in prison and has contacted Danika to intervene for him when Danika goes to meet with the king for his interrogation.

Nevertheless, Danika's act of stealing becomes apparent during the king's interrogation of him. In the interrogation described in the *Mūlasarvāstivāda Vinaya*,[34] Danika debates with the king and tries to argue that he has legally acquired the timber. When the king questions why he stole wood from his storehouse, Danika claims that the king had previously promised to give him the lumber. The king does not recall such a promise and asks Danika for clarification. Danika reminds the king that at the time of his enthronement, the king publicly "roared out a proclamation, like a lion," saying that "the Buddhist ascetics and Brahmins in my kingdom who observe the precepts, perform virtuous deeds, and do not steal may take and use all the grass, wood, and water in my kingdom as they please."[35] Danika argues that this proclamation permits him to take timber from the king's storehouse. Refuting this, the king explains that the proclamation only refers to the grass, wood, and water that is without owners, but that Danika has taken timber owned by the king. On that point, Danika sarcastically rebukes the king, saying that it is pointless for a king to promise to give religious practitioners things without owners. This last comment infuriates the king. In the *Mūlasarvāstivāda Vinaya*, the hot-tempered King Ajātaśatru grimaces, with his eyes wide open, and his hands shake. He then declares the following: "Renunciant, today you deserve to die. I cannot kill. It is better that you leave immediately. From today onward, do not do such things again."[36] In this declaration, the king considers Danika's offense punishable by death, a punishment reserved for convicted thieves. The king spells out this penalty of death for Danika in all but the *Mahāsāṃghika Vinaya*,[37] where Danika is instead lionized for having wisely saved his friend, the manager, from prison.

In all of the versions, the Buddhist legal writers have the king release Danika without imposing any punishment. In the *Sarvāstivāda Vinaya*, Danika challenges the king's authority to impose punishment on him. After confirming that Danika has taken timber from his warehouse, King Ajātaśatru tells Danika, "You have now fallen into a severe offense."[38] Danika confronts the king and says, "I am a renunciant temporarily living in your kingdom. How can you say that you will kill me?"[39] The king subsequently lets Danika leave without punishing him. In the other versions, the king decides on his own not to impose any penalty on Danika. Their reasons for this exemption vary in different texts. In most Buddhist monastic law texts, the king is reluctant to impose capital punishment on ordained Buddhists because doing so might damage his reputation as a ruler. In the *Pāli Vinaya*, King Bimbisāra explains that he is releasing Danika because he is an ordained monk and, as the king, he cannot impose corporal punishment on religious practitioners in his kingdom. The king says, "How could I flog or imprison or banish a recluse or a Brahmin who is living in my kingdom? Go, honored sir, you are freed on account of your hair, but do not do such a thing again."[40] In the *Dharmaguptaka Vinaya*, the king releases Danika because he does not want to impose the death penalty on an ordained Buddhist for having stolen a small quantity of timber.[41] In the *Mūlasarvāstivāda Vinaya*, the king simply says that even though Danika deserves to die, he, as the king, cannot kill him.[42]

In one version, the Buddhist legal writers even arrange for the king to voluntarily transfer the jurisdiction over Danika to the Buddha in the monastic community. In the *Mahīśāsaka Vinaya*, the king decides not to punish Danika, but he does not leave the case of Danika unresolved either. In this text, the king calls himself "an anointed king" who cannot imprison or kill an ordained Buddhist. Thus, he tells Danika, "I am an anointed king. How can I jail or kill a renunciant? Now, you can go back immediately to see the Buddha. The religious king himself will deal with you according to the law."[43] Here, the king's reference to the "law" is apparently referring to the Buddhist monastic law. In other words, the Buddhist legal writers depict the king transferring his jurisdiction over ordained monk criminals to the Buddha for an internal trial within the Buddhist establishment.

The Buddha's investigation soon confirms that the death penalty measured by the king complies with the state law in the kingdom. In all versions of this case, Buddhist legal writers portray the Buddha as being legally adept at working within the two systems of the state and the monastic community. The Buddha is attentive in following the proper procedures. First, he verifies whether the penalty decided for Danika accords with state law. He either sends a monk to find out what amount of stealing would lead to the death penalty in this kingdom or consults a monk who was a former governmental official. In the *Pāli Vinaya*, *Mahīśāsaka Vinaya*, and *Dharmaguptaka Vinaya*, he confers with a monk who has previously worked in the government and is knowledgeable in the kingdom's justice system. That monk informs the Buddha that a theft worth five māsaka coins is sufficient to punish an offender with flogging, imprisonment, or banishment from the kingdom.[44] In the *Sarvāstivāda Vinaya* and the

Mūlasarvāstivāda Vinaya,[45] the Buddha asks his disciple Ānanda to send a monk to find out what kind of theft would merit the death penalty in this kingdom. This monk interviews various people in public places in the city of Rājagṛha, including Brahmins, lay Buddhists, villagers, merchants, and rich householders, and reports to the Buddha that stealing goods worth five māsaka coins would bring the death penalty. In the *Mahāsāṃghika Vinaya*, the Buddha directly asks King Bimbisāra what kind of theft could lead to the death penalty, exile, or corporal punishment. The king confirms that stealing goods worth about five coins is punishable by death.

The Buddha seems to have failed to meet the king's expectations as he neither convicts nor punishes Danika. In all versions of the case, after verifying from different sources that Danika has committed a crime punishable by death according to state law, the Buddha nevertheless only scolds Danika. The justification could be that the monastic law against stealing did not exist when Danika took the timber. Yet this only means that although the Buddha, following Buddhist monastic law, could not convict him of an offense of defeat, his act still violated the state code, for which a lay offender could have been punished by death. In addition to scolding Danika, the Buddha also establishes the new rule prohibiting ordained Buddhists from stealing in the future and declares that he would impose the "not in communion" status on these offenders. The framing of this rule against the offense of defeat of stealing, however, will foreseeably provide future monks and nuns who steal—an act that breaks both the state law and the Buddhist monastic law—an opportunity to receive only internal discipline in the monastery instead of undergoing trials and punishments in the state court.

The Aftermath of Punishing Monks

To secure clerical immunity from punishment for ordained Buddhist offenders, Buddhist legal writers had to further deter laypeople from attempting to take them to the state court. They also had to convince judges in the state court to avoid punishing these monastics. To achieve these goals, they adopted a strategy of illustrating the dire consequences laypeople and judges could face if they caused monks and nuns to suffer in the state court.

Buddhist legal writers threatened laypeople with retribution were they to have caused monks and nuns hardship through adverse judgments in the state court. They warned lay litigants, both plaintiffs and defendants, of the severe losses they could face for causing physical harm to ordained Buddhists through litigation. In one case, mentioned above, the Buddhist legal writers recount the story of the husband of a runaway wife, noting how he beats the monk he finds her with and then takes him to the state court, where he accuses the monk of abducting his wife.[46] In the state court, when the wife reveals how her husband has physically abused the monk, the judge punishes the husband by confiscating his wealth. In another case recorded in the *Sarvāstivāda Vinaya*, where a Buddhist nun sues a layperson in the state court for beating her, the judge determines to have the defendant's hand mutilated.[47]

Buddhist legal writers expanded the extent of the retribution to include judges who caused any harm to convicted Buddhist monks and nuns, including for daring to impose penalties on these monastics. For example, in the *Dharmaguptaka Vinaya*, there is the case of a nun who sues over a property dispute. When the judge adjudicates in favor of the non-Buddhist plaintiff, the king confiscates the judge's wealth. Also, judges who dared torture monks during interrogation could be fired, lose all of their wealth, or even see jail time. The case that best illustrates this outcome is found in the *Mahāsāṃghika Vinaya*. It concerns a judge who tortured a monk for illegally ordaining a government official.[48] The story takes place while the Buddha is staying in the city of Rājagṛha, in the Kāraṇḍa Bamboo Grove. At that time, a monk privately ordains a government official, conferring full monkhood on him. A city guard arrests the monk for this, sends him to the state court, and tells the judge about the private ordination. In the subsequent interrogation, the judge orders that the monk be tortured as follows:

> Beat the monk to break three of his ribs, fetch his preceptor (*jieshi* 戒師) and pull his tongue, expel all ten categories of Buddhists and whip each of them eight times, and punish the fully ordained Buddhists (*shou juzujie zhe* 受具足戒者) under the extremely harsh law.[49]

The use of torture, in this case, turns in favor of the monks when King Bimbisāra suddenly intervenes. The departure of so many monks catches the king's attention as he is on his way to visit the Buddha. When he learns what has happened, the king is shocked by the punishment and immediately issues an edict that authorizes Buddhist monks to ordain anyone who wishes to be ordained. Moreover, the king summons the judge and asks him,[50] "Who is the king in this kingdom?" The judge replies, "You are the king." The king then asks, "If I am the king, why did you convict and punish people without telling me?" The king has the judge arrested, revokes his official position, and confiscates his property.

When dealing with the kings, Buddhist legal writers took a more constructive approach. Instead of threatening them, they showed how kings could benefit from protecting monks and nuns from incurring corporal penalties. To incentivize the kings to be reliable protectors, Buddhist legal writers demonstrated how doing so could win them the Buddha's reciprocal support. In the story from the *Mahāsāṃghika Vinaya*, when the king intervenes to punish the judge who had ordered the torture of a monk for ordaining a government official, the Buddha shows his gratitude by supporting the king.[51] To ease the king's concern over losing staff in his court, the Buddha promulgates a rule prohibiting monks and nuns from ordaining four types of government officials in the future: those occupying unsalaried official positions, those in salaried official positions, those salaried but without titles, and those with neither title nor salary. He further prohibits monks and nuns from ordaining all officials who have a title—salaried or unsalaried—either in this kingdom or elsewhere. Officials who are paid but have no official title could request ordination elsewhere but not in this king's kingdom. However, there are no restrictions on where unpaid officials with no official title could request ordination. These rules would certainly protect the kings from losing their staff.

Apart from threats and coercions, Buddhist legal writers also used exemplary animals, such as predatory birds and elephants, to advocate for clerical legal privileges in the Buddhist monastic law texts. In the *Mahāsāṃghika Vinaya*, Buddhist legal writers presented three stories that recount the monk Danika's previous lives, in which even predatory and enraged animals are unwilling to hurt Buddhists. In the first story we are taken back to Danika's previous life, where he is a dragon, King Bimbisāra is a gold-winged bird who preys on dragons, and the Buddha is a saint.[52] To avoid being attacked by these gold-winged birds, dragons regularly hang monastic robes on their dwellings' front doors. The birds respect these robes and will not attack places where they are hung. One day, Danika, the dragon, wanders off. The gold-winged bird, who is King Bimbisāra, spots Danika and is determined to capture him. At that very moment, the dragon puts on a monastic robe, runs along the shore, and transforms itself into a human being. The gold-winged bird then transforms itself into a Brahmin. The bird continues to hunt the dragon, curses it, and threatens to strip off its monastic robe. The dragon holds tightly to the robe, not letting it go. Finally, the dragon arrives at the dwelling of a saint—the Buddha in a previous life. The bird does not dare approach him. Instead, from afar, it vows to the saint that it will not hunt the dragon anymore.

In the second story,[53] the presence of a monastic robe discourages a six-tusked elephant king from punishing a hunter who has disguised himself as an ordained monk in order to kill him. In this story, King Bimbisāra is the elephant king, and the monk Danika is a destitute elephant hunter who has many sons to support. One day, following his wife's advice, the hunter packs some food, carries his hunting equipment, and goes to the snowy mountain to look for elephants. At that time, a six-tusked white elephant is living at the foot of the mountain. This elephant is intelligent and knows that people will hunt him for his tusks. For that reason, he has collected and stored the tusks of his dead father and grandfather. On the day the hunter arrives at the foot of the mountain, the white elephant is with some other elephants who are out searching for food. He sees the hunter and wonders if he has come to kill him. The elephant raises his trunk and signals for the hunter to come to speak with him. Fearing the elephant might kill him if he does not follow his command, the hunter goes to see him. The white elephant asks the hunter, "What did you come here for?" He replies, "I have come for your tusks." The elephant gladly offers the hunter his grandfather's tusks. The hunter is happy and leaves.

On his way home, the hunter decides to treat himself to a drink, thinking if he looks after himself, he will be able to take better care of his wife and children. He enters a wine house, carrying the tusks. The owner of the wine house sees the tusks and determines to bilk the hunter until he has taken his last penny. He volunteers to take care of the tusks, offers the hunter a lot of wine, gets him drunk, and makes him sign bills for food and drink he has not consumed. The hunter wakes up a few days later, only to find that the bills he has signed amount to the value of his elephant tusks. He ends up leaving the wine house with no money to take home. He then decides to go back to the snowy mountain to kill the white elephant for its tusks. Again, the white elephant treats the hunter with kindness and generosity, including giving the hunter its father's tusks. Again, the hunter loses the tusks to the wine house. The hunter then plans to kill the white elephant and returns a third time. On this trip, he wears a monastic robe to disguise himself as an ordained Buddhist monk. It is a hot late-spring day. The white elephant takes a bath and then rests under a tree with the other elephants. The hunter comes and shoots the white elephant with a poisoned arrow. The arrow lands between the elephant's eyes, causing blood to pour into them. The elephant lifts his head and recognizes that it is the hunter who has shot him. Despite its outrage, the elephant king tells the hunter to come to get his tusks and promises not to kill him because he respects the monastic robe the hunter is wearing. The injured elephant also protects the hunter from the other elephants, who are now attempting to kill him.

In the third story, even an elephant, who is used as an executioner, refrains from hurting a criminal after being transformed by Buddhist teachings.[54] In this story, King Bimbisāra was born as the fierce and undefeatable elephant Dashen 大身, "big body," in his previous life. In this life, the elephant's duty was to kill convicted criminals who had violated the law. The story begins when Dashen is walking out of his barn as it collapses. He continues casually walking until he arrives at the residence of some monks. He observes how well-mannered these monks are and listens to them reciting Buddhist texts that insist that killing will result in suffering and not killing will result in merit. These Buddhist teachings soften Dashen's heart. Later, a king (whose name is not specified in this story) drops a criminal who is facing the death penalty in front of Dashen. Dashen knows that his task is to kill this criminal, but he raises his trunk, sniffs the criminal three times, and shows no intention of killing him. The official monitoring the execution reports what he sees to the king, who becomes deeply worried. The king assembles his ministers for a meeting. The ministers call upon Dashen's caretaker and inquire what has happened to this elephant. When they learn that Dashen had recently gone to the monks' residence, they realize that these Buddhists might have influenced the elephant. His heart has become softer and he has lost interest in killing others. To revert Dashen to his former self, the executioner, the ministers tell his caretaker to build a gambling house, a slaughterhouse, and a prison near the elephant's barn. The caretaker brings Dashen to observe what is happening in those places. Having seen gamblers shouting, butchers brutally killing sentient beings, and people being tortured in prison, Dashen is transformed into his former self—a vicious beast. When the king sends other criminals for corporal punishment, Dashen immediately tramples them to death. In conclusion, the Buddha tells the assembled monks that in his previous life, King Bimbisāra had been a good elephant and had been delighted to see ordained Buddhist monks, including Danika, the hunter who had killed him in that life. Therefore, he forgives his stealing without imposing any penalty in this life.

A General Opposition

The Buddhist opposition to corporal punishment went beyond concerns about the extent to which monks and nuns were afflicted. As the damage caused by corporal punishment could be unbearable and irreversible, Buddhist legal writers considered it necessary to oppose these punishments more generally.

Buddhist legal writers considered corporal punishment to be intrinsically evil. They arranged for the Buddha to reject the imposition or carrying out of corporeal penalties, as he considered them to be among the three most evil deeds in the world. In one case, the Buddha offers this view in a comment on monk Danika's experience as a habitual thief in a previous life. In that life, Danika was born as a celestial being.[55] Initially, as the story goes, he and the other celestial beings take delight in meditation and need no food. Later, they indulge in delicious worldly food, the consumption of which makes them overweight, ugly, and devoid of magical power. When food becomes scarce, Danika steals it from others and refuses to quit this practice. In response, the other celestial beings establish a rule to punish thieves by beating them with heavy sticks. When they catch Danika stealing a second time, they beat him severely. Danika protests and tells them that beating a living being with a stick is an evil deed. Buddhist legal writers note that at the end the story, the Buddha summarizes the three evil deeds as stealing, speaking with arrogance, and beating a person with a heavy stick.

Buddhists legal writers defined corporal punishment as evil on account of the unbearable physical pain it causes. They present a case involving King Bimbisāra, in which they show that good governance is devoid of judgments that impose corporeal penalties, adding a lesson on how using such penalties could become a source of distress for kings.[56] In the story, the king is committed to the type of governance that uses leniency when judging criminals. During his great-grandfather's time, law enforcement officials only punished thieves by tapping their hands on the thieves' heads. During his grandfather's time, law enforcement officials placed thieves inside a circle of ashes and then immediately released them. During his father's time, thieves were exiled from the city. King Bimbisāra also exiles thieves from his kingdom. He believes that the penalties his fathers used suffice to humiliate thieves and prevent them from committing other crimes. One thief, however, challenges King Bimbisāra's principle of lenient governance. Officials have arrested and exiled this thief seven times, but the thief has returned each time to commit more crimes. When the officials catch the thief an eighth time, they ask King Bimbisāra to punish him properly. The king decides to have the thief's pinky finger cut off. After giving the order, King Bimbisāra bites his own pinky and finds the pain unbearable. He immediately regrets his decision and tries to stop the impending mutilation, but he is too late. His law enforcement officials have carried out this penalty. The thought of himself as so unkind distresses the king. He confesses to the Buddha. Instead of comforting the king, the Buddha asks the king to define the kinds of theft that would warrant the death penalty, exile, or other lesser corporal penalties. The king informs the Buddha that a theft of 4.75 units of cash would be punishable by death.[57]

Buddhists also object to corporal punishment because the harm it causes is irreversible for living beings. Buddhist legal writers illustrate the terrible consequence of corporal punishment in the case of a young mongoose in the *Mahāsāṃghika Vinaya*.[58] In this story, the mongoose is living with a Brahmin couple who have no children. The couple treats the mongoose as if he were their son. Later, the wife gives birth to a son, and the couple treats the mongoose even better, attributing the child's arrival to the young mongoose. One day, the husband goes out to run some errands, and the wife also leaves the house to borrow a rice grinder from a nearby neighbor. While both are away, their son eats some delicious bread, and the smell of the good food attracts a poisonous snake. Just as the snake is about to attack the child, the mongoose intervenes, fights the snake, and eventually tears it into seven pieces. The mongoose is proud to have protected the boy and imagines how pleased the couple will be when they see what he has done. He smears his mouth with the snake's blood and sits at the front door, waiting for the couple to come home. When the husband returns and sees the mongoose with its blood-smeared mouth, he assumes he has eaten his son. Grief and shock provoke him to strike the mongoose with a heavy stick and kill it. When the Brahmin enters his house, he sees his son sucking his fingers in the courtyard and the dead poisonous snake lying beside him. At that moment, the Brahmin realizes that he has wrongly killed the innocent mongoose. Buddhist legal writers used this case to show how the use of a corporal penalty could lead to irreversible damage.

To convince kings to abandon and forbid corporal punishment, Buddhist legal writers presented a story that further demonstrates how alternative corrective treatments can work better at transforming criminals. In this story, they contrast King Bimbisāra's remorse with another king from the Kāśī kingdom who uses kindness to transform thieves in the city of Varanasi.[59] Rather than imposing penalties on these thieves, this king sends them to a sorrow-free garden and provides them with food and musical entertainment. Soon, many people voluntarily self-identify as thieves to get into that garden. The number of thieves there soon reaches one thousand. The king has the garden cleaned and decorated and provides various foods. When he arrives at the garden with his ministers and sees the thieves wearing dirty clothes, long nails, and tangled hair, he immediately orders that they be given baths, new clothes, haircuts, and manicures, and that they be provided with good food and the wealth they need to survive. In the end, the king tells the thieves to support their parents, to take care of their homes, and to never steal again. Those thieves thus go home happily. The indication here is that leniency toward the thieves succeeds in guiding them back to a normal life.

Conclusion

The way the Buddhist legal writers introduce these cases of homicide and theft shows a Buddhist pursuit to exempt Buddhist killers from state trials as well as to exempt monk thieves from punishment in the state court. Unlike the many wrongfully accused monks and nuns who suffered during litigation in the state court, the monastics who cause others to die were only internally interrogated by the Buddha and never receive trials or punishments in the state court. In dealing with these monks and nuns, Buddhist legal writers only warned that if they repeated their offenses, they would not be allowed to live in communion with the other monks and nuns in good standing.[60]

Among the cases of homicide involving monks and nuns, we can see an interesting contrast. When the victim was a layperson, other laypeople could accuse ordained Buddhists of murder and take them to the state court. But when the victim was a fellow ordained Buddhist monk or nun, Buddhist legal writers often discouraged anyone from pressing charges against the offenders. This practice indicates that Buddhist legal writers, consciously or unconsciously, treated ordained Buddhist killers differently, depending on the composition of the litigants in each case. An ordained Buddhist charged with killing a layperson was to appear in the state court, but one who had caused a fellow ordained Buddhist to die received only an in-house trial within their monastic institution, or no trial at all. This differentiation seems to suggest a Buddhist attempt to distinguish between external homicide cases involving victims from outside the monastic community and internal homicide cases involving only victims inside the monastic community. More broadly, this distinction reveals a Buddhist perception of where to draw the jurisdictional boundary between the clergy and the state. That is to say, ordained Buddhists who committed crimes against outsiders fell within the jurisdiction of the state court, while ordained Buddhists who committed crimes against insiders within the Buddhist clergy fell within the monastic jurisdiction.

This expanded Buddhist fight for postordination clerical immunity was not devoid of interreligious legal influences. Buddhists were not interested simply in seeking reduced penalties. Instead, through their presentations of various cases of homicide and theft, they revealed a longing for ordained Buddhist convicts to be fully exempted from any penalty. This Buddhist vision of clerical legal privileges is not an idea that originated in isolation within the Buddhist institution. The social context of ancient India, where this vision emerged, was the same for the other contemporary non-Buddhist religious communities that tried to negotiate similar clerical legal privileges. The Brahmins, for instance, perceived themselves as being under the jurisdiction of the royal court in India but sought exemption from capital punishment.[61] The Brahmin legal writer Gautama, from late second century BCE, believed that "the king ruled over all except Brahmins."[62] He also insisted that kings in India should exempt Brahmins from six things: corporal punishment, imprisonment, fines, banishment, upbraiding, and abandonment.[63] Later Brahmin legal writers continued to reinforce the importance of extending such clerical legal privileges to Brahmin offenders. In his *Dharmaśāstra*,[64] the second century CE Brahmin legal writer Manu argued that a Brahmin should not receive capital punishment under any circumstances. As Manu wrote,

> Shaving the head is prescribed as the death penalty for Brahmins; but the other social classes are actually subject to the death penalty. The king should never put a Brahmin to death, even if he has committed every sort of crime; he should banish such a Brahmin from his kingdom along with all his property without causing him harm. There is no greater violation of the Law on earth than killing a Brahmin; therefore, a king should not even think of killing a Brahmin.[65]

These precedents of pursuing religious immunity and jurisdictional autonomy from the state court reveal that the Buddhists' perceptions of the parameters of their jurisdictional relationship with the state could hardly have avoided being influenced by the legal considerations entertained by pioneers in religious communities that predated Buddhism in ancient India.

4
Withered Orchid and Dead Ox

The yellow jade orchid may wither,
Yet it is still better than other flowers.
Buddhist monks may misbehave,
Or break their monastic vows,
Yet they are still better than all the non-Buddhists.[1]

The Buddha, *The Ten Wheels Sūtra*

The fight for clerical legal privileges can be described as an interactive project. Its success required constructive negotiations between the Buddhist establishment and the state. While Buddhist monastic law provided a convenient platform on which to fight, this had a fatal limitation: the monastic law texts' primary intended readers were ordained monks and nuns. Thus, the most desired audience—including kings, ministers, law enforcement officials and other laypeople—were prohibited from reading or studying these texts.[2] This chapter shows how Buddhists solved this dilemma by expanding the fight for clerical legal privileges beyond the monastic law texts into the public-facing doctrinal texts, to which access was less restricted.

Advocating for clerical privileges in these public-facing texts required Buddhists to advance their agenda with more caution. Instead of arbitrarily demanding clerical legal privileges, Buddhists sought to justify their demands by noting how reasonable they were and addressing any questions that might naturally have occurred among a lay audience. The pursuit of clerical immunity first implied that there were monks and nuns who committed crimes that were punishable in the state court. To explain how these monastics could have become criminals in the first place, Buddhists situated the need for clerical immunity as having occurred after the historical Buddha's death. In Buddhism, this was a time known as the Age of Degeneration. The Buddha's departure from this world led to the loss of his teachings and, consequently, corruption among monastic adherents, some of whom committed all kinds of crimes. The *Moon-Womb Sūtra*, a Buddhist text that contains a series of conversations between the bodhisattva Candragarbha (or Moon-Womb) and the Buddha, explains where criminal monks come from.[3] This explanation is absent in discussions on clerical legal privileges in Buddhist monastic law texts.

Buddhism in Court. Cuilan Liu, Oxford University Press. © Oxford University Press 2024.
DOI: 10.1093/oso/9780197663332.003.0005

Similarly, the demand for clerical immunity assumes that ordained Buddhists should be treated differently under the law, compared to laypeople. In the *Ten Wheels Sūtra*,[4] Buddhists present both the visible and invisible differences that separate a defendant who is an ordained Buddhist from an ordinary lay defendant who committed the same crime. Visually, the dyed monastic robe differentiates an ordained Buddhist from a layperson, because the mere presence of the robe reminds its viewers of the Buddha and his teachings. This visual reminder thus links the salvific power embodied in the robe to the monks and nuns who wear it. The invisible difference comes from the vows monks and nuns take during ordination. Their oaths to live monastic lives, guided by the vows, transform these monastics from ordinary human beings, it is thought, into those whose power to benefit other human beings transcends this lifetime. Just as a withered orchid is still more fragrant than other flowers and a dead ox or deer is still better than other living animals because they can produce medicinally valuable ingredients, such as bezoar and musk, a convicted ordained Buddhist criminal is better, Buddhist writers assumed, than a law-abiding layperson.

One noticeable difference between the campaign in the legal texts and that in the nonlegal texts was an expanded pursuit for additional immunity from financial penalty in the latter. In the nonlegal text of the *Satyaka Sūtra*, the demand for this additional immunity reflects the changed reality Buddhists faced at that time.[5] Previously, monks and nuns were at risk of being arrested, tortured, or jailed for committing crimes against state law. Later, fines and confiscation of property also became possible punitive options. Thus, an expanded campaign was necessary to protect individual monks and nuns from property loss. Buddhist institutions would also have benefited from this expansion. In Indian Buddhism, it was often a tradition for the host monastery or nunnery to inherit the possessions of their dead monks or nuns. Protecting criminally convicted monks and nuns from having their property confiscated also safeguarded their host institutions against potential future financial losses.

During their campaign, Buddhists not only vehemently protested against the state's use of violence in the legal governance of its subjects but also relied on state rulers' fear of karmic retribution should their law enforcement officials punish Buddhist criminals. In the *Sumeru-Womb Sūtra*,[6] Buddhist writers specifically forecast that those who fail to comply with the demand for clerical immunity and instead inflict physical or financial hardships on ordained Buddhists will suffer personally and professionally. Personally, hell will await them after death. Professionally, when a ruler causes a criminal monk or nun to suffer, the entire kingdom—Buddhist writers warn—will suffer from wars and natural disasters.

The presence of discussions on clerical legal privileges in multiple nonlegal Buddhist texts, as I will discuss below, is central to understanding this entire campaign's origin. In her study on the prophecy of the deterioration of

Buddhism, Jan Nattier documents the story of King Duṣprasaha of the kingdom of Kauśāmbi, wherein an exhortation urges rulers "not to punish those monks who [did] not faithfully adhere to the monastic rules." This exhortation appears only in a passage found in the Chinese translation of the *Moon-Womb Sūtra* but is absent in the Tibetan translation.[7] Moreover, Nattier was unable to locate any similar exhortations in other Indian Buddhist texts. This lack of cross-references leads Nattier to assume that such an exhortation "was added in a Chinese context in response to Chinese conditions."[8] The present chapter invites us to reconsider this assumption. It argues that the presence of this campaign in the Chinese and Tibetan translations of the *Ten Wheels Sūtra*, the *Satyaka Sūtra*, and the *Sumeru-Womb Sūtra* show how the campaign for clerical legal privileges in nonlegal Buddhist texts was not a Chinese invention but one with its origin in Indian Buddhism.

The Prophecy of Bad Monks

Why would monks and nuns misbehave and face penalties in the state court in the first place? This is the first question Buddhists faced when campaigning for clerical legal privileges in the nonlegal Buddhist texts. In ancient India, Buddhists linked the occurrence of misbehaving monks to an eschatological discourse on Buddhism's deterioration after the Buddha's death. In this discourse, a prophecy from the Buddha situates misbehaving monks in stories of war, royal devotion, and internal violence within the Buddhist community in the city of Kauśāmbi. The main elements in this story were in circulation in India no later than the second century CE and in China no later than the beginning of the fourth century CE. There are similar versions of this story in at least seven Buddhist texts that were translated into Chinese between the early fourth and early seventh centuries,[9] in two Tibetan translations dating to the eighth century,[10] and in one eighth-century Khotanese text.[11] As early as the beginning of the fourth century, these Chinese translations made it possible for Buddhists in China to engage with the idea of misbehaving monks and their immunity from punishment.

The sixth-century Chinese translation of the *Moon-Womb Sūtra* is the ideal text for understanding this story: it contains not only descriptions of how ordained Buddhist monks would misbehave in the future but also the Buddha's exhortations for people to treat misbehaving monks kindly and respectfully.[12] This text records a conversation between the Buddha and the bodhisattva Candragarbha, or Moon-Womb.[13] Here, the Buddha prophesizes that after his death, corruption and violence within the monastic community will destroy his teachings within five hundred years, with corruption beginning to erode the monastic community as soon as one hundred years after his death.[14] The Buddha also predicts that in this future time, people will seek ordination to make a living rather than for spiritual advancement. Having become ordained, they will become envious, shameless, and desirous of wealth and fame, showing no interest in reciting Buddhist texts or practicing meditation. During the daytime, they will take delight in quarreling. At night, they will enjoy a sound sleep. They will even have affairs with women, wear fine clothes, and work in secular professions to earn profits.

The Buddha prophesies that the indulgence of King Duṣprasaha, ruler of the city of Kauśāmbi, will lead these monks to another level of corruption.[15] In that future time, the city of Kauśāmbi and its Buddhist monastic community will suffer attacks from three evil kings. During their military march, these three evil kings will invade India, butchering laypeople, pillaging fortunes, burning down Buddhist monasteries and stupas, and slaughtering and robbing ordained Buddhists before they reach Kauśāmbi. There, King Duṣprasaha, who was born smeared in blood and at age seven was anointed and ascended the throne, will fight against the three evil kings for twelve years and eventually defeat them. According to the Buddha, this victory will not make Duṣprasaha happy. On the contrary, he will be extremely concerned about the karmic consequences of the deaths he had caused on the battlefield. To receive counsel, he will visit Śiṣyaka, a Buddhist monk who is learned in all three major categories of Buddhist teachings. As a remedy, this monk will advise the king to host all ordained Buddhists at a grand feast that will last for twelve years.[16] As soon as the king announces his invitation, ordained Buddhists will set out from all directions and travel to Kauśāmbi. On this journey, many will die from sickness or in attacks by bandits. At the first grand feast, monks who have safely arrived at the kingdom will inquire among each other about the whereabouts of their teachers and fellow monks. When these monks learn the news of the deaths that have occurred among their friends and teachers during their journey, they will lament and cry loudly. In vain will Śiṣyaka and King Duṣprasaha try to calm them.

The Buddha also predicts that these lamenting monks will soon find comfort in King Duṣprasaha's abundant offerings. Because many of them joined the monastic community only to make a living, twelve years of offerings from the king will lead them to indulge in material and sensual enjoyments and ignore their moral and spiritual training. They will no longer be diligent in reciting Buddhist texts, nor will they take delight in contemplative practice in solitude. Instead, in the daytime they will chat, in groups, about secular affairs, and at night, they will become so tired as to fall into a deep sleep. They will also take delight in wearing fine clothes. According to the Buddha, they will gradually fail to observe his teachings.

Ordained Buddhist monks and nuns are supposed to gather regularly to recite the monastic disciplinary rules and repent for transgressing any of these rules.

The Buddha predicts that internal corruption within the monastic community will culminate into fortnightly rituals where monks will strike each other down in deadly attacks. According to the Buddha, an exchange between the above-mentioned Śiṣyaka and an arhat monk, Sūrata, at one fortnightly gathering will provoke such a fatal assault. At this gathering, monks will learn that they are going to hear the Buddha's teachings for the last time, and they will become distressed. Śiṣyaka will be expected to preside over this last ritual but will be reluctant to do so. He will rise from his seat and confess his own failure to study and observe the monastic rules. Next, he will promise to preside over this fortnightly ritual only if a monk who is able to strictly observe all of the monastic rules will be in attendance. On that occasion, Sūrata will self-identify as such a monk and will request that Śiṣyaka proceed with the fortnightly ritual.[17]

More lively descriptions of this exchange between Śiṣyaka and Sūrata are found in other variations. In the Chinese translation of the *Miscellaneous Discourse of the Buddha*, the Buddha predicts that an administrative monk will invite Śiṣyaka to preach on the *Prātimokṣa*, a collection of versified monastic rules for fully ordained monks and nuns. Śiṣyaka, however, insists that there is no need for such preaching. Instead, he will speak to the audience and then ask them a question:

> All the disciples of the Buddha on the continent of Jambudvīpa total several millions. Among them, I am the most senior, learned in all three categories of the Buddha's teachings. Even I no longer study the monastic rules, let alone others. Therefore, to whom should I preach on the monastic rules?[18]

Next, the Buddha predicts that Sūrata will self-identify as a rule-abiding monk. He will stand up, proceed to Śiṣyaka's seat, join his palms, and speak to him:

> Venerable, please proceed to preach on the disciplinary rules. I have studied all the teachings that monks such as Śāriputra and Maudgalyāyana studied during the time when the Buddha was still alive. Although a thousand years have elapsed since the Buddha passed away, I am completely observant of all the monastic rules he established.[19]

In the Tibetan translation of the *Moon-Womb Sūtra*, the Buddha predicts that Śiṣyaka will reply with an ornate rejection, beginning with a metaphor:

> If a person is blind, and has neither nose nor ears, what is the need for a mirror? What is there to see? Even if I preach on the monastic disciplinary rules, you do not practice in accordance with them, and you do not observe them. Therefore, even if I preach on the monastic disciplinary rules, what is the benefit?[20]

The story continues to develop in the Chinese translation of the *Moon-Womb Sūtra*. In this text, according to the Buddha, the monk Aṅgada,[21] an adherent of Śiṣyaka, will read Sūrata's response as a challenge and an insult to his teacher. He will rise up, utter curse words, and kill Sūrata with a heavy stick.[22] Sūrata will be perceived as having been the last arhat. His death will cause the other monks present during the attack to cry. One demon who is also a faithful Buddhist, Dadhimukha, will become particularly outraged and kill Aṅgada.[23] Another monk, who is an adherent of Sūrata, will kill Śiṣyaka.[24]

The Buddha predicts that these deadly fights will soon lead to the complete erosion of his teachings. After that violent day, King Duṣprasaha will gather the remaining monks and continue to offer them delicious food and other provisions. He will even donate many precious jewels to build five hundred monasteries as residences for these monks. Yet when the king invites these monks to preach the Buddha's teachings, none of them will respond. After the king's repeated invitation, all of the monks will remain silent. At that moment, the monks' robes will lose their color, turn white, and fall from their seats. This will mark the end of the age of the true teachings of the Buddha.

Many Buddhist texts contain the above prophecy of the corruption of Buddhist monks, but only the mid-sixth-century Chinese translation of the *Moon-Womb Sūtra* discusses the fate of these degenerate monastics.[25] In the Buddhist chronology, these monks will live during the second age after the Buddha's death, when there is only a semblance of the Buddha's teachings. At the end of this conversation in the text, the Buddha invites people to continue to treat these monks, even in this age of semblance, with the same respect, kindness, and support they accorded the Buddha. In his prediction, the Buddha says,

> The age of semblance will last for a thousand years. Celestial beings will make offerings to those who shave their heads and wear the monastic robes, whether they obey the monastic disciplinary rules or have violated them. Do not make them short of provisions. If you make offerings to them in this way, you are making offerings to me. If for the sake of my teachings, people shave their heads and wear the monastic robes to take refuge in Buddhism, and claim to be my children, even when they break the disciplinary rules, their spiritual accomplishments will never subside. If you beat them, you are beating me. If you curse and insult them, you are destroying and insulting me.[26]

By urging people to avoid hurting or insulting ordained Buddhists, even those who violated the monastic law, what the Buddha is advocating for ordained Buddhists who misbehave is equivalent to complete immunity from verbal abuse or corporal penalty. The Buddha also speaks to Maitreya, who will become the Buddha in a future time, to secure from him additional protection for these miscreant monks. Specifically, the Buddha asks Maitreya to help robe-wearers who have violated the monastic disciplinary rules and help prevent them from dying from a shortage of provisions.

Corporal Punishment

Like the campaign for clerical legal privileges reflected in the Buddhist monastic law texts, the campaign in the nonlegal texts also seeks clerical legal privileges for both pre- and postordination crimes. In the *Ten Wheels Sūtra*, a series of conversations unfolds between the Buddha and three individuals: the bodhisattva Devagarbha, the Buddha's disciple Upāli, and the bodhisattva Kṣitigarbha. Their conversations revolve around tenfold series of actions that may either positively or negatively affect one's path to enlightenment. This text has circulated widely in three languages. It survives in two translations in Chinese, one in Tibetan, and one in the Xixia language. Its first Chinese translation, whose full title is *The Great Extended Ten Wheels Sūtra* (*Da fangguang shilun jing* 大方廣十輪經), dates to the Northern Liang (397–439 CE).[27] Over two centuries later, in 651, the aforementioned Chinese monk Xuanzang and his team produced a second Chinese translation, whose full title is *A Mahāyāna Sūtra, A Great Collection on the Earth-Womb and the Ten Wheels* (*Dasheng daji dizang shilun jing* 大乘大集地藏十輪經), at his residence in Ci'en 慈恩 Monastery in the Tang capital Chang'an 長安.[28] We know that its Tibetan translation, the *Sūtra on the Ten Wheels and the Earth-Womb Bodhisattva*, became available in either the late eighth or the early ninth century.[29] However, it is difficult to identify where this translation was produced. It could have been anywhere in Beiting, Khotan, Dunhuang, or central Tibet. A few fragmentary pages from the undated Xixia translation were found in Dunhuang.[30]

In the *Ten Wheels Sūtra*, the group of monk criminals differs from those prophesized in the *Moon-Womb Sūtra* outlined above. In the *Ten Wheels Sūtra*, the Buddha anticipates that meditating monks will commit crimes.[31] The text begins with the Buddha praising the power and virtue of bodhisattva Kṣitigarbha, or Earth-Womb. It then shifts to an exchange between another bodhisattva, Devagarbha—Divine-Womb—and the Buddha, where they are discussing the need to better support meditating monks. The Buddha informs Devagarbha that if a meditating monk does not receive proper support, he may commit crimes in order to fulfill his needs and will consequently face various corporal penalties from the king's court. As a precaution, the Buddha tells his disciple Ājñātakauṇḍinya to provide the best food and bedding to meditating monks and to exempt them from all communal duties, in order to prevent them from committing crimes to obtain the provisions they need. The Buddha notes that even when these monks commit some offenses, they should still retain their rights to access future offerings from patrons. The Buddha urges divine beings, human beings, and nonhuman beings to make offerings to all ordained Buddhists regardless of the extent of their commitment to monastic training. These include monks who have broken their monastic vows, those who always observe them, and those who have never taken these vows.

One central appeal of this Buddhist pursuit for clerical legal privileges is its call to exempt ordained Buddhist criminals from being subjected to corporal punishment in the king's court, regardless of the circumstances.[32] These penalties range from being whipped, beaten with a hammer, jailed, cursed at, and having their hands or feet cut off, to the death penalty. This topic comes up in a conversation between Devagarbha and the Buddha on criminal monks. In the earlier Chinese translation of the *Ten Wheels Sūtra*, Devagarbha asks the following of the Buddha: "Lord, if a monk meditator [becomes an offender], should a lay official whip or cut off his hands or feet?" In the later translation of 651, Devagarbha furnishes his question with more details.[33] He asks the Buddha if it is suitable for a lay official to whip, beat, jail, scold, dismember, or kill Buddhist monks who are meditators but have committed crimes. The Buddha considers it extremely unsuitable to impose corporal punishments.

The Buddha's objection to these punishments in the *Ten Wheels Sūtra* could protect all ordained Buddhists, including monks and nuns who commit the most serious crimes either before or after their ordination. The preordination crimes include the five most heinous ones and the four fundamental crimes. The most heinous ones include killing one's parents, killing an arhat, verbally causing disharmony among Buddhists or within the monastic community, and causing the Buddha to bleed. The fundamental crimes include killing a solitary Buddha,[34] raping a Buddhist nun who had attained the spiritual status of an arhat, encroaching on the communal property of the Buddhist establishment, and corrupting ordained Buddhist monks by instilling in them heretical views.[35] In theory, a layperson who commits any of these crimes is ineligible for ordination as a monk or nun. If such a violator has already been ordained, then he or she should be exiled. Yet if that wrongly ordained violator has already assumed the look of an ordained monk or nun, by shaving their head and wearing monastic robes, they would have the Buddha's protection, which would prohibit lay officials from whipping or imprisoning them.[36]

In the *Ten Wheel Sūtra*, Buddhist writers consider that the same exception is applicable to the postordination crimes of killing a human being, slandering the Buddha's teachings, having sex, stealing, or lying about having spiritual powers after ordination. In theory, such a monk or nun would face excommunication or lose the right to attend religious gatherings and enjoy communal goods.[37] Yet,

Buddhist writers still arranged for the Buddha to prohibit lay officials from whipping, jailing, or killing these clerics.

The writers of the *Ten Wheels Sūtra* only considered ordained Buddhists who contravened institutional discipline ineligible for immunity from corporal penalty. In this text, they depict the Buddha discussing this exclusion with Upāli.[38] Here, Upāli describes a situation in which an ordained Buddhist monk who is rich, knowledgeable, and eloquent, has many students, or is well connected with powerful lay patrons might disregard his own monastery's disciplinary measures. In this circumstance, the Buddha instructs the monastery to extradite this monk to the king's court, where he will be tried under state law. Upāli further describes another scenario where a monk or nun might be able to use their wealth, knowledge, eloquence to please the king and his ministers, or their connections with unlawful friends to persuade law enforcement officials not to punish them. In this type of case, the Buddha would instruct the monastery to expel the offender to prevent them from contaminating the monastic community. If the violator refuses to leave, then the Buddha should instruct the monastery to inform the king and his ministers to force the violator to relocate to another kingdom.

While this campaign tries to protect eligible Buddhist criminals from being tried and punished in the king's court, it does not exempt them from internal investigations or from incurring penalties at their host institutions. Nevertheless, Buddhist writers still present a Buddhist who is convicted of a crime as free from serious punishment. What they arrange instead is for the Buddhist institution to permit qualified individuals to verbally admonish a convicted monk or nun and only in the proper contexts. In the *Ten Wheels Sūtra*, the Buddha and Upāli discuss the procedures used for carrying out this verbal admonishment.[39] First, the institution must verify the offense to be true. Next, the administrator monks must investigate the reported offense, evaluate its gravity, and recommend a penalty in accordance with Buddhist monastic law.

There is an additional restriction on the reprimand: only senior monks who are pure in observing their vows are qualified to perform this punitive task. Ten types of people are considered unsuitable candidates for this job. These include non-Buddhists, lay Buddhist householders who do not observe the rules, individuals who have committed crimes worthy of Avīci hell, those who have slandered the Buddha's teachings, those who have defamed nobles, those who are mentally disturbed, afflicted by physical pain, or serving the monastery as lay stewards or garden keepers,[40] and ordained Buddhist monks who previously received punishment. When it is time to admonish the offender,[41] the following people are not to be present: kings, Brahmins,[42] ministers,[43] elderly and lay Buddhist householders, women, men,[44] lay stewards of monasteries, other ordained Buddhist monks and nuns, and those who have disputed with or were hateful toward the offender.

To justify this more aggressive pursuit for expanded immunity, Indian Buddhists contended that the inherent salvific power of ordained monks and nuns outweighed the trivial damage their crimes may have caused. This salvific power emits from the physical presence of the dyed Buddhist monastic robe. The Buddha describes how the sight of a monastic robe can benefit its beholders in ten ways—for example, by reminding the beholders of the Buddha and preventing them from going astray to non-Buddhists, by reminding them of the Buddha's teachings and helping them avoid violating Buddhist monastic law,[45] and by making them more charitable and resilient and less vulgar, impure, or angry. According to the Buddha, the sight of the monastic robe would entice people to start practicing Buddhism and become more diligent. It would calm them down and lead them to take delight in meditating in the mountains. It would help them cultivate wisdom and become increasingly delighted upon hearing or reading Buddhist teachings. It would make them more generous and courteous toward Buddhists. The merit of these actions would ensure that these people are reborn into rich, powerful families.

To make the teachings about the salvific potency of ordained Buddhists more relatable and easier to comprehend, the Buddha compares criminal monks to dead animals and withered plants that could produce medically beneficial substances or sensually pleasing scents. In a conversation with Devagarbha about ordained Buddhists who have broken their monastic vows, the Buddha equates them with burned incense, dead oxen or deer, and withered yellow jade orchids, when he says the following:

> Devagarbha, while such monks who have broken their vows are viewed as dead corpses in Buddhist monastic law, they still possess some remaining power [from learning and following the Buddha's teachings in preparation for ordination]. For example, after oxen and deer die and become unconscious corpses, they are still beneficial to sentient beings because a dead ox can produce ox bezoar, and a dead deer can produce deer musk. Monks who have broken their vows are like that. . . . Devagarbha, the physical form of burned incense is destroyed, but it still emits fragrant smells to make others fragrant. Monks who have broken their vows are like that.[46]

The Buddha then summarizes the essence of this argument in the following verses:

> The yellow jade orchid may wither,
> Yet it is still better than other flowers.
> Buddhist monks may misbehave,
> Or break their monastic vows,
> Yet they are still better than all the non-Buddhists.[47]

The *Ten Wheels Sūtra* also uses three analogical stories in which even beasts and demons are said to have refused to hurt criminals dressed in Buddhist monastic robes. Two of the stories are similar, with minor variations. The first story in the *Ten Wheels Sūtra* features a six-tusked elephant king who refuses to hurt hunters who disguise themselves as Buddhist monks, despite the fact these hunters have done so to kill the elephant king. The story takes place in the kingdom of Kāśī, where the six-tusked elephant lives at the foot of a snowy mountain. Instead of being pursued by a single hunter as in the *Mahāsāṃghika Vinaya*, this elephant faces five hunters who are led by a Cāṇḍāla, a low-caste untouchable in Indian society, who has been sent by the human king of Kāśī.[48] As the human king has sworn to kill all the hunters if they fail to bring him the elephant king's tusks, the Cāṇḍāla is determined to accomplish the task to avoid his own death. His plan is to dress all of the hunters in monastic robes to disguise them as ordained Buddhist monks. They carry bows loaded with arrows and arrive at the snowy mountain. A female elephant, the elephant king's partner, sees the hunters approaching and is terrified. She asks the elephant king whether the hunters intend to kill them, as they have come armed with bows and arrows. The elephant king sees that the hunters are wearing monastic robes and comforts his partner, telling her that Buddhist monks who wear monastic robes have abandoned all evil deeds and would not hurt sentient beings. The female elephant is not convinced. She suspects their arrows are poisonous; she also sees no compassion in the evil Cāṇḍāla person. The elephant king still believes that as these men are wearing dyed robes, they will not hurt him or the female elephant. He turns to his partner and says,

> Those who are wearing the dyed robes have the compassion to guide themselves. They must be converted adherents to the Buddha and have compassion over sentient beings. There is no doubt about this robe. Your worrying is unnecessary. Those who are wearing this robe are aiming to cross to the shore beyond birth and death.[49]

Just at that moment, the Cāṇḍāla hunter shoots a poisonous arrow at the elephant king. This causes the female elephant to make a loud, sorrowful sound and utter the following condemnation: "One who wears this robe must have taken refuge with the Buddha. His manner is calm, but his mind is extremely malicious. Quickly trample him to death as revenge for having shot you!"[50] The elephant king, however, would rather die than entertain such an evil thought of killing hunters who are wearing Buddhist monastic robes. Even though these hunters are malicious, the elephant king still perceives them as the Buddha's disciples. Their semblance as followers of the Buddha discourages the elephant king from harming them. Instead, when he learns that these hunters want his tusks, he pulls them off and presents them to the men as an offering to the Buddha. This story is so widely spread that today we can still see an early-Tang-dynasty (618–712 CE) depiction of the moment when the hunters aimed at the elephant king, on the south wall in Dunhuang's Mogao Cave 321 (see Figure 4.1).[51]

In the second story, a maddened elephant refuses to execute a criminal who is wearing clothes that are dotted with the color of the Buddhist monastic robe.[52] This maddened elephant lives in an unspecified kingdom in ancient India. In this kingdom, there are convicted criminals on death row, but King Fude 福德, whose name means "fortune and merit," wants to stay out of the business of executing human beings to avoid receiving bad karma. To punish this criminal without causing the king or another human being to suffer the consequences of killing a human being, a minister proposes using the maddened elephant as the executioner. The minister drops the convicted criminal in front of the elephant. The elephant seizes the criminal's feet and is about to trample him but then notices the crimson-colored dots on the criminal's clothing, thinks he is seeing a Buddhist monastic robe, and stops. He slowly puts the criminal down, sits down, faces him, and does not dare hurt him. Instead, the elephant compassionately touches the criminal's feet with his trunk. The minister witnesses the entire scene and reports it back to the king. The king marvels at such an interaction between the maddened elephant and the criminal. He then orders the people in his kingdom to pay extra respect to ordained Buddhists, and he permanently abolishes the death penalty and any other killing in his kingdom.

In the third story, hungry ogres (*luocha* 羅刹) and ogresses (*luocha mu* 羅刹母) who live in a cemetery refuse to execute a criminal who is pretending to be an ordained Buddhist monk.[53] This story takes place in the kingdom of Pañcāla, where King Prasenajit uses these ruthless ogres and ogresses as executioners of criminals on death row. When one inmate discovers that a prison guard is about to send him to the cemetery to be executed, he immediately shaves his head, finds a piece of dyed robe, and ties it around his neck. At the king's order, the guard ties the criminal's hands and feet and takes him to the graveyard. A family of ogres and ogresses immediately gathers around him, along with a retinue of five thousand. When the father ogre sees the criminal's shaved head and the piece of dyed robe tied around his neck, he circles around the criminal in a clockwise direction.[54] The father ogre tells the criminal to relax and promises not to hurt him, explaining that the shaved head and the piece of dyed robe remind him of the Buddha. The ogre's son is hungry and thirsty and protests that he wants to devour the criminal, but the mother ogress joins in to support the father ogre, affirming to her son that the shaved head and the dyed robe resemble the Buddha and that anyone who attempts to hurt this man will descend to eternal Avīci hell. These words persuade the son ogre to give up on the idea of eating the man, and he joins his parents in sauntering around the criminal in a clockwise direction.

Fig. 4.1 *The Elephant King and the Hunters*, early Tang, cave painting, Dunhuang Cave 321, South Wall, © Dunhuang Research Academy

Three more ogre families arrive with their retinues, hold similar discussions, and all end up circling the criminal without harming him. Eventually, the ogres and ogresses untie the criminal and set him free. The next morning, the freed criminal reports his experience in the king's palace.

The rare experience of this criminal who has averted his death penalty by wearing a piece of dyed robe leads to another important aspect of the Buddhist quest for clerical legal privileges. This is to codify protection over all ordained Buddhists in state law. The ogres' and ogresses' compassion toward the criminal impresses King Prasenajit and inspires him to codify his commitment to protect ordained Buddhists. All three extant translations of the *Ten Wheels Sūtra* include this code. In the earlier (fifth-century) Chinese translation, the king codifies the law as follows: "I will impose the death penalty on anyone who shows disrespect to or punishes any Śrāvaka Buddhists in my kingdom, regardless of whether these Buddhists have the potential to reach spiritual accomplishment or not."[55]

In its later translation of 651, the codified law is similar but more detailed. It reads as follows:

> From now on in my kingdom, I will impose the death penalty on anyone who assaults, bullies, or hurts ordained Buddhists who have shaved their heads and are wearing monastic robes, regardless of whether the ordained Buddhists are observing their vows, have broken them, or have made no vows at all.[56]

The law in the Tibetan translation is worded similarly to that in the 651 Chinese translation. It reads as follows:

> From now on, I will kill all who harm students of the Buddha who are residing in my kingdom and who have removed their hair and beards and are wearing a dyed robe, regardless of whether they observe their vows, have lost interest in observing their vows, have observed few vows, or have made no vows at all.[57]

This code does not explicitly demand clerical immunity for monks and nuns convicted of crimes after ordination. Yet by prohibiting anyone from hurting ordained Buddhists, even those who have committed the most heinous crimes, it has the effect of protecting ordained Buddhist criminals from any legal punishments. Unfortunately, this code only appears in the *Ten Wheels Sūtra*.[58] Unless parallels in other Buddhist or non-Buddhist sources are discovered, we should assume that this code is a desirable ideal Buddhists have pursued, but we cannot know whether it has penetrated India's legal system.

Corporal Punishment and Financial Penalty

The search for clerical immunity from corporal punishment was not sufficient to shield criminal monks and nuns from every possible penalty. In ancient India, a convicted criminal could face verbal admonishment, financial penalties, corporal punishment, jail time, or a combination of these. This wide variety of possibilities could have motivated Buddhists to expand their pursuit beyond one that sought clerical immunity from corporal punishment. In this expanded pursuit, Buddhists arrange for Mahāsatyanirgrantha,[59] a major disciple of the Buddha, to have a conversation on state governance with King Caṇḍapradyota of the city of Ujjayanī in Southern India. In this conversation, the Buddhists make Mahāsatyanirgrantha their spokesman, asking him to present King Caṇḍapradyota with their demands for jurisdictional independence and more comprehensive clerical legal privileges.[60] This conversation is documented in the *Satyaka Sūtra*, which is now preserved in a sixth-century Chinese translation and a Tibetan translation that dates to the late eighth or early ninth century.[61]

The conversation begins with King Caṇḍapradyota approaching Mahāsatyanirgrantha for advice on good governance, where he has a particular interest in the legal management of criminals.[62] Mahāsatyanirgrantha recommends that the king use extreme caution when considering convicting and punishing criminals. He advises the king to only convict a suspect when he has obtained their confession and verified that they had ill intentions when they committed their crimes. He also counsels the king that even if he could convict them, he may not want to prescribe penalties he does not feel confident enough to carry out. The king must furthermore be careful to execute a penalty in a proper manner. Mahāsatyanirgrantha instructs that when disciplining a convict, the king must speak softly and not use harsh words. If the criminal is to receive a physical or financial punishment, then the king must show compassion when sending them to jail, having them put in shackles, confiscating their property, or exiling them. Mahāsatyanirgrantha specifically notes that the king must avoid taking the life of a criminal or causing them physical harm by chopping off their hands, feet, ears, noses, or tongues or by gauging out their eyes.[63]

This requirement of punishing a criminal without taking their life or causing permanent damage to their body is central to the Buddhist perception of good governance. In his conversation with King Caṇḍapradyota, Mahāsatyanirgrantha introduces this as a universal principle that is applicable to the treatment of all criminals[64] and uses the analogy of parental discipline to explain how the state's penal system should work.[65] When children misbehave, their parents will want to discipline them to improve their manners. They may scold their children verbally and beat them but would never want to disable or kill them. Similarly,

Mahāsatyanirgrantha advises the king to discipline and punish criminals as parents would their children.

Mahāsatyanirgrantha includes misbehaving monks and nuns as one of the five categories of criminals. Other criminals range from individuals who commit crimes against the king or others, to rebels who disobey orders of the king or regional lords, to individuals such as hunters and butchers who make a living by harming nonhuman beings.[66] For all criminals, Mahāsatyanirgrantha prescribes a list of three suitable types of punishment. Depending on the offense, those enforcing the law may discipline convicts verbally, confiscate their property, or impose non-life-threatening physical punishment such as confinement, jail time, shackling, beating, or exile.[67]

Mahāsatyanirgrantha notes that a criminal may also receive a combination of multiple punishments on this list.[68] For committing a crime against the king, the criminal should lose all of their property through confiscation and also face physical punishment. When one individual commits a crime against another, the perpetrator should be physically punished and lose one-sixth of their property through confiscation. A criminal who is convicted of disobeying an order of the king or a regional lord can receive a pardon from the king and avoid all punishment if they are willing to change their ways and comply with the order. If they persist in being disobedient, they should face exile and all of their property should be confiscated. Individuals who are criminalized through professions that are perceived to be unethical (such as butchers and blacksmiths) could receive only verbal discipline but no financial or physical punishment. However, the penalties for monks and nuns who fail to follow orders or break the law are disproportionately lenient.

In his meeting with the king, Mahāsatyanirgrantha asks King Caṇḍapradyota to exempt ordained Buddhist convicts from both physical and financial punishments.[69] The only permissible penalties for convicted ordained Buddhist criminals are a restrictive form of verbal discipline and excommunication (*qubin* 驅擯) from the Buddhist monastic community. Before imposing these penalties, the leaders of the monasteries and the king must guide the convict through three steps that will help them avoid punishment. The first step is for the monastic community to try to convince the suspect to acknowledge their crime; then the community should select a sentence that accords with Buddhist monastic law. If the suspect refuses to cooperate and the king supports Buddhism, the monastic community's leader should report the suspect to the king, who would then decree a royal order to force the suspect to comply with the monastery's internal discipline. In that circumstance, the king's task is to try to convince the suspect to comply with the monastic community's instructions. If the suspect still refuses to comply, then the king should investigate the crime, before a public assembly of monks and nuns. If the offender is convicted, then the king should assist the monastic community in carrying out their punishment. This punishment, however, should not cause permanent physical damage to or take the life of a monk or nun offender. Physical confinement and financial punishment are also excluded. Further, the official carrying out the penalty should not put shackles on an ordained Buddhist criminal, beat them, remove their monastic robes, or confiscate their property. Instead, they can only verbally scold or excommunicate them.[70]

Through Mahāsatyanirgrantha's conversation with King Caṇḍapradyota, Buddhists pursue additional protections in their efforts to eradicate the possibility of convicted monks and nuns facing physical or financial harm. First, they designate as a fundamental crime any crime perpetrated against an ordained Buddhist. Examples include damaging Buddhist architecture and objects of art, seizing monastic property or valuables, and slandering ordained Buddhists.[71] Second, they discourage the state court from imposing punishment on monks or nuns who are convicted offenders. Mahāsatyanirgrantha explains this advice to King Caṇḍapradyota as follows:

> If faithful renunciants are ordained, shave their hair, and put on a dyed robe, regardless of whether they observe the monastic disciplinary rules or not, it is the third fundamental crime to jail them, put shackles on them, beat them, enslave them, subject them to hard labor, remove their monastic robes and force them to return to the laity, or take their lives.[72]

These legal recommendations for dealing with convicted monks and nuns also reveal the Buddhist pursuit of jurisdictional independence. Mahāsatyanirgrantha perceives that the king's legal intervention is occasionally necessary when the monastic community is unable to control an offender. This perception of jurisdictional independence is inseparable from the Buddhist perception that positions the Buddhist clergy as a source of legal support to the king's governance. When a king has to adjudicate doctrinal disputes among different groups of Buddhists but lacks expertise on the subject under dispute, he should rely on the opinions of learned monks before making a judgment.[73]

The Aftermath of Punishing a Monk

This outward-facing pursuit of clerical immunity from all punishment except verbal admonishment concludes with a warning to kings and their law enforcement officials who dare impose physical or financial punishment on ordained Buddhists. Two levels of retribution will be meted out on all who disregard this warning.

Buddhist writers cautioned that people who punished ordained Buddhists would descend to hell after they died. In the Chinese translation of the *Ten Wheels Sūtra*, all those who harm or kill ordained Buddhists, whether well-behaved or misbehaved, lose the ability to speak and, after they die, they descend to Avīci for eternity.[74] In the alternative Chinese translation of the same text, people who disrespect, harm, verbally abuse, beat, jail, or kill an ordained Buddhist who has committed a heinous crime have burned up all of the seeds of goodness and, consequently, must be banished from the company of wise people, and upon their death, they will fall into eternal Avīci.[75] The narrative of personal suffering for kings who mistreat ordained Buddhists also appears in the early sixth-century Chinese translation of the *Satyaka Sūtra*.[76] In this text, Buddhist writers list the following as the five heinous crimes: jailing, shackling, beating, and binding an ordained Buddhist and forcing them to do hard labor. If a king did any of the these to an ordained Buddhist and remain unaware of his mistake, he would have burned up all the seeds of goodness, causing him to descend to hell and be condemned to eternal suffering.

When a king mistreats ordained Buddhists, his act will also cause trouble for his kingdom and subjects. Kings who impose corporal penalties on ordained Buddhist convicts will incur the collective wrath of all of the creatures who are faithful to Buddhism. In the sixth-century Chinese translation of the *Sumeru-Womb Sūtra*,[77] evil human kings prosecute Buddhists, including monks, nuns, and all others who have converted to Buddhism, imposing on them corporal punishment, taxation, and even death. These behaviors then infuriate the demons, demi-gods, and hungry ghosts who are living in these rulers' kingdoms and being faithful to Buddhism. All kinds of calamities immediately occur. Among the kings' subjects, these wrathful creatures provoke wars, spread infectious diseases, and incite violent fights. In the natural world, they cause disasters in abnormally high winds, rainfall, cold, and heat that destroy all the kingdom's crops.

These calamities lead more creatures to become guardians of Buddhism and swear to punish kings who dare incarcerate monks and nuns.[78] The serpent kings are the first to join in. The recruitment begins with falsely charging serpents for having created these calamities.[79] At one point, the Buddha congratulates Śrīdevī (Gongde tian 功德天) for having fulfilled his aspirations to live in a place full of virtue. Śrīdevī notes that, on the contrary, his aspirations have only been partially fulfilled, because in the place where he lives, all kinds of serpents are misbehaving and causing calamities. The Buddha then turns to the bodhisattva named Sumeru-Womb and inquires how to end such calamities. Sumeru-Womb assumes that the malicious serpents are the culprits and promises to discipline them and stop them from creating more catastrophes.

At the same time, several serpent kings are sitting among the audience.[80] They immediately refute this false accusation. The first one to speak is the serpent king Shanzhu 善住, "kind dweller." He rises from his seat, exposes his right shoulder, joins his palms, and then speaks to the Buddha. His defense begins with a statement that all serpents are kind toward Buddhism and Buddhists, and even follow the Buddha's teachings. They are also kind toward everyone in the kingdom where they reside and have no intention of causing harm. The serpent king further explains that because these serpents believe that ordained Buddhists who wear the dyed monastic robe are precious, they see them as embodying the hope of enlightenment and the elimination of all suffering. In his defense, he elaborates on his understanding of the significance of the dyed robes of Buddhist monks and nuns as follows:

> All of the Buddhas in the past have always empowered this dyed robe. This dyed robe is then the seed of all bodhisattvas and the proper path that leads toward nirvana. So, too, it is the steel knife that can cut off affliction and thus the seed of nirvana. So, too, it is always a luminous lamp for those who have strayed from the path.[81]

The serpent king claims that his appreciation of the salvific power of the ordained Buddhist's dyed robe is the main reason for his unconditional support of Buddhists and his pledge to never harm them. This is why serpent kings require all serpents to avoid bringing any disaster to kingdoms where human kings are faithful to Buddhism, rule by the law, and treat ordained Buddhists kindly.

While noting the serpents' lack of intention to cause any of the calamities under discussion, the serpent king also explains why these calamities occur. This explanation, and the subsequent corroborating testimonies of two other serpent kings, Nanda and Upananda, explicitly attest that serpent kings have become scapegoats for evil human kings.[82] The primary cause, they explain, is evil human kings who mistreat Buddhism and ordained Buddhists. The serpent kings' implicit message, which is probably more important for this text's intended audience, shows what can happen in one's kingdom if a human king mistreats an ordained Buddhist by imposing corporal punishment, taxation, or the death penalty. An unexpected outcome of this false accusation is the serpent kings' voluntary commitment to punish kings who dare punish monks and nuns. The serpent kings swear that if any king causes Buddhism or ordained Buddhists to suffer in the future, they will immediately return to punish them.

The serpents' commitment inspires a celestial musician to join them as a guardian and offer to carry out the same revenge for ordained Buddhists.[83] At this meeting, a celestial musician named Yaosheng 药生 rises from his seat and joins his palms.[84] He swears to the Buddha that if, in the future, any warrior kings dare cause distress to fully ordained Buddhist monks and nuns or anyone whose head is shaven and wears a dyed robe, he will ensure that those kings will receive a corresponding karmic retribution. Specifically, he will cause those kings to lose everything—their kingdom and families—to their enemies. Moreover, he will also stir up internal conflict and rebellion, dry up rivers or cause them to overflow, spread disease, allow bandits to increase in number, and disturb all human beings, ghosts, and animals.

Conclusion

This expanded public-facing campaign embedded in the nonlegal Buddhist texts was crucial for Buddhists' successful negotiations over legal privileges with the state. Preaching on the necessity for Buddhist monastic law texts to grant monks and nuns immunity from pre- or postordination crimes was important for gaining internal support within the Buddhist community. But the success of this campaign relied on these legal ideas gaining external recognition beyond the monastic community. Thus, the nonlegal Buddhist texts provided an ideal platform for disseminating these ideas to the lay interlocutors for whom the Buddhists had crafted their campaign in the first place. Unlike the monastic law texts, access to the nonlegal texts was not restricted. On the contrary, Buddhists encouraged kings, ministers, and other laypeople to engage with these nonlegal texts in multiple ways. They could have attended oral teaching sessions on these texts, copied them by hand or commissioned others to do so on their behalf, or appreciated the visual illustrations carved on walls in Buddhist caves and temples. These features of the nonlegal texts made the campaign for clerical legal privileges most effective in reaching out to a lay audience.

This campaign's appearance in multiple doctrinal texts challenges the earlier scholarly assumption that it was a Chinese invention. Its presence in the Chinese translation and its absence in the Tibetan translation of the *Moon-womb Sūtra* do not suffice to prove it was apocryphally added by Chinese translators. There are numerous cases in which discrepancies between a Buddhist text's Chinese and Tibetan translations resulted from the use of different root texts. While the *Moon-Womb Sūtra* is one text that documents this campaign in detail, the traces of the campaign's many elements in the Chinese and Tibetan translations of the *Ten Wheels Sūtra*, the *Satyaka Sūtra*, and the *Sumeru-Womb Sūtra* further attest to this campaign's origins in Indian Buddhism.

The core objective of this Buddhist pursuit was to retain jurisdiction over monks and nuns within the Buddhist establishment. To that end, Buddhists sought to exclude the state's intervention in the interrogation and punishment of ordained Buddhist offenders. The first step was to remove ordained Buddhists from the state court, in the first place, by preventing them from initiating lawsuits as plaintiffs in this court. At the same time, Buddhist writers also threatened laypeople not to file charges against ordained Buddhists that would result in their being taken to the state court as defendants. In case this first step failed, the campaign's next focus was to prevent state law enforcement from imposing punishment on monks or nuns who were convicted criminals. In ancient India, Buddhists crafted the campaign to gain clerical immunity from both corporal and financial penalties. Even when the court permitted the lightest penalty of verbal admonishment to be meted out to Buddhist convicts, Buddhists asked the court to avoid inviting laypeople to carry out the admonishment, specifying that only ordained Buddhists in good standing could perform the punishment and that no lay onlookers could be present.

As I have pointed out in Chapter 3, this Buddhist campaign for clerical legal privileges was not devoid of contemporary influences. Its approach fit a historical pattern of how other religious establishments negotiated their legal relationships with the state in ancient India. In the subsequent chapters, I will show how these close associations with unique legal and religious cultures in ancient India created challenges for Chinese Buddhists who attempted to transplant the campaign for clerical legal privileges to Chinese soil. To minimize any repercussions from directly transposing the campaign from India to China, Chinese Buddhists had to reimagine what a feasible campaign would look like in the legal, cultural, and religious contexts of China at the time.

PART II
IN THE CHINESE COURTROOM

5
Hybrid Courts, Hybrid Laws

> Since ordained Buddhists and laypeople are different, their laws should also be different.[1]
>
> Emperor Yuan Ke, 508 CE

Chinese Buddhists were never merely onlookers when emperors were trying to expand the state's jurisdiction.[2] Instead, they were vital collaborators in shaping that expansion. To deter the state from infringing on the Buddhist establishment's jurisdiction, many monks worked for the ruling emperors of their time by helping draft laws that governed Buddhist criminals. These endeavors offered them leverage in negotiating the jurisdictional boundary between the state and the Buddhist establishment.

One Buddhist monk, Zhizang 智藏 (458–522), however, took a risky step in this Buddhist project. Instead of being obedient to the rulers, Zhizang directly confronted one emperor who had been attempting to seize more jurisdictional control over Buddhists. During the Southern Liang dynasty (502–557), some Buddhist monks and nuns began to neglect their duty to study and recite Buddhist scriptures.[3] The chief monastic official, a layman the state had appointed to prosecute clerical offenders, consulted state law when investigating complaints over these monks and nuns. This official's incompetence displeased Emperor Xiao Yan 蕭衍 (464–549; reign 502–549) of the Southern Liang, who subsequently proposed that he could appoint himself as the new chief monastic official. This proposal led Zhizang to confront the emperor.

While many monks endorsed the emperor's proposal, Zhizang firmly objected to it. At a gathering in a palace hall, the emperor explained to Zhizang that he had only proposed this self-appointment to correct the misuse of excessive punishment on monks and nuns. He also argued that although the Buddhist establishment should have been responsible for handling its misbehaving monks and nuns, the Buddha had also permitted kings to intervene. Zhizang did not consider alleviating these monks and nuns from excessive punishment to be the solution. Instead, he argued that Buddhist monastic law, if properly implemented, could suffice. In his opinion, appointing a layperson to manage the Buddhist monastic community would do more harm than good. The real solution, he believed, was to abolish this appointment altogether. Thus, he petitioned the

Buddhism in Court. Cuilan Liu, Oxford University Press. © Oxford University Press 2024.
DOI: 10.1093/oso/9780197663332.003.0006

emperor to completely exempt offending monks and nuns from punishment because most ordained Buddhists could not follow all the Buddhist monastic law codes. This confrontation showed that while Chinese rulers vigorously tried to gain more jurisdictional control over monks and nuns, Buddhist leaders sought clerical legal privileges and jurisdictional autonomy, with equal enthusiasm.

The tension over jurisdiction and clerical legal privileges that played out in this confrontation is representative of the ongoing legal negotiations between Chinese rulers and the Buddhist establishment of the time. From the fourth to the early twentieth centuries, Chinese rulers and Buddhist leaders frequently discussed the Buddhist establishment's jurisdictional autonomy and the legal privileges accorded its ordained members.[4] Historically, negotiations of this sort centered around three questions: where to try ordained Buddhist offenders, what law to use for their trials, and how to measure the penalties for convicted clerical offenders. These points of debate placed many rulers in imperial China in a persistent conundrum over how to adjudicate Buddhist monastic offenders while maintaining their public image as supporters of Buddhism. The act of approving eminent Buddhist monks' petitions calling for Buddhist institutions to be entrusted with handling clerical offenses would have been cast as recognizing the Buddhist establishment as an independent jurisdictional body beyond the state's jurisdiction. Conversely, to insist that all clerical cases be tried in the state court would have drawn protests from these Buddhists.

The jurisdictional boundary between the state and the Buddhist establishment in China never remained static. Its instability was reflected in the inconsistent assignment of trial venues for clerical offenses. Scholars propose three approaches to understanding this instability.[5] The work of the Chinese American sociologist C. K. Yang discusses the first approach. He focusses on the choice of the trial venue and proposes differentiating internal cases from external ones, emphasizing how a litigant's social identity affected the choice of trial venue.[6] Lawsuits between ordained Buddhists were treated as internal cases. Conversely, external cases involved both ordained Buddhists and lay or non-Buddhists. Depending on the composition of the litigants, a clerical offense may have been tried in one of two possible venues. One venue was the state court, which had jurisdiction over external clerical cases and clerical offenses that violated state law. The other was a new office that was located within the state administrative system and staffed by state-appointed monastic officials with jurisdiction over monastic offenders who had violated only Buddhist monastic law.[7] Today, "hybrid court" refers to a court where more than one legal system operates. In this book, I use the term to refer to the latter trial venue, where both Buddhist monastic law and Chinese state law are referred to when interrogating ordained Buddhist offenders.

The second approach proposed by scholars considers the distinction between civil and criminal cases as contributors to the unstable jurisdictional boundary. The Chinese historian Chen Dengwu explains how ordained Buddhists charged with civil and criminal offenses were tried in different courts. Most civil lawsuits involving ordained Buddhists only required local government officials and three principal monastery administrators (*sangang* 三綱) to mediate these trials. The state court only prosecuted crimes causing damage to the state, society, or individuals, or civil disputes involving property of significant value.[8] This kind of criminal prosecution required that ordained Buddhist criminals be defrocked so the state court could prosecute them as lay offenders. The state court could immediately drop this requirement for prosecuting monks and nuns if the crimes they committed were serious, such as engaging in illicit sexual intercourse, theft, or the murder of a disciple, and thus required more substantial penalties. The distinction between civil and criminal cases also affected the severity of the penalties convicted monks and nuns faced. While ordained and lay offenders faced the same penalties in civil cases, ordained Buddhists whose trials involved criminal cases were usually punished more severely than lay offenders.[9]

The third approach considers how the severity of the clerical offenses contributed to the unstable jurisdictional boundary. In his study on Buddhism and the law in the Tang dynasty, Zhang Haifeng differentiates serious clerical offenses from minor ones. The three principal administrators in the offender's host monastery often had the authority to handle minor clerical offenses internally. The state court, on the other hand, had jurisdiction over severe clerical offenses, such as murder, illicit sexual intercourse, and theft.[10]

These three approaches partially reveal some aspects of the battle over jurisdiction between the Buddhist establishment and the state in imperial China. Each one on its own fails to uncover the full movement of the jurisdictional boundary. To paint a fuller picture of how this boundary shifted over time, we must uncover how these three approaches became intertwined over a long historical period.

An analysis of Chinese legal codes—as well as legal regulations promulgated in edicts, memorials, and historical writings—from the fourth to the early twentieth centuries shows how the Buddhist establishment worked with the state to introduce hybrid laws and the institution of the hybrid court as a third venue beyond the state and monastic courts, initially designing it to prosecute exclusively clerical offenders.[11] This hybrid court dismantled the existing dichotomous structure of the state and monastic courts to form a new tripartite legal infrastructure. This change forced state rulers and Buddhist leaders to fight over the hybrid court whose jurisdiction directly affected the jurisdiction of both state and monastic courts. Buddhist leaders and state rulers worked in collaboration to employ distinctions between internal and external, civil and criminal, and serious and minor offenses as tools to determine a cleric's trial venue among the three types of courts. Collectively, these entities constantly re-demarcated the jurisdictional boundary between the state and the Buddhist establishment.

The Hybrid Court

The jurisdictional landscape of China underwent a significant reconfiguration during the Northern Wei dynasty (386–535 CE). After Buddhism's arrival in the country around the first century, monks and nuns who had committed crimes were tried in either the state or monastic court. The state court operated under state law and was the primary venue for interrogating lay offenders. Alternatively, a clerical offender could have been tried in a monastic court. This was the judicial body within which the Buddhist establishment conducted trials under Indian Buddhist monastic law. In later dynasties, the monastic court also adopted the *Pure Rules* (*Qinggui* 清規) as its legal guidelines. The *Pure Rules* were a set of indigenously developed Chinese monastic community bylaws that had been established and implemented either in individual monasteries and nunneries or in several allied monastic institutions across China.

A new development in the Northern Wei destabilized this jurisdictional configuration between the state and the Buddhist establishment. Sometime after the year 396,[12] the Northern Wei rulers envisioned a new mechanism with which to exert jurisdiction over the Buddhist establishment, establishing the Office for Overseeing Meritorious Works (Jianfu cao 鑒福曹) to handle exclusively regional and national Buddhist affairs.[13] They placed this office within the state's administrative system and staffed it with state-appointed monastic officials. This new mechanism created a third potential trial venue for Buddhist clerical offenders: the hybrid court, where laws from multiple sources are consulted.

This hybrid court remained functional throughout the Northern Wei. By 462, it had been renamed the Office for the Illumination of Mysteries (Zhaoxuan cao 昭玄曹)[14] in a change that was indicated by the appointment of the Buddhist monk Tanyao 曇曜 as the Buddhist Controller (Shamen tong 沙門統) the same year.[15] After the Northern Wei moved its capital to Luoyang, the hybrid court was relocated adjacent to the south of the Yongning 永寧 Monastery, which was built in the new capital in 516.[16]

One of this hybrid court's major duties was to deal with clerical offenders. In the autumn of 508, the first year of the Yongping 永平 era, Emperor Yuan Ke 元恪 (483–515; reign 499–515) issued an edict prescribing the jurisdiction of this court as follows:

> Since ordained Buddhists and laypeople are different, their laws should also be different. From today onward, prosecute all Buddhist monks who have committed murder or any more severe crimes the way lay offenders are prosecuted. Leave all of their other crimes to the Office for the Illumination of Mysteries to handle following the Buddhist monastic law and the *Rules for Monks and Nuns* (*Sengni zhi* 僧尼制).[17]

This edict clearly recognized the jurisdictional boundary between the state court and the hybrid court.

This hybrid court did more than prosecute Buddhist criminals. It also had the authority to review applications for the construction of new Buddhist monasteries.[18] In the winter of 518, the first year of the Shengui 神龜 era, the Minister of Works (Sikong gong 司空公), Wang Cheng 王澄, submitted a lengthy memorial complaining about the excessive number of Buddhist institutions in the capital city. He argued that as an established tradition, Yongning Monastery should have been the only Buddhist institution situated within the capital city's inner circle. In its outer circle, one Buddhist nunnery was allowed. Yet the capital had over five hundred Buddhist institutions, in many of which only three to five monks resided. To address this breach, Wang proposed that, starting from 518, only communities with over fifty ordained Buddhist monks in the region (*zhou* 州) outside of their capital city could propose building new Buddhist monasteries. First, the applicants had to submit a proposal to the regional office. Next the proposal would go to the Office for the Illumination of Mysteries for review. Finally, the emperor would review the proposal before deciding on it.

This hybrid court was not merely a theoretical construction devoid of the authority to practice legal proceedings. Officials in the Northern Wei treated it as a viable legal venue for dealing with monk offenders. In 511, Gao Zhao 高肇 (?–515), the Director of the Imperial Secretariat (Shangshu ling 尚書令), wrote a memorial to Emperor Yuan Ke in which he petitioned the emperor to have several Buddhist monk officials prosecuted in the Office for the Illumination of Mysteries.[19] The accused included two Buddhist rectors (Du weina 都維那):[20] Sengluo 僧暹 and Sengpin 僧頻. Gao had accused them of mistreating approximately two hundred monastic households.[21] These had previously been military households, situated in Liangzhou 涼州, that passed over to monastic use in 476, at the request of the former chief monastic official Tanyao. Monastic household members worked for the Buddhist establishment, but they did not belong to any individual Buddhist institution. Their main task was to store grain in case of famine. In his memorial, Gao accused the two Buddhist rectors of violating these arrangements, consequently causing over fifty people from this community to take their own lives by either hanging or drowning themselves. At the end of the memorial, Gao petitioned the emperor to prosecute these two Buddhist rectors, following Buddhist monastic law.[22] The emperor, however, decided to pardon the accused monk officials, without providing an explanation.

Despite the political turnover in subsequent dynasties, each new ruler always reserved an office where the hybrid court could deal with clerical matters. At the national level, this court resided in an office that oversaw national religious affairs pertaining to Buddhist and Daoist clergy. In different dynasties, rulers gave this office different names, placed it under the supervision of different government units, and assigned it different degrees of jurisdiction.[23] During the Northern Qi (550–577), its name was changed to the Court for the Illumination of Mysteries (Zhaoxuan si 昭玄寺). During the Sui (581–618), it became the Bureau for the Veneration of Mysteries (Chongxuan shu 崇玄署) within the Court for Dependencies (Honglu si 鴻臚寺).[24] Subsequently, during the Tang, the host of this hybrid court became, at different points, the Bureau of Sacrifices (Cibu 祠部),[25] the Bureau for the Veneration of Mysteries,[26] the Commissioner for the Cultivation of Merit and Virtue (Xiu gongde shi 修功德使),[27] the Court of State Ceremonial (Honglu si 鴻臚寺), the Commissioner for Merit and Virtue of the Left and Right Avenues of the Capital (Liangjie gongde shi 兩街功德使), the Office of Foreign Relations (Zhuku 主客),[28] and the Office of the Buddhist Registry for (Monasteries Situated along) the Avenues of the Capital (Zuoyou jie senglu si 左右街僧錄司).[29] The last host continued to hold jurisdiction over Buddhist clerical affairs during the Song.

When the Mongols ruled during the Yuan dynasty, they introduced major changes to the hybrid court's status in the central government. They downgraded the Office of the Buddhist Registry of the Tang from a central institution to reconfigure it as a regional office.[30] They then established three new institutions to oversee national Buddhist affairs: the Supreme Control Commission (Zongzhi yuan 總制院), the Bureau of the Commissioner for Merit and Virtue (Gongdeshi si 功德使司), and the Commission for Buddhist and Tibetan Affairs (Xuanzheng yuan 宣政院). The Yuan Emperor Kublai (1215–1294; reign 1260–1294) invested much interest in these reforms. In 1264, after establishing the Supreme Control Commission to oversee Buddhist monks and the administration of some nearby Central Asian areas, Kublai further appointed as its head the imperial preceptor 'Phags pa Blo gros rgyal mtshan (1235–1280), a Tibetan Buddhist monk of the Sa skya School. Later imperial preceptors continued to lead this office after its reorganization as the Commission for Buddhist and Tibetan Affairs in 1288.[31]

In the Ming, a short-lived Bureau for Buddhist Patriarchs (Shanshi yuan 善世院) emerged, in 1368, to adjudicate Buddhist clerical matters. In 1371, the fourth year of the Hongwu era, the Ministry of Rites replaced the Bureau for Buddhist Patriarchs to become the hybrid court's new host. Soon afterward, in 1382, the Office of the Buddhist Registry regained its jurisdictional control over the national Buddhist establishment. A notable reform occurred in 1396, the twenty-ninth year of the Hongwu era, when the Ministry of Rites was renamed the Bureau of Sacrifices (Ciji qingli si 祠祭清吏司) and began to share its jurisdiction over ordained Buddhists with the Office of the Buddhist Registry. During the Qing, these two offices continued to share jurisdiction over ordained Buddhists.[32]

Outside the capital, the hybrid court had different hosts at different regional levels. During the Tang, the hosts for the regional hybrid courts on the frontier differed from those in the core regions. In remote frontiers, such as in the town of Dunhuang in the Hexi Circuit, the regional hybrid court was under the supervision of the Office of the Buddhist controller (Dusi 都司),[33] which oversaw religious affairs.[34] In the core regions, the court found accommodations at the district or prefecture level. In districts or prefectures with populations over twenty thousand, the Adjutant of the Personnel Manager (Sigong canjun shi 司功參軍事) supervised the hybrid court in its dealings with Buddhist clerical matters. For those areas with populations less than twenty thousand, the Adjutant of the Director of Granaries (Sicang canjun shi 司倉參軍事) performed this role.[35]

In the Song, the regional hybrid court operated at two levels.[36] At the prefecture level, it operated in the Office of the Buddhist Rector (Sengzheng si 僧正司). At the district level, the Buddhist Chief (Sengshou 僧首) oversaw this court.[37] During the Yuan, the regional hybrid court operated at the three levels: the route (*lu* 路), the superior prefecture (*fu* 府), and the prefecture (*zhou* 州). In each route, the hybrid court was located in the Office of the Buddhist Registry.[38] In the superior prefectures, it was situated in the Office of Buddhist Discipline (Senggang si 僧綱司). In the prefectures, it operated within the Office of the Buddhist Rector.

During the Ming, the regional hybrid court operated at four different levels: in the capital, and at the prefecture (*fu* 府), subprefecture (*zhou* 州), and district (*xian* 县) levels. Two operational changes made this possible. First, the Office of the Buddhist Registry was restored in the capital along with its authority to oversee national clerical affairs. Second, an extra office was added at the district level. On the second day of the fourth month of 1381, the fourteenth year of the Hongwu era, Emperor Zhu Yuanzhang 朱元璋 (1328–1398; reign 1368–1398) established the Office of the Buddhist Registry in the capital, the Office of Buddhist Discipline in the prefectures, the Office of the Buddhist Rector in the subprefectures, and added a new Office of the Buddhist Assembly (Senghui si 僧會司) in the districts. In 1382, on the eighteenth day of the sixth month in the fifteenth year of the Hongwu era, Zhu Yuanzhang closed the Office of the Buddhist Assembly in the districts and assigned the Office of Buddhist Discipline to oversee all Buddhist clerical matters at the district and subprefecture levels.[39] The Office of the Buddhist Assembly, the Office of the Buddhist Rector, and the Office of Buddhist Discipline continued to exist throughout the Qing.[40]

Hybrid Law

The success of the hybrid court required a set of laws to guide its operations. This was a role neither state nor Buddhist monastic law alone could fulfill. To address this challenge, Chinese rulers invited Buddhist monks to create a new code that would integrate the relevant rules from both state and Buddhist monastic laws to exclusively govern the prosecution of Buddhist clerical offenders. Given its hybrid nature, in this book, I refer to the new set of laws as the hybrid law.

Collaborations on creating this hybrid law date to as early as the Northern and Southern dynasties (420–589). During this period, both the state and the Buddhist establishment actively participated in creating, implementing, and revising a set of laws for dealing with clerical offenders. In the Southern dynasty (420–479), rulers had attempted to create this hybrid law in the early fifth century. They were concerned about ordained Buddhists who had committed crimes of adultery and murder. These offenses led Emperor Liu Yu 劉裕 (363–422; reign 420–422) to issue an edict requiring senior monks to carefully assess the resident monks in their monasteries.[41] In this edict, Liu Yu warned that if, in the future, an ordained Buddhist committed a crime, then both the offender and all of those involved in the crime would be severely punished. To that end, he urged the primary administrators of Buddhist institutions to create and immediately implement the *Articles and Regulations* (*Tiaoge* 條格), which became the earliest reference to the hybrid law.

Whether the Southern Song was able to create and implement the hybrid law remains unknown, but the succeeding Southern Qi dynasty (479–502) saw the circulation of a one-scroll-long hybrid law, the *Rules for Monks* (*Sengzhi* 僧制), attributed to Xiao Ziliang 蕭子良 (460–494), the younger son of Emperor Xiao Ji 蕭賾 (440–493; reign 482–493) of the Southern Qi.[42] The need for this hybrid law continued in the Southern Liang 梁 (502–557), whose emperor, Xiao Yan, had appointed the Buddhist monk Fayun 法雲 (467–529) as abbot of the newly established Guangzhai 光宅 Monastery and had asked him to create a set of laws, which were also titled the *Rules for Monks* (*Sengzhi* 僧制).[43]

In the north, there had been equally strong interest in creating a hybrid law. In 493, the seventeenth year of the Taihe 太和 era, Emperor Yuan Hong 元弘 (467–499; reign 471–499), of the Northern Wei (386–534), issued an edict elaborating on the need to create a set of *Rules for Monks and Nuns* (*Sengni zhi* 僧尼制).[44] A now-lost version reportedly consisted of forty-seven articles.[45] This version of the hybrid law was apparently used in legal practices in the Northern Wei. In the autumn of 508, Emperor Yuan Ke issued an edict decreeing that ordained Buddhists who had committed lesser crimes (that is, crimes less serious than homicide) were to be adjudicated under Buddhist monastic law (*neilü* 内律) and the *Rules for Monks* (*Sengzhi* 僧制).[46] A year later, in the winter of

509, Buddhist controller monk Huishen 惠深 reported to Emperor Yuan Ke that he had drafted a version of the *Rules for Monks* in consultation with Buddhist masters who were learned in Buddhist monastic law.[47] However, implementing this law in the Northern Wei was not without its problems. In 518, a lay official complained about how the *Rules for Monks* that had been established in 508 and revised in 509 had been created in vain because they were not being followed. Therefore, this lay official petitioned officials who, at the time, were investigating the illicit construction of new Buddhist monasteries, asking them to consult the *Rules for Monks*.[48] New versions of this hybrid law continued to appear. In the Northern Qi (550–577), which was ruled by the Gao family, the Buddhist monk Huiguang 慧光, who had held high-ranking government positions as a Buddhist controller, drafted a set of laws, also titled the *Rules for Monks* (*Sengzhi* 僧制), consisting of eighteen articles.[49]

The state and the Buddhist establishment continued to collaborate in drafting the hybrid law during the Sui dynasty, producing at least two hybrid legal texts. The first hybrid text resulted from a collaboration between Emperor Yang Jian 楊堅 (541–604; reign 581–604) and the Buddhist monk Yancong 彥琮 (557–610). In 595, Yang Jian had been eager to establish a suitable legal code to deal with Buddhist clerical offenses because it had been unfeasible to enforce state law in prosecutions of ordained Buddhist offenders. To compile this legal text, Yancong and his collaborators consulted disciplinary rules found in various Buddhist doctrinal texts in the Theravāda and Mahāyāna traditions. In 595, Yancong presented the emperor with the final version of the ten-scroll *Laws and Ordinances from Various Scriptures* (*Zhongjing fashi* 眾經法式).[50]

The second hybrid legal text from the Sui was also titled the *Rules for Monks and Nuns* (*Sengni zhi* 僧尼制), which the Buddhist monk scholar Lingyu 靈裕 (517–605) had drafted during the Kaihuang 開皇 era (581–600).[51] This version consisted of rules written on scrolls, but its contents remain unknown.[52] Its author Lingyu was a monk from the Daci 大慈 Monastery in Xiangzhou 相州, located in today's Hebei Province.[53] At different times during his life, Lingyu received multiple invitations from Emperor Yang Jian to serve in his court. In 583, Xiangzhou's Regional Chief (Cishi 刺史) Fan Shulüe 樊叔略 (536–594) recommended that Emperor Yang Jian appoint Lingyu as the Chief Buddhist Controller (Dutong 都統). When the rescript for the appointment arrived, Lingyu declined it. Eight years later, in 591, the emperor again invited Lingyu to serve in the court but in a different position. This time, Lingyu accepted the invitation and stayed at the Xingshan 興善 Monastery in the capital, according to the arrangements the emperor had made for him. That same year, the emperor again tried to recruit a Buddhist Controller (Sengtong 僧統). His officials unanimously recommended Lingyu, who once again declined the invitation.

These hybrid laws from the Sui did not impress rulers during subsequent dynasties. Instead of inheriting the hybrid laws from their predecessors, each new dynasty's ruler became more interested in crafting his own laws. This trend continued when the Tang replaced the Sui. In 626, the Tang's first ruler, Emperor Li Yuan 李淵 (566–635; reign 618–626), noticed that greedy and cunning laypeople, after becoming ordained Buddhists, committed various offenses and tarnished the reputation of the Buddhist establishment. To purge them from the Buddhist community, Li Yuan issued an edict that urged for the creation of a hybrid law:

> Let all Buddhist monks and nuns and Daoist priests and priestesses who are diligent in their practices and obey the disciplinary rules live in big monasteries and temples. The government should provide them with clothes and food and never let them experience a shortage of supply. As for those who are unable to practice diligently and have erred in carrying out their disciplinary rules, do not supply them with provisions. Force them to abandon their practices and return to their places of origin. The relevant department should explicitly establish the *Articles and Ordinances* (*Tiaoshi* 條式) and [guide] them to follow the teachings of their religions. All behaviors against the *Rules* (*Zhi* 制) must stop.[54]

This project soon came to a standstill when Li Yuan abdicated later that year. Fortunately, the next ruler, Emperor Li Shimin 李世民 (598–649; reign 626–649), was also interested in creating this hybrid law. In 629, he issued an edict stating that he would show no leniency toward ordained Buddhists who had committed serious crimes, including but not limited to falsely claiming to be possessed by ghosts or spirits, spreading rumors, claiming to be a witch doctor to gain profit, immolating themselves to shock the public, or corrupting government officials during office visits. Li Shimin considered these offenses destructive to the longevity of Buddhism. Therefore, he swore to protect Buddhism by inviting the relevant departments to "explicitly create the *Articles and Rules* (*Tiaozhi* 條制) by consulting Buddhist monastic law and state law."[55] A few years later in 635, in the tenth month of the ninth year during the Zhenguan 貞觀 era, Li Shimin received a memorial from the Buddhist monk Xuanwan 玄琬 (562–636), who died shortly afterward.[56] In this memorial, Xuanwan criticized the practice of prosecuting ordained Buddhist offenders the same way lay offenders were prosecuted. He petitioned the emperor to send ordained Buddhists offenders to their host institutions for trial in accordance with Buddhist monastic law (*senglü* 僧律).[57]

This long-desired hybrid law was finally ready to implement by the time of the third Tang ruler, Emperor Li Zhi 李治 (628–683; reign 649–683). At the beginning of his reign, however, this emperor was not enthusiastic about implementing the hybrid law.[58] Instead, he preferred prosecuting certain monastic offenders in the state court. In 655, the sixth year of the Yonghui 永徽 era, Li Zhi issued a rescript permitting "complicated cases involving ordained Daoists or Buddhists to be investigated in accordance with the procedures for investigating crimes committed by laypersons."[59] Some judges in remote areas abused this rule in their legal practices, misinterpreting the purpose of the edict. Whether the charge was big or small, in the state court they put shackles on ordained Buddhist offenders and beat them with heavy sticks during trials. Li Zhi's attitude toward the hybrid law soon changed after the eminent monk scholar Xuanzang sent him a list of complaints about the mistreatments and insults lay judges inflicted upon ordained offenders. In his memorial, Xuanzang urged the emperor to prevent lay judges, in state court, from ordering the beating of ordained Buddhist offenders. Li Zhi fully supported Xuanzang's petition. On the twenty-third day of that month, he issued a rescript ruling that offenders who had been ordained Buddhists and Daoists should not be tried under state law but in accordance with the *Articles and Rules* (*Tiaozhi* 條制). Xuanzang subsequently submitted two memorials to express his gratitude to Emperor Li Zhi. In both memorials, he reiterated the emperor's position as expressed in the edict. In particular, he highlighted the emperor's prohibition against prosecuting ordained Buddhist offenders under the same state law for lay offenders. He also reiterated the need to prosecute them under the "old regulations" (*jiuge* 舊格) for ordained Buddhists and to abolish the rule permitting cases involving ordained Buddhists from being investigated under the same state laws that were used for the laity.

These efforts, however, were apparently insufficient in ensuring that ordained Buddhist offenders were tried under the hybrid law, nor did they eliminate the abuses these offenders incurred in the state court. A complaint from a lay official clearly illustrates this double failure. In 741, in the first month of the twenty-ninth year of the Kaiyuan 開元 era, Qi Han 齊澣 (675–746), the Regional Chief of Bianzhou 汴州 and the Investigation Commissioner (Caifang shi 採訪使) of the Henan Circuit submitted a memorial to Emperor Li Longji 李隆基 (685–762; reign 712–756).[60] In this memorial, Qi urged that ordained male and female Daoist and Buddhist offenders be tried under the *Regulations for Daoists* (*Daoge* 道格). He also petitioned the heads of the districts and prefectures not to prosecute Daoist and Buddhist clerical offenders on their own and not to punish those clerical offenders who had disobeyed state law. The emperor granted these requests in a rescript. This exchange between Qi Han and the emperor clearly shows that by this time, the hybrid law that recommended trying ordained Buddhist offenders had been updated to the now-lost *Regulations for Daoists*, which later became a primary source used when drafting the *Regulations for Daoists and Buddhists* (*Daoseng ge* 道僧格).[61]

The far-reaching impact of the *Regulations for Buddhists and Daoists* went beyond China. This Tang version of the hybrid law traveled to Japan, where it gained even higher legal status to become statutes in the *Penal Code and Administrative Statutes of the Yōrō Period* (*Yōrō ritsuryō* 養老律令). They were promulgated in 757 and appeared as the *Statutes for Monks and Nuns* (*Sōni ryō* 僧尼令), of which twenty-seven articles have survived to this day.[62]

These twenty-seven articles became a main source for understanding the legal negotiations between the state and the Buddhist establishment over the treatment of Buddhist clerical offenders. They show how the state attempted to expand control over the Buddhist establishment and its interactions with lay society. Through the hybrid law, the state claimed jurisdiction over clerical offenders whose acts violated both state and monastic laws. Examples of such acts include crimes of murder, rape, theft, and lying about having supernatural powers, which are comparable to the four most serious offenses in Buddhist monastic law.

Moreover, these twenty-seven articles also show the state's encroachment on the Buddhist establishment's jurisdiction as it claimed authority over ordained Buddhists whose behaviors were inappropriate but not in violation of state law. These articles allowed judges to use state law to prosecute ordained Buddhists who had been involved in a wide variety of activities. These included providing astrological observations and interpretations, telling fortunes, providing medical treatment, studying military books, making music, playing games, drinking alcohol, eating meat, consuming the five pungent ingredients,[63] wearing clothes of forbidden colors and materials, sharing a room with an adult of the opposite sex, entering the monastic residences of members of the opposite sex, failing to show respect to government officials in accordance with their rank, changing one's name, possessing or trading property for profit, providing or receiving illicit ordinations or forcing others to do so, preaching to laypeople door-to-door, and accepting slaves, animals, or weapons as offerings. This jurisdictional expansion shrank the Buddhist establishment's jurisdiction while the state's increased.

These articles outlined the penalties judges could assign to convicted clerical offenders, which ranged from chastisement (*kushi* 苦使) to being forcibly returned to lay society.[64] They also gave the state greater jurisdictional control over the Buddhist establishment and limited the monastery's authority's ability to adjudicate offenses whose convictions required penalties that went beyond chastisement but kept short of forcing convicted monks and nuns to return to the laity. That is, within the Buddhist legal system, monastic officials, such as principal administrators, could only impose disciplinary actions on ordained offenders, but they had no authority to impose physical punishment or confinement.

Despite the extent of its jurisdictional control, these twenty-seven articles offered one advantage to monastic offenders. They allowed monks and nuns to use their religious privileges to eliminate or substitute certain punishments. Article 21 describes how this conversion worked. To avoid a penalty of one or more years of penal servitude (*tu* 徒), a monk or nun could voluntarily disrobe. For beatings that entailed fewer than one hundred blows with a heavy stick, a monk or nun could choose to receive ten days of chastisement for every ten blows. They could also seek penalty reductions. To defray one year of penal servitude, they could surrender their ordination certificates. If one's crime required more than one year of penal servitude, the offender could convert their remaining penalty to chastisement by surrendering their ordination certificate.

The other advantage these twenty-seven articles offered to Buddhists was a relaxed restriction on conducting litigation in state court. Article 17 of this hybrid law permitted ordained Buddhists who litigated in a state court for personal matters to be treated as ordinary lay litigants, but they would not have received any special honorific treatment.[65] Yet when the monastery's principal administrators appeared in a state court for reasons pertaining to the institution's communal affairs, the court was to show them respect by offering them seats. This indicated that monks and nuns were not prohibited from litigating in state court for nonpersonal matters. In other words, this hybrid law lifted this restriction in Buddhist monastic law.

The Serious-versus-Minor-Offenses Approach

In the early sixth century, when Chinese legislators were deciding on the jurisdiction in which to try an ordained Buddhist offender, they proposed that the trial venue should be selected based on two aspects of the offense: if the offense was serious or minor, and if it was an internal dispute among monastics or a dispute involving members from outside of the Buddhist monastic community. These deliberations provided legislators in subsequent dynasties a basic model, which they continued to adapt to accord with the social and political contexts of their times. The venue in which a monastic offender would have been tried depended on the particulars of their case. A few centuries later, in the Yuan dynasty, a monastic offender may even have had a fourth option, which would have been to receive a joint investigation (*yuehui shenli* 約會審理) attended by jurisdictional representatives of all parties involved. I will discuss this joint investigation in the next section.

Efforts to distinguish between serious and minor offenses began no later than the early sixth century. In the autumn of 508, in a nationally promulgated edict, the above-mentioned Northern Wei emperor, Yuan Ke, elaborated on the importance of differentiating between these two types of offenses. In this edict, Yuan Ke considered laypersons and ordained Buddhists to be different. As such, he considered that the laws that applied to them should also be different. To highlight this difference in legal practice, the emperor proposed that Buddhist offenders be tried in either the state court or the hybrid court (for the pattern of jurisdiction distribution, see Figure 5.1). The state court would prosecute ordained Buddhists who committed homicide or similar serious offenses. The hybrid court, which had been hosted in the Office for the Illumination of Mysteries, would prosecute Buddhist clericals who committed lesser offenses in accordance with Buddhist monastic law and the hybrid law as laid out in the *Regulations for Monks* (*Sengzhi* 僧制).[66]

This jurisdictional arrangement continued throughout the Tang. Ordained Buddhist offenders continued to receive trials in separate courts under separate laws, depending on whether they had committed serious or minor offenses. Article 11 in the *Statutes of the Tang* (*Tang ling* 唐令) provided similar instructions on which laws to use when prosecuting ordained Buddhist offenders. The *Statutes of the Tang* are no longer extant. But the *Statutes of the Tiansheng Era* (*Tiansheng ling* 天聖令), a thirty-scroll collection of statutes promulgated in 1029, under the reign of the Northern Song emperor Zhao Zhen 趙禎 (1010–1063; reign 1022–1063) in the seventh year of the Tiansheng era,[67] still exists. It records an article that was subsequently repealed during the Song. Its section on prison administration (*yuguan* 獄官) consists of fifty-nine articles from contemporaneous statutes of the Song dynasty and twelve articles from the *Statutes of the Tang*. The repealed article 11 states the following:

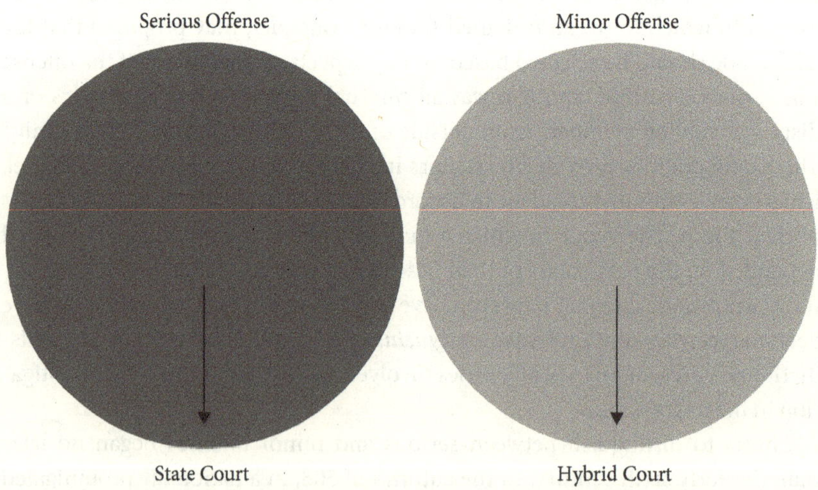

Fig. 5.1 Jurisdictional arrangement in the Northern Wei and the Tang

> All male and female ordained Daoists and Buddhists who have committed an offense for which the penalty would be penal servitude and above, as well as [offenses of] illicit sexual intercourse, theft, wrongful claims [of obtaining supernatural power], or taking off their religious robes, should be investigated and receive a judgment under the state law. For committing other offenses, they should be investigated and receive a judgment under the *Laws for Buddhists and Daoists* [*Daosengfa* 道僧法].[68]

In Japan, lawmakers added more items to this Tang list of serious offenses. In the Japanese *Statutes for Monks and Nuns*, which continually cited the Tang dynasty's *Regulations for Daoists and Buddhists*, the first article required the following crimes to be prosecuted in a state court under state law:

> For making astrological observations, wrongly proclaiming disasters and auspicious phenomena, criticizing the state, misleading the public, as well as studying military technology, committing homicide, having illicit sexual intercourse, and lying about having achieved enlightenment, all monks and nuns will be sent to the state court for investigation and sentenced under state law.[69]

This basic model mapped out in Figure 5.1 continued to function during the Song, but new legislators embarked on a major reform.[70] They still insisted that ordained Buddhist offenders should be tried in different courts, depending on the offense.[71] Yet they perceived the monastic court, and not the hybrid court, to be a more suitable venue for prosecuting minor clerical offenses. In the 963 compilation of the *Detailed Revised Collection of Criminal Law Arranged by Categories from the Jianlong Era during the Song* (*Song Jianlong chong xiangding xingtong* 宋建隆重詳定刑統), monks and nuns who had been involved in internal disputes within their monastic communities could only seek mediation from the head of their host institutions. They could only ask that their cases be transferred to a state court when these cases became so complicated that the heads of their host institutions would have been unable to adjudicate them.[72] In the absence of a clear definition of what constituted a difficult case, we can safely assume that serious offenses were more likely to have qualified as such. Figure 5.2 illustrates the Song's revised pattern for jurisdiction distribution.

In so doing, the Song legislators restricted jurisdiction over ordained Buddhist offenders to state and monastic courts but excluded the hybrid court as a possible venue. The Song legislators' intention, here, can be seen in their decision to repeal article 11 from the *Statutes of the Tang*, a legal document that had included the hybrid court as a possible venue for prosecuting clerical offenses.[73]

When the Mongols took control in the Yuan, new legislators retained the serious-versus-minor-offenses approach to determining the trial venue for

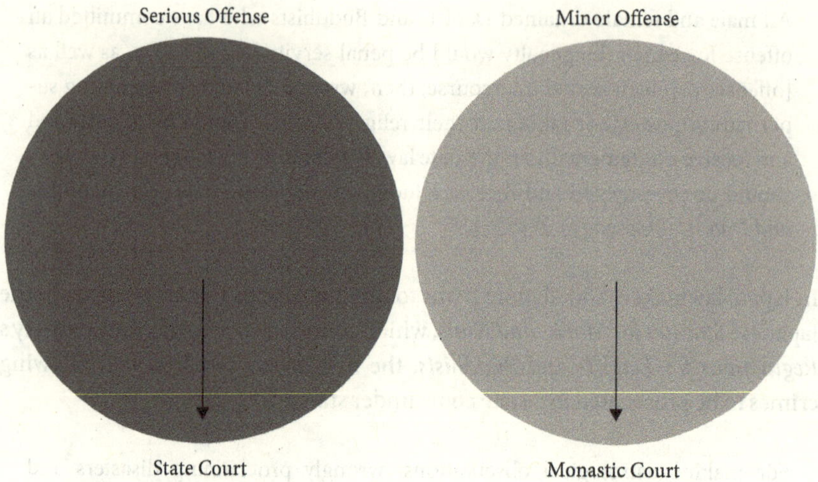

Fig. 5.2 Jurisdictional arrangement in the Song

ordained Buddhist offenders. In an edict issued in 1297, during the fifth month of the first year of the Dade 大德 era, Emperor Temür (1265–1307; reign 1294–1307) ruled that ordained Buddhists and Daoists who had committed the serious offenses of illicit sexual intercourse or theft were to be tried in the state court.[74] Meanwhile, the Yuan legislators also transformed the existing jurisdiction's distribution by introducing a second internal-versus-external approach, which will be discussed in the next section.

This Yuan transformation apparently impressed the succeeding Ming legislators, who had not only adopted both the serious-versus-minor and internal-versus-external approaches to court selection but had also reintroduced the hybrid court to replace the monastic court in their legal landscape. In 1382, on the second day of the fourth month of the fifteenth year of the Hongwu era,[75] Emperor Zhu Yuanzhang issued an edict stating that the monastic courts in Buddhist and Daoist establishments were to have complete jurisdiction over members who had committed offenses that violated Buddhist monastic law. This edict also prohibited the state court from intervening in those cases. Now, the state court could only prosecute and recommend penalties in clerical cases that involved military and laypeople.

In the *Ming Code with Collected Commentaries and Sub-statutes Appended* (*Da Ming lü jijie fuli* 大明律集解附例), promulgated in 1397, Ming legislators further outlined the trial procedures for ordained Buddhist offenders who had committed serious crimes.[76] If a monastic official stationed in the capital committed an offense, then the law enforcement official was to inform the emperor before prosecuting him in a state court. If the monastic official was stationed outside of the capital, then the local court could immediately proceed to trial and prosecute the offender. When ordinary ordained Buddhists committed crimes, such as having illicit sexual intercourse, committing theft or fraud, or being corrupt, these acts would stain their religious practice, and the state court could immediately prosecute and defrock them. When an ordained Buddhist faced punishment for committing crimes while on official duty, due to a collective punishment, or by mistake, they could pay a fine and retain their clerical status. The following Figure 5.3 illustrates the jurisdictional arrangement adopted during the Ming.

These approaches aided the Ming in its efforts to exert tight jurisdictional control over the Buddhist establishment. Ming legislators no longer considered the Buddhist establishment a legitimate legal entity for adjudicating clerical offenses. Instead, they arranged for the hybrid court and the state court to share the jurisdiction over Buddhist clerical offenders.

Qing legislators did not follow the Yuan model but continued to adopt the serious-versus-minor approach, while showing little interest in the internal-versus-external approach. Qing law only emphasized the state court's jurisdiction over serious clerical offenses. In the *Code of the Great Qing* (*Da Qing lüli* 大清律例), the first article in the section on the five punishments (*wuxing* 五刑) required the immediate arrest of monastic officials who had committed crimes considered serious enough for prosecution. When ordinary ordained Buddhists and Daoists committed the serious offenses of illicit sexual intercourse, theft, fraud, or any form of corruption, it was required that they first be defrocked and then receive a penalty that would have been decided under state law.[77]

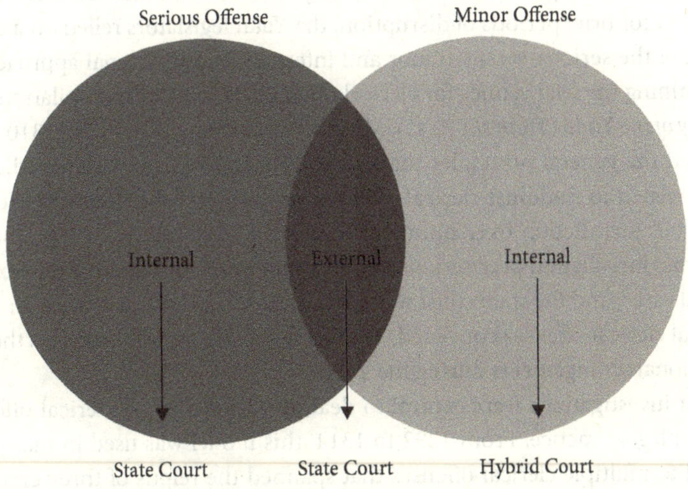

Fig. 5.3 Jurisdictional arrangement in the Ming

Internal-versus-External Approach

Mongols embraced the strategy of dividing up legal jurisdictions based on whether clerical offenses were serious or minor. But when they spotted an oversight in the system, they also saw room for fine-tuning. The existing system had failed to differentiate clerical offenses involving non-Buddhists from those without them. Their solution was to split legal cases into two categories: internal cases that only involved ordained Buddhists and external cases involving ordained Buddhists and lay or non-Buddhists. Non-Buddhists could be ordinary laypeople, ordained Daoists (*xiansheng* 先生), or Confucian scholars (*xiucai* 秀才).

This solution primarily entailed dividing up the jurisdiction that dealt with minor clerical offenses. It aided the state in further restricting the Buddhist establishment's jurisdiction and in expanding the state's jurisdiction by introducing a new trial model: the joint investigation, where representatives from all involved communities were invited to join lay officials in adjudicating external cases involving both ordained Buddhists and lay or non-Buddhist religious practitioners. These jurisdictional representatives included civil officials (*guanmin guan* 管民官),[78] abbots of Buddhist monasteries,[79] abbots of Daoist monasteries, and the head of the Confucian scholars. Throughout the Yuan, legislators often designated as Buddhist representatives the abbots of the monasteries that hosted the offenders or monastic officials who represented the office in charge of overseeing religious affairs. This unique joint investigation reshaped the legal governance of Buddhism during the Yuan and subsequent Ming dynasties. It also created a fourth trial strategy that extended beyond the three established legal venues of the state, hybrid, and Buddhist monastic courts.

Except for brief periods of disruption, the Yuan legislators relied on a combination of the serious-versus-minor and internal-versus-external approaches in determining the trial venues for clerical offenses. In his 1369 compilation of the *History of the Yuan* (*Yuan shi* 元史), Ming historian Song Lian 宋濂 (1310–1381) outlined the general principles that guided Yuan's dealings with jurisdictional issues related to Buddhist clerical offenses, as follows:[80] the Buddhist monastic court had jurisdiction over minor offenses that were internal cases; the state court had jurisdiction over serious offenses that were both internal and external clerical cases; and the state court was also where joint investigations over minor external clerical offenses convened. The following Figure 5.4 illustrates these jurisdictional arrangements during the Yuan.

Joint investigations were central to dealing with Buddhist clerical offenders in Yuan legal practice. From 1292 to 1314, this model was used in many trials related to multiple clerical offenses that spanned the reigns of three emperors. Emperor Kublai was a firm supporter of joint trial. He had explicitly committed

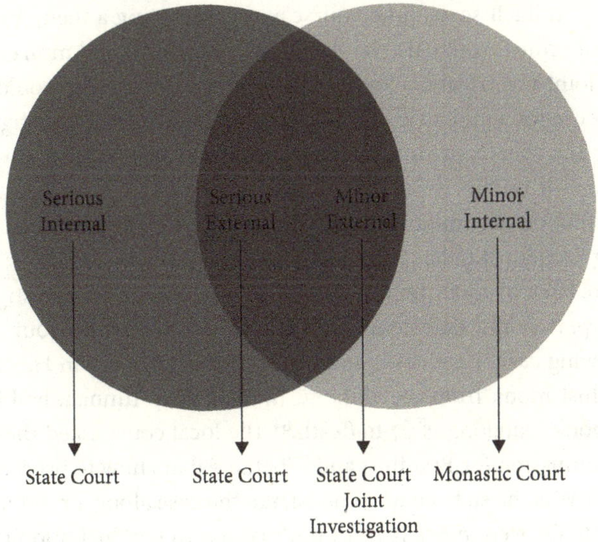

Fig. 5.4 Jurisdictional arrangement in the Yuan

to joint investigations in at least two edicts. In an edict issued in 1292, Kublai requested that the abbot of the Buddhist offender's host monastery join civil officials in investigations of disputes between laypeople and ordained Buddhists; he further prohibited civil officials from intervening in disputes among ordained Buddhists.[81] This edict shows that the Yuan ruler differentiated between internal and external clerical cases. He also designated the state court as the legal venue for joint investigations. A year later, in 1293, Kublai issued another edict that reinforced his support for joint investigations being held in state court for an increasingly diverse body of litigants. In 1293, on the ninth day of the first month of the thirtieth year of the Zhiyuan 至元 era, the Fujian branch secretariat (*xingsheng* 行省) sent a memorial to Kublai, inquiring about the venue in which legal cases involving ordained Buddhists and Daoists and Confucian scholars were to be adjudicated. In his reply, Kublai quoted his 1292 edict and recommended not allowing civil officials to try these cases alone in the state court. Instead, the state court was to convene a joint investigation in the presence of civil officials, the head of the Confucian scholars, and the abbots of the relevant Buddhist and Daoist institutions.[82]

The next supporter of joint investigations, Emperor Temür (1265–1307; reign 1294–1307), embraced and proposed expanding this model's jurisdiction. In 1298, in the third month of the second year of the Dade era, Temür issued an edict that outlined his plan for jurisdictional assignments: the state court and its civil officials were to have sole jurisdiction over clerical offenses that included participating in illicit sexual intercourse and committing a theft, fraud, or forgery; the state court would also be the venue where civil and monastic officials conducted joint investigations over minor clerical offenses. It would also have been an offense for a monastic official to fail to attend a joint investigation.[83] By authorizing the state court to prosecute minor internal offenses through joint investigations of ordained Buddhists, Temür stripped the Buddhist monastic court's jurisdiction over minor internal clerical offenses, a right it had previously held during Emperor Kublai's reign.

Two years later, in 1300, Temür continued to endorse joint investigations but transferred part of the state court's jurisdiction to the hybrid court, as shown in the following case. Previously, at an unspecified time, Duan Haichang 段海長, a Buddhist monk from the Taihe 太和 district in Yunnan, had beaten the Buddhist monk Liangong 連公 to death.[84] The local court asked the Censorate and the Commission for Buddhist and Tibetan Affairs how to proceed with the prosecution: Was the state court to prosecute the case alone, or did it fall to the hybrid court? Or were officials from both courts to conduct a joint investigation? In an edict, Emperor Temür provided instructions for the procedure: a joint investigation in a state court required that both minor and serious offenses perpetrated between laypeople and ordained Buddhists—and serious offenses between ordained Buddhists, such as the case reported above—be investigated and tried in a hybrid court. This edict did not specify where minor internal offenses were to be tried; the venue could have been a hybrid court or a monastic court. What is noteworthy is that this edict ruled that civil officials alone had jurisdiction over external Buddhist clerical offenses, whether serious or minor, and that Buddhist abbots had jurisdiction over internal clerical offenses that occurred in their own monasteries. The cases here and in Temür's edict became precedents that were cited in later judicial inquiries. In 1300, in the first month in the fourth year of the Dade era, the Censorate and the Commission for Buddhist and Tibetan Affairs reiterated this instruction from Emperor Temür in its reply to an inquiry from the Office of the Buddhist Registry on the Ruizhou 瑞州 route in Jiangxi, regarding where to prosecute crimes that resulted in severe injury among ordained Buddhists. In its reply, the commission recommended the following: "When ordained Buddhist monks have committed serious offenses among themselves, the Office of the Buddhist Registry should prosecute them accordingly."[85] This meant the hybrid court gained significant jurisdiction over serious clerical offenses. However, it remained unclear whether jurisdiction over minor internal clerical offenses would go to the hybrid or monastic court.

Within two years, in 1302, Temür decided to further expand the usage of joint investigations by requiring that they prosecute all clerical offenses. In 1302, during the first month of the sixth year of the Dade 大德 era, the Buddhist monk Shi Zujin 石祖進 sued and laid ten charges against Zhu Qing 朱清 and Zhang

Xuan 張瑄.[86] This reference did not specify what these ten charges were, nor did it clarify whether the defendants had been lay or ordained Buddhists. Given that the subsequent discussion focused on procedures for dealing with ordained Buddhist offenders, we can assume that these defendants had likely been ordained Buddhist monks. The complaint reached Temür, who immediately ordered the Censorate to investigate the charges. Temür further promulgated an edict stating that the Censorate and the Commission for Buddhist and Tibetan Affairs were to collaborate in prosecuting all offenses committed by Buddhist monastic officials and ordinary ordained Buddhists. Temür's edict also noted that if the officials from the Commission for Buddhist and Tibetan Affairs failed to rule justly, then the Censorate was to take over the case and investigate the offenses alone.[87]

This move to promote the use of joint investigations in all clerical offenses was met with resistance, and the operation ended a year later, in 1303. The resistance had begun with Buddhist leaders refusing to attend joint investigations. On many occasions when ordained Buddhists committed crimes of lying, robbery, illicit sexual intercourse, or homicide, the abbots of their host monasteries refused to attend the joint investigations that had been set up to prosecute these cases. In one case, when state court officials traveled to these monasteries to summon these abbots to court, they were met with physical assaults carried out under the abbots' instructions.[88] These abbots' refusal to cooperate led to significant delays in trials and lay victims' prolonged waits for justice. In 1303, on the twenty-fourth day of the second month during the seventh year of the Dade era, the Imperial Secretariat (Zhongshu sheng 中書省) submitted a memorial to the emperor requesting a solution to this dilemma. The document briefly summarized how previous emperors had only permitted state court to prosecute serious external clerical offenses. It then proceeded to describe how the current emperor's decision to impose joint investigations resulted in significant damage to Yuan's legal practice, as outlined above. In response, Emperor Temür eliminated this requirement and restored the state court's sole jurisdiction over serious clerical offenses. A year later, in the eleventh month of the eighth year of the Dade era, Emperor Temür publicly reiterated these changes in another edict.[89]

When Emperor Ayuur Balbad (1285–1320; reign 1311–1320) was about to assume power, he renewed the attempt to expand the state court's jurisdiction and reduce that of the Buddhist establishment. According to Ayuur Balbad's plan, the state court should be overseen by civil officials and also be the sole venue in which to try all Buddhist offenders. To accomplish this, the first step would be to abolish all of the regional hybrid courts and retain only two hybrid offices in the central government: the Commission for Buddhist and Tibetan Affairs and the Bureau of the Commissioner for Merit and Virtue. This project began in 1311, while Ayuur Balbad was still a crown prince. In 1311, on the twenty-seventh day of the second month of the fourth year of the Zhida 至大 era, the crown prince ordered that all offices overseeing Buddhist religious affairs at the route, prefecture, and district levels were to be abolished, their official seals were to be destroyed, and their officials were to be dismissed.[90] Two months later, on the twenty-sixth day in the fourth month, the newly enthroned Ayuur Balbad issued an edict that announced his decision to implement these action plans.[91]

Ayuur Balbad's decision to eliminate the hybrid court immediately encountered challenges. Officials from those hybrid offices ignored the order to disband. Two months after the plan had been made known, on the twenty-third day of the fourth month, some former officials in the disbanded hybrid offices began harassing monks in the Baoci 報慈 Monastery in Changshu 常熟 in the Jiangzhe 江浙 branch secretariat.[92] These officials demanded that the monastery provide the names of all senior monks over eighty or ninety years old; they further asked the monastery to provide them with food, wine, and money. The official promulgation to disband these regional hybrid offices came three days later. Yet the monks at the monastery still had to reach out to government officials for help, most likely due to the delay of this edict's implementation in regions far from the capital. It was the monk Zu 祖 who reported the issue of harassment to the route government. On the twenty-fifth day of the fifth month of that year, the Jiangzhe branch secretariat sent inquiries to the Imperial Secretariat in the central government, asking what to do. In its reply, the Imperial Secretariat reiterated its position of forbidding former officials of disbanded hybrid regional offices to harass Buddhist institutions.

Ayuur Balbad's proposal to disband the hybrid offices also disrupted ordained Buddhists' internal legal governance. After the hybrid offices that oversaw these offices were disbanded, ordained Buddhists and Daoists went to the state court at the branch secretariat level to sue the abbots who had performed unjust and illicit acts.[93]

These combined challenges forced the newly enthroned Ayuur Balbad and his officials to reconsider their treatment of the hybrid offices. In 1312, on the sixth day of the fourth month during the first year of the Huangqing 皇慶 era, the Jiangzhe branch secretariat reported its judicial opinion of the need to limit the state court's jurisdiction to serious Buddhist clerical offenses and to entrust the monastic court with all other Buddhist clerical offenses.[94]

This short-lived reform ended with Ayuur Balbad's restoration of the earlier policy to split jurisdiction over ordained Buddhist offenders among the state court, the monastic court, and the use of joint investigations. In 1313, the second year of the Huangqing era, officials from the branch secretariat and the Commission for Buddhist and Tibetan Affairs proposed reinstating the joint investigation procedure and the policy to distinguish between external and internal offenses.[95] This proposal recommended authorizing civil officials to prosecute serious clerical offenses in the state court, including for acts of illicit sex, theft, fraud, and forgery and for causing fatal injuries. Leaders of the offenders' monasteries were to handle disputes among ordained Buddhists in the monastic court, and joint investigations were to decide on offenses involving both ordained Buddhists and laypeople.

Before submitting their new proposal to Emperor Ayuur Balbad, the officials shared it with the imperial preceptor, the highest-ranking monastic official overseeing national religious affairs, who later supported presenting it to the emperor.[96] On the seventeenth day of the sixth month of that year, Ayuur Balbad announced the new proposal in an edict.[97] The edict forbade civil officials from intervening in cases involving ordained Buddhist monks. Civil officials could only try serious Buddhist clerical offenses. The abbot of the host monastery could adjudicate minor disputes among monks internally, but they were to join civil officials in the state court to resolve land disputes between ordained Buddhists and laypeople. If the abbot failed to appear at a joint investigation, the civil official could prosecute the case alone. One month later, the branch secretariat reiterated the requirement to protect the Buddhist establishment's jurisdiction over internal cases and to restrict the state court's jurisdiction to trying serious clerical offenses.[98]

By 1314, a new dilemma forced the joint investigation procedure to change: if the abbot of the offender's host institution had the authority to handle internal clerical offenses, who would prosecute an internal clerical dispute involving the abbot? This was the dilemma in the case between the monk Chonggui 崇圭 and his abbot.[99] In 1314, during the eighth month of the first year of the Yanyou 延祐 era, this monk sued (*gao* 告) his abbot in the district court of Qiantang 錢塘 for having illicit sexual intercourse with laywomen. When the district official Wu Shouzhi 吳壽之 accepted the complaint, the Surveillance Commission (Lianfang si 廉訪司) in East Zhejiang cited the above-mentioned edict of 1313 and accused Wu of accepting bribes in return for intervention in internal clerical cases. Finally, the Department of Justice determined that when ordained Buddhists sued their abbots, an abbot from a nearby monastery should prosecute the case.

Despite supports from the three emperors, during the Yuan era many opposed the use of the joint investigation. Opposition first came from monastic officials who represented religious communities, then from the Buddhist abbots, and later from lay civil officials. In 1298, Ayuur Balbad promulgated an edict stating that a monastic official's failure to appear at a joint investigation would be an offense.[100] By 1303, the abbots of offenders' host monasteries replaced the monastic officials in these joint investigations. In many cases, these abbots deliberately chose not to attend joint investigations, causing delays in the prosecution of ordained Buddhist offenders. Ayuur Balbad solved this problem by authorizing civil officials to prosecute serious clerical offenses without the abbots being present. In 1313, Ayuur Balbad reiterated his threat to allow civil officials to handle these cases alone if the abbots failed to attend joint investigations.[101]

By 1317, the commissioner of the Commission for Buddhist and Tibetan Affairs had become the new representative for ordained Buddhist offenders. However, this official's absence at joint investigations had caused delays in prosecutions. In one case, for instance, when an external lawsuit between an ordained Buddhist and a layperson in East Zhejiang required the commissioner's presence, it was reported that the commissioner was away buying donkeys.[102] The civil official in charge of this case determined that the prosecution had to wait until the commissioner returned. Yet, over a year after he had returned, the commissioner still failed to attend that trial. In 1317, on the twelfth day of the tenth month of the fourth year of the Yanyou era, the Surveillance Commission of East Zhejiang submitted an inquiry asking the secretariat what to do about the case. When the commissioner still failed to appear for the joint investigation, officials in the central government decided to follow the edict of 1313, thereby permitting a civil official to prosecute this external case alone.

Civil officials caused joint investigations to fail in similar ways. For example, in 1320, on the fourteenth day of the fourth month of the seventh year of the Yanyou era,[103] officials from the Jiangxi Branch Commission for Buddhist and Tibetan Affairs asked the local government to adjudicate cases involving ordained Buddhists in accordance with an earlier edict. They cited this edict when arguing that ordained Buddhists who committed serious offenses should be tried in the state court and that disputes between ordained Buddhists and laypeople should be jointly investigated by civil officials, officials from the branches of the secretariat, and the commissioners of the Commission for Buddhist and Tibetan Affairs and the Pacification Commission (Xuanwei si 宣慰司). In practice, some state court officials refused to cooperate in these joint investigations, noting they lacked experience working with the abbots of Buddhist monasteries. The proposed solution, which the emperor approved, was to punish these officials for refusing to attend these trials.

Buddhist Reaction

Buddhists in China had, by and large, embraced the project that created the hybrid court and hybrid laws. Many monks had assisted the state in drafting the laws for guiding the operations of the hybrid court. A trial in the state court under the hybrid law may not have been ideal, but when it became unavoidable for ordained Buddhist offenders to face a trial in the state court, they could benefit from a trial that proceeded under the hybrid law instead of the state law.

Buddhists also saw how the hybrid law worked in their favor. The Tang Buddhist monk scholar Daoxuan 道宣 (596–667) appreciated how the hybrid law could prevent ordained Buddhists from committing offenses against people who were not part of their monastic community.[104] In the opinion of Zanning 贊寧 (919–1001), a Song monk scholar, the hybrid law could also effectively shield ordained Buddhists accused of committing severe crimes from being sentenced to death.[105] Beginning in the fourth century, these opinions could have encouraged numerous high-profile Buddhist monks and monastic officials to embrace, endorse, and aid the state in its efforts to pursue these hybrid legal projects by drafting laws and accepting appointments in the hybrid court.

More importantly, Buddhists in China felt an urgency to support these hybrid projects as they addressed several challenges they continued to face in state courtrooms and beyond, including torture, humiliation, excessively severe penalties, and discrimination. The use of physical torture on ordained Buddhist offenders in the state court was a key issue in the negotiations between the Buddhist establishment and the state. During the Tang, eminent monks made earnest efforts to oppose the use of torture during trials of ordained Buddhists. As mentioned above, in 655, the Buddhist monk Xuanzang petitioned Emperor Li Zhi to prevent officials from beating ordained Buddhists in the state court. Despite edicts forbidding this practice, the use of torture on Buddhist clerical offenders during legal proceedings continued. In the ninth month of 765, the first year of the Yongtai 永泰 era, after the reciting of Buddhist scriptures was perceived to have been effective in averting a Tibetan military invasion of the Tang capital in Chang'an, Emperor Li Yu 李豫 (726–779; reign 762–779) felt the need to issue an edict that once again forbid lay officials from beating ordained Buddhist offenders in the state court. In the edict, Li Yu urged that "civil officials in the state court must not beat or humiliate Buddhist monks and nuns."[106]

Ordained Buddhist convicts also faced humiliating penalties in the state court. During the Yuan, in addition to being beaten in the state court, they could also face branding, a punishment commonly inflicted on lay offenders, though not women and Mongol offenders. In 1279, the sixteenth year of the Zhiyuan 至元 era, Buddhist monk Zhang Wentong 張文通 stole clothes and money from a monk named Li Baoyue 李寶月.[107] The thief received a penalty of being branded on his arm. In 1299, the third year of the Dade era, Buddhist monk Sun Yiji 孫義吉 stole a horse. The judge originally recommended the penalty of branding this monk's face but later changed it to being branded on his arm.[108]

The high probability of receiving an excessively severe penalty was another reason ordained Buddhists feared the state court. If convicted, an ordained Buddhist offender could anticipate receiving a heavier penalty than lay offenders would for the same crime. Article 57 and its commentary in the *Tang Code* instructed judges to consider the nature of the crime (illicit sexual intercourse or rape), the relationship between those involved in the offense (kinship), and their social identities (commoners, slaves/retainers/bondsmen, officials, Daoists, or ordained Buddhists) when deciding on a penalty for a convicted sex offender.[109] Ordained Buddhist offenders who had been accused of a sexual crime were disadvantaged in three ways.[110] First, judges could reduce a commoner offender's penalty but not the penalty imposed on an ordained Buddhist offender who had engaged in illicit sexual intercourse with a noncommoner of a lower social status, such as a slave, personal retainer, or bondsman. Second, for illicit sexual intercourse with a commoner, the penalty would be one degree heavier for a clerical offender. Later in the Song dynasty, the penalty would be two degrees heavier.[111] Third, the penalty would be two degrees heavier for an ordained Buddhist monastic official convicted of having illicit sexual intercourse with individuals under their jurisdiction. Even when an ordained Buddhist's offense was exposed after they had been defrocked, the now defrocked offender would still receive a heavier penalty, since the offense occurred while the offender was still an ordained Buddhist.[112] Legal codes during the Song, Ming, and Qing followed the same principle of deciding heavier penalties for monastic officials.[113]

Ordained Buddhist convicts continued to be haunted by a fear of the state court in their postmonastic life. Immediately after their conviction in the state court, an ordained Buddhist offender was first to be defrocked and then to begin serving their sentence.[114] At the end of a trial, the judge would write the nature of the crime and the date of the conviction on the offender's ordination certificate.[115] The offender was then obliged to surrender the marked ordination certificate to the local government. If a monk offender died, fled, or was defrocked due to a criminal conviction, their abbot was then to submit their ordination certificate to the state, and if they failed to do so, the abbot could receive a flogging of sixty blows with a heavy stick. The civil official who received the ordination certificate of a defrocked monk or nun was to destroy it immediately. If they failed to do so, they could receive a penalty of a flogging of one hundred blows with a heavy stick.[116] In 1265, the second year of the Zhiyuan 至元 era, Emperor Kublai also issued an edict requiring that monks who had officiated the earlier ordinations of the clerical offenders collect the offenders' ordination certificates and Buddhist ceremonial robes (from the defrocked), after which they were to subject the offenders to corvée (that is, forced, unpaid) labor and other duties, similar to other lay convicts.[117]

Not only would defrocked Buddhists lose all the privileges typically granted to religious practitioners, but they would also face much discrimination in their future lay lives. During the Yuan, the court could send defrocked former monks to the frontier to cultivate farmland or to become eagle hunters.[118] These former monks would lose the right to set up households. Instead, they could only become dependents of the royal family.[119] After being defrocked for committing such crimes as homicide, arson, poisoning, fraud, concealing military weapons, privately slaughtering horses or cattle, gambling for profit, or privately making wine or vinegar, many former monks would also lose their commoner status. In 1311, the Department of Justice articulated these guidelines during the adjudication of a homicide case involving the Buddhist monk Cheng Pushan 程普善 in Huizhou 徽州, who had been accused of strangling Buddhist monk Wang Miaoyuan 汪妙遠 over a dispute.[120]

Discrimination in the marriage market would also await former monks who chose to disrobe. In the middle of the third month in 1296, the second year of the Yuanzhen 元貞 period, Buddhist monk Li Fuzheng 李福證 chose to disrobe, grow his hair, and propose to his newly widowed sister-in-law.[121] The woman declined his proposal because she wanted to marry another man, one of her own choice. The former monk sued his sister-in-law in the state court. The judge ruled that because the brother-in-law was a former monk who returned to the laity, the widowed sister-in-law should be allowed to marry the man of her choice. This judgment seemed to imply that if the man had not formerly been a monk but an ordinary layperson, the judge might not have excluded him from the right to marry his sister-in-law.

The fear of postmonastic discrimination also came from the fact that many offenses could result in defrocking. In eighth-century Japan, ordained Buddhist offenders who had been sentenced to penal servitude or worse faced the additional punishment of being defrocked; this included sentences for committing theft,[122] marrying another man's wife, lying about having attained enlightenment, engaging in illicit sexual intercourse, getting drunk and fighting with others,[123] making music or performing for profit,[124] wearing lay clothes,[125] or deceitfully using another person's name for their own gain.[126]

In China, similar offenses could also lead to defrocking. On the seventh day of the fifth month of 955, the second year of the Xiande 顯德 era, Emperor Guo Rong 郭荣 (921–959; reign 954–959) of the Later Zhou dynasty issued a rescript that outlined the treatment of ordained Buddhist offenders. He specified that those who committed crimes of theft, robbery, illicit sexual intercourse, gambling, getting drunk, causing harm, or committing fraud would be punished under state law and incur the additional penalty of defrocking. If they had been sentenced to death for their crimes, the state was to execute them without leniency.[127] During the Song, ordained Buddhist offenders would trigger defrocking penalties if their sentences involved penal servitude or exile; repeat offenders would be flogged with a heavy stick in addition to the defrocking.[128] Specific examples of these offenses included losing an ordination certificate,[129] robbery, intimidation, gambling, intentionally injuring others, fleeing after committing a crime, committing any crime severe enough to require the punishment of exile while on duty, or committing any personal crime where the punishment was penal servitude.

Buddhist Jurisdictional Autonomy

When Buddhists in China collaborated in these hybrid projects, they sought more than compliance. They wanted greater jurisdictional autonomy. In the monasteries, abbots created community bylaws for governing resident monks and nuns and guiding the internal trials of clerics who had committed minor clerical offenses. Outside of these monasteries, eminent monks negotiated with emperors in efforts to eliminate or reduce the state court's jurisdiction over ordained Buddhist offenders. Through these efforts, Chinese Buddhists aimed to transform the monastic legal infrastructure to ensure that Buddhist institutions were trustworthy legal venues capable of hearing cases and imposing penalties.

In the Buddhist pursuit for jurisdictional autonomy in China, it became a priority to improve the legal infrastructure within Buddhist institutions. Such improvements were guided by a new set of monastic community bylaws known as the *Pure Rules of Baizhang* (*Baizhang qinggui* 百丈清規), which dated to the late eighth and early ninth centuries and was applied exclusively to resident monks and nuns of one or several allied Buddhist communities.[130] These bylaws proposed new rules, many of which are devoid of an Indian origin, to address new situations that arose in Chinese Buddhist communities. These were disciplinary rules the Chan Buddhist monk Baizhang Huaihai 百丈懷海 (749–814) crafted to manage residential life in his monastic communities. They have survived in an abridged version, a version written in verse, and three commentaries on the verse version.[131] These texts continue to guide monastic life in monasteries and nunneries in China today.

One bold feature of these Chinese *Pure Rules* was the incorporation of physical and financial punishments, which were absent in Indian Buddhist monastic law. Instructions for physical punishment first appeared in two Song dynasty commentaries on the *Pure Rules of Baizhang*.[132] These commentaries stipulated that as soon as an ordained Buddhist had been convicted of an offense that was punishable by being expelled, the relevant monastery's law-enforcement monks were to beat the convict with a walking staff. Next, monks in the monastery were to assemble to destroy the convict's robes, begging bowls, and other religious possessions. In the end, the monastery would expel the convict, forcing him to exit from a side gate. Later commentators in the Yuan and Qing cited these procedures word for word in their commentaries on the bylaws.[133] All four commentators on the *Pure Rules of Baizhang* noted how the reimagined expulsion procedure could benefit both the Buddhist establishment and the state.[134] First, expelling convicts would prevent damaging the reputation of the Buddhist monastic community. Second, destroying the offenders' religious possessions would prevent these convicts from posing as ordained Buddhists and, thus, from continuing to disgrace the Buddhist establishment. Third, this procedure would relieve civil officials in the state court from excessive trials of clerical offenses. Fourth, dealing with clerical offenders in-house within the monastery would keep their offenses unknown to outsiders and thus protect the reputation of the Buddhist establishment.

The proposal to integrate financial punishment in the community bylaws came from the Ming Buddhist monk Zhuhong 袾宏 (1535–1615). In 1571, Zhuhong began to restore the long-neglected Yunqi Monastery in Hangzhou, in today's Zhejiang Province. In the community bylaws he wrote, the *Regulations for Communal Life at Yunqi Monastery* (*Yunqi gongzhu guiyue* 雲棲共住規約),[135] he outlined punishments for resident monks who had committed offenses. When an offense was serious enough to merit expelling, the offender, in order to remain in the monastery, would have to kneel on both knees and pay a fine. For serious offenses, the fine was five hundred coins; for a medium offense, fifty coins; and for minor offenses, five coins.[136]

While Zhuhong was the first to integrate fines into these monastic bylaws, the practice of imposing financial punishment on Buddhist clerical offenders predated him. In the early fifteenth century, the option to pay a fine to reduce or waive a punishment in the state court was a desirable alternative. When the offense was minor, a convicted Buddhist could pay a fine to remain in the monastic community. When judges in the state court eliminated this option and forced all ordained Buddhist convicts to return to the laity, leaders from the Buddhist community fought to reverse this decision. On the twenty-fifth day of the sixth month of 1456, the seventh year of the Jingtai 景泰 era, the imperial preceptor Shajia 沙加 submitted a memorial where he complained about how civil judges forced all clerical offenders to be defrocked.[137] The imperial preceptor petitioned the judicial office for the right to prosecute clerical offenses in accordance with the practices of the Yongle 永樂 (1403–1424) and Xuande 宣德 (1426–1435) eras, when the state court required only ordained Buddhists convicted of serious offenses to be defrocked but allowed those convicted of minor offenses to pay a fine and thereby retain the right to remain in the Buddhist monastic community. The judicial office rejected this petition. It insisted that defrocking all convicted clerical offenders complied with current state law and that the judgments during the Yongle and Xuande eras had been short-lived exceptions.[138]

The Buddhist pursuit for jurisdictional autonomy also required that a monastic court be capable of enforcing legal judgments. Chinese Buddhists saw two challenges to building this capable monastic court. If convicted monks and nuns refused to comply with the rulings of these courts, then what could the monastery do? And when Buddhist monastic law was unsuitable for prosecuting a monk offender who had contravened worldly orders and violated state law, what could the monastery do? Buddhists in China proposed a simple solution.[139] The guiding principle was to protect the entire Buddhist establishment. The monastery was to stop sheltering offenders if covering for them jeopardized the entire Buddhist monastic community. This meant if the offenses were minor, the Buddhist establishment could take care of the offender in accordance with the community bylaws, but if the offenses were serious and the offenders were incorrigible, cunning, and undisciplined, the monastery should send the offender to the state court to be tried under state law.

Buddhist monks in China had to work very hard to convince the state to recognize these Buddhist community bylaws. One strategy was to demonstrate engagement with the state law by integrating its rules into their community bylaws. In their commentaries on the *Pure Rules of Baizhang*, the Yuan Buddhist monk Dehui and the Qing Buddhist monk Yirun both quoted articles from the *Compendium of Statutes and Sub-statutes of the Yuan* (*Yuan dianzhang* 元典章) on how to adjudicate serious clerical offenses (internal and external) and minor internal clerical offenses. Both monks specified that the Buddhist monastic court should try internal clerical offenses under community bylaws.[140] The rules in these Buddhist monastic community bylaws aligned with the Yuan state law that authorized the state court to hear serious clerical offenses, the monastic court to hear internal minor offenses, and the joint court to hear external minor offenses.

The other strategy was to demonstrate loyalty to the state law. Leaders of China's Buddhist communities did not perceive community bylaws as having the power to override the state law. Rather, they urged that resident monks and nuns obey the state law. In the ten rules Zhuhong had created for the resident monks in his community, the first rule required that monks obey the state law, and anyone who deliberately disobeyed them would face the possibility of being expelled.[141]

Conclusion

From the fourth century onward, Chinese emperors showed sustained interest in increasing state control over religion. They used the legal system as a major apparatus for this purpose, and their efforts in this endeavor led to a series of reforms to China's legal structure. These reforms began in the fourth century, when emperors recognized the need to differentiate ordained Buddhist offenders from ordinary lay ones.

In collaboration with eminent Buddhist monks, the state proposed a two-step solution to tackle this challenge. First, it introduced a set of laws along with a legal office that was solely dedicated to adjudicating clerical offenders. Trials of ordained Buddhist offenders were to take place in the state court, the monastic court within a Buddhist institution, or the hybrid court. Judges overseeing these trials also had the option of using the state law, Buddhist monastic law, or the newly established hybrid law in these trials. From the fourth century to the Qing, state lawmakers continually changed the names, content, and host institutions of the hybrid law and hybrid court in accordance with the social, political, and religious contexts of their time.

Next, the state lawmakers explored two approaches to determining which one of the three legal venues and laws to use in trials for clerical offenses. They began with an approach that focused on the differences between serious and minor offenses and between criminal and civil ones. Later, they expanded this approach to assess an additional dimension of clerical offenses: internal versus external. This later development led to the invention of a fourth trial strategy, the joint investigation, which was introduced during the Yuan but gradually fell out of use in later dynasties.[142]

On the other end of the negotiating table, leaders of the Buddhist establishment continued their attempts to persuade the emperors and their lawmaking teams to allow the Buddhist establishment to retain some degree of jurisdictional autonomy. Eminent Buddhist monks repeatedly submitted petitions that prosecutions of ordained Buddhists no longer take place in the state court and that the use of torture be disallowed during interrogations.

Ultimately, the state's goal in these reforms was to exert tighter control over Buddhism by reducing the Buddhist establishment's jurisdictional autonomy. Through this project, the state not only controlled the jurisdiction of ordained Buddhists accused of committing serious crimes, such as murder and theft, but they also extended their control over matters that had previously been exclusively under the Buddhist establishment's jurisdiction. To consolidate their efforts to reduce the Buddhist establishment's jurisdictional autonomy, Chinese emperors also elevated the legal status of the hybrid law by formally incorporating it into the state legal system as regulations, statutes, or announcements in edicts. The invention of the hybrid court and hybrid law thus enabled Chinese rulers to compromise without relinquishing control of the courts.

In recent decades, increasing revelations of clerical offenses have brought forward discussions on religious law's place in the state justice system. This chapter shows how similar discussions on the place of Buddhist religious law in the Chinese legal system unfolded in historical contexts. From the fourth century to the early twentieth century, China's Buddhist establishment and the state continued to collaborate in demarcating, maintaining, and redrawing their jurisdictional boundaries. The transformation of a bipartite legal infrastructure into a tripartite one and the distribution of jurisdictional power between the three legal venues of the state, monastic, and hybrid courts allowed the state court to retain absolute jurisdiction over serious clerical offenses while also providing a buffer zone for negotiating jurisdiction over minor clerical offenses. Seeing the interactions between the two legal systems of the Buddhist establishment and the state in China thus provides a more balanced understanding of the patterns of the interactions that have developed between religion and the state; it also enables Buddhism to have a place in global conversations on the legal relationship between religion and the state.

6
A Fallen Abbot

> We have received the report and begun an investigation.
>
> State Administration of Religious Affairs, August 2, 2018

On August 1, 2018, a ninety-five-page report went viral on social media in China and gained immediate domestic and international attention.[1] In this report, a high-ranking Chinese Buddhist monk named Xuecheng 學誠 was accused of sexual harassment and assault against several ordained Buddhist nuns, of embezzling monastery funds, and of illegally constructing new buildings in his monastery without permits from the city of Beijing. Xuecheng was the abbot of Longquan 龍泉 Monastery, also known as Dragon Spring Monastery, situated on the outskirts of Beijing. In just over a decade, this monastery had earned an international reputation for recruiting highly educated intellectuals, from prestigious academic institutions in China, to become monks and nuns. Its successful use of social media, advanced technology, and artificial intelligence also helped establish its public identity as a prominent Buddhist institution in contemporary China.[2] In addition to being the abbot of this leading Buddhist monastery, the accused was also the president of the Buddhist Association of China, the highest state-recognized organization overseeing national Buddhist affairs. Xuecheng's case rose to national prominence in connection with developments in the #MeToo movement in China,[3] which had surged a few weeks earlier when victims of sexual assault or harassment made a series of allegations against high-profile scholars, activists, and influential journalists. This case should not have been circumscribed exclusively within the sexual harassment movement, however, as this obscured its significance to the broader scope of legal interactions that were taking place at the time between religion and the state in China.

The negotiations over jurisdictional boundaries between the state and religious establishments are central to the legal relationship between the two entities. Scholars have proposed two theories to explain how these negotiations unfolded between the Buddhist establishment and the state in China.[4] One theory considers the Buddhist submission to the state's jurisdictional governance to be a distinctive feature in the Chinese transformation of Buddhism. Kenneth Ch'en, an influential proponent of this theory, argues that the Buddhist clergy in China betrayed the Indian tradition as it became Sinicized and took root in Chinese

Buddhism in Court. Cuilan Liu, Oxford University Press. © Oxford University Press 2024.
DOI: 10.1093/oso/9780197663332.003.0007

society.[5] Their abandonment of the Indian tradition of requiring royal kings to pay homage to ordained Buddhists among Chinese Buddhist clergy is cited as evidence of this betrayal. According to Anthony C. Yu, the tradition of royal rulers paying homage to ordained Buddhists illustrates the Indian Buddhist monastic community's "essential independence" from the state.[6] Yet Yu challenges the validity of Ch'en's claim that the clergy submits to state jurisdiction. He argues that even if the Chinese Buddhist establishment "might have indeed come to terms by and large with the supremacy of the state," some individual Buddhists are exceptions. One was the pilgrim monk Xuanzang, during the early Tang, willingly risked violating state law to travel to India when crossing the border had been prohibited.[7] To Yu, such incriminating actions by individual Buddhists indicate a belief in "a demand, a summons, and a law that were higher than any norm or form of authority sanctioned" by the individual's native traditions.[8]

Another theory highlights the contrast between the harsh state control over religion according to the law and the lax enforcement in practice. Holmes Welch sees this contrast as having existed during the late Qing, where extremely harsh state laws on Buddhism were rarely implemented in practice, leaving ordained Buddhists in a legal limbo.[9] Citing missionary reports of ordained Buddhist offenders who were spared from punishment,[10] Welch suggests that a criminal could have avoided prosecution by entering the Buddhist order. This fantasy is most elaborately entertained in the fourteenth-century classical novel *Water Margin*, introduced earlier, featuring the murderer Lu Da, who escapes prosecution by becoming an ordained Buddhist monk. Welch presents two reasons for the laxity in enforcing state laws on ordained Buddhist offenders.[11] First, law enforcement officials might have been less antagonistic toward Buddhism and Buddhists. Second, the office overseeing monks and nuns was powerless. Nevertheless, Welch believes that this contrast between harsh codes and lax applications of the law had served the state. A flexible enforcement allowed the state to show benevolence toward ordained Buddhist offenders while also reserving the right to lawfully prosecute any monk who became "even slightly involved in something heretical or subversive," because the "district magistrate could consult the code and strike him down with at least twenty dire regulations that he had been breaking (like most other monks) throughout his career."[12]

The actual handling of Xuecheng's case in 2018 illustrates a different pattern of how the tension between the Buddhist and state jurisdictional boundaries unfolds in legal practice in contemporary China. The nature of the charges against Xuecheng made it difficult to immediately ascertain which court had jurisdiction over this case. For an ordained Buddhist monk, having sexual intercourse violates one of the four fundamental precepts in Buddhist monastic law. Thus, in theory, the host monastery should expel the offender from the monastic community.[13] Moreover, in the contemporary context, an ordained Buddhist monk who sexually harasses or assaults others is also violating Chinese law. As such, both the state and the Buddhist establishment could claim jurisdiction over anyone accused of such allegations. The presence of two other third-party institutions further complicates the determination of jurisdiction in this case: the Buddhist Association of China, staffed by state-approved Buddhist officials, and the State Administration of Religious Affairs, staffed by state-appointed lay officials. Each of the four institutional powers is a potential investigator.

The day after the report about Xuecheng appeared on the internet, the State Administration of Religious Affairs assumed responsibility for investigating the charges. How this decision was made, who made it, and why all remain a mystery. The previous chapter shows how the state and the Buddhist establishment collaborated in establishing a tripartite legal system, beginning in the fourth century, to replace the dichotomous lay and monastic courts and laws. In this chapter, I argue that authorizing the State Administration of Religious Affairs, a third-party hybrid agency, to conduct a preliminary investigation of criminal, civil, and administrative accusations against an ordained Buddhist monk illustrates the continued influence of this dynastic tripartite legal infrastructure in contemporary China.

The Allegations

Two monks from Longquan Monastery coauthored the report against Xuecheng. In this report, they disclosed their legal names, national identity card numbers, cell phone numbers, and explanations of their connections to this monastery. The first author, Xianjia 賢佳 (lay name Liu Xinjia 劉新佳), self-identified as a monk. He had graduated from Tsinghua University with a PhD in engineering, in 2003. A year later, he was ordained at Longquan Monastery. The other coauthor was the monk Xianqi 賢啟 (lay name Du Qixin 杜啟新), who had also completed a PhD in engineering at Tsinghua University, in 2000. He was ordained at Longquan Monastery in 2006. Both monks had worked on the monastery's supervisory committee until January 2018. While staying at the monastery, Xianjia also worked as a disciplinarian (*dujian* 都監) and as Xuecheng's personal attendant (*shizhe* 侍者) for many years.

Their coauthored report named at least five nun victims, all of whom remained anonymous. The accusations of sexual harassment and assault were primarily built on the victims' testimonies and on privately exchanged text messages. These included a photocopy of the handwritten last words that victim Nun A wrote as a precaution, a typed statement of her experience, the text messages exchanged between Xuecheng and the victims, and snapshots of the sexually abusive messages that Xuecheng had exchanged with the victims on the popular Chinese social media platform WeChat.

Nun A reported experiencing verbal sexual harassment via text messages from the accused. She was born in 1984 in Guangxi, China. On April 25, 2014, she began working at Longquan Monastery as a resident volunteer. A year later, on October 2, 2015, the monastery sent her to Jile 極樂 Nunnery in Fujian Province, where she became a lay steward in preparation for the next step toward ordination.[14] This nunnery was subordinate to Longquan Monastery. On March 16, 2016, Nun A was ordained as a novice. Six months later, on October 16, 2016, she and seventy-seven other novice nuns from the same nunnery received full ordination at Zhongde 種德 Monastery in Fujian Province. On December 21, 2017, the nunnery sent Nun A and another nun, Nun B, to Beijing to study English for three months before assigning them to go overseas to expand Longquan Monastery's global influence. Finally, on December 25, 2017, Nuns A and B arrived in Beijing, where they stayed at the Rixin 日新 Dharma Center.

On December 27, 2017, Nun A's interaction with Xuecheng began with text messages. Her nunnery provided her and Nun B with a cell phone to share while they were in Beijing. Three days later, on December 30, she received the first harassing text message from the abbot. In her written testimony, Nun A reported that the abbot probed her dating history and asked whether she was still a virgin. Over the next two weeks, the abbot used graphic language to demand sexual favors, ranging from touching to sexual intercourse. On February 5, 2018, Nun A wrote a one-page letter of her last words by hand, expressing fear and anxiety for herself and her parents. Feeling her life was in danger, in her letter she had even asked for help regarding her parents' care. On February 11, 2018, Nun A resolved to cease communicating with the abbot, to terminate her English-language studies in Beijing, and to leave the nunnery permanently. With the help of the monk Xianqi, with whom she had worked on an editing project earlier in 2017, Nun A managed to flee from her residence at the Rixin Dharma Center. On February 14, 2018, she wrote a twenty-five-page statement describing how the abbot had sexually harassed her. This statement was included in the monks Xianjia and Xianqi's report, which went viral online.[15]

The second victim, Nun B, had been Nun A's companion during their time in Beijing. Nun A's statement described Nun B as a college graduate born in 1994. While still in college, Nun B had already become a regular volunteer at Longquan Monastery. In 2016, she received her novice ordination at Jile Nunnery and was fully ordained a year later, in April 2017. The document did not contain testimony from Nun B. Still, the transcriptions of text messages exchanged between another nun, Nun C, and the abbot, dated January 7, 2018, indicated that the abbot had sexually harassed Nun B the same way he had harassed Nun A.[16] The snapshot of two other nuns' WeChat conversations about Nun B, included in the report, also indicated that the abbot had already had sexual intercourse with Nun B.[17]

The third victim, Nun C, was revealed in transcribed text messages she and the abbot had exchanged on January 23, 2018.[18] Like Nun B, Nun C did not provide any first-person testimony. The transcribed text messages show that the abbot had asked nun C to compose a pornographic description of having imagined sex with him and text it to him. According to nun A's statement, Nun C had already become mentally ill by about February 2017, almost a year before the abbot had demanded the pornographic text. The snapshot of a WeChat conversation between Nun C and another unidentified nun also indicated that the abbot had already had sexual intercourse with Nun C.[19] In the report, the two monks stated that Nun C had reported Xuecheng's sexual assault to five administrative monks, including Xianjia, at Longquan Monastery on June 25, 2018. At the same time, Nun C had also reported having witnessed Xuecheng's sexual assault of another nun, who remained unidentified.

The fourth and fifth victims were Nuns D and E. Unfortunately, we know very little about these victims. The report only included three transcriptions of the text messages between Nun D and the abbot. These messages indicate that the abbot had demanded that Nun D have virtual sex with him and indicated that Nun D had helped send another nun (Nun E) to the abbot's bed.

These nun victims and the monks who supported them initially intended to deal with these abuses internally within Longquan Monastery. So, after learning about Nun A's experience, Xianqi first went to verify the accusations. Then on February 17, 2018, Xianqi circulated a written petition among the monastery's administrators. In this petition, Xianqi asked the monastery to refer to Buddhist monastic law to encourage the abbot to confess his misdeeds. But this failed.

Unable to resolve this critical issue within the monastery, the victims and their supporters sought external intervention. On June 29, 2018, accompanied by Xianqi and three other monks, Nun C went to file a police report at the local police station in Haidian District, the jurisdiction of Longquan Monastery. Nun C told the police that Xuecheng had sexually assaulted her and several other Buddhist nuns, but the police did not file the case. On July 15, 2018, the monks Xianjia and Xianqi emailed their report to over a thousand monasteries and individuals to uncover Xuecheng's sexual assaults and harassments.[20]

After repeated denials, the accusations finally went public online on August 1, 2018, and immediately went viral. This forced Longquan Monastery to issue an official statement, on the same day, wherein it denied all charges against its abbot and accused the monks Xianjia and Xianqi of making false accusations and forging evidence against the abbot.[21] While discussions on this case continued to swirl around, online and off, these monks and nuns sent a copy of the report of the accusations to the State Administration of Religious Affairs in Beijing. In their report, the two monks and the victims demanded that specific actions be taken against Xuecheng. First, they asked that Xuecheng be removed from all his appointments in religious and social organizations and that he be defrocked. Furthermore, they asked that Xuecheng's contact with his followers be blocked and that he be moved to a solitary retreat where he could receive help reflecting on his behavior. On August 2, that year, the State Administration of Religious Affairs officially announced receipt of the report and the initiation of an immediate investigation of the accusations.

The Legal Context

It is important to understand the development of Xuecheng's case within China's legal context in 2018. In that year, Chinese legislators were still working on refining the definitions of sexual harassment and assault. At the assembly of the National People's Congress on August 28, 2005, Chinese legislators first introduced the concept of sexual harassment in an updated version of the *PRC Law on the Protection of Women's Rights and Interests* (*Zhonghua renmin gongheguo funü quanyi baozhang fa* 中華人民共和國婦女權益保障法). This law first came into existence on October 1, 1992. In the 2005 version, article 40 prohibited sexual harassment against women and provided victims the right to submit a complaint to the relevant employers or other relevant officials. Four years later, on May 4, 2009, the Standing Committee of the People's Congress in Beijing proposed a plan for implementing this law in Beijing. This proposal provided a more detailed description of sexual harassment and the specific venues for dealing with it.[22] Article 38 prohibited anyone from sexually harassing women verbally, through texts, images, or electronic information, or through bodily contact. This proposal also provided victims with two options. They could either file an administrative complaint, whether with their employer, the perpetrator's employer, or the All-China Women's Federation (Quanguo funü lianhe hui 全國婦女聯合會) and other relevant offices, or they could initiate a lawsuit in court. The National People's Congress kept revising its understanding of sexual harassment. On August 27, 2018, legislators proposed defining sexual harassment as "verbal or physical sexual advances against the victim's will," in article 1010 from the section on personality rights in the *Civil Code* (*Minfa dian* 民法典). This proposed article would enable victims to sue their perpetrators. On May 28, 2020, the National People's Congress passed this law, effective January 1, 2021.

For Buddhist nuns, however, suing their perpetrators was not the preferred option. Buddhist monastic law prohibits nuns who are victims of sexual crimes from filing suits in the state court. Instead, it encourages ordained Buddhists to resolve internal offenses, involving only ordained Buddhists, within the institution. This rule was found in the section discussing the probationary offenses in the *Mahīśāsaka Vinaya*,[23] which I analyzed above in Chapter 1. In sum, a nun who was the victim of abuse was to first seek help from her family members, fellow monks and nuns, and lay Buddhists to resolve the matter privately. If she sued the perpetrator without first making these efforts to privately settle her case, she committed a confessable probationary offense. It is important to note that this prescriptive procedure was not universal. Beyond the *Mahīśāsaka Vinaya*, no parallels have been found in Buddhist monastic law texts transmitted from the other traditions, including the *Dharmaguptaka Vinaya*, the dominant text guiding ordination ceremonies and the regular study of monastic discipline among Chinese Buddhists.

These legal notions expressed in the *Mahīśāsaka Vinaya*, however, may have continued to affect how Buddhist nuns in China evaluated their options if they became victims of sexual crimes. While the *Dharmaguptaka Vinaya* had been the dominant monastic law in China, the Chinese Buddhist community also circulated and used laws that had been transmitted from the Mahīśāsaka, Sarvāstivāda, Mahāsāṃghika, and Mūlasarvāstivāda traditions.[24] Buddhists in China today still actively consult these other Buddhist monastic law texts, such as the *Mahīśāsaka Vinaya*. In their report, the two monks Xianjia and Xianqi cited articles from both the *Mahīśāsaka Vinaya* and the *Dharmaguptaka Vinaya* to corroborate their accusations against the abbot of administrative and financial misconduct.[25] They also cited the writings of various historical and contemporary Buddhist monks to argue why it is fundamentally wrong for ordained Buddhists to have sex. These contemporary engagements with the *Mahīśāsaka Vinaya* suggest that nun victims in China may still feel pressured to refrain from suing their perpetrators in the state court.

These complicated realities foster a legal context in which nun victims of sexual violence may agonize over suing their perpetrators in the state court, or at least not consider litigation as the first choice. In the case of Xuecheng, the nun victims' reactions affirm how these concerns still affect the Buddhist community in contemporary China.

Buddhist Jurisdiction

In 2018, the Buddhist Association of China received a copy of the report on Xuecheng's case.[26] Earlier scholars considered the historical predecessors of this association to be mediators. In his study of the Buddhist revival in China, Holmes Welch describes the Buddhist Association in modern China as "an intermediary" between the monasteries and the official organs.[27] In another book discussing Buddhism during the Mao era, Welch equates the role of this association with that of monastic officials (*sengguan* 僧官) in imperial China.[28] In 2018, however, this association did not assume a mediating role in investigating the accusations against Xuecheng. A conflict of interest likely prevented it from leading the investigation into allegations against its president. Yet its lack of action in this case belies how much, from its debut in 1912 to the present day, this association has fought for jurisdictional control over the Buddhist establishment, its monastic properties, and its individual members.

Historically, the Buddhist Association of China has faced turbulence. China's leadership has changed dramatically between 1912 and the present, from frequent changes in military power during the Republican era (1911–1949) to the Communist takeover in 1949 and the significant reforms that have taken place since then. During this period, different groups of Buddhists have attempted to establish similar national organizations to oversee Chinese Buddhists and have also competed to lead these organizations. In the ensuing chaos, the successive national organizations that were established came with slightly different names at different times and locations. Between 1912 and 1929, Buddhists in China made at least eighteen attempts to form a new national association or to revive one that had been terminated.[29] After initially recognizing the Buddhist Association of China as an official organization in 1912, the government subsequently forced it to dissolve in 1915 and again in 1919, before finally licensing it as a legitimate organization in 1932.[30] Civil war and war with Japan also forced the association to go dormant from time to time. This turmoil helps explain why its name changed from the General Buddhist Association of China (Zhonghua fojiao zonghui 中華佛教總會) in 1912, to the Buddhist Association of China (Zhonghua fojiao hui 中華佛教會) in 1917, to the Buddhist Academy of China (Zhongguo fojiao xuehui 中國佛教學會) in 1928, back to the Buddhist Association of China (Zhongguo fojiao hui 中國佛教會) in 1929, and finally to the Buddhist Association of China (Zhongguo fojiao xiehui 中國佛教協會) in 1953.[31]

To understand how this association's own perception of jurisdiction changed over time, we should refer to the multiple versions of its charter as it was promulgated at different times. This legal document is not only a guide for the association's operations; it is essential for its existence. Its charter changed several times between 1912 and 1949. The first charter was drawn up in February 1912, and there were major subsequent revisions in April 1912, 1913, 1915, 1919, 1929, 1935, 1936, and 1948. After 1949, the People's Republic of China (PRC) founded its own Buddhist association on June 3, 1953, which was then approved as a registered organization by the Ministry of the Interior on June 20, 1953.[32] The association passed its first charter of the PRC era on June 3, 1953.[33] Since then, the association's national assembly has revised its charter eight times, in 1957,[34] 1980,[35] 1987,[36] 1993,[37] 2002,[38] 2010,[39] 2015,[40] and 2020.[41]

The association's relentless pursuit of jurisdiction over monastic properties put it on a collision course with the government. The presence or absence of jurisdiction in its negotiations with the government manifested the association's struggle with writing its jurisdictional powers into its charter. This occurred in four phases: the phase of aggressively pursuing jurisdiction, from 1912 to 1915; the phase of abandoning this pursuit in exchange for the association's survival, from 1917 to 1934; the phase of a renewed battle over jurisdiction, from 1935 to 1949, after the government's jurisdictional encroachment threatened its very existence; and the phase of making no mention in the charter of the issue of the association's jurisdictional power, from 1953 to 2021, in the PRC.

The association's aggressive pursuit of jurisdiction was a hallmark in its first phase, from 1912 to 1915, under the administration of the General Buddhist Association of China. At that time, this association played an important role as the legal representative for individual monasteries and nunneries in lawsuits over the encroachment of their monastic properties.[42] The multiple versions of its charter, presented to the Ministry of the Interior, attested to its ambition to gain and secure jurisdictional control over Buddhist institutions and individuals. This ambition also resulted in the association being forced to close down in 1915.

The association's journey had begun in 1912. Newly founded at the beginning of that year, it drafted the *Charter of the General Buddhist Association of China* (*Zhonghua fojiao zonghui zhangcheng* 中華佛教總會章程), composed of twenty-three articles.[43] On February 12, 1912, the Ministry of the Interior and the Ministry of Education both approved this charter and praised the association's aspirations to support education and promote Buddhism.[44] In the document, the association assumed absolute jurisdiction in several areas. First, it asserted complete control over the admission of new members.[45] All candidates were required to obtain an ordination certificate from the association, without which their ordination would be invalid. Also, any ordained monks and nuns who were without such a certificate were prohibited from becoming an association member. Second, the association claimed custody of all monastic properties,[46] which it considered to be collectively owned by the entire Buddhist establishment but not by individuals or Buddhist institutions. Monasteries and nunneries had the right only to use and maintain monastic properties. Without the association's approval, they had no right to sell or transfer them. The association had sworn to fight anyone who dared encroach on these monastic properties.[47] Third, it claimed the right to mediate disputes between the residents of these monasteries and nunneries.[48] When local monasteries and nunneries needed to interact with outside entities, or when conflicts arose among their residents, the county offices of this organization would have been the first to intervene to mediate the issue. If anything proved too complicated to resolve at that level, the monasteries and nunneries would have to report to one of the association's provincial or central offices.[49] Fourth, the association asserted its responsibility to protect registered members, and this required state law to provide equal protection to support the legal acts of monks and nuns,[50] but the association also declared its lack of intention to cover up for members who had been convicted of crimes against state law.[51]

Within six months, the Ministry of the Interior expressed regret for having approved this charter. Agreeing to give the association jurisdiction over the monastic property was the primary basis of this regret. In a written response to an inquiry from the military governor of Hunan Province, published on August 23, 1912,[52] the Ministry of the Interior required the association to resubmit a revised charter for re-evaluation and re-approval. The official reason was that the new government had just been established when the approved charter was submitted and laws were not yet in place. The approval the ministry granted to the 1912 charter was temporary. Now that the nation had settled down, it was time for the Ministry of the Interior to revisit the legal documents it had hastily approved under extraordinary circumstances. The association presented a revision on November 2, 1912,[53] but the Ministry of the Interior was not convinced it warranted approval. In its reply to the state council, published on December 8, 1912, the Ministry of the Interior requested further revision.[54] The association promptly presented the *Revised Charter of the General Buddhist Association of China* (*Zhonghua fojiao zonghui xiugai zhangcheng* 中華佛教總會修改章程), which appeared in print on December 9, 1912. This version consisted of twenty-seven articles. The Ministry of the Interior approved this revision on March 4, 1913. A slightly tweaked final version was printed in the first issue of the association's official journal, which occurred on the Buddha's birthday, May 13, 1913.[55]

The *Revised Charter* had added four more articles—a total of twenty-seven, as noted above—and provided further details on many of the articles in the original. What did not change was the association's claim of having jurisdiction over monastic property. Taking a much more aggressive stance than it had in 1912, the association announced that nobody should intervene in its governance over Buddhist communities.[56] The association further announced its absolute right to supervise the promotion of Buddhism, mediate disputes between Buddhist adherents, and handle any disputes over monastic property. Additionally, the association cited a state council policy that demonstrated its determination to protect monastic property from illegal encroachment.[57] That policy prohibited law enforcement from punishing the host monastery if a resident monk had committed a crime, permitting only personal punishments for individual offenders.

The association's persistence in asserting control over monastic properties provoked the Ministry of the Interior to require it to revise its charter again. On June 8, 1914, the Minister of the Interior submitted a petition to the president, requiring the association to revise its 1913 charter and resubmit it for approval.[58] In this petition, the minister attacked many more articles, such as those requiring monks and nuns to become registered members of the association in order to receive communal benefits, including the right to use accommodations at different monasteries and nunneries. The minister argued that these articles violated the freedom of individual monks and nuns to practice their religion. He also attributed the increasing number of lawsuits over monastic property taking place in many provinces to the association's claim of jurisdiction over monastic property. In September 1914, the association requested that the National Assembly hold a meeting to discuss the revisions.[59] Afterward, the association attempted to satisfy the Ministry of the Interior's requirement and revised its charter multiple times. However, the ministry was determined not to approve it. By October 1915, the association was still unable to officially register itself as a legitimate organization and thereafter became inactive.[60]

The second phase of the association's pursuit of jurisdiction took place from 1917 to 1929. This phase featured repeated compromises in its charter in exchange for gaining the government's approval to reestablish the association that had previously been forced to disband. In 1917, the Mongolian Buddhist monk Lcang skya Blo bzang dpal ldan bstan pa'i sgron me (1890–1957) and the Chinese Buddhist monk Qinghai 清海 initiated the association's first attempt to reestablish. On May 3, 1917, the Beiyang government approved their request to form the Buddhist Association of China (Zhonghua fojiao hui 中華佛教会).[61] This approval came at the cost of significantly revising its charter, resulting in twenty-six rewritten articles.[62] The new charter no longer addressed the association's jurisdiction, legal rights, or legal duties. It also completely dropped the earlier articles that had asserted authority over monastic properties, ordination, and the appointment of monastic leaders. Furthermore, it removed articles that claimed equal protection for ordained monks and nuns under state law. These compromises in the new charter did not save the association for long. In May 1919, after the association's short revival of two years, the Ministry of the Interior declared its founding to be illegal and removed it from the government registry.[63] However, in October 1929, a second attempt to revive the association succeeded, under the name of the Buddhist Association of China (Zhongguo fojiao hui 中國佛教會). This came at the expense of further restricting the association's rights and powers as codified in its *Charter of the Buddhist Association of China* (*Zhongguo fojiao hui huizhang* 中國佛教會會章). The new charter, published in 1929, contained just sixteen articles, which discussed only its administrative organization.[64]

In the third phase, from 1935 to 1948, the recurrence of an old threat motivated the association to revisit its charter. This threat was a proposed plan to confiscate monastic property to support the establishment of secular schools. On July

18, 1935, the association passed the *Revised Charter of the Buddhist Association of China* (*Xiuzheng zhongguo fojiao zhangcheng* 修正中國佛教章程), this time with thirty-two articles.[65] One highlight of this revision was that it tightened its restrictions on who would have been admitted to the association. Specifically, article 6 defined as inadmissible the mentally ill, incarcerated convicts, those addicted to unhealthy habits, those without citizenship rights, and those who had violated the bylaws of Buddhist communities.[66]

A significant disruption occurred in 1936, when the Central Department for Military Training of the Nationalist Party of China (Guomin dang zhongyang minxu bu 國民黨中央民訓部) linked the increasing disputes between ordained Buddhist monks and nuns to corruption in the Chinese Buddhist community. To improve the situation, they believed, reform was necessary, which started with revising the association's charter. The department's director, Zhang Tinghao 張廷灝, reportedly consulted Master Taixu 太虛 and Master Yuanying 圓瑛, in person, in Shanghai, before writing the *Draft Charter for the Buddhist Association of China* (*Zhongguo fojiao hui zhangcheng cao'an* 中國佛教會章程草案), along with seventy articles that were to be discussed at the association's upcoming national assembly.[67] In June 1936, this draft was published in the association's official journal.[68]

This new draft provoked unprecedented debate among monastics, lay Buddhists, and governmental officials. Both proponents and opponents openly joined the discussions. They stormed government offices and the editorial offices of Buddhist journals, voicing their comments, criticisms, suggestions, and clarifications regarding the revisions.[69] From July to September 1936, the influential Buddhist journal *The Voice of the Ocean Wave* (*Haichao yin* 海潮音) published three special collections of comments on the proposed charter, by monks, lay patrons, and officials from the Ministry of the Interior. Around August 23, 1936, the association's official journal also published twenty-five comments by Buddhists who had criticized the revision.[70] A complaint from the Buddhist monk Guangwen 廣文 dated July 7, 1936, decried how the new charter would overburden monks and nuns in Sichuan Province.[71] The new charter required monks and nuns to rejoin the association and pay an annual membership fee of one Chinese yuan. Guangwen predicted this would be a substantial financial burden for monks and nuns in his home province, as many of them still struggled to acquire food and other basic provisions. The Buddhist monk Benseng 本僧, who had been affiliated with the Buddhist association in Anhui Province, complained that the article on revoking membership was too abstract and unfeasible to implement in practice and recommended it be removed.[72] The monks and nuns who had sent complaints about the new policy were not the only ones who had expected to suffer. The above-mentioned director, Zhang Tinghao, reported that the comments he received focused on four articles. These included the article requiring ordained Buddhists to join the association while excluding lay Buddhists; the article on defrocking ordained Buddhists who had violated the laws of the monastic community or the state; the article requiring Buddhist institutions to submit financial reports; and the article requiring monasteries and nunneries to make mandatory donations to the state government, according to their annual revenue.[73]

Despite these numerous unwelcome articles, what the June 1936 draft charter did for the association was reclaim some of the jurisdiction it had previously lost. Specifically, it gave the association the ability to function as an adjudicator for internal disputes between different Buddhist institutions, as well as between ordained Buddhist monks and nuns.[74] This is reflected in multiple articles. Article 8 specified the association's duty to "mediate all disputes among Buddhist monasteries and nunneries, as well as those among ordained Buddhist monks and nuns."[75] Article 25 specified the right of ordained Buddhist members of the association to "seek mediation from this association when one has disputes with monks and nuns from one's hosting monastery or nunnery or with those from other monasteries and nunneries."[76] This article also aided Buddhist institutions and individual members who had faced ill-treatment, unavoidable disasters, or great difficulties. Article 54 further specified that the association's supervisory board was responsible for providing mediation. Despite these invitations for Buddhists to self-govern, the Central Department for Military Training of the Nationalist Party of China still emphasized the state court's general jurisdiction over ordained Buddhists. Article 26 specified that a monk or nun's membership could be revoked if they committed offenses against state law or Buddhist monastic law or indulged in gambling or other reckless behavior that might damage the reputation of the association and the dignity of their fellow monks and nuns.

In the wake of the protests over the unfavorable articles in this version of the charter, Buddhists lost more than they gained. The debate concluded with the approval of a further revised charter, reduced to thirty-eight articles, at the association's eighth national assembly in November 1936,[77] the version that remained in circulation under the Nationalist government in 1948.[78] This enabled Buddhists in China to revise any unreasonable articles, such as those requiring all ordained Buddhists to become members of the association and forbidding any lay Buddhists from becoming members. Despite this success, the Nationalist government rescinded its offer to legalize the Buddhist Association of China's jurisdiction over internal disputes among ordained Buddhists.

This lost judicial power was never reinstated in the association's future charters under the PRC. After 1949, the association drafted its first charter from scratch. This one bore little resemblance to its predecessors from the Republican period. The entire charter under the PRC shifted to its legal responsibilities. The first two versions in 1953 and 1957 did not address any legal or jurisdictional issues.

In 1980, the third charter began to emphasize the association's legal duties in two main areas. First, it was to ensure that ordained Buddhist monks and nuns studied the state's laws, regulations, and policies concerning religion. Second, it was to help them to obey state laws and be patriotic. In 1993, the charter further expanded the association's legal duties to include a third area: supervising Buddhist institutions' self-management and enforcement of monastic discipline as well as establishing regulations and rules for monasteries and nunneries. Later versions of the charter consistently limited discussions on legal issues within these parameters.

The association's loss of jurisdictional control in one battlefield did not discourage Buddhists from passing *The Regulations on the National Management of Chinese Buddhist Monasteries* (*Quanguo hanchuan fojiao siyuan guanli banfa* 全國漢傳佛教寺院管理辦法). Articles in these regulations recommend dealing with clerical offenders on three levels: the host monastery or nunnery, the Buddhist Association of China, and the state court. First, article 18 permits the hosting monastery or nunnery to convene an internal investigation on clerical offenders who have committed severe crimes, disobeyed community bylaws, or refused to correct their behavior. The monastery or nunnery's administration team would have the authority to expel the offender (*qiandan* 遷單). At the next level, the hosting monastery or nunnery was to report to the local Buddhist association any severe offenses that could damage the reputation of the entire Buddhist establishment and also recommend and implement punishment by revoking the offenders' membership within the clergy, transferring their household registrations from the hosting institutions to their places of origin, and forfeiting their ordination certificates (*dudie* 度牒) and certificates attesting to their receipt of the precepts (*jiedie* 戒牒). Finally, external adjudication in the state court was required for clerical criminal offenses that violated state law. In recent decades, the association has also become increasingly involved in protecting the economic interests of monasteries and nunneries in their disputes with lay heirs over estates of deceased monks and nuns. This is the topic of Chapter 7, where I will analyze a series of lawsuits over estates of deceased monks and nuns, between 1984 and 2020.

State Governance

It is no accident that the State Administration of Religious Affairs assumed the leading role in investigating Xuecheng's case in 2018. In contrast to the Buddhist Association of China's fluctuating jurisdictional control over ordained Buddhists, the state had always sought to expand its jurisdictional control over them. This expansion relied on an increasingly secularized government organ staffed with state-appointed lay officials managing religious affairs. During the Republican era, the Ministry of the Interior carried out the duty of managing religious affairs. After 1949, that duty was taken up by what is now known as the State Administration of Religious Affairs.[79] From 1913 to 1929, the Republican governments carried out at least six legislative experiments where they explored ways to manage Buddhist affairs. These experiments resulted in revised government policies on managing Buddhist institutions. They also showed how the state aggressively sought greater jurisdiction over ordained Buddhists,[80] with the State Administration of Religious Affairs becoming an increasingly influential agency in exercising that jurisdictional control.[81]

The state's pursuit of jurisdiction over ordained Buddhists began in the 1910s. The earliest legislation focused on handling Buddhist monastic property. On June 9, 1913, the Beiyang government promulgated the *Temporary Regulations on Managing Monasteries* (*Siyuan guanli zanxing guize* 寺院管理暫行規則). None of the seven articles in this legislation mentioned ordained Buddhist offenders.[82] Articles imposing the state's full jurisdictional control over the Buddhist establishment soon appeared in a revised charter promulgated in 1915, and these were retained in the 1921 revision.[83] In 1915, the Beiyang government revised this legislation as the *Regulations on Managing Monasteries* (*Guanli simiao tiaoli* 管理寺廟條例). This revision contained thirty-one articles divided into six sections on general rules, temple property, ordained Buddhists and Daoists of the various monasteries, temple registration, punishments, and an appendix. Article 14 in the third section permitted the Buddhist clergy to hold community meetings to deal with issues concerning the observance of monastic rules by its ordained members. Article 23 in the fifth section on punishments required the state's judicial offices to investigate ordained Buddhist monks and nuns who had committed civil or criminal offenses. This article further authorized local government officials to handle Buddhist clerical offenders who had committed offenses against Buddhist monastic law.[84] These rules were reiterated in articles 15 and 19 in the *Modified Regulations on Managing Monasteries* (*Xiuzheng guanli simiao tiaoli* 修正管理寺廟條例), revised in 1921.

When the Nationalist government replaced the Beiyang government in 1928, it attempted to tighten its jurisdictional control over the Buddhist establishment. However, this met with strong resistance from the Buddhist community. On January 25, 1929, the Nationalist government promulgated the revised *Regulations on Managing Monasteries* (*Simiao guanli tiaoli* 寺廟管理條例). This revision immediately provoked strong opposition. Influential lay Buddhists and eminent monks sent telegraphs expressing criticisms of almost every article to the Nationalist government in Nanjing.[85] The strongest opposition focused on articles 4 and 17. Article 4 permitted the government to close a monastery and confiscate its property when an individual monk or nun from that institution had been convicted of violating the law of the Buddhist monastic community, the Nationalist Party, or social customs. In these cases, the local government or a public organization would have been entitled to confiscate or claim the monastic property for various uses.[86] On March 15, 1929, in a telegraph to the government in Nanjing, Buddhists from Sichuan province criticized article 4 for "destroying Buddhism in the name of protecting it."[87] These Buddhists refuted article 4 by arguing that no government department had ever been closed when officials working in that unit had committed a crime; by the same token, they asserted that a Buddhist monastery should not be punished for offenses committed by its members. Several such criticisms appeared in Buddhist journals.[88] Five monks and four lay Buddhists on the standing committee of the Buddhist Association of China directly submitted a joint petition to the Legislative Yuan (Lifa yuan 立法院)—a legislature of the Nationalist government that is still in existence in Taiwan today—demanding the latter to consider revising the proposed legislation.[89]

In the same telegraph, the Sichuan Buddhists also opposed article 17.[90] This article proposed that the state court prosecute criminal and civil cases involving ordained Buddhists. These Buddhists argued that ordained Buddhist monks and nuns were under the protection and governance of state law, just as all other laypeople were. For this reason, when an ordained Buddhist committed an offense against state law, they should be prosecuted under state law, just as an ordinary lay offender would be. Article 17 thus was an unnecessary repetition of common sense and therefore should be removed. Furthermore, these Sichuan Buddhists also demanded jurisdictional independence to consult Buddhist monastic law to determine the penalty for convicted criminals. If such offenses required punishment beyond a confession under the Buddhist monastic law, then the abbot of the offenders' hosting monastery would have been the authority to punish these offenders by expelling them.

The Nationalist government took these protests from the Buddhist community seriously. On March 28, 1929, the Executive Yuan (Xingzheng yuan 行政院) asked the Minister of the Interior to discuss the issues Buddhists from Jiangxi Province had brought forward and to revise the January 1929 legislation.[91] On April 3, the Executive Yuan further forwarded the protests from the Sichuan Buddhists to the Ministry of the Interior.[92] In May, the Minister of the Interior asked the Legislative Yuan to review the legislation that had been promulgated in January 1929.[93] On May 25, the Nationalist government asked the Legislative Yuan to postpone implementing the January 1929 legislation.[94] In June and July, that year, the Minister of the Interior sent notices to local governments to delay adjudicating any case related to Buddhist temples until the new legislation was announced. On August 30, the Nationalist government urged the Minister of the

Interior to immediately submit a revised draft of the legislation to the Legislative Yuan.[95] It made the same request again on September 7 and November 7.[96]

These earlier negotiations between the government and the Buddhist establishment strengthened the state court's jurisdiction over ordained Buddhists convicted of violating state law. On one hand, the government removed articles granting Buddhists jurisdictional control over ordained Buddhist offenders. After discussions at four meetings, the Legislative Yuan concluded that the legislation proposed in January 1929 was too difficult to implement. Instead, the Legislative Yuan presented a significantly revised draft.[97] In this draft, the controversial article 4 had been removed and article 17 had been split into articles 19 and 20. Article 19 permitted the Buddhist clergy to adjudicate only clerical offenses that violated Buddhist monastic law. In the draft version, article 20 had authorized the government to prosecute ordained Buddhists who had committed offenses under articles 8 and 10–19, which primarily concerned ordination, the management of temple property, and the observance of state law. On December 7, 1929, the Legislative Yuan promulgated a final version of this legislation,[98] deleting all the articles concerning the treatment of Buddhist clerical offenders. It only kept article 11 stipulating that abbots who had committed offenses must be sent to the state court for investigation. This 1929 legislation continued to be used in Taiwan until it fell out of use in 2006.

The government, on the other hand, insisted on affirming the state court's jurisdiction over ordained Buddhist criminals. My translations of articles 23, 19, and 17 from the regulations promulgated in 1915, 1921, and 1929 suffice to demonstrate this persistence. Article 23 in the 1915 *Regulations on Managing Monasteries* stated the following:

> When ordained Buddhists, Daoists, and abbots from any monastery do not obey their monastic rules, the official in the local district should discipline or expel them. Those whose offenses are serious should receive penalties. When their offenses are related to civil disputes and criminal offenses, they should be adjudicated by the judicial offices following the law.[99]

Article 19 in the 1921 *Modified Regulations on Managing Monasteries* inherited this position:

> When ordained Buddhists, Daoists, and abbots from any monastery do not obey their monastic rules, even when violations constitute serious transgressions, the official in the local district should discipline them or expel them. When their offenses are related to civil disputes and criminal offenses, they should be adjudicated by the judicial offices following the law.[100]

Article 17 in the 1929 *Regulations on Managing Monasteries*, effective January 25, 1929, continued in the same vein, stating that "all civil disputes and criminal offenses of ordained Buddhists and Daoists, as well as their abbots, should still be prosecuted by the judicial offices following the law."[101]

In contemporary China, the state's obsession with jurisdictional control over Buddhists continues to mark its legal interactions with the Buddhist establishment. A distinctive feature of this control is the Communist Party's firm emphasis on the state's right to criminally prosecute clerical offenders. In post-1949 China, the earliest legislation on religious affairs only came into existence in the 1990s. On January 31, 1994, the state council published the *Regulations on Managing Religious Venues* (*Zongjiao huodong changsuo guanli tiaoli* 宗教活動場所管理條例), which went into effect on the same day. This legislation contained twenty articles focusing on the management of religious practitioners, organizations, and venues. Article 15 stipulated that, depending on the nature of the offense, those who had violated this legislation would face criminal prosecution in the judiciary or punishment by the police as outlined in the *PRC Regulations on Penalties for Administration of Public Security* (*Zhonghua renmin gongheguo zhi'an guanli chufa tiaoli* 中華人民共和國治安管理處罰條例).[102] Ten years later, the Communist Party abolished the 1994 legislation and replaced it with a new legislation, *Regulations on Religious Affairs* (*Zongjiao shiwu tiaoli* 宗教事務條例). On July 7, 2004, the state council passed this new legislation, effective on March 1, 2005. Article 45 outlined the consequences for religious practitioners who violated the state law or government regulations: they will face prosecution and risk losing their status as religious practitioners.[103] This principle to impose criminal prosecution continues to exist in the latest revision of this legislation. On August 26, 2017, the state council passed its latest revision of the *Regulations on Religious Affairs* that went into effect on February 1, 2018.[104] Article 73 in this version outlined the various violations against state law that would require a religious practitioner to face criminal prosecution.

The Actual Procedure

On August 2, 2018, the State Administration of Religious Affairs received the monks Xianjia and Xianqi's report on Nun A's case against the Buddhist abbot Xuecheng and immediately began investigating. On August 23, 2018, it posted the results of its investigation on its official website.[105] First, it confirmed that the accused had committed sexual harassment through texting, which it viewed as a violation of Buddhist monastic law. It thus recommended that the host monastery and the Buddhist Association of China take serious actions to follow up in accordance with the relevant Buddhist regulations and the *Charter of the Buddhist Association of China*. Second, it did not confirm whether the accused had committed the alleged sexual assault but did report that the Beijing city police had officially filed a complaint and started an investigation. Third, it found the allegations of administrative and financial misconduct to be credible and noted that the relevant local government offices had taken over the case to follow up with further investigation and charges.

As of October 2018, Xuecheng had been convicted of sexually harassing the nun victims via text messages. The State Administration of Religious Affairs recommended correlating the penalty for this abbot with Buddhist monastic law and the *Charter of the Buddhist Association of China*. However, this charter only addresses issues concerning the administrative and financial management of Buddhist institutions in China; it makes no reference to any penalty for sexual misconduct. In addition, the *PRC Law on the Protection of Women's Rights and Interests* outlines legal options for victims. Still, it does not specify what punishment should be imposed on the convicted. Buddhist monastic law holds sexual intercourse to be one of the four serious offenses for an ordained Buddhist monk, but it does not discuss punishments for verbal sexual harassment.[106] The absence of sentencing guidelines in these two laws may have contributed to Xuecheng's evasion of an official penalty.

Unofficially, his punishment had begun even before the results of the investigation became available. While the State Administration of Religious Affairs was still investigating, Xuecheng quietly offered to resign from his position as president of the Buddhist Association of China. At its ninth national meeting on August 15, 2018, the association accepted his resignation. To this day, Xuecheng's whereabouts remain unclear.[107]

The outcome of this case is far from satisfactory. Many unanswered questions continue to obscure the truth about what occurred. Moreover, the lack of a defense from Xuecheng is further dissatisfying to the followers of this case. It remains unclear whether Xuecheng had any defense, whether his defense had been kept confidential, or whether he had been forced to remain silent during the investigation. The investigation would have been more convincing if the announcement from the State Administration of Religious Affairs had included an explanation for the absence of his defense.

The lack of a report on the validity of the evidence presented in the coauthored report also left many people ruminating over whether the abbot had indeed committed the alleged sexual assaults and harassments. The primary evidence includes transcribed text messages and snapshots of WeChat messages. When the allegations against Xuecheng were exposed in 2018, digital records such as text messages had not yet been legally recognized as evidence in civil disputes in Chinese courts. Text messages and WeChat records only became legitimate digital evidence one year later, on October 14, 2019, when the Supreme People's Court of China authorized their use in civil disputes.[108]

The authenticity of the texts and WeChat messages is another source of suspicion. The two coauthors stated that they retained lawyers to consult the Ministry of Public Security, technicians for digital forensics at the Supreme People's Procuratorate, and chief technology officers in the mobile communications industry. They reported that the consensus among these authorities is that it would have been impossible to alter or forge records of digital messages stored on servers. The two monk coauthors stated that they followed the requisite legal procedures to obtain the text messages sent from the cell phone number owned by Xuecheng, but they never explained or provided evidence on how they did so legally.

Conclusion

The coexistence of four institutional powers in contemporary China complicates the distribution of jurisdictional authority in Xuecheng's case. Among the four possible investigators, three did not react. Alternatively, authorizing the State Administration of Religious Affairs to investigate indicates that the other three investigators had been either been disqualified or excluded. Their exclusion fits the historical pattern of assigning jurisdiction in imperial China. In that pattern (discussed in Chapter 5), internal offenses involving only members within a monastic community were treated differently from those involving lay Buddhists or non-Buddhists. The jurisdiction for serious and minor crimes also differed. This framework makes it much easier to understand why the State Administration of Religious Affairs had been assigned the leading role in Xuecheng's case.

This framework excludes the state court as a possible venue. In the Chinese legal system, the jurisprudential understanding of sexual harassment and assault are still in the early stages of development. Thus, in 2018, Xuecheng's offenses would not have been considered serious crimes requiring prosecution in the state court. The composition of the litigants in this case also rendered the state court a less likely investigator. The accusations against Xuecheng primarily involved offenses internal to a Buddhist monastery and its subordinate nunnery. This internal case was, thus, unsuitable for prosecution in the state court, and this factor could have kept local police from filing a report.

Longquan Monastery hosted both the accused and the victims. Its administrators could have been the ideal investigators. Yet as the monastery's abbot was the accused, this created a conflict of interest. However, there are historical precedents showing how to resolve this type of conflict of interest and retain the investigation within the monastery. In the eighth month of 1314, during the Yuan dynasty, the Buddhist monk Chonggui 崇圭 sued his monastery's abbot for committing illicit sexual intercourse with a laywoman.[109] At that time, Yuan law permitted abbots of host monasteries to handle internal lawsuits between ordained Buddhists. In this case, when an abbot was the accused, the Department of Justice's solution was to appoint an abbot from a nearby monastery to oversee the adjudication. In 2018, Longquan Monastery likewise could have invited an abbot of another monastery to lead the investigation into Xuecheng's case. However, his case did not proceed in that manner.

A conflict of interest also excluded the Buddhist Association of China from being involved in the investigation. The association's failed pursuit in writing its jurisdictional power into its charter might have further complicated or overshadowed its chance of leading Xuecheng's investigation. The collapse of imperial China in 1911 gave way to a new legal system, providing opportunities to renegotiate the Buddhist clergy's legal status and jurisdiction vis-à-vis the state. The need to protect Buddhist monastic property from state and military encroachment had forced Buddhists to tolerate the loss of many personal and collective clerical privileges under the new legal system introduced in 1929. In imperial China, those personal clerical privileges could have ranged from immunity from trial in the state court to leniency when convicted of a crime.[110] At that time, this compromise was justified, as in the early twentieth century it came in exchange for the badly needed protection of monastic property against forced government confiscation.

To secure this protection, Buddhists had to assume the identity of ordinary citizens, submitting to the governance of state law. The Nationalist government of Republican China gladly recognized monks and nuns as ordinary citizens. On June 9, 1932, the Minister of the Interior, Huang Shaofang 黃紹竑, defined ordained Buddhists monks and nuns as citizens with voting rights.[111] Being ordinary citizens also put monks and nuns under the additional scrutiny of state law. On June 10, 1937, the Jiangsu provincial government asked the Minister of the Interior whether an ordained Buddhist who had smoked opium could be appointed as abbot of a Buddhist monastery.[112] In its reply, dated on June 28, the minister noted that he considered smoking opium an offense against state law and that this required punishment in accordance with the same set of laws. This minister further recommended that a monk's host institution consider a penalty for the opium smoker that reflected comparable penalties under Buddhist monastic law. The minister concluded that an opium smoker would absolutely be disqualified from becoming an abbot, given that article 11 in the *Charter of the*

Buddhist Association of China prohibited membership to anyone who had developed an unvirtuous addiction, violated the laws of the Buddhist monastic community, or committed other offenses. The lack of specific references to ordained Buddhists in the constitution and other criminal and civil law codes also indicates the state's treatment of ordained Buddhists as ordinary legal subjects within the state legal system.

In the end, Xuecheng did not have to publicly stand trial in court. The State Administration of Religious Affairs quickly and confidentially carried out the investigation. Given the abbot's roles as leader of his monastery and of the Buddhist Association of China, this was probably the best arrangement to allow him to save grace. Xuecheng's experience, however, may not have been representative of ordinary Buddhist offenders, as these people would have faced much different trials at much different venues. Yet, an adequate appreciation of how his case was handled still sheds light on the legal dynamics in the broader Buddhist establishment.

The development of Xuecheng's case reveals a high level of legal sensitivity among monks and nuns in contemporary China. As victims of sexual harassment and assault, Nuns A and C first approached fellow monks in their community for help. When these monks became aware of the case, they provided the required assistance and reached out to the administration in the offender's hosting monastery about assisting them with handling it internally. When an internal resolution was unattainable, Nun C and her monk supporters then reached out to the local police to intervene externally. In each step, the victim nuns and their monk supporters had complied with the necessary procedures prescribed by Buddhist monastic law and state law in contemporary China.

The previous chapter examined the realignment of relations between the state and the Buddhist clergy in imperial China. In this chapter, the legal procedures adopted in the handling of Xuecheng's case help us understand how that realignment has come to shape the state's control over religion through legal practice in China today. Before involving the police and local government, the state allowed a third-party agency between the state and the Buddhist establishment to conduct the preliminary investigation. After the initial investigation, this third-party agency designated the host monastery and the Buddhist Association of China as the parties that would address the confirmed offense of sexual harassment under Buddhist monastic law. This agency designated the local police to investigate the allegation of sexual assault and the local government to further investigate the allegations of financial and administrate misconduct. In handling this case, external law enforcement was only invited to intervene when internal mediation failed. The entire process reveals that, despite its legislative control over religion and constitutional claims on ordained Buddhists as ordinary citizens under the state law, the Chinese state nevertheless shows leniency, in its legal practice, toward ordained Buddhist offenders, or at least toward one high-profile state-appointed monk official. The analysis herein furthers our understanding of how the legacy of jurisdictional boundaries between the state and the Buddhist establishment in imperial China continues to prevail in twenty-first century China.

7
Dead Monks, Living Heirs

> It is a problem that remains unsolved through legislation. This court is unable to provide a jurisprudential explanation.[1]
>
> The Supreme People's Court of the People's Republic of China
>
> October 13, 1994

Late on the night of January 26, 2010, the Buddhist abbot Yongxiu 永修 opened the doors to his residence at Pudu 普度 Monastery in Yuxi, Yunnan Province, to two young men seeking accommodations. Pudu Monastery is subordinate to Lingzhao 靈照, a much larger local monastery where Yongxiu had been abbot since 1988. A few hours after the abbot welcomed these men to his monastery, they murdered him and fled with a few thousand Chinese yuan in cash, a used cell phone, and some other personal belongings of the victim. The victim had been married and had fathered a two-year-old-daughter prior to his ordination in 1979. After the murder, the abbot's now-adult daughter worked with Lingzhao Monastery to check on her father's possessions. They discovered that he had bank accounts with balances amounting to 4,740,000 Chinese yuan (roughly US$700,000). At that time, China's *Law of Succession*, from 1985, gave the biological children of the deceased the right to inherit.[2] The victim's daughter cited this law to claim ownership of the discovered money. The monastery, however, also asserted that it had a right to that money, for two reasons. First, in Chinese Buddhism it is a long-established tradition for the host monastery to inherit the estate of its deceased monks. Second, the Buddhist Association of China legally endorsed this traditional practice in its 2006 guidelines for monastic life in Chinese Buddhist monasteries and nunneries.[3] Unable to reach an agreement with the monastery, the daughter initiated a lawsuit on January 26, 2012. Five months later, the Yuxi Intermediate People's Court of Yunnan Province heard the case, and on September 20, 2012, it issued a judgment rejecting the daughter's suit.[4] The daughter then appealed to the Yunnan Higher People's Court, which dismissed this appeal, thereby upholding the Yuxi Intermediate People's Court's initial judgment of November 22, 2012.[5] This case attracted extensive media attention in China. Phoenix New Media even created a webpage dedicated to the theme on its official website, featuring similar historic cases, opinions from legal scholars and Buddhist leaders, and comments from Chinese netizens.[6]

Buddhism in Court. Cuilan Liu, Oxford University Press. © Oxford University Press 2024.
DOI: 10.1093/oso/9780197663332.003.0008

This lawsuit is one of the most widely reported in China, partly due to the abbot's violent death and partly due to the large sum of money involved. But this is neither the first nor the latest of its kind to attract public attention in China. In fact, at least fifteen disputes over the estate of deceased monks and nuns were reported between 1984 and 2020.[7] In each case, children, relatives, and caregivers of the deceased had challenged the deceased Buddhists' host monasteries over their rights of inheritance. In only one case were the roles reversed, when a local Buddhist association sued a nun's niece in August 2020. This was a case over the estate of a deceased nun, Huilin 慧玲 (lay name Nie Juxiang 聶菊香) in Fuzhou, Jiangxi Province.[8] Before her death, the nun had been living in a room within a much larger complex in the city's Linchuan District, which had been a venue for religious activities supervised by the district's local Buddhist association. When the county's office for property expropriation and compensation demolished the dwelling of the deceased nun, it paid 205,358.80 Chinese yuan in compensation to the nun's niece Nie Xiaolan 聶小蘭. The Buddhist association in Linchuan District contested the niece's right to that compensation, arguing that even if the deceased nun had been the rightful owner of the demolished dwelling, her death would have made the district's Buddhist association her sole heir. Designating the niece as heir to a religious property, it claimed, not only "infringed upon the plaintiff's rights" but also damaged the Buddhist tradition and severely "violated the religious policy of the Communist Party and state."[9] The Buddhist association in Linchuan District initially filed a suit, in the Nancheng County People's Court in Jiangxi Province, against the office that had overseen the property's demolition. Then on August 21, 2020, before the trial began, the plaintiff changed to sue the government of Linchuan District. Because of that change, the court declined to hear the case, as it did not have jurisdiction over the district government. In all the other reported cases, the lay heirs sued the host monastery or nunnery of the deceased.

These lawsuits have been occurring in complicated legal, political, and religious contexts in China since 1984. The Buddhist Association of China considered the religious policy during the Cultural Revolution (1966–1976) to have been a major culprit in this legal complication. Apart from a few nephews and one caregiver, most of the lay litigants had been the biological children of the deceased monks or nuns in question and, therefore, the first legal heirs of the disputed property. Some were children from marriages prior to a monk or nun's ordination. This had been particularly common among retirees who had decided to spend the rest of their lives in a monastery. Many others, according to the Buddhist Association of China, had been forced to disrobe during the Cultural Revolution and then got married, had children, and eventually returned to the monastery after the end of the Cultural Revolution.[10] During their time in these monasteries, some monks had been appointed to administrative positions, enabling them to accumulate more wealth. Other monks may have retained title to property they had acquired before joining the monastery. When these monks passed away, they left property, and also left behind surviving children and other relatives. The combination of sizable estates, aggrieved surviving lay heirs, and continuing reliance on the *Law of Succession* led to an unprecedented number of lawsuits between lay heirs and host monasteries and nunneries.

Chinese legal prohibitions against religious organizations registering property under their own names further contributed to this confusion. Until recently, religious organizations in China could only open corporate bank accounts and register property in the names of actual persons. For Buddhist entities, holding title to institutional property only became possible after April 1, 2019.[11] Before then, many Buddhist institutions opened bank accounts and registered purchased property under the name of their abbots or other administrative monks, which made it difficult to assess the nature of the money and property that had been registered under the names of the individual monks and nuns when they died.

Legal scholars in China have written on the contradictions in jurisprudence between the state's *Law of Succession* and the Buddhist religious law reflected in some of these lawsuits, and they have proposed potential solutions to this persisting legal confusion.[12] In particular, the most recent of these lawsuits, between 2012 and 2020, are of interest for several reasons. These trials entailed more than the final settlement of a dead monk's property, account balances, and other valuable belongings. Trial outcomes define the preeminence of laws that conflict with other laws and set precedents for which law should apply in similar future conflicts. This potential long-term impact compelled more parties, other than lay heirs and monasteries, to become involved in such trials. Buddhist leaders, China's regional and central court judges, the National People's Congress, the Buddhist Association of China, and the State Administration of Religious Affairs have all assumed different roles at various stages of these litigations. The rich records of the dynamic interactions among these different entities offer a unique window into negotiations that have taken place over the jurisdictional boundaries between religion and state in China. These records, spanning the period between 1984 and 2020, illuminate the Buddhist Association of China's important role in negotiating the legal spaces between the Buddhist establishment and the state in contemporary China. Its various legal interventions show how the tripartite legal infrastructure of the monastic, state, and hybrid courts continue to influence the operation of law in China today.

Understanding these lawsuits and how they played out in China's courtrooms sheds light on contemporary issues and adds a new perspective to the current conversation on religion and law in China. The outcomes of these cases fly in the face of the dominant discourse that purports to show that China has used the law to restrict, reduce, and dismantle religious practices and organizations.

For example, in its 1997 report "China: State Control of Religion," Human Rights Watch criticized China, noting that "increasingly the government is citing violations of Chinese law as its pretext for dismantling churches, monasteries, mosques, temples or congregations that refuse to adapt, especially targeting those individuals and organizations that attempt to operate outside official bureaucratic control."[13] Contributing to this discourse is a report titled "China: Religion and Chinese Law," which the Law Library of Congress in the United States prepared and submitted to the US Department of Justice in June 2018. The report argues that China's law and regulations have restricted religious freedom and "substantially reduced the scope and effectiveness of the constitutional protection of religious freedom," citing the Chinese legal scholar Qianfan Zhang.[14] I do not dispute the fact that China has used law to exercise state control over religion. Rather, I intend to highlight an important—yet unreported—dimension of the legal interaction between the state and religion in China, in which religion often appears to have gotten the upper hand. Lawsuits over the estates of dead monastics reveal that China's state law, National People's Congress legislators, and court judges have almost uniformly leaned toward protecting the economic interests of Buddhist institutions over those of lay litigants when existing state law and religious law are in conflict or are ambiguous.

The Buddhist Position

Chinese Buddhists have perceived ordained monks and nuns as religious practitioners with different legal rights and duties than ordinary lay citizens. Buddhist institutions and the Buddhist Association of China at the regional and national level have consistently taken this position in every reported dispute over monastic estates. In many of these lawsuits, the Buddhist Association of China assumed a significant role in representing the interests of the Buddhist institutions. Its official interventions in a case in 1998 and another one in 2002, which I will discuss below, stand out as poignant illustrations of how this association acted as a third-party agency when negotiating legal conflicts, over the estates of dead monastics, between the state and the Buddhist establishment. In both episodes, the Buddhist Association of China openly published written statements expressing its support for the host monasteries as the rightful heirs of the disputed estates. These two statements paint an apt picture of how Buddhists viewed themselves in the legal world of post-1949 China.

The Buddhist Association of China's intervention in 1998 is the background for the first statement. That year, a Buddhist monk from Shengshui 聖水 Monastery in Mianyang, Sichuan Province, died and left an estate. The surviving record does not include any details of the dispute over this property. What we know is that the Buddhist Association of China's regional office in Sichuan Province reached out to its national office in Beijing, asking what to do with the dead monk's estate. On October 26, 1998, the association's national office issued a public statement elaborating its position on this dilemma. The statement later appeared in the organization's official publication, *The Voice of Dharma* (*Fayin* 法音).[15] It began with an editorial comment, followed by a one-page official statement, and ended with an appendix of doctrinal references to corroborate its arguments.

This statement reveals how the lack of clarity in the *Law of Succession* frustrated Buddhists in China. The editorial comment claimed that China's legal experts considered the lay heirs of deceased monks ineligible to inherit monastic property; yet the lack of clarification in the *Law of Succession* encouraged lay heirs to contest monastic claims to what they felt were their rightful inheritances. The editorial comment purported that some unnamed legal experts in the legislature had said that "jurisprudentially, lay family members and relatives cannot inherit monks' estates."[16] Yet for various reasons, the *Law of Succession* did not provide explicit instructions on how to distribute estates of dead monks and nuns. The lack of legal clarification thus led to challenges against individual monasteries when lay relatives and family members claimed rights to those estates.

By publishing the statement in its official journal, the Buddhist Association of China intended to provide some much-needed clarification, as lawsuits of this kind continued to increase over those years. The association considered the inquiry from its provincial office in Sichuan to be representative of the struggles other Buddhist institutions were facing in similar cases. On December 26, 1998, with approval from its president, Zhao Puchu 趙樸初, the association provided a written statement in response to this inquiry, hoping it would provide a guideline the entire Buddhist community could use to deal with similar lawsuits in the future.

This written statement does not seem to have achieved its intended goal, however, because new lawsuits compelled the Buddhist Association of China to reiterate its position again in another written statement, which it released four years later, in August 2002. That year, the Buddhist monk Youjin 有錦 from Guangxiao 光孝 Monastery in Guangzhou died, leaving money in his bank account. Three parties each presented their own distribution proposals.[17] His lay relatives used the *Law of Succession* to claim that the money was their rightful inheritance. The host monastery claimed itself to be the legitimate beneficiary. The bank holding the account of the deceased monk claimed that neither party was the legitimate beneficiary and that these savings should be handed over to the government. Eventually, the association's regional office in Guangdong Province submitted an inquiry to its national office in Beijing. On August 20, 2002, the association published a third written statement in its official journal,[18] which was longer than the first version. It consisted of three pages: one for the statement and two containing an editorial comment elaborating on the rules from the three Buddhist sources, many of which had already been noted in the 1998 version.

The Buddhist Association of China expressed its position quite clearly in these two statements: the host monastery was the sole beneficiary of any estate left by a deceased monk. In both statements, the association argued that ordained Buddhists cannot be treated as ordinary citizens. For that reason, the *Law of Succession* was not applicable when deciding on the distribution of a dead monk or nun's estate. Instead, such a distribution should be guided by existing Buddhist practices.

The Buddhist Association of China defended its position in three steps: first, it identified doctrinal endorsements from three Buddhist texts that instructed host monasteries to take possession of property left by resident monks or nuns. The first cited endorsement came from the *Maudgalyāyana Inquiring on Five Hundred Heavy and Light Matters in the Buddhist Monastic Law Narrated by the Buddha* (*Foshuo mulian wen jielü zhong wubai qingzhong shi* 佛說目連問戒律中五百輕重事).[19] This text records a conversation between the Buddha and one of his major disciples, Maudgalyāyana, on the topic of the rules in Buddhist monastic law.[20] In the tenth chapter, Maudgalyāyana asks the Buddha what to do with the possessions of deceased monks. The Buddha replies, "All belongings of a deceased monk belong to the monastic community."[21]

The second cited endorsement came from an indigenous Chinese legal text, the *Pure Rules of Baizhang* (*Baizhang qingui* 百丈清規). Buddhists in China had followed the principles outlined in Indian Buddhist monastic law texts, such as the *Dharmaguptaka Vinaya*, and had established rules for dealing with deceased Buddhists' estates in the *Pure Rules of Baizhang*, which the Tang Buddhist monk Baizhang Huaihai 百丈懷海 (749–814) had established for resident monks and nuns of Chan Buddhist communities. In its statement, the Buddhist Association of China claimed that this text states, "When a Buddhist monk leaves home, he stays in the monastery while alive and is buried in a monastic cemetery with a pagoda after death."[22] The *Pure Rules* also provide detailed instructions on how to divide up a deceased Buddhist monk or nun's estate. These instructions required the host institutions of deceased Buddhists to sort the contents of these estates into two categories: heavy (*zhong* 重) items, such as gold and silver, land, gardens, and real estate, and light (*qing* 輕) items, such as robes and household items. Next, the heavy items were to go to the monastery's communal fund. Then the host monastery's monk administrators were to create an inventory of the light items, which were to be auctioned off at the monastery. The proceeds from the auction were to be divided into three portions: one third was to be used to cover the funeral costs of the deceased; one third was to go to the monastery's communal fund to compensate for the expenses related to providing care for the deceased prior to their death; and one third was to be used as an honorarium for the monks and nuns who had participated in the funeral rituals for the deceased. Based on these references, the Buddhist Association of China argued that it was already an established tradition for host monasteries to take possession of the estates of deceased Buddhist monastics. Moreover, it also argued that the Buddhist ordination ceremony marked a monk or nun's severance from their legal, financial, and familial ties with their biological families and the establishment of new ones with the monastery. Starting from that moment, lay family members and relatives lost their legal right to any property from the deceased. China's *Law of Succession*, however, does not recognize this claimed severance of the legal relationship between ordained Buddhists and their lay families.

The third cited endorsement came from Chinese commentaries on Indian Buddhist monastic law. In both statements, the Buddhist Association of China pointed to a passage from *A Further Explanation on Exercising the Buddhist Monastic Law Code* (*Pini zuochi xushi* 毗尼作持續釋), a fifteen-scroll word-by-word commentary on Buddhist monastic law, divided according to ten subjects. This commentary, composed by the Tang Buddhist monk Daoxuan 道宣 (596–667), explains how to understand and follow disciplinary rules from the Buddhist monastic law codes. In the section discussing the eighth subject, "Various Methods for Distributing Clothes (*Zhuyi fenfa* 諸衣分法)," Daoxuan explains what to do with the belongings of a deceased Buddhist. A similar explanation was also found in another commentary by the same author, the *Randomly Selected Ecclesiastical Proceedings: Abridgements and Emendations to the Dharmaguptaka Vinaya* (*Sifen lü shanbu suiji jiemo* 四分律刪補隨機羯磨).[23] Both explanations comment on a passage in the *Dharmaguptaka Vinaya*.[24] This passage recommended dividing a deceased Buddhist monk's possessions into two categories: those that should go to the monastery as communal wealth and those that could be redistributed among members of the monastery. Those that were not to be divided for redistribution included immovable assets such as real estate, gardens, and fruit trees; household items such as vases, axes, candleholders, beds, seating covers, bedding, vehicles, garden keepers, water pitchers, bath barrels, staffs, fans, and all items made from iron, wood, clay, leather, or bamboo.[25] Items that could be redistributed among ordained members in the community included woolen blankets and fabrics, razors, robes, alms bowls, seats, needle holders, and other small items. These regulations on what to do with a deceased monk's possessions appear to have already been common practice in India because a similar scheme for dividing redistributable and non-redistributable items also appears in the Buddhist monastic law from the Mūlasarvāstivāda tradition, the *Assembled Buddhist Monastic Law from the Mūlasarvāstivāda Tradition* (*Genben sapoduo bu lüshe* 根本薩婆多部律攝),[26]

which the Tang Buddhist monk Yijing 義淨 (635–713) had translated into Chinese.

In the second step, to advance its defense, the Buddhist Association of China skillfully adopted a principle regarding heirs in the *Law of Succession*. Here, articles 12 and 13 weigh in on an heir's engagement in caring for the deceased when deciding whether to allow a more caring heir not only to inherit in general but to inherit a larger portion.[27] This principle led the association to propose evaluating the claimants' right to inherit by assessing whether they had fulfilled their duties to the deceased. It argues that after ordination, Buddhist monks and nuns rely on their host monasteries and nunneries for food, shelter, medical care, and nursing. These institutions also cover funeral expenses and pay off the debts of the deceased upon their death. In this context, it is the host monastery, and not the lay family members and relatives, that provide financial and emotional support and care for monastics prior to their death. Therefore, when ordained monks or nuns die, the host monasteries should automatically become their legitimate beneficiaries.

In the third step, the Buddhist Association of China used precedents to defend the host monastery's right to inherit. It argued that Chinese Buddhism established a tradition in history for the host monasteries to take over the deceased monks' estate. This tradition continued in contemporary China. After 1949, the newly founded communist government in China abolished many outdated Buddhist practices, such as scarring a candidate's head with a burning incense stick during their ordination ceremony. Yet the government never banned Buddhist monasteries from acquiring deceased monks' possessions. The Buddhist Association of China interpreted the lack of that ban as an indication of the Chinese government's legal acceptance of monasteries acquiring the estates of their dead clerics as a legitimate religious practice.

This is a flawed argument, however. Historically, the host monastery was not always the sole beneficiary. In his research on the privately held property of Buddhist monks and nuns in China, Cao Shibang shows how, up to the late eighth century, multiple stakeholders could split and share the property of deceased monks.[28] Prior to 767, the government used to confiscate deceased monks' estates. In some cases, the government could only claim half of the estate, leaving the other half to the deceased's close disciples. Buddhist monasteries only officially replaced the government as the principal beneficiary in 767. In the *Biographies of Eminent Monks Compiled during the Song* (*Song gaoseng zhuan* 宋高僧傳), written by the Song scholar Zanning 贊寧 (919–1001), we can find the official record of this change in the biography of the Buddhist monk Shengru 乘如 from Anguo 安國 Monastery in the Tang capital. According to this biography, on the twenty-seventh day in the eleventh month of 767, Emperor Daizong Li Yu 李豫 (726–779; reign 762–779) issued a rescript (*chi* 敕) regulating that "from today onward, when ordained Buddhists die, their belongings will go to the monastic community."[29]

This rescript did not fully stop monks and nuns from bequeathing their estates to various beneficiaries, including but not limited to their host monasteries and nunneries. Away from central China, ninth-century manuscripts documenting religious practices in the Dunhuang Buddhist community, on the Silk Road, attest to this practice in at least two last wills and testaments respectively left by a Buddhist monk and a Buddhist nun. Sometime in the mid-ninth century, affluent Buddhist monk Chong'en 崇恩 wrote a last will and testament where he provided detailed arrangements for dividing up his estate. This document found in the Mogao Cave 17 in 1900 is now preserved as manuscript Pelliot chinois 3410 (see Figure 7.1) in the Bibliothèque Nationale de France, Paris. This last will and testament listed items for distribution, including real estate, other land, chariots, horses, donkeys, cows, furniture, tools, fabric, clothes, gold and silver, and a maid the monk had bought.[30] For each item, he specified beneficiaries ranging from local government offices, to monasteries, to close disciples, to monastic friends, to cousins and nephews from his lay family.

Nuns in Dunhuang also enjoyed the right to distribute their estates as they pleased. The Chinese manuscript S. 2199 (see Figure 7.2), which comes from the same Mogao Cave 17, documents that on the twenty-third day in the tenth month in the sixth year during the Xiantong 咸通 era (865), the Buddhist nun Linghui 靈惠 fell ill and decided to leave a last will and testament. Her wish was to give her maid, who had been her only possession, to a niece named Panniang 潘娘. To avoid any dispute over this arrangement after her death, this nun assembled her younger brother, two other nieces—one of whom was also a nun and the other a laywoman—three nephews, and two officials at the same time to witness and sign her will. Whether Linghui's will was honored or not remains unknown.

Apart from expressing its support for the host monasteries in the official statements of 1998 and 2002, the Buddhist Association of China also took the impressive step of advancing its defense by legalizing host monasteries' right to inherit the estate of dead monastics under the state legal system. The rescript issued in the Tang dynasty in 767 was the earliest legal regulation permitting Buddhist institutions to acquire the estates of the deceased Buddhists. Seeing an opportunity to integrate this regulation into China's contemporary state legal system, the association convened a national assembly on February 25, 2006, where members decided to insert a new article, article 14, into the *General Principles and Regulations for Living in the Chinese Buddhist Monasteries* (*Quanguo hanchuan fojiao siyuan gongzhu guiyue* 全國漢傳佛教寺院共住規約). This document had been revised from an earlier version the association had promulgated at a national assembly on October 21, 1993. The 1993 version contained fourteen articles but did not address issues concerning the estates of deceased Buddhists.[31]

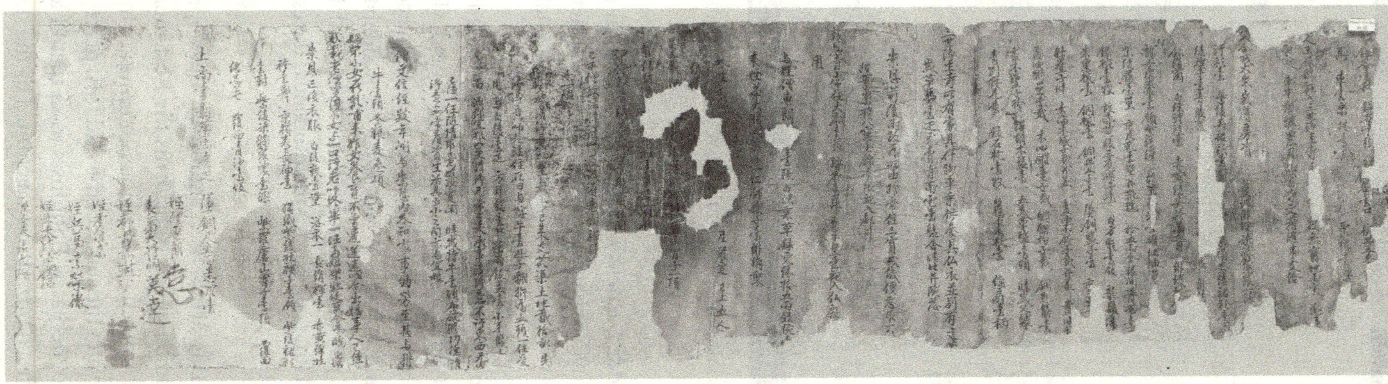

Fig. 7.1 Monk Chong'en's last will and testament, Pelliot chinois 3410, © Bibliothèque Nationale de France

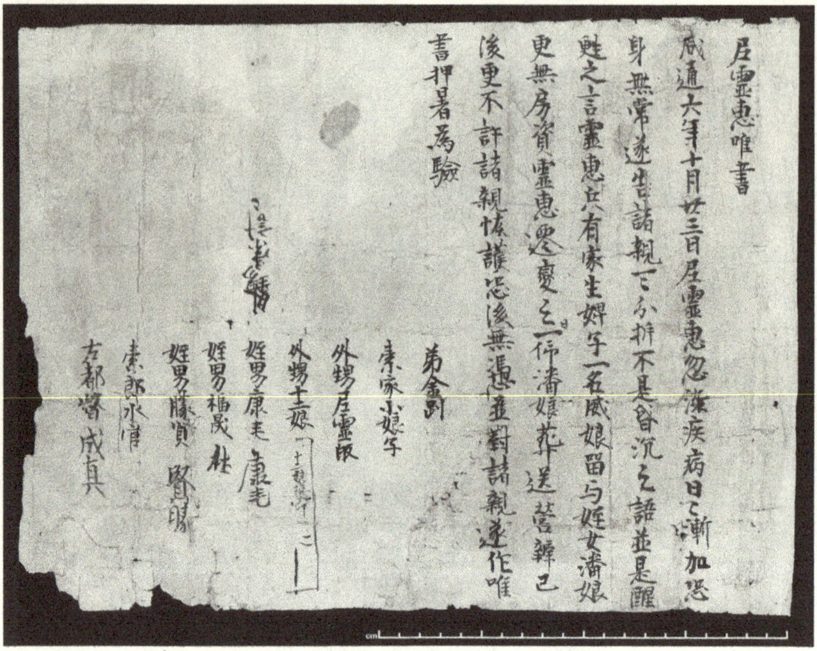

尼靈惠唯書
咸通六年十月廿三日尼靈惠忽染疾病日日漸加恐
身無常遂告諸親一一分拆不是昏沉之語並是醒
甦之言靈惠只有家生婢子一名威娘留與姪女潘娘
更無房資靈惠遷變之日一仰潘娘葬送營辦已
後更不許諸親恡護恐後無憑並對諸親遂作唯
書押署為驗
弟金剛
索家小娘子
外甥尼靈皈
外甥十二娘
姪男康毛 康毛
姪男福晟
姪男勝賢 賢
索郎水官
左都督成真

Fig. 7.2 Nun Linghui's last will and testament, S. 2199, © British Library Board

In 2006, the newly added article 14 passed a regulation explicitly stating that when ordained Buddhists passed away, the host monastery was to take care of their funerals and was to inherit these dead monastics' estates.

> Under the tradition established by the Buddha, while ordained Buddhists stay in the monastery, the monastery's communal fund will supply them with provisions. When ordained Buddhists become aged, the communal fund will pay for their care and nursing. When ordained Buddhists become sick, the communal fund will pay for their medical care. When ordained Buddhists pass away, the communal fund will pay for their funerals. The estate of the deceased Buddhists will go to the communal fund.[32]

The introduction of this article is a significant development in complicated lawsuits over monastic estates. It transforms the host monasteries' right to inherit from a practice confined to a religious community into a part of the apparatus of state law. It elevates the status of the Buddhist practice of host institutions acquiring the estates of deceased Buddhists from that of a religious practice to that of a legal practice recognized and sanctioned by the state. Theoretically, this should have put an end to the persisting legal disputes over deceased monks' possessions. In legal practice, however, it does not seem to have helped establish host monasteries as legitimate heirs. Lay litigants and their lawyers condemn article 14 as unlawful because it contradicts the *Law of Succession*.[33] Judges cite it in their jurisprudential analysis but see that it lacks lawful authority because it is only applicable to religious practitioners and not to everyone in the country.

The Buddhist Association of China's defense also entails compromise. While defending its position of protecting the host monasteries' right to inherit the estates of deceased monks and nuns, the association recommends—in order to make it easier to settle disputes—that financial subsidies be offered to the lay heirs of deceased Buddhists. This compromise was a new development in the Buddhist Association of China's second official statement in 2002. There, it recommended that host monasteries offer some humanitarian support for the struggling lay survivors of the deceased monks. At the end of the official statement to the Buddhist Association of Guangdong Province, the Buddhist Association of China wrote the following:

> After the death of the Buddhist monk Youjng from Guangxiao Monastery in your office's jurisdiction, his bank savings should be inherited by Guangxiao Monastery in Guangzhou as a communal fund. We hope you will follow this principle, with the aid of the Bureau of Religious Affairs in Guangdong Province, to assist Guangxiao Monastery in Guangzhou in requesting access to the deceased monk's bank savings. If the monk's lay family members are experiencing hardship in life, the monastery could provide a suitable subsidy to reflect Buddhism's spirit of unconditional compassion and benevolence. But the lay family members cannot receive the deceased monk's estate.[34]

This amendment illustrates the association's determination to defend the economic interests of the monastic institutions and its openness to make minor compromises in settlements. What is not specified but is apparent in the 2002 reply is its concern over the public's view of Buddhism, its institutions, and the monastic community. By showing empathy for the needy and offering them financial assistance, this amendment would have softened any tension between the winning monasteries and the losing lay heirs. This may have served to offset the perception, among the wider lay community, that Buddhist institutions were greedy and litigious. This is a valued service because Buddhist monastic communities in China depend on the financial support and spiritual attachment of the lay community, so this needs to remain vital.

The potential rewards of this gesture are not just hypothetical. For example, when the abbot monk Juezhao 覺照 (lay name Li Hetong 李鶴童) passed away at Bixia 碧霞 Monastery in Lianyungang, Jiangsu Province, on February 18, 2016, his savings in multiple bank accounts amounted to 3,440,956 Chinese yuan. He was also the registered owner of a seventy-five-square-meter apartment. After his death, the monastery met with the monk's six living siblings, his elder sister and five brothers, and offered them a death gratuity of one million Chinese yuan and the apartment. In return, the siblings unanimously affirmed the monastery as the sole beneficiary of the deceased abbot's bank savings. On January 16, 2018, the same host monastery was forced to sue the lay family members in the Haizhou District People's Court because the bank holding their deceased brother's account had refused to release the money to this monastery.[35] The bank argued that the lack of a will prevented it from allowing the monastery to withdraw this money. This forced Bixia Monastery to sue the monk's living siblings to obtain a court judgment confirming the monastery as the sole beneficiary, thereby forcing the banks to release the money. The monk's siblings cooperated and supported the monastery's case throughout the lawsuit.

Lay Refutations

The case of Bixia Monastery is not representative of a typical dispute over monastic estates. In almost all other cases, lay heirs and their legal representatives have refuted the validity of Buddhist laws and regulations and challenged the host institutions. They believed the state court should only consider the *Law of Succession* and the 1994 jurisprudential explanation of the Supreme People's Court in disputes over a deceased monk's estate. For most lay heirs, Buddhist laws and traditions as well as regulations and statements issued by the Buddhist Association of China apply only to ordained Buddhists, not to all citizens. In their view, religious vestiges are subordinate to the universal *Law of Succession* and have no place in the courtroom.

In their challenges, lay litigants openly criticize the Buddhist Association of China for making "illegal" statements and promulgating rules that contradict state law. Lay heirs and their legal representatives in a dispute over the estate of the Buddhist monk Benyuan 本愿 (lay name Yang Fangzhou 楊方洲) were particularly vocal in this regard. Ordained in 1951,[36] Benyuan had been the abbot of Xiangyan 香岩 Monastery in Anshan, Liaoning Province, until his death in 2008. At the time of his death, his estate included a car and 280,000 Chinese yuan held in a bank account in his name. The lawsuit over the inheritance of this estate was heard first in the Qianshan District People's Court, then in the Anshan Intermediate People's Court, and finally in the Liaoning Higher People's Court. On June 10, 2008, the lay litigants' lawyer, Yang Yunhua 楊蘊華, argued that "from the legal perspective, the Buddhist Association of China's regulations on the distribution of deceased monks' estates contradict the *Law of Succession*, and that contradiction renders those Buddhist regulations illegal."[37]

The lay heir in another case over the estate of a Buddhist nun, in 2016, was even more critical of the legality of the Buddhist regulation entitling the host monastery to inherit this nun's estate. On December 7, 2014, the Buddhist nun Yanche 演徹 (lay name Kou Shuhua 寇淑華) committed suicide at Mituo 彌陀 Nunnery in Liaoning Province, where she had been its abbess since 2002. At the time of her death, she left behind a total of 1,833,000 Chinese yuan in her bank accounts. She also left a note for her disciple nun Kuanxin 寬歆 to look for "Mituo Nunnery's money" in a metal cabinet, where the password to her bank accounts could be found. The nunnery took care of the abbess's funeral and assumed custody of her note, identity card, bank cards, and a diary. On December 25, 2016, the abbess's ex-husband and their son forced Kuanxin to hand over the abbess's identity card and bank cards. The next day, the son withdrew all the money from the deceased abbess's bank accounts. The nunnery sued the son in the Chaoyang Intermediate People's Court in Liaoning Province. In the initial trial, the court declared that the disputed money had not been the abbess's private property for three reasons. First, she had very limited sources of income other than donations from lay patrons. Second, she left a will instructing her disciple to look for the nunnery's money in the metal cabinet, where details on the bank accounts were found. Third, letting the host institution inherit its deceased monastics' estates had been an established Buddhist tradition. The son challenged the legitimacy of the note left by the abbess as a legal last will and testament because it lacked a signature and other elements required in a valid will. Nevertheless, the court ruled in favor of the nunnery. The son then appealed in the Liaoning Higher People's Court, where a judge heard the case on April 14, 2016. Here, the son challenged the legality of the Buddhist Association of China's statement regarding the handling of estates left by deceased nuns or monks. He also challenged the Chaoyang Intermediate People's Court's citation of that statement in the initial trial, where he stated:

> The *Reply on the Estates of Buddhist Monks* (*Guanyu siyuan sengren yichan wenti de fuhan* 關於寺院僧人遺產的復函) was a reply from the Buddhist Association of China to the inquiry on what to do with the estates of deceased monks, from the Guangdong Provincial Association of Buddhism. This was an internal document for the religious community. This was not a regulatory document universally applicable to all. In the initial trial, the Intermediate People's Court cited this document and followed the Buddhist tradition by declaring Mituo Nunnery the heir of Kou Shuhua's personal savings. This judgment violated the existing law on property ownership and blood-based inheritance rights. It damaged the legal order and provided religious organizations legal means to interfere with social affairs.[38]

Judges in the Liaoning Higher People's Court took this criticism seriously. On May 20, 2016, the chief judge Sun Weiliang 孫維良 acknowledged that the citation of the 2002 reply from the Buddhist Association of China had been inappropriate. He wrote the following at the end of his judgment for the final trial:

> The Buddhist Association of China is a Buddhist autonomous religious organization in China. Its *Reply on the Estate of Buddhist Monks* [2002, article 128] is not universally applicable. Plus, the current case is not a dispute over succession. Citing this document in the judgment of the initial trial was inappropriate. This court thus corrects it.[39]

The Higher People's Court, however, still upheld the original judgments of the lower courts.

Other lay heirs also refuted another major accusation against them from the host institutions: that legal heirs have failed to fulfill their duty to their deceased monastic relations. Many monasteries and nunneries have argued that the lay children and relatives did not care for the deceased when they were alive and thus failed to fulfill their responsibilities as legal heirs. This was true in some cases in which the lay heirs resided at a distance from the monks or nuns in question. But in some cases, the lay heirs had lived close by and had been actively involved in caring for these monks or nuns when they were alive. One example is the above-mentioned case concerning the monk Benyuan.[40] The three children of the deceased monk had lived close to the monastery. They argued that their extended families had continued to care for and support not only the monk but the entire monastery. The monk's adult children and their spouses regularly cared for the monk, gave him money, and bought him medicine. In the last year of the monk's life, his grandson-in-law had spent many days and nights attending to the monk's needs. This rebuttal, however, still failed to change the outcome of the lawsuit.

Noncooperative Banks

Another unexpected complication came from the banks where much of the disputed money had been deposited. This did not happen in every lawsuit over the estates of deceased monks and nuns; but in a few cases, banks had refused to release the deceased's money to the host monastery or nunnery. One example is a case from 2001 in which a bank had refused to release the disputed bank savings of the monk Youjin to his host monastery, Guangxiao.[41] Instead, the bank argued that since the monk had no heirs, his money should be handed over to the government. It is understandable that these banks would have taken precautions. Releasing the deposited funds of the deceased to anyone without proper legal documents could have legally jeopardized these banks.

Different banks refused to cooperate with host monasteries for different reasons. Some banks refused to hand over the funds of deceased monastics because no legal documents existed to establish these monasteries as the sole legal beneficiaries. This had been the case for the bank account of a Buddhist monk whose lay name was Cao Guixin 曹桂昕.[42] This monk had been a resident of Wenfeng 文峰 Monastery in Yangzhou, Jiangsu Province. From July 2007 to February 2012, he had been in charge of attending to visitors at the monastery. When he passed away on February 18, 2012, the monastery found money on his bank card. But when the monastery went to withdraw the money, the bank refused to release it. In 2016, the monastery sued the bank in the Guangling District People's Court in Yangzhou, Jiangsu Province, but lost its case in the first trial. It then appealed to the Yangzhou Intermediate People's Court, where the case was heard on February 17, 2017. During the investigation, the court discovered that the monk had had an heir: a daughter who was still in high school. Because the monk had not left a will to bequeath his money to the monastery and because of the existence of the monk's daughter, the intermediate court did not grant the monastery access to the disputed money. The final outcome of this dispute remain unknown.

Other banks refused to release the money of deceased monastics because their monasteries had failed to produce notarized documents. In a lawsuit over the bank savings of the Buddhist monk Xinmiao 心妙 (lay name Shi Xiaozhai 施小齋) between his host Donghua 東華 Monastery, and the China Construction Bank,[43] which I will introduce in more detail in the next section, the bank required either a notarized certificate specifying the host monastery as the legal heir or a court order to release the money. Because the monastery was unable to obtain such notarization, the China Construction Bank refused to release the money for two reasons. First, the bank was not a law enforcement entity and was not able to investigate the situation of the deceased monk's family. Therefore, it was unable to verify whether the monk had had any living family members as legal heirs to his money. Second, there were concerns over the deceased monk's will. As it had not been notarized, the China Construction Bank could not verify whether it was authentic and legal. In the end, the monastery sued the bank in court to get a court order for it to release the money. During the trial, the court searched but could not find any living family members of the deceased monk. Therefore, the court issued a judgment ordering the China Construction Bank to release the deceased monk's money to his host monastery.

The Judiciary

The promulgation of the *Law of Succession* in 1985 was an important watershed for litigation over the estates of deceased monks and nuns. After that year, court judges adopted different principles in their adjudications. But the establishment of the *Law of Succession* had no substantial impact on the outcome of lawsuits over questions regarding the legitimate beneficiaries of the estates of dead monastics. From the first documented lawsuit in 1984 to the most recent case in 2020, Chinese courts at various levels overwhelmingly ruled in favor of the host monastic institutions.

Before 1985, "Buddhist tradition" was the basis for ruling in favor of Buddhist institutions. In the legal vacuum prior to 1985, judges mostly relied on Buddhist rules, traditions, and interpretations to designate host monasteries as beneficiaries. This is what occurred in the dispute over the estate of the Buddhist monk Juzan 巨贊, who had been the vice president of the Buddhist Association of China until the time of his death.[44] Juzan passed away in Beijing on April 7, 1984. After his death, Juzan's nephew insisted that he was the rightful beneficiary of this monk's estate and demanded he be accorded his inheritance, which at the time was being held at Guangji 廣濟 Monastery, the headquarters of the Buddhist Association of China. When his demand was rejected, the nephew sued the association in the Beijing Intermediate People's Court. Because no law existed to provide clear guidance on how to adjudicate such cases, the court solicited opinions from the legislature, legal experts, and Buddhist leaders. Finally, the court declared the Buddhist Association of China to be the legal beneficiary and deemed the monk's nephew to have no legal right to inherit his deceased uncle's estates.

After 1985, the newly promulgated *Law of Succession* created a brief disruption in courtrooms as some judges had not adhered to the earlier consensus of ruling in accordance with Buddhist tradition. This disruption occurred during the case of the Buddhist monk whose lay name was Qian Anding 錢安定. The Shanghai Higher People's Court heard this case in 1986. On September 26, 1984, Qian Anding passed away at Shanghai's Yufo 玉佛 Monastery, where he had been a resident monk since 1981. Upon his death, the monastery took care of his funeral. The monk left behind 4,200 Chinese yuan and 100 yuan's worth of treasury securities. Upon his death, Qian Anding's nephew, the son of his elder brother, claimed the right to inherit his uncle's estate. Before coming to Yufo Monastery, Qian Anding had previously been a monk at Qingliang 清涼 Monastery until 1949. Later he returned to lay life and married a woman, but they had no children. In 1973, his wife passed away. At the time of this monk's death, his younger brother ceded any rights to this estate. Soon after the monk's death, his elder brother also died. This left his nephew as his only living heir. After securing a notarized certificate, the nephew withdrew 1,500 Chinese yuan from the monk's personal bank account. However, when he requested the remaining 2,700 yuan and the treasury securities that were being kept at the monastery, the monastery refused. The nephew countered by filing a lawsuit in the Shanghai Higher People's Court.

The judges in the court disagreed on how to adjudicate the case. Some supported the Buddhist monastery, arguing that the monastery should take possession of the money for having taken care of the monk when he had been alive and for attending to his funeral needs. This was consistent with the position of the city's Office for Religious Affairs and the Buddhist Association of China's local office in Shanghai. Other judges, however, argued that the newly promulgated *Law of Succession* protected the nephew's right to inherit his uncle's estate. Moreover, this law did not differentiate between the estate of a Buddhist monk and that of lay citizens. On September 4, 1986, the court rendered its final opinion, as follows, and submitted it to the Supreme People's Court of China for confirmation:

> Our country's constitution, general civil law, and *Law of Succession* all require protecting the inheritance rights of citizens' private possessions. The *Law of Succession* does not treat the estates of Buddhist monks as exceptions. Therefore, these monks' heirs can legally inherit. Because this case involves religious policy, in order to treat it with extra caution, we are submitting this report to your court for instruction.[45]

Despite this local court's split decision in Shanghai, its final opinion clearly tended to support the lay heir. The outcome of this lawsuit, however, remains unknown.

Dissenting voices did not last long. Conflicts between Buddhist law and the *Law of Succession* forced judges to think creatively. They soon found a solution that later became the dominant guiding principle for all future disputes over the estates of deceased monks and nuns. Rather than concentrating on who had the right to inherit these estates, judges redirected their attentions to focus on the nature of the estate: was it a deceased Buddhist's private property, or was it property the host monastery had acquired through—and kept under the name of—the now deceased Buddhist? Such an examination would, theoretically, proceed in one of two directions: either the lay heirs were to prove that the estate was the deceased's private property, or the host monastery needed to prove that the property constituted part of its communal possessions. In the courtroom, if both entities failed to provide solid evidence to demonstrate the nature of the disputed estate, then the lay heirs were much more likely than the host monasteries to lose their cases.

Courts supported the host monastic institutions in all cases where lay heirs could not prove decisively that the disputed estate had been the deceased's personal property. The cases of the monks Farong 法融 from Xinglong 興隆 Monastery,[46] the monk from Shengshui Monastery in Sichuan, the monk Youjng from Guangxiao Monastery in Guangzhou, the monk Yongxiu from Lingzhao Monastery in Yunnan, and the monk Benyuan from Xiangyan Monastery in Liaoning all clearly illustrate this outcome. In the case of the monk Benyuan, his lay heir argued that his car was his personal property because it had been registered in his name. The judge and the host monastery, however, argued that the car was the monastery's communal property because it had been purchased with the monastery's money. Regarding bank deposits in the name of deceased monks or nuns, monasteries often argued that the money came from lay patrons who had intended it as donations to the monastery. Lay heirs, however, viewed this money as personal gifts made to the now deceased monks or nuns. In the absence of sound evidence from both parties, most judges ruled in favor of the host institutions.

Even when lay heirs clearly demonstrated that the disputed estate had been the deceased Buddhist's private property, judges still managed to grant part of the disputed estate to the host institution. Consideration of an additional factor—the wills of the deceased monks—had made this possible for the court. When the dispute was over whether a Buddhist monastery was the beneficiary, the court often accepted a will as an important document establishing the host monastery as the sole or partial beneficiary. A dispute over the estate of the Buddhist monk Hanjing 含淨, in 2003, illustrates how this was done. On March 22, 2003, Hanjing passed away at Longquan Monastery on Mount Wutai, Shanxi Province.[47] Before his death, Hanjing had left a notarized will giving two properties in Beijing to his host monastery. His deceased wife had been the owner of one property that consisted of sixteen rooms and was located in Xuanwu District, and the monk and his daughter had co-owned the other property, which consisted of nine rooms and was located in Xicheng District. When the monastery approached the daughter for the titles to both properties, the daughter refused to turn them over. The monastery then filed a lawsuit against the daughter in the Xicheng District People's Court. The court recommended the following settlement: the property with sixteen rooms currently in the deceased wife's name belonged to the daughter, and the property with nine rooms co-owned by the monk and his daughter belonged to the monastery. Both parties accepted this settlement, after which the monastery withdrew its suit. In this case, the judge had given significant weight to the monk Hanjing's will.

But judges did not treat all wills of deceased Buddhists equally. When a monk's will designated the host monastery as the beneficiary, judges generally ruled or tried to facilitate a settlement according to the will. This was how they had mediated Hanjing's case, wherein they had granted the host monastery half of the disputed estate. Judges' inclinations to rule in favor of host monasteries can also be seen in the outcome of a 2016 suit, in which a legally invalid will was used as important evidence to rule in favor of the host monastery.[48] On August 29, 2015, the Buddhist monk Xinmiao 心妙 passed away at Donghua 東華 Monastery, in Guangdong Province, where he had been living for over ten years. When he died, he left behind money in a bank account. On August 7, 2015, about three weeks before his death, Xinmiao left a will that bequeathed all of his estate to his host monastery, including the money in his bank account. This monk's last will and testament read as follows:

> Declarant: Religious name Venerable Xinmiao; lay name Shi Xiaozhai, male, born on May 23, 1957. Han Chinese. Currently resides at Donghua Chan Monastery in Guangdong Province. National identification card number: [redacted].
>
> I am fifty-eight years old. While leaving this last will and testament, I am of sound mind and rational thought. Because physical afflictions could lead to accidents, I am leaving this will. The witness is Master Venerable Foyuan, my junior religious brother. Here is my will:
>
> First, in the early days when I first became ordained, I received support from faithful adherents from all over the place. The donations I have received were due to the influence of my master and the monastic residential community. Therefore, I am leaving all my possessions to the monastic community.
>
> Second, I am a resident in this Chan monastery. Today, I designate Venerable Foyuan, who is both my master's disciple and my junior religious brother, to be the witness of my last will and testament, and Master Zhongdao as the executor of my will. There are three copies of this will: one for myself, one for the executor of my will, and one for the witness of my will. The executor will be in charge when the succession begins.
>
> Declarant: Shi Xiaozhai
> Witness: Zhang Liwei
> Executor: Qiu Lu
> August 7, 2015[49]

After this monk's death, the host monastery arranged his funeral and covered all expenses. In December 2015, when the monastery went to the bank to withdraw the monk's savings, the bank refused to release it because the monastery could not provide either a court order or a certificate showing it to be the legal heir of the money in the bank account. The monastery then sued the bank in the People's Court of that county.

During the trial, the court found the will to be invalid. As it had not been notarized, the court could not verify its authenticity or legality. In its final judgment, however, the court still took it as a decisive document in declaring the host monastery to be the legal heir of the disputed money in the bank account. The judge arrived at this finding based on the following three conditions. First, the court could not identify any living legal heir of the deceased monk. Second, the will left by the monk expressed his willingness to give his estate to the host monastery. In the judgment, the chief judge Feng Kaixuan 馮開選 wrote:

> Shi Xiaozhai left a last will and testament on August 7, 2015, with Zhang Liwei and Qiu Lu as witnesses. His will states that he would like to "leave all possessions to the resident community." This was an expression of his genuine will. There were two or more witnesses present, which complied with the legal requirement. Its contents should be protected by law.[50]

Third, the chief judge cited Buddhist tradition in which the host monastery assumed possession of its deceased monks' estate. In sum, the judge concluded that Shi had been a resident monk at Donghua Monastery. As the designated beneficiary of his will, Donghua Monastery had the right to his bank savings.

The unequal treatment of a will is also apparent in the 2016 case between Mituo Nunnery and the son of the Buddhist nun Yanche, which was analyzed in detail above. This nun had left a casual note that contained no signature and had been neither witnessed nor notarized. Legally, the note could not have been treated as the nun's valid will. Yet in the initial trial in the Chaoyang Intermediate People's Court, the judge referred to this note as the "last will and testament" of the abbess and used it as an important piece of evidence to establish the disputed money as being the monastery's communal property. During the second trial in the Liaoning Higher People's Court, the chief judge avoided the previous affirmation of the note as a "legal will" but nevertheless included it as evidence to support the court's concurrence with the initial judgment.

In defending the economic interests of Buddhist institutions, judges went so far as to discard legally notarized wills of a deceased monks even when lay persons had been explicitly designated as the beneficiaries. This is what happened to the will of the Buddhist monk Benyao 本耀, the abbot of Shifo 石佛 Monastery in Shaoxing, Zhejiang Province.[51] Benyao passed away in 2003. Before his death, the abbot had left a will that contained instructions to use part of his cash and his bank account savings to cover his funeral expenses and to give the remainder to a woman who had cared for him for a long time. After he passed away, the caregiver could not obtain the monk's inheritance for her, so she had to sue the monastery. In two rounds of trials, the court ignored the deceased monk's will and denied the caregiver's petition based on a "lack of evidence" to prove that the money in the abbot's bank account balance had been his private property.

Most of these lawsuits were eventually settled in the district, city, or provincial courts. Only in rare cases did the regional courts reach out to the Supreme People's Court of China before making a final judgment. This happened at least twice. The Supreme People's Court of China first got involved in 1987 in the case of the Buddhist monk Qian Anding, which I analyzed in detail above. On October 16, 1987, the court delivered a reply by telephone to the Shanghai Higher People's Court. Its position was both firm and vague. First, it recognized a citizen's right to inherit as legally undeniable in this case, stating, "The current law in our country contains no special regulations regarding the personal property of ordained Buddhist monks. Therefore, with regard to the Buddhist monk who was also a citizen, we cannot deny the legal rights of those who are legally eligible to inherit his estate after his death."[52] Intertwined with the Supreme People's Court's firm stance in defending the authority of Chinese law vis-à-vis individual property rights was a reluctance to have state law override or diminish Buddhist monastic law and customs. In the case of the estate of Qian Anding, the Supreme People's Court acknowledged the complexity of the dispute between the monastery and the monk's nephew, but it would not designate which party in the case was ultimately the legitimate heir to the disputed money. It simply instructed the Shanghai Higher People's Court to provide mediation between the litigants. In so doing, the Supreme People's Court of China avoided giving any jurisprudential interpretation on the specifics of the lawsuit.

This reluctance remained unchanged when the Supreme People's Court had to reiterate its position in 1994. It is unclear what might have provoked another round of inquiry. Apparently, the State Administration of Religious Affairs had submitted an inquiry to this court asking what to do regarding the dead monks' estates. On October 13, 1994, the Supreme People's Court reiterated the position it had expressed in its 1987 reply to the Shanghai High People's Court:

> Our country's current laws have no exceptional regulations on the succession to the estate of Buddhist monks. Thus, for Buddhist monks who are also citizens, after their death, we cannot deny the rights of their relatives who are legally eligible to receive their inheritances. The succession of a Buddhist monk's estate is a new problem that emerged after the *Law of Succession* and the *General Principles of the Civil Law* had been promulgated. It is a problem that remains unsolved by legislation. Therefore, this court is not able to provide a jurisprudential explanation. We recommend you reach out to the Legislature for a solution through legislation.[53]

What was new in the Supreme People's Court's 1994 reply was its explicit explanation as to why it had been unable to solve this problem. The court's new reply conceded its inability to intervene in conflicts between state law and Buddhist religious law and tradition. Furthermore, it considered this dilemma to be a new issue requiring legislative intervention. Therefore, the Supreme People's Court declined to adjudicate the legitimacy of parties with claims as heirs in disputes over the estates of deceased Buddhists. To improve matters, the court recommended litigants seek a solution from the legislators.

China's legislators are equally reluctant to meddle in conflicts between state law and Buddhist religious law. The *Law of Succession* that had been in force in China since 1985 was scheduled to expire on January 1, 2021. On this very day, an updated version of the *Law of Succession* was integrated into the newly promulgated *Civil Code* (*Minfa dian* 民法典). This was a golden opportunity for China's legislators to revisit the *Law of Succession* and make necessary clarifications on handling ordained Buddhists' estates. Repeated struggles over such lawsuits at various court levels had amply demonstrated the urgency of this clarification. Even after the Supreme People's Court of China had specified the need for legislative intervention in 1994, China's legislators failed to confront this jurisprudential challenge. The newly revised 2021 *Law of Succession* still avoided addressing the dilemma over how to distribute the estates of deceased monks and nuns. On December 29, 2020, the Supreme People's Court of China even rescinded its own 1994 reply "to ensure that the country's laws are consistent, correct, and applicable,"[54] but provided no clarification on the succession of ordained Buddhists' estates in the updated *Law of Succession*. When explaining the new law within a few months of this revision, judges from the Supreme People's Court of China specifically pointed out that this court had changed its mind and would continue to adhere to its 1994 reply to the inquiry on what to do with the estates of dead monks, because even though the reply addressed the treatment of monastic property, its reply was not a jurisprudential document and its positions were not contradictory to the section in the *Civil Code* that contains the *Law of Succession*.[55] Such legal indecisiveness and ambiguity demonstrate the significant challenges inherent in resolving this dilemma, which continues to haunt litigants, judges, and legislators to this day.

Conclusion

The development of lawsuits over monastic estates illustrates how the legacy of the hybrid courts and laws continue to influence the operation of the law in China to the present day. After 1949, communist China inherited the hybrid court from imperial China but split it into two branches: the State Administration of Religious Affairs, located within the state government, and the Buddhist Association of China, which is more closely affiliated with the Buddhist establishment. In Chapter 6, we saw how the State Administration of Religious Affairs functioned as a third-party agency, leading investigations of criminal charges against ordained Buddhist monks. The current chapter shows how the Buddhist Association of China assumed the role of a third-party agency mediating monastic institutions, lay heirs, the judiciary, and the legislature.

When the Buddhist Association of China intervened in lawsuits between lay heirs and host Buddhist institutions over the estates of deceased monks and nuns, its role exceeded that of a national organization overseeing religious affairs. This role ranged from legal consulting and interpreting jurisprudence to lawmaking, all of which served to protect the economic interests of the relevant host institutions. Normally, the jurisdiction of the Buddhist Association of China would have been limited to the community of ordained Buddhist monks and nuns, and disputes over estates involving lay litigants would have been outside of that jurisdiction. Yet, in contemporary China where jurisprudential contradictions remain a legal hot potato that even judges and legislators avoid touching, the Buddhist Association of China's engagements in these lawsuits can be seen as neither reckless nor out of place. On the contrary, they reflect how the dynastic legacy of a tripartite legal infrastructure made up of monastic, state, and hybrid courts continues to operate in subtle and direct ways in the contemporary context.

The influence of the hybrid law is also present in the development of these lawsuits. A typical example of a later hybrid law is the *General Principles and Regulations for Communal Living in Chinese Buddhist Monasteries*, which the Buddhist Association of China first passed in 1993. Originally, it contained fourteen articles; in 2006, it was amended to contain fifteen articles; and in 2019, it contained sixteen articles. In all three versions, these articles merged Buddhist and state legal concepts. On one hand, they regulate the institutional behavior of resident monks and nuns in accordance with historical expectations within the Buddhist monastic community. These include obeying the teachings of the Buddha, monitoring one's behavior in accordance with monastic disciplinary rules, participating regularly in religious practices and rituals, and respecting the requirements of attire, hairstyle, diet, and fundraising. All three versions of this document also integrate state law into monastic regulation. Article 1 requires all resident monks and nuns to strictly obey China's constitution as well as all other laws, regulations, and policies. The impact of this hybrid legal document—its 2006 iteration in particular—is reflected in its ubiquitous use in the adjudication of all lawsuits over the distribution of monastic estates. Judges in courts at every level give it consideration. Some even directly cite it to justify their deliberations in final judgements.

This hybrid document is not the only Buddhist legal text to have gained traction in contemporary courtrooms. While defending the authority of state law, as represented in the *Law of Succession*, regional and central court judges, in lawsuits over inheritances and succession, use extra caution when working around established Buddhist traditions and legal assumptions. They comment on and cite references from Indian Buddhist monastic law texts, their Chinese commentaries, indigenous community bylaws established in Chinese monasteries and nunneries, and the Buddhist Association of China's promotion of granting disputed estates to the host monasteries and nunneries. Although the *Law of Succession* applies to all citizens, in some ways judges in China's judiciary have given more weight to Buddhist laws and regulations, which supposedly only apply to the monastic members of a much smaller religious community.

This inclination to support the Buddhist position is also passively reflected in the state judiciary and legislature's ongoing avoidance of addressing the central issue in these disputes over monastic property: who is ultimately the legitimate heir? Instead, they turn to temporary solutions that rely on marginal details focusing on the nature of the disputed estates and the sources of the money used to accumulate the estate. Legislators also ignore the petition for legislative clarification.

The lack of a timely legislative clarification may contribute to more conflicts in the courtroom in the years to come. Unlike in earlier times, monks and nuns today can accumulate legitimate personal wealth in any number of ways. Monks and nuns who were ordained after completing successful careers might have acquired savings, real estate, and other valuables prior to their ordinations. Others might have inherited wealth from deceased family members. Increasing numbers of ordained Buddhist monks and nuns are working as paid academics. If these monks and nuns were to become residents of monasteries and nunneries, their earnings and wealth could hardly be considered anything other than personal wealth. In such circumstances, the lack of jurisprudential clarification on the rights of heirs to monastic estates would make adjudication next to impossible.

Epilogue

We need to focus on the institution, not the individual priests.[1]

Martin Baron, *Spotlight* (2015)

This book traces the origins and transformations of a two-millennia-old Buddhist campaign for clerical legal privileges that would exempt ordained monks and nuns from facing court trials and judgments that administer punishments. Contrary to earlier scholarly arguments, this Buddhist project was not a Chinese invention but one deeply rooted in Indian Buddhism. Indian Buddhists envisioned a religious institution that could provide sanctuary to ordained monks and nuns who had committed crimes that violated state law, whether prior or subsequent to these clerics' ordinations. They further wove these legal ideas into the fabric of both legal and nonlegal Buddhist texts. In China, Buddhists engaged with this project creatively. Instead of trying to transplant the idea of clerical legal privileges into Chinese soil, they collaborated with the state in building a hybrid court and setting up hybrid laws that would maximize the Buddhist establishment's jurisdictional control over its ordained members.

Understanding the origins and transformations of this Buddhist project in Asia is important and relevant today. Confusion over clerical legal privileges has direct impacts on how abuses that take place within the contemporary Buddhist community are treated. In recent decades, accusations of clerical sexual abuse in the Tibetan, Japanese, Chinese, and Southeast Asian Buddhist communities have emerged at accelerating rates.[2] But unlike the many Catholic victims who have now gained the confidence needed to seek justice in the courtroom, Buddhist victims today are still at a loss over their legal options.

Many cases of abuse within Buddhist communities remain unknown.[3] Some victims have revealed their experiences but never sued their perpetrators in court,[4] and some have filed lawsuits but ended up settling out of court. The first documented public attempt to take a Buddhist clerical offender to court occurred in 1994, when a female student, under the pseudonym Janice Doe, filed a lawsuit, in the Superior Court of California in Santa Cruz, accusing the Tibetan Buddhist teacher Sogyal Rinpoche (1947–2019) of sexual abuse.[5]

The next breakthrough occurred over two decades later, in Canada, in 2021, when the Buddhist community saw some progress in pursuing clerical offenders

Buddhism in Court. Cuilan Liu, Oxford University Press. © Oxford University Press 2024.
DOI: 10.1093/oso/9780197663332.003.0009

through civil law and the courts. On April 15, 2021, the Supreme Court of British Columbia heard an unusual case that concerned a high-profile Buddhist religious leader and marked a global awakening to the fact that Buddhist clerical abuses were being swept under the rug.[6] The claimant Vikki Hui Xin Han was a former nun who had been ordained to practice Tibetan Buddhism. At the time, the respondent—the seventeenth Karmapa, Ogyen Trinley Dorje[7]—had been an ordained Buddhist monk and leader of the Karma Kagyu school of Tibetan Buddhism. In an earlier petition submitted on July 17, 2019, Han had sought child support from the respondent. She claimed the respondent was the father of her daughter, born on June 19, 2018, after he had sexually assaulted her on October 14, 2017, during a meditation retreat at a Buddhist monastery in New York State. In the new hearing, Han sought to amend her earlier petition by adding a request for spousal support, claiming she had established a virtual marriage-like relationship with the respondent through communications over text messages. The judges stated that "the facts alleged by the claimant do not fit within a traditional concept of marriage" because the secret relationship "never moved into the physical world."[8] But on May 17, 2021, these judges nevertheless approved Han's request to have spousal support added to her earlier petition.

The court had scheduled a trial for April 11, 2022, but in October 2022, the claimant chose to discontinue the lawsuit.[9] Except for the May 2021 ruling to approve adding the additional claim for spousal support, all the other court documents remain inaccessible because the lawsuit had been filed as a family law proceeding in the Supreme Court of British Columbia and access to case documents for these types of cases is restricted to those involved in the case and to their legal representatives. Despite the mystery of its development, this case is still significant. It marks the Buddhist community's progress in seeing Buddhist plaintiffs succeed in taking a high-profile Buddhist leader to court. However, this case shows only limited improvements: the claimant, understandably, only sued the respondent for child and spousal support but did not press criminal charges for the sexual assault.

These ongoing challenges within Buddhist communities mirror a global and transreligious urgency to investigate the origins and contexts of clerical legal privilege. Clerical sexual abuse today has become a pressing crisis across countless religious establishments worldwide. In 2002, the Catholic community was forced to confront its failures in this regard head-on, when *Boston Globe* journalists exposed a pervasive pattern of clerical sexual abuse and institutional cover-ups within Catholic churches and institutions. These revelations upset everyone involved: abusive priests had to be prosecuted criminally, churches had to overcome a crisis in public trust, and victims were subject to interrogations about long-concealed injuries. If there is one positive takeaway from this collective religious catastrophe, it would be that the 2002 conviction of the former priest John

Joseph Geoghan (1935–2003) significantly challenged the pattern of legal immunity from prosecution in civil courts for Catholic priests. Geoghan's conviction also provided an empowering precedent that could be used to support victims of clerical abuse who were seeking justice through the law.[10] But more importantly, this case inspired a quest to uncover the much deeper systematic cause for the Catholic Church's having indulged and tolerated such expansive clerical abuses for decades. In the 2015 film *Spotlight,* based on this story, *Boston Globe*'s editor Martin Baron asks his journalists not to focus on individual Catholic priests who had abused children but to question the institutional practices that have systematically tolerated and covered up those individual crimes. In Buddhism, what is the larger story behind the individual cases of Buddhist abuses?

This larger story concerns a rarely discussed illusion of clerical legal privilege, in Buddhism, that has both emboldened perpetrators and intimidated victims. This illusion has nourished the core active ingredient for cultivating a "toxic secrecy," a term Lama Willa B. Miller used to describe the climate after having experienced sexual abuse at the hands of the teacher who had been instructing her in the Tibetan Buddhist tradition.[11] This toxic institutional culture of secrecy has been indulging the communal practice of concealing clerical misconduct and criminal behavior and handling these privately within the Buddhist establishment across Buddhist communities in and beyond Asia. At the core of these victims' fear of litigating was the lack of a proper understanding of the opacity of the clerical legal privileges that have been perpetually reinforced through popular literature, institutional interpretations, and personal interactions with these perpetrators. Dispelling that fear requires demystifying the doctrinal origins of clerical legal privileges in Buddhism, their reception and transformation in Buddhist regions, and their impact on the legal practice. By demystifying the historical trajectory and (il)legitimacy of the clerical legal privileges in Buddhism that have fed and enabled the Buddhist practice of legal secrecy, this book engages with scholars and practitioners of Buddhism—and beyond—to help clear the way for justice to be achieved in the courtroom and for internal restoration within the Buddhist community.

Beyond China

The continuing tension over the jurisdictional boundary between the Buddhist establishment and the state is not a unique Chinese phenomenon but a shared challenge in the pan-Asian context. Depending on Buddhism's place in each country's religious landscape, Buddhists in Asia have utilized different strategies to cope with this challenge. These differences make it impossible to map out a neat pan-Asian pattern to describe the legal interactions between Buddhist establishments and the state. Thus, how Buddhist practitioners and state rulers in China have engaged with the legal tensions between them could hardly lead us to any general conclusions about how the rest of Asia has coped with this critical matter. Yet, given China's influence in East Asia and the transnational connections Chinese Buddhists have established with South and Southeast Asia, the Chinese approach is indispensable in serving as a reference point for gaining a panoramic pan-Asian view of that messy map.

The Chinese approach is filled with persistence, collaboration, and mutual compromise on the part of both the Buddhist establishment and the state. Buddhists in China persisted in seeking their jurisdictional autonomy. By no later than the fourth century CE, they had facilitated the acquisition and translation of Indic Buddhist texts that contained discourses promoting clerical legal privileges for ordained Buddhists. Eminent monks enthusiastically lobbied the Chinese rulers of their times to seek more legal privileges for clerics. In the creative project of designing a third legal venue—the hybrid court—for exclusively adjudicating religious practitioners, many monks volunteered or agreed to royal invitations to collaborate with governmental officials in drafting the hybrid law that incorporated both the state and Buddhist monastic law to guide the operations of the hybrid legal venues. Many monks further accepted appointments to staff positions in those venues. These collaborations earned some eminent Buddhist monks the capital to directly petition Chinese emperors for clerical legal privileges.

The state, the other party involved in wrestling for jurisdictional control, has been equally persistent in defending its legal territory. Instead of favoring a single religious group, Chinese rulers have been more interested in cultivating religious diversity to encourage competition among peers to maintain a dynamic balance within China's religious landscape. One effort to keep this balance was in never officially acknowledging the Buddhist establishment's jurisdictional autonomy. Even during Buddhism's peak influence in the royal court, when eminent monks such as Xuanzang and Xuanwan were able to directly present petitions to the emperors, the state's position remained firm on defending its jurisdiction over ordained Buddhists. At the most, some of those petitions resulted in short-lived periods during which ordained Buddhists could be exempted from trials and torture in the state court. Overall, the state tolerated discussions and experiments to delineate the jurisdictional boundary between the Buddhist establishment and the state. Yet for the most part, the state was only willing to give the Buddhist establishment limited power to participate in shaping the jurisdictional boundary between them.

From the fourth century to the present, China experienced at least two substantial legal ruptures: one in 1911, when imperial rule ended during the final days of the Qing Empire, and the other, in 1949, when a Republican China, which had no significant objections to religion, transitioned to a Communist China that officially let a Communist ideology overrule religious beliefs. Despite these substantial ruptures, this pattern of engagement between the Buddhist establishment and the state changed very little.

The state court's dealings with lawsuits over estates left by dead monks and nuns show how mutual compromise, collaboration, and persistence are still alive in China today. The state's judiciary was neither willing to let state law overrule Buddhist monastic law and tradition nor to allow the latter to overrule state law. Even the Supreme People's Court of China and the Chinese legislature were unwilling to let the state's *Law of Succession* discredit the validity of the Buddhist legal custom that allowed host institutions to confiscate the estates of deceased monks or nuns, regardless of whether these deceased monks or nuns had bequeathed their estates to someone else in a written will.

Among China's neighbors in East Asia, one vignette from Japan in the seventh century suggests that Japanese Buddhists and state rulers were also engaged in this type of legal negotiation. In April 623 CE, a Buddhist monk killed his grandfather with an ax.[12] This crime outraged Suiko Tennō 推古天皇 (554–628; reign 592–628), Empress Suiko, who subsequently ordered an extensive investigation of all monks and nuns and also ordered that all who had been convicted of criminal offenses should face severe punishment. However, the foreign Buddhist monk Gwalleuk, from the Korean kingdom of Paekche, intervened to dissuade the empress from having her orders carried out. This Buddhist monk argued that Buddhism had only reached Japan barely a hundred years ago and thus monks and nuns in Japan committed crimes because they were still learning the Buddhist laws. Gwalleuk then petitioned Empress Suiko to drop the plan to investigate all of the other monks and nuns and instead only punish monks who had committed murder. While this anecdote was presented to explain the beginning of the establishment of the system for appointing Buddhist monastic officials in Japan, it also illuminates how Japanese Buddhists and state rulers engaged in negotiations over the treatment of Buddhist criminals.

This Chinese approach to seeking clerical legal privileges illuminates many regional similarities and differences among Asia's legal systems, the most startling similarity being a shared state legal practice with zero tolerance for serious clerical crimes in contemporary Asia. Today, Buddhist institutions are unable to provide sanctuary to ordained Buddhists who commit crimes before or after their ordinations. For committing crimes of murder, rape, or theft, for example, which violate both state and Buddhist monastic law, ordained Buddhist criminals must face arrest, court trials, jail time, and other punishments, just like lay offenders. Domestic and international arrests, trials, and sentencings are common in East and Southeast Asia. In international cases, state courts try and adjudicate foreign monks. For example, in August 2015, the Nagasaki District Court in Japan sentenced the seventy-year-old South Korean Buddhist monk Kim Sang-ho to six years in prison for having stolen 360 volumes of Buddhist scriptures from a Japanese temple.[13]

In domestic cases, arrests and punishments are even more common in East and Southeast Asia. In Japan, on May 22, 1916, the Tokyo District Court sentenced the ordained Buddhist monk, veteran, and serial killer Daimai Ryuun 大米龍雲 to death, for having raped, robbed, and killed multiple victims between 1905 and 1915.[14] In Korea, on September 19, 2010, the Seoul Central District Court sentenced a Korean Buddhist monk, whose surname was Hong, to six months in jail for threatening to kill Japan's ambassador to South Korea, Toshinori Shigeie.[15] This court subsequently delayed the start of Hong's sentence for one year. In China, monk killers face fines and jail time. On October 10, 2021, the Intermediate People's Court in Ningbo, Zhejiang Province, convicted a seventy-six-year-old Buddhist monk, with the surname Wang, who was also the abbot of an unspecified Chan Buddhist monastery in Zhejiang Province, of manslaughter in the death of a woman with whom he had been maintaining a romantic relationship since April 25, 2018. This monk received a sentence of six years in prison and a fine of 900,000 yuan to be paid to the victim's family.[16]

In Southeast Asia, criminal monks and nuns have faced similar treatments in court. In Sri Lanka, on July 6, 1962, the Buddhist monk Talduwe Somarama was hanged for assassinating the Sri Lankan prime minister. This monk assassin seemed to have struggled with his religious identity in the court. When he was attending his court trial, he did not wear his monastic robe. Two weeks before his execution, he gave up his status as an ordained Buddhist monk. Two days before his execution, an Anglican priest baptized him a Christian.[17] In another Sri Lankan case, on February 21, 2012, the Tangalle High Court sentenced the thirty-seven-year-old Buddhist monk Gomadiye Sarana to death for having stabbed and killed a layperson named Makumburage Dharmadasa, on January 10, 2000, prior to the killer's ordination. The high court judge asked the killer to remove his robe prior to receiving his judgment during the trial, but the killer refused.[18] In Thailand, arrests of ordained Buddhist monks have become increasingly common. In October 2018, the criminal court in Bangkok convicted the already jailed Buddhist monk Wirapol Sukphol of two additional crimes of kidnapping and sexually abusing children, increasing his sentence from 114 years to 130 years in prison.[19] On June 15, 2020, Thai police arrested the fifty-seven-year-old Buddhist monk Phra Um Deeruenrom, the abbot of Wat Ban Nong Bua in Thailand, who stabbed and killed his ex-girlfriend, a married woman who was eight-months pregnant.[20] In Myanmar, the forty-two-year-old monk Tun Naing Win was detained and charged with murder for stabbing and killing Ko Zaw, a Muslim teenager, on June 18, 2020.[21]

The Chinese Buddhist proposal to try and prosecute Buddhist clerics is also connected to the rest of Asia through regional agencies that oversee religious affairs in the respective central governments. Two agencies deal with Buddhist affairs in most Asian countries. One is located within central government departments that oversee their respective countries' religious affairs; the other is a national organization staffed with ordained Buddhists who handle Buddhist affairs. In contemporary China, these two agencies are the State Administration of Religious Affairs and the Buddhist Association of China. In the rest of Asia, we find the equivalents of the first one in the Japan's Religious Division within the Agency for Cultural Affairs; South Korea's Religious Affairs Office within the Ministry of Culture, Sports, and Tourism; Thailand's National Office of Buddhism; Sri Lanka's Department of Buddhist Affairs in the Ministry of Buddhasasana and Religious and Cultural Affairs; and Myanmar's Department of the Promotion and Propagation of Sāsana in the Ministry of Religious Affairs and Culture.

The messiness starts with the presence of the second agency, a national organization dedicated to the supervision and management of Buddhists and Buddhist affairs that is staffed by ordained or lay Buddhists. In China, the Buddhist Association of China plays this role. Other organizations that play similar roles include the Japan Buddhist Federation; the Korea Buddhist Federation; the Saṃgha Supreme Council, in Thailand; and the Supreme Council of Abbots, in Myanmar.[22] Sri Lanka, however, lacks such a national organization. Nevertheless, this absence does not indicate a lack of organization. Instead, in Sri Lanka, multiple organizations for Buddhist groups have been formed through alliances based on denomination, region, gender, or age.

Southeast Asia also stands in startling contrast to East Asia for its ability to establish and maintain full-fledged monastic courts, which East Asia lacks even today. Thailand, Sri Lanka, and Myanmar have all established functional Buddhist monastic courts that adjudicate and impose decisions on disputes involving Buddhist practitioners or Buddhism, but only the monastic courts in Myanmar and Thailand have support from the state to enforce monastic court judgments.[23]

The establishment of Buddhist monastic courts in Myanmar was a winding journey that began in 1949, when Buddhists successfully lobbied the Burmese government to legislate the *Buddhist Court Case Act* (*Vinicchaya Act*).[24] This law was later rescinded after the military coup of 1962. In 1965, Buddhists appealed to have the *Buddhist Court Case Act* reinstated and offered a compromise that would limit the Buddhist establishment's jurisdiction to matters only over Buddhist monastic law within each Buddhist order's monastic lineage. This compromise still failed to secure the establishment of monastic courts. Having a monastic court only became possible after the government and compliant senior monks in the country collaborated to establish the Supreme Council of Abbots in 1980. Since then, the supreme council established the Buddhist monastic courts and these coexisted with the state's criminal and civil courts as the country's three major judicial venues. This Buddhist monastic court's jurisdiction is limited to adjudicating disputes over religious matters, and to civil or criminal cases involving religious matters.

What differentiates these Buddhist monastic courts from traditional state courts is that instead of having fixed venues and relatively stable judges, Buddhist monastic courts, such as those in Myanmar, are often temporary, ad hoc compositions entailing different judges, depending on the cases they are assigned to adjudicate. In Myanmar, a five-monk committee from the State Supreme Council of Abbots decides and appoints monk judges for specific temporary courts.[25] These monk judges must come from a pool of three hundred monks who are permanent members of the State Central Saṃgha Executive Committee.

In Sri Lanka, the Buddhist monastic courts operate similarly, with one significant difference: it is more challenging to enforce rulings that come from the monastic courts, compared to those from the state court, because the country's state court system does not officially recognize these rulings as enforceable. For example, in the Rāmañña Buddhist Order, Sri Lanka's youngest but "second-largest unitary monastic fraternity" among the island's three major Buddhist schools,[26] full-fledged Buddhist monastic courts exist on three levels: the regional court, the high court, and the supreme court. Fifty monk judges staff the regional courts, and three senior monk judges staff the high courts. The supreme court is the final venue for appeals; it is staffed by twelve senior monks, a judicial chief, and a chief judicial registrar. In practice, this system still encourages litigants to seek mediation first and then a trial within their monastery before launching an official lawsuit in the regional monastic court. Even though the Sri Lankan government tolerates the existence of these Buddhist monastic courts, judges in the state court "do not treat the decisions given by Buddhist monastic judges as authoritative sources of law or as legally binding precedents that state courts are obliged to follow."[27] However, some of these state court judges do treat decisions made by monk judges in the monastic court "as important evidence or advisory opinions" when formulating their own judgments.[28]

Beyond Buddhism

Immunity from facing trials and penalties in the state court has been a desirable clerical privilege for religious establishments around the globe. When juxtaposed with the handling of similar issues in the Christian tradition, the Buddhist fight for clerical legal privileges enhances an increasingly important dialogue on law and religion in the wider context of world religions. Having Buddhism as an interlocutor in this dialogue allows us to decentralize the existing Eurocentric understanding of the relationship between religion and the state based on the Christian tradition as the norm.

The Buddhist campaign paralleled, but differed from, similar ones in the Christian context. Both Buddhists and Christians have discouraged adherents from litigating in state court.[29] However, they have had completely different priorities and have sought different degrees of immunity. Buddhists were primarily interested in monks and nuns having complete immunity from facing penalties adjudicated in the state court, but they offered a compromise on clerical defendants' obligations to appear in the state court—if a lay judge had requested that they appear there, then they were obliged to obey. Christians, on the contrary, defended the trial venue but compromised on the penalty. They insisted on a cleric's right to be tried in the ecclesiastical court and resisted considering capital punishment but compromised by accepting alternative forms of punishment. Christian offenders who had successfully claimed the benefit of clergy still faced property forfeitures, degradation from orders, relegation to a monastery, whippings, brandings, serving time in correction houses, and later, being transported to America.[30]

Buddhists and Christians took different approaches to regulating access to clerical privileges. Buddhists controlled access to these privileges more tightly. They only extended clerical immunity from punishment to ordained Buddhist convicts, thereby excluding even practicing lay Buddhists. To be eligible for sanctuary in a Buddhist institution, a lay fugitive must first have been officially ordained into the monastic order. These restrictions limited the beneficiaries of Buddhist clerical legal privileges to a much smaller pool of novice monks and nuns, probationary nuns, and fully ordained monks and nuns.[31]

In Christianity, the pool of eligible claimants was much larger and changed over time. Christian churches opened their doors of sanctuary to anyone identifying or willing to self-identify as Christian. Initially in England, only ordained clerks and monks could claim "the benefit of clergy."[32] In 1350, the English King Edward III (1312–1377; reign 1327–1377) relaxed this requirement, in an ordinance for the clergy that expanded the benefit of clergy to "all manner of clerks as well as secular religious," which Cross interpreted to include all who could read.[33] In legal practice, offenders who claimed the benefit of clergy during this time were often only required to read, usually a verse from Psalm 51, to prove their literacy. When the literacy rate improved in society, the rule changed again, limiting nonclerical Christians to claiming the benefit of clergy only once in a lifetime. Ordained clerks, though, could still make this claim as many times as they needed.[34] On February 14, 1707, during the sixth year of her reign, Queen Anne (1665–1714, reign 1702–1707) officially abandoned the reading test as a requirement for claiming the benefit of clergy.[35]

Beneath the control over access to clerical legal privileges lay different Buddhist and Christian perceptions about the jurisdictional boundary between the clergy and the state. Buddhists and Christians pursued different levels of jurisdictional autonomy. Christians aimed at comprehensive jurisdictional autonomy over all religious affairs and all individuals who self-identified as Christians. They were interested in having jurisdiction over ordained clergy and monastics as well as over lay Christians in disputes over religious matters. During Anglo-Saxon times, from the fifth to the eleventh centuries, bishops and sheriffs cooperated in trying civil and criminal cases in local English courts.[36]

Buddhists were not nearly as ambitious. In ancient India, they showed no intention of advocating for Buddhist monks or nuns to participate in the operations of the state's legal system. They only envisioned a modest jurisdiction for the Buddhist clergy. Unlike English Christians who had aggressively tried to seize power over religious matters in and beyond the ecclesiastic courts, the Buddhist establishment in ancient India appeared to be obedient, submissive, courteous, and extremely careful about avoiding upsetting state rulers. In return, these Buddhists expected the state rulers in India to be reciprocally considerate, courteous, and willing to temporarily concede part of their jurisdiction over certain clerical cases that called for the death penalty.

Lastly, Buddhists and Christians sought to achieve different goals through clerical legal privileges. Buddhists sought clerical immunity from facing trials and penalties in the state court primarily to protect the Buddhist establishment's jurisdiction over its ordained members. However, for Christians, the introduction of the benefit of clergy and its implementation in England fulfilled a significantly different role. Through examinations of criminal cases in England, Cross notices that applications of the benefit of clergy in England's legal practices aided in correcting inadequacies in its legal system. Specifically, in the eighteenth and early nineteenth centuries, offenders of minor crimes could have faced capital punishment. Granting the benefit of clergy thus allowed judges to avoid using the death penalty for offenders of minor crimes and, instead, impose penalties adequate to these offenses.[37]

These contrasts between how Buddhists and Christians handled their legal relationships with the state are crucial for unpacking and correcting Orientalist assumptions about Buddhism's "lawlessness."[38] In the Christian tradition, the battle between church and state centered around redistributing legal power from the church to the king. Buddhists had a different agenda in that they struggled to survive in ancient India's legally and religiously pluralistic society. Buddhists there envisioned a submissive and reciprocally courteous and cooperative approach that was key to Buddhism's very survival. Unfortunately, the legally and religiously Orientalist discourse labeled this Buddhist approach as "lawlessness." This book shows that despite adopting a less aggressive strategy to settle jurisdictional boundaries with the state, the Buddhist establishment was not only interested in creating and implementing a Buddhist monastic law for internal governance; it was also legally ambitious and strategic about securing legal privileges and jurisdictional autonomy in its interactions with the state.

Notes

Introduction

1. For the original reference in Chinese, see Shi and Luo 2005: 79.
2. For Lu Da's killing of the butcher and his ordination in the Buddhist monastery, see Shi and Luo 2005: 40–72.
3. Chapters 6 and 7 show how new forms of the hybrid court continued to be functional in contemporary China. Recently, I reviewed an excellent article titled "The Hybrid Court at Work: The Local Practice of the Buddhist Office in Qing China," for the journal *Buddhism, Law & Society*. Examining clerical legal cases from the Baxian County Archive in Sichuan, this article reveals that lay people frequently used the hybrid court to press charges against ordained Buddhist monks and nuns in Qing China.
4. The data comes from the Pew Research Center and is cited for general reference. See "Global Religious Landscape: Buddhists."
5. For an excellent overview of the history of the sanctuary institution, see chapter 3 in Rabben 2016.
6. See Baker 1971: 585.
7. See Rabben 2016: 39–40.
8. Title 13 in this code says: "Persons who flee for sanctuary to the churches shall be safe within fifty paces outside the doors. Unrestricted entrance shall be available to a bishop who is visiting prisons." See Pharr 1952: 483.
9. See Rabben 2016: 43.
10. See Rabben 2016: 53.
11. For an overview of the history of the Sanctuary movement in the US, see González 2020; Chinchilla, Hamilton, and Loucky 2009. The Sanctuary movement was also the subject of a notable dissertation. See Matters 1994.
12. See Rabben 2016: 39–40.
13. See Rabben 2016: 39–40.
14. See Rabben 2016: 39–40.
15. Rabben 2016: 52.
16. Rabben 2016: 52.
17. For a general study on Catholic canon law's influence on the church's ecclesiastical jurisdiction, see Helmholz 2004.
18. A bishop's court refers to *episcopalis audientia*. Sirks suggests interpreting it not as a court with a judge but as "a place for mediation and reconciliation." See Sirks 2013: 88. For a detailed discussion of the recognition of clerical exemption in Catholic Canon law, see Duggan 2007.

19. On this conflict between King Henry II and Becket, see Cheney 1936; Dunggan 1962; and Fraher 1978.
20. For a historical study on the benefit of clergy, see Gabel 1969; Poole 1933. For a discussion on the concept of clerical immunity, see Downs 1941. For an additional discussion on clerical immunity in France, see Campbell 1964.
21. In this letter, King Henry II wrote, "We have conceded . . . that a clerk shall not in future be brought in his own person before a secular judge for any criminal matter, nor concerning any wrong, except a wrong of my forest, and except lay fee whence lay service is owed to me or another secular lord." Ralph de Diceto (c. 1120–c. 1202) recorded this letter in his chronicle *Ymagines historiarum*. For the text, see Stubbs 1876: vol. 1, 410. The English translation of the quotation cited above is from Duggan 2007: 89.
22. For a discussion on the development of the benefit of clergy in England until its elimination in 1827, see Cross 1917.
23. Dalzell 1955: 45.
24. Dalzell 1955: 266. For a discussion on the status of clerical immunity in the US, see Stewart 2008.
25. See discussion in Chapters 2 and 3.
26. See discussion in Chapter 4.
27. For example, an early-Tang mural painting in Dunhuang on the south wall of Mogao Cave 321 depicts the story of a white elephant king who refuses to harm the hunters disguised as monks, even though they were trying to kill him.
28. See the discussion of the Buddhist monks Xuanwan and Xuanzang's petitions in Chapter 5 in the section on "Hybrid Law".
29. See Granoff 2018.
30. For the edited volume, see French and Nathan 2014. The first English academic journal dedicated to the study of Buddhism and law, *Buddhism, Law & Society*, was established in 2015. In 2021, Tom Ginsburg and Benjamin Schonthal organized a series of workshops on "Buddhism and Comparative Law," which attracted an international assembly of thirty scholars from law, religious studies, history, anthropology, politics, and regional studies. For papers that resulted from these workshops, see Ginsburg and Schonthal 2022.
31. See Clarke 2014b.
32. See Oldenburg 1879; Oldenburg 1880; Oldenburg 1881; Oldenburg 1882; Oldenburg1883.
33. See Horner 1938; Horner 1940; Horner 1942; Horner 1951; Horner 1952; Horner 1966.
34. See Roth 1970; Hirakawa 1982; Prebish 1975; Prebish 1996; Wang 2007; Karma Lekshe Tsomo 1996; Heirman 2002.
35. See Clarke 2014a; Schopen 1997; Schopen 2004; Schopen 2005; Schopen 2014.
36. See Ruskola 2013: 4.
37. See French and Nathan 2014: 14.
38. Witte 2012:335.
39. For this interim report, see Witte 2012. An earlier literature review on law and religion from Vogel provides a detailed description on the development of law and religion as

a field in the US, starting in the 1970s, highlighting the contribution of scholars such as Harold J. Berman, who had worked and written tirelessly on the importance of studying the interaction between law and religion. See Vogel 1983. A third literature review by Sullivan and Yelle provides a detailed overview of the history of the separation between law and religion. See Sullivan and Yelle 2005.

40. For example, see Schonthal 2016; Ashin and Crosby 2017; Lammerts 2018; Wallace 2015; and Jansen 2018.
41. For a discussion on the hybrid court, see Chapter 5.
42. See Nattier 1992: 195–96.
43. Zürcher 2007: xi.
44. For example, Zhang Haifeng's *Law and Buddhism in the Tang Dynasty* discusses how Buddhist legal ideas and literary traditions influenced the development of the legal culture in the Tang dynasty (618–907). See Zhang 2014. In the last quarter of this book, Zhang Haifeng also discusses how the Tang imposed rules over the Buddhist establishment's administration, criminal offenses, and economic engagement. Another major book in this direction is Zhang Jingzhen's *The Administration of Buddhism during the Sui and Tang from a Legal Perspective*. See Zhang 2018. This book discusses Buddhism's influence on the legal culture during the Tang and Tang law's regulation of Buddhism. As a major departure, half of this 2018 publication focuses on the historical development, reconstruction, and interpretation of the *Regulations on Daoists and Buddhists* (*Daoseng ge* 道僧格), which is a legal text containing state rules on penalties for ordained Buddhists and Daoists for misbehavior. First promulgated in Tang China, these rules are no longer extant in Chinese. They have survived in Japanese as *Statutes on Monks and Nuns* (*Sōni ryō* 僧尼令) and were promulgated in Japan in 701 as part of the *Taihō Code* (*Taihō ritsuryō* 大宝律令). For a general discussion on how the Chinese concept of law is influenced by Confucianism, Legalism, and Buddhism, see Lee and Lai 1978. See also Yang 2008.
45. For a recent survey of extant Vinaya texts and manuscripts in various Indic and East- and Central-Asian languages, see Liu and Andrews 2017: 1–16.
46. Ideally, this requires a thorough examination of legal cases involving ordained Buddhist monks and nuns in different periods in China from the fourth century to the present. In this book, I choose to analyze two types of cases in contemporary China to see if the historical negotiations over jurisdictional boundaries have been respected in legal practices due to restraint of time and space. Fortunately, scholars working on other historical periods have begun to publish excellent studies on this subject. For instance, for a series of studies on cases involving Buddhist monks and nuns at the various state court, hybrid court, and community meetings recorded in the Baxian County Archive in the nineteenth century, see Chen 2019; Chen 2022.
47. The cases cited in the Buddhist monastic law texts can be of different natures: some are cases that describe offenses that occurred in the present, some are cases that describe offenses that occurred in people's previous lives, and some are hypothetical cases that may happen in the future.
48. See Clarke 2021 for a detailed discussion on how the *Mūlasarvāstivāda Vinaya* presented six cases without having established a rule on the killing of a human being.

49. For instance, the section in the *Mūlasarvāstivāda Vinaya* that discusses murder recounts the story of the Buddhist nun Yuanman who accidentally killed sixty thieves by offering them vinegar to drink. When other nuns informed her that all the sixty thieves died after drinking the vinegar she gave them, the nun Yuanman doubted them, saying, "Isn't it true that I have committed an offense of defeat (*jiang fei wo fan tasheng zui ye* 將非我犯他勝罪耶)?" See T1442: 665b22–b23.
50. Apart from ordained Buddhists, there are also lay Buddhist men (Skt. *upāsaka*; Tib. *dge bsnyen*; Ch. *jushi* 居士, *youpo sai* 优婆塞) and women (Skt. *upāsikā*; Tib. *dge bsnyen ma*; Ch. *jushi* 居士, *youpo yi* 优婆夷).
51. Apart from the offense of defeat and rules for probationary offenses, which I will introduce in detail below, there are also rules whose violation requires the forfeiture of the improperly acquired goods and a public confession (Skt. *naiḥsargika pāyantika*); rules whose violation requires expiation (Skt. *pāyantika*); rules whose violation requires disclosure to others (Skt. *pratideśanīya*); rules on the qualities to be learned (Skt. *śaiksa*) and whose violation results in being accused of wrongdoing (Skt. *duṣkṛta*), which I will discuss shortly below; and the seven rules on settling disputes (Skt. *saptādhikaraṇasamatha*). For monks, there is an extra category of two rules of uncertainty (Skt. *aniyata*) regarding a monk's interaction with women in a nonpublic area—an act that may lead to two different offenses.
52. For a nun, there are four additional acts that could lead to an offense of defeat: touching a man, failing to observe the eight rules of respect (Skt. *gurudharma*), concealing the offenses of others, and providing robes, alms bowls, and other necessities to a nun who is under discipline.
53. In the *Pāli Vinaya,* this term "not in communion" is discussed in the section explaining the offense of defeat: stealing. For an English translation of the discussion, see Horner 1938: vol. 1, 128.
54. See T1443: 918c5–c8. A similar explanation is found in the section on the first offense of defeat for monks: sex. T1442: 630c11–c15.
55. The fortnightly retreat (Skt. *poṣadha*; Tib. *gso sbyong*; Ch. *baosa tuo* 褒灑陀, *busa* 布薩) refers to a "semimonthly ceremony (observed on the new and full moon) in which monks and nuns are to assemble within a specific boundary to recite the monastic rules of conduct" set out in the versified version of the Buddhist monastic law known as the *Prātimokṣa*. For further explanations of this term, see Buswell and Lopez 2014: 943.
56. The term is translated in Chinese as *suiyi shi* 隨意事 or *zizi* 自恣 and in Tibetan as *dgag dbye*. They both correspond to the Sanskrit term *pravārṇā*. This refers to a ritual held at a retreat at the end of the summer rainy season, when resident monks invite others to "point out any wrongs he may have committed that were either seen, heard, or suspected." For further explanation of this term, see Buswell and Lopez 2014: 674. There is a Chinese translation of a collection of rules concerning the *pravārṇr* ritual in T1446.
57. In the Chinese translation, this is translated as *danbai* 單白, "single announcement." The Tibetan translation for this term, in the corresponding passage mentioned above,

is *gsol ba'i las*. This term is explained as *gsol ba zhu ba lan gcig*, "a one-time request" for the monastic rule to become a novice monk or nun, in Zhang 2004: vol. 2, 3034.

58. This is translated as *bai'er* 白二 in Chinese. For its interpretation in Tibetan as *gsol ba dang gnyis kyi las*, see Zhang 2004: vol. 2, 3034.
59. Heirman interprets this phrase (Skt. *jñapticaturtha-karman*; Tib. *gsol ba dang bzhi'i las*; Ch. *baisi jiemo* 白四羯磨) as "a formal act consisting of one motion (*jñapti*), three propositions (*karmavācanā*), and a conclusion." See Heirman 2008: 114n39.
60. Note that in the section discussing the offense of defeat against sex in the *Sarvāstivāda Vinaya*, the explanation on this term mentions that the punishment for "not in communion" include prohibiting fourteen types of persons from attending ecclesiastical proceedings. See T1435: 2c18–c21. The text provides the same explanation on "not in communion" in the section commenting on the terms for the second offense of defeat, stealing, see T1435: 4b14–b16. In another text from the same Sarvāstivāda tradition (T1458) translated by Yijing, we find a commentary on the fourteen types of persons as the fourteen types of persons that should not be scolded. See T1458: 573c25–574a8.
61. See T 1442: 630c11–c15.
62. Note that in this explanation, the list of prohibitions included prohibiting those who had committed the offense of defeat from sharing "religious food" and "tasty food." These may be referring to the spiritual food of the Buddha's teaching and edible tasty food. We also find a similar explanation in the Tibetan translation of the *Mūlasarvāstivāda Vinaya*, on the same offense of defeat 1 on sex for monks, see *'Dul ba rnam par 'byed pa, Bka' 'gyur*, vol. 5, 92: "*gnas par mi bya ba'o zhes bya ba ni dge slong rnams kyis de dang gso sbyong dang / dgag dbye dang / gsol ba dang / gsol ba dang gnyis dang / gsol ba dang bzhi'i las la gnas par mi bya'o / gang zag bcu gnyis po dag tu bsko bas mi bya ba ste / de na gnas par mi bya'o zhes gsungs so.*" This Tibetan translation does not mention "religious food" or "tasty food."
63. This text does not provide an explanation for "not in communion" in the sections discussing the first three offenses of defeat—sex, killing, and stealing—for monks. But in the section discussing the offense of defeat for nuns who have had bodily contact with men, it provides an explanation of "not in communion." See T1425: 515c9–c11. In the *Sarvāstivāda Vinaya*, in the section on the offense of defeat 1 on sex, we find an explanation of "not in communion" in the section providing a word-for-word commentary. See T1435: 2c18–c21. The text repeats the same elaboration on "not in communion" in the section commenting on the terms for the offense of defeat on stealing. See T1435: 4b14–b16.
64. See the explanation for "not in communion" in the word-for-word commentary in the section discussing the first offense of defeat, sex, in the *Mahīśāsaka Vinaya*. T1421: 4c23–c26.
65. For instance, in the *Dharmaguptaka Vinaya*, a convicted offender of the offense of defeat will lose the privilege of participating in two communal activities: attending ecclesiastical proceedings (*jiemo* 羯磨) and the fortnightly retreat to recite the monastic rules (*shuo jie* 說戒). The text states, "What does 'not in communion' mean? There are two communions: to attend the ecclesiastical proceedings together and to attend the fortnightly retreat together. Because [one who has committed the offense of defeat] is

not permitted to attend those two activities, it is called 'not in communion.'" For the original Chinese translation, see T1428: 571c8–c10.

66. In all but the Pāli Vinaya traditions, these offenders were given a penitent (Skt. *śikṣkdattaka*; Tib. *bslab pa byin pa*; Ch. *yuxue* 與學) status. For a detailed study on this reduced penitent status of monks who had committed the offense of defeat, see Clarke 2009a. Buswell and Lopez interpret the term *asaṃvāsa* as follows: "The monk who is *asaṃvāsa* is not permitted to participate in any of the official monastic proceedings or ecclesiastical acts (*karman*): thus, he is effectively ostracized from the formal activities of the monastery. Although this term has sometimes been interpreted as 'expulsion,' *asaṃvāsa* does not necessarily mean that the monk is banished from the monastery but simply that he is "no longer in communion" with the work, rules, and training of the monastic community as a whole. Indeed, there is evidence from virtually all recensions of the Vinaya (except the Pāli recension of the Theravāda school), that *pārājika* monks continued to live in the monastery even after their transgressions, under the special status of *pārājika* penitents (*śikṣkdattaka*)." See Buswell and Lopez 2014: 69.
67. See T1425: 257c3–c5.
68. Clarke discusses this exception and considers this exception to be comparable to *nullum crimen*. See Clarke 2021: 16–17. The full term, *nullum crimen sine lege*, "no crime without law," refers to a legal principle prevents the conviction of a person does something before a law is established to prohibit that act. See Garner 2019: 1286. In the US criminal law system, it is comparable to a "case of first impression." It is important to note that in the US legal system, a judge can legally convict the offender in a case of first impression. For further explanation on the case of first impression, see Garner 2019: 266.
69. In the *Pāli Vinaya*, the text says that "there is no offense if it was unintentional, if he did not know, if he were not meaning [to cause a] death, if he was out of his mind, a beginner." See Horner 1938: vol. 1, 136.
70. See T1421: 9a9-a10. Note that in the *Mahīśāsaka Vinaya*, at the end of the section discussing the offense of defeat on sex, it says T1421: 5a27-a28: 不犯者。狂心亂心病壞心初作。此四種不犯。下一切諸戒皆如是. This seems to suggest that the four circumstances in which an offender can't be convict of the offense of defeat is applicable to all the subsequent offense of defeat cases.
71. In the *Mahāsāṃghika Vinaya*, a killer will not be convicted of the offense of defeat for killing a human being if the killer is "wild, mad, or mentally disturbed (狂癡心亂)." See T1425: 257c7-c8.
72. For a list of circumstances in which the killer will not be committing an offense of defeat after having caused someone else to die, see T1428: 577b6-b12. Note that in most of the circumstances on this list, the lack of intention to kill will cause it insufficient to convict the killer of murder.
73. For a list of exemptions in the *Mūlasarvāstivāda Vinaya*, see T1442: 668c10-c11. Note that here this text included an additional situation when someone killed another person before a rule prohibiting such killing was established.
74. The *Sarvāstivāda Vinaya* mentions none of the two "no-offense (不犯)" exceptions.

75. Here, I adopt the English translation for *saṃghāvaśeṣa* provided in Buswell and Lopez 2014: 752.
76. The following description of the redemption of an offender for having committed a probationary offense is based on instructions provided in the various *Prātimokṣa* texts. Additionally, in the *Dharmaguptaka Vinaya* and the *Sarvāstivāda Vinaya*, we also find instructions on what to do with an offender who commits a probationary offense. In the *Dharmaguptaka Vinaya*, we find a detailed description on what to do with a monk who had committed a probationary offense. If a monk had concealed his probationary offense, then he was to first request a penance for having concealed the offense (*fucang jiemo* 覆藏羯磨). If he committed the offense again during this period, then he was to start his penance over again. After having completed his penance, the offender could then request a six-night *mānatva* penance. If he repeated the offense again during this step, he would have to request a *mānatva* penance without repeating the penance of living separately from other monks (*monachui benrizhi jiemo* 摩那埵本日治羯磨). Once this step was completed, next, he could request an ecclesiastical proceeding to allow him to exit the penance (*chuzui jiemo* 出罪羯磨) If a monk had not concealed his offense, he could directly request a six-night *mānatva* penance. If he repeated the offense during this period, he would have to request a *mānatva* penance without having to repeat the penance of living separately from other monks. Once this step was completed, the offender could request an ecclesiastical procedure consisting of one announcement and three confirmations to exit from the penance (baisi jiemo chuzui 白四羯磨出罪). See T1428: 896b25-903c20. In the *Sarvāstivāda Vinaya*, if the offender had not concealed the offense, they could perform the six-night *mānatva* penance then request to exit from the penance (*chuzui*出罪). If the offender committed the offense again, the offender was to perform the six-night *mānatva* without repeating the first step (*monachui benrizhi* 摩那埵本日治), and then request to exit from the penance. If the offender had concealed their offense, they were to perform the first step of living separately for as many days as the offense had been concealed. Next, the offender could perform the six-night *mānatva* penance. After that, the offender could ask to exit the penance. See T1435: 232c7-c10.
77. These three steps are discussed at the end of the section discussing probationary offense 1, in the *Pāli Vinaya*: *parivāsa* (probation), *mānatta*, and *āvarhaṇa* (rehabilitation). See Horner 1938: vol. 1,196-197. In the *Mūlasarvāstivāda Vinaya*, at the end of the section discussing the 13 probationary offenses, the four-step penance is required. See *'Dul ba rnam par 'byed pa*, vol. 6, 76-77; and T1442: 710a15-a23.
78. For further explanation on the term *parivāsa*, see Buswell and Lopez 2014: 631.
79. Many of these texts mention performing this step for six days and six nights, see T1426: 550c16-c17; T1436: 472b8; T1422: 195c27-c28; T1429: 1016c26-c27; T1454:502b1; T1455: 510b25. An exception is found in T1455 and T1423, where the text states that this step should last "half a month." See T1423: 208b23 and T1455: 510b25.
80. For an explanation of this term, see T2788: 621c18-c19.
81. This step is known as *āpattivyutthānam* or *āvāhana* in Sanskrit, *dbyung ba* in Tibetan, and is transliterated as *afuhena* 阿浮訶那 or translated as *chuzu*i 出罪 in

Chinese. Note that this step is absent in the *Mūlasarvāstivāda Vinaya* but is found in the *Mahāsāṃghika Vinaya* (several references), the *Dharmaguptaka Vinaya* (two references), the *Mahīśāsaka Vinaya* (several references), and the *Sarvāstivāda Vinaya* (once). Discussions on this step are found in the *Prātimokṣa* texts (*jieben* 戒本), rules of the Vinaya that are compiled in verses, for monks in the *Sarvāstivāda Vinaya*, for both monks and nuns in the *Mahīśāsaka Vinaya*, and for nuns in the *Mahāsāṃghika Vinaya*. See T1436:472b9; T1427: 558b12; T1422: 195c28; T1423: 208b23-b24. The same rules, however, are not found in the other *Prātimokṣa* texts for monks and/or nuns in the other Vinaya traditions. In the *Dharmaguptaka Vinaya* and the *Sarvāstivāda Vinaya*, in the sections discussing what to do with those who had committed an offense while on probation, this step is described as *chuzui jiemo* 出罪羯磨, the ecclesiastical proceeding for exiting the penance. In the *Sarvāstivāda Vinaya* in this section, it only mentions *chuzui* 出罪, but does not mention *afu hena* 阿浮訶那. In the *Mūlasarvāstivāda Vinaya* at the end of the section on probationary offense 13, the term for the existing penance period is *chuzui* 出罪. See T1442: 710a19. Soothill and Hodous 1937: 289 interprets this term as "the calling of a monk or nun into the assembly for penance, or to rid the delinquent of sin." For a further explanation this term in Chinese Vinaya texts, see T2788: 621c22-c29; T1462: 770c11-c15.

82. Note that a nun who committed a probationary offense during probation would have to publicly confess the offense in front of twenty persons twice, once in front of the monks, once in front of the nuns. See T1427: 558b12-b13; T1423: 208b24-b25; T1455: 510b27-b28; T1431:1033b23-b24.
83. For descriptions of the following types of penance in the different *Prātimokṣa* texts for nuns from different Vinaya traditions, see T1423: 208b22-b25; T1427: 558b11-b17; T1431: 1033b21-b26; T1437: 481b22-b26; T1455: 510b24-c1.
84. Among the five Chinese translations of the *Prātimokṣa* texts, only the *Prātimokṣa* texts for nuns in the *Mūlasarvāstivāda Vinaya* states that a penance is imposed on nuns who had concealed the probationary offenses, see T1455: 510b25. The other *Prātimokṣa* texts for nuns do not indicate whether this is a penance for nuns who had tried to conceal their transgressions. Clarke 2002: 387 also notes the two-week *mānatva* penance for nuns convicted of a probationary offense; he notes that these *Prātimokṣa* texts also lack the punishment of probation (*beizhu*別住) for nun offenders for having committed a probationary offense.
85. For a full list of these six circumstances, see Clarke 2002: 392.
86. For a discussion on this penance, see Clarke 2002: 393-395.
87. See T1463: 843a9-843a17.
88. For reference to this method of penance, see T1462: 733c18-c24.
89. In the *Pāli Vinaya*, in the section discussing offense of defeat 2 on taking what is not given, the text differentiates between three types of violations related to taking what is not given: *pārājika, thullaccaya*, and *dukkata*. See Horner 1938: vol. 1, 76-77. In the Chinese translations of the offense of defeat 2 on taking what is not given, the texts mention three levels of transgressions in this category: *boluoyi* 波羅夷, *toulanzhe* 偷蘭遮, and *tujiluo* 突吉羅 in the *Mahīśāsaka*, *Dharmaguptaka*, and *Sarvāstivāda Vinaya* texts. They correspond to *pārājika*, *sthūlātyaya*, and *duṣkṛta*. In

the *Mahāsāṃghika Vinaya* and the *Mūlasarvāstivāda Vinaya*, these texts split *duṣkṛta* into two further subcategories. In the *Mahāsāṃghika Vinaya*, it became *yuebini* 越比尼 and *yuebini xinhui* 越比尼心悔. See T1425:237c2-c3. In the Chinese and Tibetan *Mūlasarvāstivāda Vinaya*, we see a differentiation between *boluoyi* 波羅夷/*pham pa*, *sutu luodi* 窣吐羅底/*nyes pa sbom po*, *ezuo* 惡作/*nyes bya*, and *yuefa zui* 越法罪/*'gal tshabs can*. There, in these texts, *duṣkṛta* is split into *ezuo* 惡作/*nyes byas* and *yuefa zui* 越法罪/*'gal tshabs can*. Note that Hirakawa identifies the original Sanskrit expressions for *yuebini* 越比尼 as *deśanā-gami-vinayātikrama*, an offense which requires the offender to reflect on it and confess it to another person, and *yuebini xinhui* 越比尼心悔 as *saṃvara-gāmi-vinayātikrama*, an offense that only requires the offender to repent to herself. Both expressions were translated as "a light infringement of the Vinaya rules," see Hirakawa 1982: note 10, 105-106.

90. See 1463: 849b19: 心念懺悔即除. Note that the author of *Lüjie benshu* 律戒本疏 considers requiring the offender to confess to others for a *duṣkṛta* offense, but the offender who had committed the *śaiksa* offense could privately confess to themselves. See T2788: 639a17-a21.

Chapter 1

1. See T1428: 719a20–a23.
2. For Xuanzang's description of Ayodhyā's Buddhist communities, see T2087: 896b4–b12.
3. For the citation of Xuanzang's description, see Supreme Court of India 2019: 690.
4. See Supreme Court of India 2018a and Supreme Court of India 2018b for two judgments regarding the Buddhist man Maurya's writ petition.
5. For example, the Buddha Education Foundation filed similar petitions in the Supreme Court of India in 2003 and 2011. For a record of the 2011 petition, see Supreme Court of India 2011. Menon mentions an earlier petition submitted in 2003, but I am unable to obtain that petition. See Menon 2011.
6. The Archaeological Survey of India (ASI) conducted the early surveys and excavations at Ayodhyā. Its founder, Alexandra Cunningham, conducted the first survey from 1862 to 1863. From 1889 to 1891, the ASI's team, led by Alois Anton Führer, conducted a second survey. The most recent excavation and survey were conducted in 2002. On February 17, 2003, a corporate entity commissioned by the Archaeological Survey of India, under the order from the Allahabad High Court, submitted a report on this excavation. For an analysis of this 2003 report, see Supreme Court of India 2019: 507–99.
7. See Supreme Court of India 2019: 588.
8. Patrick Olivelle identifies two types of judges in ancient India. The first one is the *dharmastha* mentioned in Kauṭilya's *Arthaśāstra*, a treatise on statecraft composed in the mid-first century CE. It refers to "a governmental official" who is "permanently located in villages and towns and responsible for a variety of functions relating to

the maintenance of public order and morals and the resolution of disputes." In other words, this judge's duties included but were not limited to the adjudication of judicial cases. Olivelle further points out that by the first century BCE, "there existed in ancient India a court system where disputes between individuals and between groups such as guilds and villages resulting in lawsuits were recorded." The other one was the *prārvivāka* in the Dharmaśāstra tradition, which mainly "function[ed] solely within the confines of a court and [was] responsible for interrogating witnesses." This judge was delegated to perform judicial functions in the presence of the king. See Olivelle 2016: 305–13.

9. Olivelle 2004: 167.
10. See Olivelle 2004: 167. This requirement that only Brahmins could be appointed as chief judges was also confirmed in the *Bṛhaspati Smṛti*, 1.24, where it is mentioned that only the king or a twice-born could officiate as a chief judge. "Twice-born" refers to three groups of people in the upper castes: the Brahmins, the warriors, and the merchants. See Jolly 1889: 280.
11. See Manu's *Dharmaśāstra*, 8.1, on the court, in Olivelle 2004: 167.
12. See Gautama's *Dharmasūtra*, 11.19–20, on the judicial process, in Olivelle 1999: 97.
13. See Gautama's *Dharmasūtra*, 1.18, on the king, in Olivelle 1999: 159.
14. See Vasiṣṭha's *Dharmasūtra*, 19.40–43, on criminal justice, in Olivelle 1999: 301.
15. See Vasiṣṭha's *Dharmasūtra*, 19.40–43, on criminal justice, in Olivelle 1999: 301.
16. See Gautama's *Dharmasūtra*, 11.19–20, on the judicial process, in Olivelle 1999: 97.
17. See Manu's *Dharmaśāstra*, 8.20–22 on the Śūdras as legal interpreters, in Olivelle 2004: 168.
18. This scenario is clearly illustrated in the *Mūlasarvāstivāda Vinaya* in the section elaborating on the second offense of defeat—taking what had not been given (i.e., stealing)—where the redactors of this legal text considered two forms of land acquisition by ordained Buddhists to be acts of skillful theft (*toudao fangbian* 偷盜方便): by litigating before a judge or by planting trees around land, digging holes in land, or building fences to encircle land. The Tibetan translation mentions only that "there are three things related to land (*sa gzhi ni gsum ste*)." For the Chinese translation of this case, see T1442: 641a10–641a20; for its Tibetan translation, see '*Dul ba rnam par 'byed pa*, vol. 5, 184–85. Note that the Tibetan translation of the *Mūlasarvāstivāda Vinaya* explicitly lays out two possibilities for an ordained Buddhist to resolve a land dispute: through a local head (*'og gzu*) or through an ordained senior monk (*bla grwa*). The Chinese translations of the *Dharmaguptaka Vinaya* and the *Mahāsāṃghika Vinaya* mention seeking adjudication before a lay judge (*duanshi guan* 斷事官, *duanshi ren* 斷事人).
19. In her analysis of religious communities' relationships to the royal court in Indian literature, Granoff examines two cases: one from the *Pāli Vinaya* and one from the Chinese translation of the *Mahāsāaghika Vinaya*. In these, both Buddhist and Jain legal texts prohibit ordained members of their clergies from litigating. See Granoff 2018: 289–310.
20. For further analysis on concerns that state courts were places of injustice, see Granoff 2010: 377–98.

21. See T1435: 108a21–b13. The first case presented in this section elaborates on *pāyantika* rule 58, prohibiting monks from touching silver or gold, and take place while the Buddha is staying in Vaiśālī.
22. T1428: 691b13–692c4. This case is presented in the section elaborating on *pāyantika* rule 82.
23. T1435: 281c15–282a1. This case is presented in the section elaborating on miscellaneous rules.
24. T1435: 116a2–b6. This case appears in the section discussing *pāyantika* rule 71 on travelling with thieves.
25. T1435: 462c5–462c26. This case is presented in the fourth section on karma and cause (*yinyuan pin* 因緣品).
26. T1435: 462c15–c16.
27. T1425:381b6–381c27. This case appears in the section introducing the *pāyantika* rule prohibiting monks from travelling with women. In the *Mūlasarvāstivāda Vinaya*, *pāyantika* rule 70, there is another case regarding monks travelling with woman. In this case, the woman is a weaver's daughter. Her husband is violent and abusive. When she runs away, she meets a monk and travels with him. When the husband finds the monk and his wife, he beats the monk badly and almost kills him, but does not take the monk to the court. See T1442: 852b11–c13.
28. Schopen points out that the *Pāli Vinaya* and the *Mūlasarvāstivāda Vinaya* "have a rule making it a monastic offense for a nun to go to court—to sue—for recovery of debt or property—in both this is a probationary offense and there is no counterpart to it in the rules for monks, suggesting, perhaps, that nuns were thought to be particularly prone to litigation by the compilers of these codes." See Schopen 2012: 595. As I will show below, monks are subject to the same rule.
29. See probationary offense 4 on litigating in T1425: 517c12–518a20. For an English translation of entire case, see Hirakawa 1982: 138–42. For an earlier analysis of this case, see Granoff 2018: 297–98.
30. The following English translation is based on but revised from Hirakawa's translation in Hirakawa 1982: 140–42. To save space, I have omitted the word-by-word commentary on the terms in the middle. For the reference in the Chinese translation, see T1425: 518a8–a20.
31. The term *chuzui sengjia poshisha* 初罪僧伽婆尸沙 refers to one of the two categories of probationary offenses. For violating rules in this category, the offenders' act immediately constitutes a probationary offense. In the other category, the offenders would only be committing a probationary offense if they still refused to give up committing the acts after being admonished three times.
32. The term for this offense *is yuebini* 越比尼. Hirakawa provides its Sanskrit as *deśana gāmi vinayātikrama* and considers it to correspond to *dukkaṭa* in the *Pāli Vinaya*. See Hirakawa 1982: 104–5.
33. The Chinese term for this offense is *yuebini xinhui* 越比尼心悔. Hirakawa provides its Sanskrit as *saṃvara gāmi vinayātikrama* and considers it to correspond to *dubbhāsita* in the *Pāli Vinaya*. See Hirakawa 1982: 104–5.

34. The Taishō version of the *Mahāsāṃghika Vinaya* has Buddhist nun (*biqiuni* 比丘尼), but in four other versions of the Buddhist canon, the term here is Buddhist monk (*biqiu* 比丘. See T1425: 518a19n5. In the context, "Buddhist monk" makes better sense because going to the palace of the king is, as explained above, a heavier probationary offense for Buddhist monks. Hirakawa translates the term here as *bhikṣu*, "Buddhist monk." See Hirakawa 1982: 142.
35. T1428: 718c21–719b06. This case appears in the section elaborating on the probationary offense 4 for Buddhist nuns regarding litigating in the state court. For an English translation of this case, see Heirman 2002: pt. 2, 331–32.
36. The Chinese translation of this text addresses the new occupant as a female non-Buddhist (*nü fanzhi* 女梵志), which the text later explains as referring to a woman who had been ordained in a religious tradition other than Buddhism. For this case, see T1428: 719a26–a27.
37. T1428: 719a2–a3: 世尊制戒。不得詣斷事官相言。
38. T1428: 719a4–a5: 自今已去若有喚應往。
39. The following translation is slightly modified from Heirman 2002: pt. 2, 334–35. To save space, I have chosen not to translate the middle section that provides a word-by-word commentary on the terms. For the original in Chinese, see T1428: 719a20–b6.
40. For an explanation on the term *chufa* (初法), see *chuzui* (初罪) in Endnote 33 in this chapter.
41. T1435: 309a14–309c5.
42. T1435: 309a29–b1.
43. This Chinese translation transliterated her name as Xiumuqu 修目佉.
44. The penalty of cutting off the offender's hand that was used to perform the assault complies with the Indian Dharmaśāstra law. Manu ruled that for physically assaulting another person, the punishment entailed cutting off the limb the assailant had used in the assault. For an English translation of this article, see Olivelle 2005: 182. For a discussion on bodily punishment in India, see Olivelle 2011.
45. See T1435: 309b21–c5. My English translation omits the word-by-word commentary in the middle.
46. This appears in the section discussing the probationary offenses for nuns. For the rule, see T1435: 309a14–c6. This rule is listed under the category of the seventeen nonidentical rules (*bu gongjie* 不共戒). See T1435: 307a3. This concept is also present in the *Mahīśāsaka Vinaya*, where a monk learned in Buddhist monastic law should be skillful in seven things, one of which was to have knowledge about the identical and non-identical rules (*zhi gongjie bugongjie* 知共不共戒). See T1421: 122a28–b2. I thank Shayne Clarke for reminding me to check these terms *gonjie* 共戒 and *bugong jie* 不共戒. My interpretation of these two terms is based on the Chinese translation of the commentary on the Chinese translation of the *Sarvāstivāda Vinaya* within the same tradition, where the terms were used. For instance, see T1440: 520b10–b11. I must note that two Buddhist nuns practicing in the Chinese tradition, Venerable Xinchan 心禅 and Venerable Rongdao 融道, both shared that one contemporary Buddhist interpretation of the term *gongjie* 共戒 is that it is referring to a rule that

applies to both monks and nuns, and the term *bu gongjie* 不共戒 refers to a rule that is not shared by monks and nuns but applies only to monks or only to nuns.

47. For discussion on the nonidentical rule (*bu gongjie* 不共戒) and identical rule (*gongjie* 共戒), see T1440: 519b8–b28.
48. This is the *pāyantika* offense.
49. See T1428: 719b1–b3. This is the section explaining the probationary offense 4. An offense of wrongdoing (Skt. *śaikṣa*) was considered a much lighter offense, which only required the offenders to confess their transgressions to themselves.
50. This case was presented in the section elaborating on the probationary offense 1 for nuns. For the original Pāli text, see Oldenberg 1882: vol. 4, 223–25; for an English translation of this story, see Horner 1942: vol. 3, 177–81. Granoff also analyzed this case. See Granoff 2018: 296–97.
51. This is the original English translation from Horner 1942: vol. 3, 179–81.
52. This case appeared in the section elaborating on probationary offense 7 for nuns. See also T1421:80b14–80c9.
53. T1421: 80b22–b23: "我等不捨此地。勿使詣官言汝更大輸物。"
54. T1421: 80c2–c9.
55. See T1442: 641a11–a16. For the Tibetan translation of this rule, see *'Dul ba rnam par 'byed pa*: vol. 5, 184.
56. This is an offense of defeat. The Tibetan translation clearly states it as "*pham par 'gyur*." The Chinese translation only says that the monk will commit the offense mentioned above, which should be understood as the offense of defeat of stealing.
57. T1442: 641a12–a16.
58. This case was found in the Chinese and Tibetan translations of the *Mūlasarvāstivāda Vinaya*. For the case in the Chinese translation, see T1443: 936b3–c5; for the case in the Tibetan translation, see *Dge slong ma'i 'dul ba rnam par 'byed pa*: vol. 9, 296–99. For discussion on this case, see Schopen 2000: 7.
59. *Dge slong ma'i 'dul ba rnam par 'byed pa*: vol. 9, 298: "*gal te khyod kyis 'di nga la ma byin par 'gro na rgyal po'i pho brang du dbul lo*." Note that the nun's threat to go to the king's court only appears in the Tibetan translation of this story and is never mentioned in the Chinese version.
60. *Dge slong ma'i 'dul ba rnam par 'byed pa*: vol. 9, 298: "*chags rgya len par byed*."
61. T1428: 739c17–740a26. This case was presented in the section elaborating on the *pāyantika* rule 78 regulating what Buddhist nuns should have been doing with their night soil.
62. For a discussion on the nuns in the group of six, here, and those in the group of twelve, see Liu 2013: 179–95.
63. Her story was found in the *Pāli Vinaya*, the *Dharmaguptaka Vinaya*, and the *Mahīśāsaka Vinaya*. The versions in the first two only recount how she was raped by the Brahmin youth. The *Mahīśāsaka* version provides a more detailed account on her life before ordination. The following summary is based on the version presented in the *Mahīśāsaka Vinaya*. Different Vinaya texts use her story to elaborate on different rules. In the *Pāli Vinaya*, her case appears in the section discussing offense of defeat 1—sexual intercourse for Buddhist monks. In the *Mahīśāsaka Vinaya*, her story

appeared in the section discussing one of the thirty *naiḥsargika pāyantika* (*sheduo* 捨墮) rules for monks. For the original passage in Pāli, see Oldenberg 1881: vol. 3, 35. For an English translation of the story, see Horner 1938: vol. 1, 53–54. For her story in the Chinese translations of the *Dharmaguptaka Vinaya* and the *Mahīśāsaka Vinaya*, see T1428: 929c28–930a9; T1421: 25a8–c9. Note that in the *Dharmaguptaka Vinaya*, Uppalavaṇṇā escapes from an attempted rape. When the Brahmin youth catch her and attempt to rape her, Uppalavaṇṇā persuades the rapist to go to a different place, where she attacks the rapist by smearing cow dung over his body. The Brahmin youth fights back by throwing stones at Uppalavaṇṇā's head and injuring her eyes. Her name translates as Lianhua se 蓮華色 in the Chinese translations of the Vinaya texts, as her name means the one with skin the color of the blue lotus.

64. See Horner 1938: vol. 1, 61–62.
65. T1421: 80b15–80c9. Note that this advice is absent in the sections elaborating on the same probationary offense in all the other Vinaya texts.
66. See 1421: 80b4–b6.
67. For the Chinese translation of these incidents, see T1451: 285b22–285c10; for its Tibetan translation, see *'Dul ba phran tshegs kyi gzhi*: vol. 10, 574–75.
68. The king's court is mentioned as *rgyal po'i pho brang* in the Tibetan translation and as *wangjia* 王家 in the Chinese translation.
69. T1451: 285c9–c10: "成就衣鉢卒難可得。"
70. T1428: 982a7–982a10. This case is found in the section elaborating on the offense of defeat for having killed a human being.
71. For these exceptions, see the paragraph on no offense in the section discussing probationary offense 1 in Horner 1938: vol. 1, 181; T1428: 719b3–b6; *Dge slong ma'i 'dul ba rnam par 'byed pa*: vol.9, 298.
72. See T1443:936b3–c5. The *Mūlasarvāstivāda Vinaya* permitted nuns to collect promissory notes as payments to the nunnery but not to themselves. This permission is not mentioned in the Tibetan translation of this text, but a commentary on the Tibetan translation does mention that nuns who litigated to collect a debt for their nunnery or monastery would not have been committing an offense. For an analysis of this exception, see Schopen 2000: 7.
73. In the *Pāli Vinaya*, a nun was allowed to do so by issuing a general lawsuit that did not accuse any individual. See Horner 1938: vol. 1, 181. In the *Sarvāstivāda Vinaya*, there was no offense if a nun cursed the offender in anger in a concealed place (privately) but did not reveal the details of the offense. See T1435: 309c5.
74. See T1425:518a8–a20.
75. See T1435: 309c5.
76. See the rule prohibiting monks from seizing land through litigation in the *Mūlasarvāstivāda Vinaya* (T1442: 641a12–a16), which I discuss in detail in the section "Ban for Monks and Nuns" in this chapter.
77. This is discussed at the end of the section on probationary offense 1 on dispute over donated properties. See Horner 1942: vol. 3, 180.
78. See Schonthal 2016; Schonthal 2020; Schonthal 2021; Schonthal 2022; Ashin and Crosby 2017; Lammerts 2018.

Chapter 2

1. T1443: 936a19–a20: "若依法殺戮便傷佛教我招惡響。若今釋放復損刑科。"
2. Eugen Hultzsch dates Aśoka's coronation to 264 BCE. See Hultzsch 1914: 950.
3. Three such inscriptions survive on three rock pillars in Rupnath, Sahasram, and Bairat.
4. For this event, see the Nigali Sagar pillar inscription in Hultzsch's *Inscriptions of Asoka*. Hultzsch 1925: 165. The date is from his article "The Date of Asoka." Hultzsch 1914: 951.
5. For this event, see the Rummindei pillar inscription in Hultzsch 1925: 164–65. The date is from "The Date of Asoka." Hultzsch 1914: 951.
6. This pillar was found near a shrine of Hanūmān on the first or lower platform on the summit of a hill near Bairāt. For a description and English translation of this edict, see Hultzsch 1925: xxv, 172–74.
7. This edict survives on two pillars in Samchi and Sarnatha. For the edict that has been inscribed on these two pillars, see Hultzsch 1925: 160–64. In this book, I use "defrock" to describe monks and nuns who were forced to leave the monastic community after committing offenses. Later in this book, I also use "disrobe" to describe monks and nuns who choose to leave the monastic community without committing any offense.
8. See Olivelle 1999: 72 (*Dharmasūtra of Āpstamba*: bk. 2, ch. 29).
9. See Jolly 1889: 282 (*Bṛhaspati Smṛti*: bk. 1, ch. 31).
10. Olivelle 2017: 182.
11. Patrick Olivelle and Mark McClish argue that the legal domain had four levels in ancient India: customary rules for certain private groups (*caritra*), more universal rules governing public transactions (*vyavahāra*), general and broad common-sense justice (*dharma*), and lastly the king's edicts (*rājaśāsana*). An investigation of a legal dispute will start at the lowest level and move to the next level if it cannot be solved. The king's court is the final legal venue for reaching a decision on a legal dispute. See Olivelle and McClish 2015. See also McClish 2019: 301.
12. See Bühler 1898: 165–67.
13. See Olivelle 2013: 251–52.
14. See Olivelle 2005: 187.
15. The following discussion on theft is based on the section on litigation against theft in *Manu's Code of Law*. See Olivelle 2005: 183–85.
16. Olivelle 2005: 184.
17. The Buddha mentioned these punishments to define what constituted a convicted criminal in the *Mahāsāṃghika Vinaya*. See T1425: 520b7–b9.
18. This prohibition speaks to the probationary offense. It is worth mentioning that the *Mūlasarvāstivāda Vinaya* discusses a total of four rules on ordaining disqualified women as nuns. Apart from probationary offense 10, which discusses the illegal ordination of convicted women criminals, we also found three more rules in the *pāyantika* section: rule 117 on ordaining a combative woman (T1443: 1006c21–1007a14), rule 118 on ordaining a sorrowful woman (T1443: 1007a15–a29), and rule 160 on ordaining a prostitute (T1443: 1014a8–a17).

19. In the *Pāli Vinaya*, the king's name was Pasenadi. This case is presented in the section explaining probationary offense 2 on ordaining unsuitable candidates. For the original text, see Oldenberg 1882: 225–27; for its English translation, see Horner 1940, vol. 2: 182–85.
20. T1428: 719b7–720a5. This was also the only case presented in this *Dharmaguptaka Vinaya* to illustrate probationary offense 5 pertaining to ordaining unsuitable candidates.
21. T1435: 309c14–310b18. This case was presented to illustrate probationary offense 8 on ordaining unsuitable candidates.
22. See T1435: 310a12–a13.
23. T1435: 310a19–a20.
24. T1421: 79b6–c24. See the section on probationary offense 3.
25. T1421: 79b20–b21.
26. T1421: 79b22–b23: "今已出家不可追罪."
27. T1421: 79b23–b24: "凡有此罪不復得治亂我國矣."
28. T1443: 935c11–936b3. See the section elaborating on probationary offense 10 concerning the ordination of women.
29. T1443: 935c17–c18.
30. T1443: 936a2.
31. T1443: 936a4.
32. For a discussion on the nuns in the band of twelve, see Liu 2013.
33. T1443: 936a19–a20: "若依法殺戮便傷佛教我招惡響. 若今釋放復損刑科."
34. T1443: 936a22–a23: "所立嚴令衆並同知. 如何此女王欲違制而釋放耶."
35. T1443: 936a23.
36. *Dge slong ma'i 'dul ba rnam par 'byed pa*: 293–96.
37. *Dge slong ma'i 'dul ba rnam par 'byed pa*: 293–94: "*bdag cag gis ni ri brags pa logs pa'i rnams 'dul ba byed na rang gi chung ma dag gdul bar mi nus sam khrims bca' gor ma chag.*"
38. *Dge slong ma'i 'dul ba rnam par 'byed pa*: 294: "*gal te 'di chas pas ma bcad par byur na bdag cag gis kyang khrims dral bar bya'o.*"
39. *Dge slong ma'i 'dul ba rnam par 'byed pa*: 294: "*bdag gis khrims bcas la bdag gis dral du ga la rung.*"
40. *Dge slong ma'i 'dul ba rnam par 'byed pa*: 295: "*rab tu 'byung bar mi 'dod dam.*"
41. *Dge slong ma'i 'dul ba rnam par 'byed pa*: 294: "*dpog bed kyi bu mo sde can ma 'di ni sangs rgyas la skyabs su song ba / chos la skyabs su song ba / dge 'dun la skyabs su song ba / nga la skyabs su 'ongs pa / khyed cag la skyabs su song ba yin gyis ma gsod cig.*"
42. *Dge slong ma'i 'dul ba rnam par 'byed pa*: 294: "*lha ci khyims dral bar bgyis a'm?*"
43. *Dge slong ma'i 'dul ba rnam par 'byed pa*: 294: "*ga la dral gyi steng du legs par rab tu bsrung mod kyis 'on kyang 'di'i phyir mchog zhig sbyin par bya'o.*"
44. T1425: 519b2–519c6.
45. T1425: 519b16–b17.
46. T1425: 519c10–c11.
47. T1425: 519c19.
48. T1425: 519c19–c20.

49. T1425: 520a16–b14.
50. For an explanation of the probationary offense and its punishment, see T1442: 681b6–b10.
51. T442: 936a27–a29. If ordained Buddhist nuns had knowingly ordained women who had committed unlawful deeds, were despised by the public, had been abandoned by their husbands, and their deeds have been reported to the kings, these ordaining nuns would have committed a probationary offense.
52. T1428: 719b23–b26.
53. T1421: 79b24–b26: "凡有此罪不复得治乱我国矣."
54. These include the *Pāli Vinaya*, the *Mahāsāṃghika Vinaya* (Chinese), the *Dharmaguptaka Vinaya* (Chinese), the *Sarvāstivāda Vinaya* (Chinese), the *Mahīśāsaka Vinaya* (Chinese), and the *Mūlasarvāstivāda Vinaya* (Chinese and Tibetan).
55. For instance, Li Tianyou 力天佑 used a fake identity to become a Buddhist monk after having murdered a man in 2002, but was eventually arrested in 2018. For a report of his case, see Shen 2018.

Chapter 3

1. T1435:4a1–a2: 我出家人寄住王國。云何殺我。"
2. T1421: 5c17–c18: 我是灌頂王。如何當因沙沙門。如今便可速還。詣佛法王自當以法治汝。
3. For this case, see the section on the offense of defeat of killing a human being in T1442: 654b29–655c15.
4. Olivelle dates Aśvaghoṣa to the first century CE. See Olivelle 2008: xix.
5. This reference to the legal texts composed by Bṛhaspati and Śukra, which their fathers were unable to produce, is found in the reconstructed Sanskrit version of the *Buddhacarita* by Aśvaghoṣa as well as in its Tibetan translation. For this reference in Aśvaghoṣa's *Buddhacarita* reconstructed in Sanskrit, see Olivelle 2008: 1.46, pp. 14–15. In its Chinese translation, *Fo suoxing zan* 佛所行讚, the Brahmins mention what the two sons have composed, but what their fathers have not, to be the "Treatise on the King" (*Diwang lun* 帝王論). See T192: 2b4–b7. For this reference in the Tibetan translation, see *Sangs rgyas kyi spyod pa zhes bya ba'i snyan dngags chen po*: 9. The names of the two fathers are shes ldan for Aṅgiras and Ngan spong for Bṛgu in Tibetan, according to the Tibetan glossary *Sgra bye brag tu rtogs byed chen mo skad gzhi shan sbyar ma* 2015: 288, 295. The first-century author Kauṭilya saluted both Śukra and Bṛhaspati at the beginning of his *Arthaśāstra*. See Olivelle 2013: 63.
6. We know little about Bṛhaspati, but Jolly dates his work *Bṛhaspati Smṛti* to the sixth century CE. See Jolly 1889: 281.
7. Granoff 2018: 295.
8. The only exception is the Chinese translation of the *Mūlasarvāstivāda Vinaya*, where six cases of homicide were presented before the case of Mṛgalaṇḍika, but those cases

did not lead to the establishment of the offense of defeat of homicide. For a detailed analysis on these six cases and why they were included but did not lead to the establishment of this rule, see Clarke 2021.

9. For a discussion on the punishment for those having committed this offense, see the section on the "The Buddhist Legal World" in the Introduction.
10. His crimes have been documented in all the extant traditions of Buddhist monastic law. The story of this monk was found in the sections in all of the extant Vinaya texts that discuss the offense of defeat of killing human beings. For its occurrence in the *Pāli Vinaya*, see Horner 1938: vol. 1, 116–23. For its occurrence in the Chinese translations, see T1421: 7a27–7c9; T1428: 575c11–577b12; T1435:7b21–10b29; T1425: 253c25–254a16; 254b11–255a11; and T1442: 659c21–660b3. For its occurrence in the Tibetan translation, see *'Dul ba rnam par 'byed pa*: vol. 5, 325–42. The killer's name was transliterated or translated differently in different texts. In the *Pāli Vinaya*, the killer's name is Migalaṇḍika. In Chinese translations, this name was phonetically transliterated as Wudaojianan 勿刀伽難 in the *Dharmaguptaka Vinaya* or Milin zhantuoluo 彌隣旃陀羅 in the *Mahīśāsaka Vinaya*. In the *Sarvāstivāda Vinaya*, the *Mahāsāṃghika Vinaya*, and the *Mūlasarvāstivāda Vinaya*, his name was translated as Luzhang 鹿杖. In the Tibetan translation, his name was Ri dags zlog dge sbong sbel. These Chinese and Tibetan translations of the killer's name could be reconstructed as Mṛgalaṇḍika in Sanskrit. Note that Clarke has reconstructed the Sanskrit name of this killer as either Mṛganaṇḍika or Mṛgadaṇḍika. See Clarke 2021: 68, note 28–29.
11. Horner 1938: vol. 1, 125–26. This final version is amended from a previous promulgation that only prohibits the murder of a human being or providing knife to the victim, but it does not mention the crime of praising death.
12. Such post-rule cases are not found in the *Mahīśāsaka Vinaya*, the *Dharmaguptaka Vinaya*, or the *Mahāsāṃghika Vinaya*.
13. For a definition of involuntary manslaughter, see Garner 2019: 1153.
14. T1442: 664c8–665b28. In this text, we also find the case of another monk caregiver who had killed a sick monk by offering the latter salty vinegar with the intention of curing the sick monk. See T1442: 664b16–c4. The case of this nun is also found in the Tibetan translation of the *Mūlasarvāstivāda Vinaya* after the Buddha had already established this rule against the killing of human beings in the section discussing the offense of defeat, for monks, of homicide. There, her name is nun Skyong ma. For the case in the Tibetan version, see *'Dul ba rnam par 'byed pa*: vol. 5, 367–72.
15. T1442: 665a27–a29.
16. T1442: 665b22–b23: 將非我犯他勝罪耶。
17. T1442: 665b24.
18. T1442: 665b24–b25.
19. T1442: 665b25–b26.
20. T1442: 665b27–b28.
21. For a discussion on this offense, see the "Buddhist Legal World" section in the Introduction.

22. See T1435:10b29–c9; T1442: 664a5–b15; and *'Dul ba rnam par 'byed pa*: vol. 5, 362–65. My analysis below is based on the more elaborate versions in Chinese and Tibetan translations of the *Mūlasarvāstivāda Vinaya*. For an English translation of the full story in one of the Tibetan versions, see Clarke 2009b: 321–22.
23. In the Tibetan version, it was a girl, or the daughter (*bu mo*) of the Caṇḍāla woman who had given birth to a baby (*gtum mo'i khyim du bu mo zhig la khye'u zhig btsas nas*). See *Bka' 'gyur*: vol. 5, 364.
24. T1442: 664b9; *Bka' 'gyur*: vol. 5, 363.
25. The story of Danika (Pāli: Dhaniya; Tib. Nor can; Ch. Dannijia 但尼迦) is found in the section discussing the offense of defeat of taking what is not given, or stealing, in the Buddhist monastic law texts in all six extant traditions. For the original passage in Pāli, see Oldenberg 1881: vol. 3, 44–45; for its English translation, see Horner 1938: vol. 1, 64–72. For other editions of this case in Chinese translations, see T1442: 635c23–637b22; T1435: 3b8–4b3; T1428: 572b6–573b12; T1421: 5b1–6a8; T1425: 238a27–241c12. For its appearance in the Tibetan translation, see *'Dul ba rnam par 'byed pa*: vol. 5, 135–52. My analysis of the case below is based primarily on the Chinese translation of the *Mūlasarvāstivāda Vinaya*, where the case was furnished with more details. Significant variations in other versions are noted when necessary.
26. Furthermore, we also find cases of theft occurring after the Buddha's articulation of the offense of defeat of stealing, as found in the *Mūlasarvāstivāda Vinaya*, the *Sarvāstivāda Vinaya*, and the *Pāli Vinaya*.
27. Note that the king's name is Bimbisāra in both the *Pāli Vinaya* and the *Mahāsāṃghika Vinaya*.
28. T1442: 636b10–b13.
29. T1435: 3c22–c24.
30. T1442: 636c7–c12; *'Dul ba rnam par 'byed pa*: vol. 5, 144.
31. T1421: 5c9–c13.
32. See T1428: 572c22–c26; Horner 1938: vol. 1, 68–69.
33. T1425: 239a4–a12.
34. For a description of the following interrogation, see T1442: 636c14–c26.
35. T1442: 636c20–c21.
36. T1442: 636: c25–c26: 沙門汝今合死。我不能殺。汝宜速去。從今已往更不得如此。This declaration is, however, absent in the Tibetan translation of the *Mūlasarvāstivāda Vinaya*. See *'Dul ba rnam par 'byed pa*: vol. 5, 146.
37. T425: 239a25–a28.
38. T1435: 4a1: 汝今墮大罪中。
39. T1435: 4a1: 我出家人。寄住王國。云何殺我？
40. Horner 1938: vol. 1, 69–70.
41. T1428: 573a8–9.
42. In the Chinese translation of the *Mūlasarvāstivāda Vinaya*, the king simply says that the monk Danika deserves to be killed, but he cannot give the order to carry out capital punishment. See T1442: 636c25–c26. This statement is, however, absent in the

Tibetan translation of the *Mūlasarvāstivāda Vinaya*. See *'Dul ba rnam par 'byed pa*: vol. 5, 146.

43. T1421: 5c17–18: 我是灌頂王。如何當囚殺沙門。如今便可速還。詣佛法王自當以法治汝。
44. What I have rendered as five coins here refers to the one *pāda* or five *māsaka*s in the original Pāli text. Olivelle writes that eighty-eight white mustard seeds equal one silver *māsaka*. See Olivelle 2013: 143. Horner was not sure whether the *māsaka* and *pāda* were coins, so she left them untranslated in her translation of the *Pāli Vinaya*. See Horner 1938: vol. 1, 71n2.
45. T1435: 4a18–a27; T1442: 637a3–a13.
46. I discuss this case in Chapter 1 in the section "The Dreadful Courtroom." For the case, see T1425: 381b6–c27.
47. T1435:309a14–c5. For a further discussion on the punishment of lost lay defendants, see Liu 2020b: 109–11. It is important to note that this penalty was also applicable to offenders who had beaten or injured other laypeople. Therefore, mutilation was not a specific penalty for having injured ordained Buddhists.
48. T1425: 419c26–420a18. This case is found in the section elaborating on miscellaneous rules concerning ordaining unsuitable candidates.
49. T1425: 419c29–420a2.
50. For the following conversation between the king and the judge, see T1425: 420a6–a8.
51. T1425: 420a11–a12. This case was found in the section of the *Mahāsāṃghika Vinaya* elaborating on miscellaneous rules concerning ordaining unsuitable candidates.
52. T1425: 240a18–b23.
53. For the story of the six-tusked elephant, see T1425: 240b23–241a20.
54. T1425: 241a21–b25.
55. T1425: 239b17–240a18.
56. T1425: 242b25–243a6.
57. The king explains that for stealing something worth a quarter of nineteen units of cash (*qian* 钱), the offender will receive the death penalty. See T1425: 242c22–c23.
58. For this case, see T1425: 243b27–c27. I thank Yu Meng for identifying the Chinese phrase *najuluo chong* 那俱羅蟲 as the transliteration of mongoose, or *nakula* in Sanskrit, in this text and for her suggestion to look for the original story in Sanskrit in the *Pañchatantra*, where the second story in book 5 tells of a Brahmin's wife who had mistakenly killed a mongoose who saved her son from a snake's attack.
59. For this story, see T1425: 243a10–b15.
60. Clarke 2009a shows how even when monks and nuns were convicted of the severest offense of defeat in the Buddhist legal world, they were able to avoid excommunication and continue to live in the monastic community.
61. I thank David Brick for suggesting that I check the Dharmaśāstra literature for the rules concerning Brahmin immunity.
62. Olivelle 1999: 96.
63. Olivelle 1999: 90.
64. This is a legal textual tradition that began with compositions written in an aphoristic style (*sūtra*), shifting to a verse style (*śloka*) that appeared in the first century

CE and later to a commentary style (*bhāṣya*) that appeared in the ninth century CE. For an introduction to the history of the Dharmaśāstra literary tradition, see Olivelle 2010: 28–57. For a study on the four major Dharmaśāstra texts, see Olivelle 2000.

65. Olivelle 2004: 187.

Chapter 4

1. T411: 737a15–a16; T410: 694b24–b25. For its Tibetan translation, see *'Dus pa chen po sa'i snying po'i 'khor lo bcu pa zhes bya ba theg pa chen po'i mdo*: 349.
2. For the restriction on laypeople's access to Buddhist monastic law, see T1442: 672c4–c5; T1425: 338a22–a29; T1425: 448b22–c2.
3. For the Chinese translation of this text, see T397a.
4. The reconstructed Sanskrit title of this text is *Daśacakra Kṣitigarbhasūtra Sūtra*. For its two Chinese translations, see T410; T411.
5. For the Chinese translation of this text, see T271; T272.
6. The reconstructed Sanskrit title of this text is *Sumerugarbha Sūtra*. For the Chinese translation of this text, see T397b.
7. Nattier 1991: 185.
8. Nattier 1991: 185.
9. See T2029, T2028, T99, T2042, T383, T1545, T397a.
10. See *Las brgya tham pa* and *'Phags pa Zla ba'i snying pos zhus pa'i mdo*. The former text is the Tibetan translation of *Karmaśataka*. Nattier dates it to no later than the second half of the eighth century because the title of this translation appeared in the Tibetan catalogue *Lan kar ma*. The latter text is the Tibetan translation of the *Moon-Womb Sūtra*. See Nattier 1991: 51.
11. For an introduction to this Khotanese version, see Nattier 1991: 173.
12. See T397a.
13. In the Chinese translation of the *Moon-Womb Sūtra*, the Buddha is initially talking to the bodhisattva Candragarbha, but then turns to speak to Yuedeng pusa 月燈菩薩, bodhisattva Moon-Lamp. In the Tibetan translation of the *Moon-Womb Sūtra*, the Buddha is only talking to Candragarbha. See *'Phags pa Zla ba'i snying pos zhus pa'i mdo*: 618.
14. For this conversation in the *Moon-Womb Sūtra*, see T397: 375b28377b23; T2029: 9c29–11b11; T2028: 7a29–8c24. In T2028, the monk Kātyāyana, but not the Buddha, describes how Buddhism would deteriorate and perish in the future. This is not framed in the context of the time immediately following the Buddha's passing away. It is worth mentioning that in the *Great Sūtra of Lady Māyā* (T383), the Buddha provides a more specific timeline that maps the progress of this corruption over a much longer span of fifteen hundred years after his death. This text does not record the invasion of the three evil kings, nor the twelve-year defense against them, nor offerings of a grand feast to all ordained Buddhists, nor a description of these monks' misbehavior after having received the kings' abundant offerings. In T383,

at the request of Lady Māyā, the Buddha's principal disciple, Ānanda, reports that the Buddha predicted the gradual decline of Buddhism taking place after his death. According to the Buddha, within seven hundred years of his death, there will still be monks capable of preaching his teachings and guiding people toward enlightenment, but their number will decrease; eight hundred years after his death, monks will take delight in good clothes and entertainment and only one or two in 100,000 will become accomplished in their training; nine hundred years after his death, male slaves will become monks and female slaves will become nuns; a thousand years after his death, monks will start to hear teaching on contemplations on impurity and other things; after 1,100 years, monks will get married, provide matchmaking services, and publicly slander Buddhist monastic law; after 1,200 years, monks and nuns will engage in impure acts and give birth to children; after 1,300 years, the dyed monastic robes will fade and no longer be able to be dyed; after 1,400 years, like hunters, all people will take delight in killing people of the Buddhist community and destroying their belongings; after 1,500 years, the first phase of corruption will culminate and lead to the end of Buddhism. See T383: 1013b16–1014a3.

15. For the full story, see T397: 377c1–380b2. A detailed description of the misbehaviors of ordained Buddhists described here can also be found in T1545: 918b3–b9; T2042: 127a29–127b7; and T99: 178b10–b18.
16. In the Tibetan translation of the *Moon-Womb Sūtra*, the kings are shown to have had the same motivation for offering this grand feast. In T99 and T2042, King Duṣprasaha aspires to make a grand offering to restore the Buddhist monastic community that had been severely damaged by the three evil kings during a twelve-year war. In T2029 and T2028, the king is pleased with Śiṣyaka's teachings and decides to make a grand offering. T1545 does not specify the king's motivation, and T383 does not mention the grand feast.
17. In T2029, Śiṣyaka offers to preach to the assembly, but Sūrata challenges Śiṣyaka's qualifications to teach because he considers Śiṣyaka ignorant in the Buddha's teachings. In T2028, Śiṣyaka offers to preach but is challenged by two other monks. One of them is Sūrata. Both monks claim to be qualified teachers, and they volunteer to preach. In T99, T397, and the *Zla ba'i snying pos mdo*, an administrator monk invites Śiṣyaka to preach the rules of the *Prātimokṣa* to the assembled monks, but Śiṣyaka believes there is no need to do so because he expects there will be no monks who can study or observe these rules. In T2042, Śiṣyaka admits that he is incapable of preaching on the monastic rules and invites anyone who can do so to identify themselves. In T383, Sūrata sits on an elevated seat as he preaches on the *Prātimokṣa* and instructs the monks on which things to do and which to avoid. In T1545, Śiṣyaka is to give a concise sermon on the *Prātimokṣa*, but Sūrata requests a more extensive sermon.
18. T99: 179a10–a13.
19. T99: 179a22–179a25.
20. *'Phags pa Zla ba'i snying pos zhus pa'i mdo*: 635.
21. The reconstruction of this name is obtained from Nattier 1991: 159.
22. T99 reports that the arhat monk was killed with a sharp knife.

23. The arhat monk's name was transliterated as Qutanti 佉檀提 in T397, Datimuqu 大提木佉 in T99, and Lemian 樂面 in T2042, the latter of which Jan Nattier has translated as "joyful face," but its meaning is unspecified in the other texts.
24. T2029 and T2028 do not mention the arhat monk's death. In T99 and T2042, an anonymous disciple of the arhat monk kills Śiṣyaka. See T2042: 127c26–c27; T99: 197c13–c14. In the Chinese translation of the *Moon-Womb Sūtra*, this disciple is an evil monk Jiduoluo 雞多羅 who kills Śiṣyaka with a stick. See T397: 378c10–c11. In the Tibetan translation, the demon Dadhimukha kills Śiṣyaka but not Aṅgada. T1545 records both accounts. In one, the arhat monk's disciple kills Śiṣyaka. In the other, the faithful Buddhist demon kills him. See T1545: 918c9–c11.
25. For this exhortation, see T397: 379c10–c17.
26. T397: 379c9–c17.
27. See T410. Zhiru Ng notes that this text was mentioned in the sixth century in Chinese catalogues of the Buddhist canon. For a discussion on the dating of T410, see Ng 2007: appendix 1.
28. For this text, see T411. The arrangements in the two Chinese translations are slightly different. T410 contains fifteen chapters in eight scrolls (*juan*), while T411 contains eight chapters in ten scrolls. This may indicate that these two Chinese translations used different root texts.
29. For this translation, see *'Dus pa chen po sa'i snying po'i 'khor lo bcu pa zhes bya ba theg pa chen po'i mdo*. The structure of the Tibetan translation of the *Ten Wheels Sūtra* is identical to the 651 Chinese translation by Xuanzang, so it was likely translated from Chinese to Tibetan. Its translators are listed as a Chinese monk whose name is Zab mo and a Tibetan monk called Rnam par mi rtogs pa. We know very little about the Chinese monk, partly because he was only mentioned by his Tibetan name, which means "profound." Apart from working with the Chinese monk, the Tibetan translator Rnam par mi rtog pa had also collaborated on the translation of two other Buddhist texts, no later than 789, with a Khotanese monk, Śīladharma, who was fluent in Sanskrit and Chinese. Śīladharma worked with the Tang pilgrim monk Wukong 悟空 (731–812) at Longxing 龍興 Monastery in Beiting, in present-day Xinjiang, on the translation of T287 and T998. The Tang monk Wukong returned to Chang'an on the thirteenth day of the ninth month of the year 789. In the *Princeton Dictionary of Buddhism*, Buswell and Lopez noted that Śīladharma had gone to Chang'an with the Chinese monk Wukong in 790 and then returned to Khotan, but the authors of this entry did not specify the source of this statement. See Buswell and Lopez 2014: 822. The Tibetan translation is divided into eight chapters (*le'u*). Its colophon states that a team led by the Chinese *mkhan po* monk (Tibetan: *hwa shang*) Zab mo and the chief translator (*zhu chen lo ts'a ba*) monk (*ban de*) Rnam par mi rtog translated, proofread, and finalized this Tibetan translation. They also translated another text: *Ting nge 'dzin gyi mi mthun pa'i phyogs rnam par gzhag pa*.
30. This text has also been translated into the Xixia language of the Tangut people. At least two Xixia fragments survive. Both are now housed in the Dunhuang Academy in China. For a detailed study on these two Xixia fragments, see Wang 2017.

31. For a discussion on these meditating monk criminals, see T410: 693c1–c16; T411: 735c21–736a11; *Sa'i snying po 'khor lo bcu pa*: 340–42.
32. See chapters 5 and 6 in T410: 692c25–702a16; chapter 3 in T411: 734c28–748b22; and *'Dus pa chen po sa'i snying po'i 'khor lo bcu pa zhes bya ba theg pa chen po'i*: 335–412.
33. See T410: 693c17–694b25. The Tibetan version later describes this potential scenario as follows: "They would break the law of the king and the great minister" (*rgyal po dang blon po chen po'i khrims dang yang 'gal bar byed de*). See *'Dus pa chen po sa'i snying po'i 'khor lo bcu pa zhes bya ba theg pa chen po'i mdo*: 340. In the later Chinese translation, T411, the examples of corporal penalty expand to include whipping, beating with a hammer, jailing, cursing, cutting off hands or feet, and the death penalty. See T411: 736a12–a15.
34. This refers to the Pratyeka Buddha, "an arhat who becomes enlightened through his own efforts, without receiving instruction from a Buddha in his final lifetime." See Buswell and Lopez 2014: 673.
35. T410: 694c4–c13.
36. T410: 694b26–c3.
37. T410: 695a7–a13.
38. T410:696a20–b18.
39. See T410: 695c5–696a7; T411: 738c9–739a5.
40. The lay steward was translated from its Sanskrit original, *kalpikāraka*. This term was often translated as *jingren* (淨人) in Chinese and *phyogs bzhi'i dge 'dun gyi rung bar byed pa* in Tibetan. For a further explanation on this term, see Buswell and Lopez 2014: 409–10.
41. See T410: 695c11–696a1; T411:738b25–739a5; *'Dus pa chen po sa'i snying po'i 'khor lo bcu pa zhes bya ba theg pa chen po'i mdo*, 359–360.
42. In the Tibetan translation, this person is referred to as *kun du rgyu ba*, "wandering mendicant."
43. T410 mentions members from the royal family before mentioning the ministers.
44. T410 mentions children but does not mention the assembly of men.
45. Such forbidden things included killing human beings (including a fetus forty-nine days along in gestation), taking what had not been given, having sex, lying about having supernatural powers, and drinking alcohol, among other infractions.
46. T411: 736c16–737a3. Cf. T410: 694a29–b13. For the Tibetan translation, see *'Dus pa chen po sa'i snying po'i 'khor lo bcu pa zhes bya ba theg pa chen po'i mdo*: 347–48.
47. T411: 737a15–a16; T410: 694b24–b25. For its Tibetan translation, *'Dus pa chen po sa'i snying po'i 'khor lo bcu pa zhes bya ba theg pa chen po'i mdo*, 349.
48. For the following story, see T410: 697c10–698b6; T411: 741c7–742b12; *'Dus pa chen po sa'i snying po'i 'khor lo bcu pa zhes bya ba theg pa chen po'i mdo*, 375–377.
49. T410: 697c27–698a1. For the same quote in the other translations, see T411: 741c24–c27; *'Dus pa chen po sa'i snying po'i 'khor lo bcu pa zhes bya ba theg pa chen po'i mdo*: 376–77.
50. T410:698a4–a7. For the same quote in the other translations, see T411:742a1–a4; *'Dus pa chen po sa'i snying po'i 'khor lo bcu pa zhes bya ba theg pa chen po'i mdo*: 377.

51. For the dates and identification of the mural painting as depicted based in the *Ten Wheels Sūtra*, see introduction on Mogao Cave 321 at www.e-dunhuang.com.
52. T410: 699a25–b9; T411:743b19–c1; *'Dus pa chen po sa'i snying po'i 'khor lo bcu pa zhes bya ba theg pa chen po'i mdo*, 385.
53. T410: 698b6–699a25; T411: 743b19–743c20; *'Dus pa chen po sa'i snying po'i 'khor lo bcu pa zhes bya ba theg pa chen po'i mdo*: 379–84.
54. The father ogre is absent in T411, where the interaction begins with the mother ogress, followed by the son ogre.
55. T410: 699a16–a18.
56. T411: 743b1–b4.
57. For the Tibetan translation of the rule, see *'Dus pa chen po sa'i snying po'i 'khor lo bcu pa zhes bya ba theg pa chen po'i mdo*: 383–384.
58. A reference to some similar laws can be found in the Chinese translation of the *Mūlasarvāstivāda Vinaya*, where a maid reminds her mistress that "killing a monk violates the law" of their country and that the killer "will become a slave permanently." See T1442: 863a1–a2.
59. The Chinese translation of his name is Sazhe Niqianzi 薩遮尼乾子 in T271 and Da Sazhe Niqianzi 大薩遮尼乾子 in T272. In the Tibetan translation, his name was translated as Gcer bu pa'i bu bden smra.
60. King Caṇḍapradyota's name was transliterated as Yanchaboshuti 旃茶鉢樹提 in T271 and translated as Yanzhi 嚴熾 in T272—Gtum po rab snang in Tibetan. The Tibetan scholar Bsod nams rgyal mtshan (1343–1347) described King Caṇḍapradyota as the ruler of one of the four kings who were contemporaries of the historical Buddha. The other three kings were King Prasenajit of Śrāvastī; King Bimbisāra of Rājagṛha; and King Udayana of Kauśāmbi. For the English translation of this Tibetan reference, see Bsod nams rgyal mtshan 1994: 56; Bsod nams rgyal mtshan 1996: 36. The name of this kingdom was transliterated as Youchanyan 優禪延 in T271 and Yusheyan 鬱闍延 in T272, and as Phags rgyal in the Tibetan translation. The Sanskrit name of this kingdom is from Beal 1884: 270–71. The Chinese monk Xuanzang mentioned a Wushe yanna 鄔闍衍那 city, or Ujjayanī in Sanskrit, in Southern India. See Xuanzang 1985: 922–25.
61. The Chinese translation was found on a ten-scroll text the Indian monk Bodhiruci 菩提留支 (d. 572) had translated in 520, in Luoyang. See T272. In the first year of the Zhengguang 正光 era (520), Bodhiruci, who had arrived in the Northern Wei capital Luoyang in 508, translated this text upon the commission of Yuan Yue 元悅 (494–533), the Lord of Runan 汝南 of the Northern Wei. For references to the date, the commissioner, the translator, and the place of translation, see T2034: 85c17; T2149: 287a11–a12. Its Tibetan translation was produced in the late eighth and early ninth centuries by the Indian scholar Prajñāvarma and the Tibetan monk translator Ye shes sde. At the end of the Tibetan translation, they give the Sanskrit title of this text as *Bodhisattvagocaropāyaviṣayavikurvāṇanirdeśa*. The Tibetan monk translator Ye shes sde was a prolific late eighth and early ninth century translator who has been credited with translating over three hundred texts that are preserved in the Tibetan Buddhist canon. For a study on Ye shes sde and a list of the texts credited as having

been translated by him, see Rhaldi 2002. For the Tibetan translation, see *'Phags pa byang chub sems dpa'i spyod yul gyi thabs kyi yul la rnam par 'phrul pa bstan pa*. For an English translation of this Tibetan translation, see *The Range of the Bodhisattva* 2010.

There was an earlier fifth-century Chinese translation of a similar text in three scrolls, noted as having been translated by the central Indian scholar Guṇabhadra 求那跋陀罗 (394–468), who arrived in China in 435 and died there in 468. See T271. The length and the structure of this earlier Chinese translation is significantly different from the later Chinese and Tibetan translations. This discrepancy indicates that its root text was likely different from the one used for the latter two translations. The Sui dynasty scholar Fajing 法經 identified this eight-scroll T272 and the three-scroll T271 as being different translations of the same text. See T2146: 117a15–a16. The title of this text was also recorded as *dasazhe niqianzi shouji jing* 大薩遮尼乾子受記經. See T2034: 85c17; T2149: 268c23.

62. This conversation on governance occurs in chapter 5 (王論品) in the Chinese translation, and chapter 6 (*Rgyal bo'i tshul*) in the Tibetan translation.
63. T272: 333b5–b27.
64. T272: 333b23–b26; *'Phags pa byang chub sems dpa'i spyod yul gyi thabs kyi yul la rnam par 'phrul pa bstan pa*: 273–274. See also T272: 334c12–c22; *'Phags pa byang chub sems dpa'i spyod yul gyi thabs kyi yul la rnam par 'phrul pa bstan pa*: 277–278.
65. T272: 333b27–c15.
66. See T272: 333c16–334a19; *'Phags pa byang chub sems dpa'i spyod yul gyi thabs kyi yul la rnam par 'phrul pa bstan pa*: 275–278.
67. See T272: 334a20–a27; *'Phags pa byang chub sems dpa'i spyod yul gyi thabs kyi yul la rnam par 'phrul pa bstan pa*: 276.
68. For the following summaries on different punishments, see T272: 334a28–c22; *'Phags pa byang chub sems dpa'i spyod yul gyi thabs kyi yul la rnam par 'phrul pa bstan pa*: 276–78.
69. For reference to the following summary, see T272: 334b28–c22; *'Phags pa byang chub sems dpa'i spyod yul gyi thabs kyi yul la rnam par 'phrul pa bstan pa*: 277–78.
70. T272: 334c9–c11; 334c3.
71. T272: 336a29–336b12.
72. T272: 336b5–336b9. The Tibetan translation does not contain an elaboration of this fundamental crime for kings who torture or kill ordained Buddhist criminals. The term for renunciant is *shamen* 沙門, or *śramaṇa* in Sanskrit.
73. See T272: 334c12–c22; *'Phags pa byang chub sems dpa'i spyod yul gyi thabs kyi yul la rnam par 'phrul pa bstan pa*: 277–78.
74. T410: 698a20–a28.
75. T411:742b1–b8.
76. For the following summary, see T272: 336b5–b13.
77. See T397: 389b22–b29. The Central Asian monk Narendrayaśas translated this text into Chinese in 559. This text has five chapters. The discussion on the disastrous consequences of mistreating ordained Buddhists appears in chapter 4 on Buddhist chants (*dhāraṇī*).
78. The following summary is based on T397: 388a25–389a19.

79. Ng reconstructs Śrīdevī as the Sanskrit spelling of the Chinese translation Gongde tian 功德天. See Ng 2007: 37.
80. The following summary is based on T397: 389a20–c20.
81. The English translation is from Ng 2007: 40. For the original reference, see T397: 389b7–b9.
82. For this explanation, see T397: 389b22–c6; for additional testimonies from the two other serpent kings, see T397: 389c29–390a26.
83. In Buddhist literature, the *gandharva* mentioned in the text often refers to a celestial musician who survives by eating fragrance.
84. For reference to the following summary, see T397: 391a6–a22.

Chapter 5

1. Wei 1974: 3040.
2. This chapter is revised from Liu 2019.
3. For the interaction between Zhizang and the emperor, see Zhizang's biography in Daoxuan, T2060: 466b9–c21. The date of this interaction appears to be inaccurate. The biography states that the interaction occurred in the Datong 大同 era (535–546), but the same text also records that the monk Zhizang passed away in 522, the third year of the Putong 普通 era (520–527).
4. The legal governance of ordained Buddhist offenders in the earlier period remains to be investigated, as primary legal sources on the subject predating the fourth century are yet to be found.
5. The office overseeing religious affairs and the monk officials who were appointed to this office were the subjects of a number of earlier works. C. K. Yang provides a brief general discussion on the role of this office. See Yang 1967: 190–92. Stanley Weinstein explores this subject in more detail for the period from the fourth century to the Tang. See Weinstein 1987: 9–11. The most recent summary on this subject with added attention to its practice in the Ming and Qing is found in Barrett 2014. My introduction of the legal courts and codes in this chapter was built on descriptions found in these earlier works, but it is more comprehensive and analytical. In recent decades, Chinese scholars working on Buddhism and the law during the Tang pay particular attention to the mutual influence between Buddhism and state law. Zheng Xianwen points out how state law in Tang China treated lay and ordained Buddhist offenders differently. See Zheng 2004a: 258–59. Zhang Haifeng further elaborates on this in his book where he discusses the mutual influence between Buddhism and state law during the Tang. He presented more Tang edicts that addressed the need to treat lay and ordained Buddhist offenders differently, discusses the reasons the state did so, and points to three penalties that were only applicable to ordained Buddhist offender (surrendering their ordination certificate in return for a reduced penalty, incurring chastisement, and being forced to return to the laity). See Zhang 2014: 254–56, 321–26. Scholars working on Buddhism and the law during the Song also noticed how

penalties for convicted Buddhist clerical offenders were measured differently. See Liu 2012: 29–34; Chen 2015: 88–97.

6. Lawsuits would have included both civil disputes and criminal cases. In contemporary China, state prosecutors prosecute criminal cases. In premodern China, however, charges against criminal offenders were brought up by the victims or their representatives.
7. Yang 1967: 210.
8. Chen 2009: 68.
9. Yan 2007:187–88.
10. Zhang 2014: 321–23.
11. Recent studies on the Baxian County Archive from Sichuan reveals that in the nineteenth century, many laypeople brought ordained Buddhists to the hybrid court. These cases have been discussed in an anonymous article I recently reviewed for *Buddhism, Law & Society*, whose title is "The Hybrid Court at Work: The Local Practice of the Buddhist Office in Qing China."
12. This translation is from Weinstein 1987: 9. Hucker translates the name of this office as the Superintendency of Buddhist Happiness. See Hucker 1985: 147. Wei Shou wrote in his *Book of the Wei* that the Northern Wei established the *cao* 曹 unit in 396, the first year of the Huangshi 皇始 era. See Wei 1974: vol. 113, 2972. This reference led Xie and Bai to date the establishment of the Jianfu cao to 396 or 399, the second year of the Tianxing 天興 era. See Xie and Bai 1990: 55. Weinstein quoted Yamazaki and dated the establishment of this office to circa 396, but this may not be correct. See Weinstein 1987: 9; Yamazaki 1942: 499.
13. For a reference to the establishment of this office in the *Book of the Wei*, see Wei 1974: 3040. Apart from this reference, the Office Overseeing Meritorious Works remains little known. For an introduction to monastic official systems from the fifth century to the Tang, see Weinstein 1987: 9–11. For a study of the development of official monastic systems in China, see He 1958; Mingfu 1981; Xie and Bai 1990. For updated versions, see Xie 2009; Bai 2003; Zhou 2021.
14. Weinstein cites Yamazaki and dates this name change to around 460. See Weinstein 1987: 9; Yamazaki 1942: 9.
15. See T2122: 875b16–b17.
16. In his publication *A Record of Buddhist Monasteries in Luoyang* (*Luoyang qielan ji* 洛陽伽藍記), completed sometime after 534, the Northern Wei historian Yang Xuanzhi notes that the Yongning Monastery was built in the first year during the Xiping 熙平 era and that it was situated adjacent to the Office for the Illumination of Mysteries. See T2092: 999c10–c12.
17. For reference to the following example, see Wei 1974: 3040.
18. Wei 1974: 3044–47.
19. Wei 1974: 3042.
20. For a detailed discussion on this term, see Silk 2008: 127–35.
21. The monastic household (*sengqi hu* 僧祇戶) worked for and paid taxes to Buddhist monasteries. Together with the Buddha's household (*fotu hu* 佛圖戶), members of the monastic household were an important part of the Buddhist monastic economy.

22. Wei 1974: 3042.
23. The following introduction on the transition of these offices during the Tang is based on Bai 2003. See also Xie 2009: 88.
24. Note that this court's name remained the same from the Sui to the Tang but its functions changed. As such, Hucker translates this term differently for its usage in the Sui and Tang dynasties. See Hucker 1985: 264.
25. The Bureau of Sacrifices regained exclusive jurisdiction over the Buddhist establishment after Emperor Li Shi 李適 (742–805; reign 779–805) abolished the position of the Commissioner for the Cultivation of Merit and Virtue, in 779. In 788, the Bureau of Sacrifices once again began to share jurisdiction over ordained Buddhists with two other commissioners: the Commissioner for the Bureau of Merit and Virtue of the Left and Right Avenues of the Capital and the Commissioner for Merit and Virtue in the Eastern Capital (Dongdu gongde shi 東都功德使).
26. Following the reign of Empress Wu Zetian 武則天 (624–705; reign 683–690), the Bureau of Sacrifices assumed jurisdiction over ordained Buddhists in 694. In 736, during the reign of Emperor Li Longji, the Bureau for the Veneration of Mysteries temporarily resumed its jurisdiction over the Buddhist establishment, after which this jurisdiction was again transferred to the Ministry of Rites, starting in 737.
27. At the end of the Tianbao 天寶 (742–756), the Bureau of Sacrifices began to share jurisdiction of the Buddhist establishment with a newly established Commission for the Cultivation of Merit and Virtue (Xiu gongde shi 修功德使), a position staffed by eminent Buddhist monks who, under the supervision of the Court of State Ceremonial, "were charged with regulating the issuance of ordination certificates and the state obligations of Buddhist monks throughout the country." See Hucker 1985: 248.
28. In 845, the Department of Foreign Relations assumed jurisdiction of ordained Buddhists during the reign of Emperor Li Chan 李瀍 (814–846; reign 840–846).
29. In 807, the Commission for the Bureau of Merit and Virtue of the Left and Right Avenues of the Capital assumed sole jurisdiction over Buddhist affairs. In 846, the Bureau of Sacrifices and the Commission for the Bureau of Merit and Virtue of the Left and Right Avenues of the Capital resumed jurisdiction over ordained Buddhists.
30. From the Tang to the Qing, four different Buddhist offices were established at different levels: Senglu si 僧錄, Senggang si 僧綱司, Sengzheng si 僧正司, and Senghui si 僧會司. Charles Hucker translated all of the names of all of the offices to the Buddhist Registry but located them at different levels: the Central Buddhist Registry, the Prefectural Buddhist Registry, the Subprefectural Buddhist Registry, and the District Buddhist Registry. These translations led to confusion when a name used to refer to an office of a Buddhist registry in the capital was later also used to refer to a regional Buddhist registry. To avoid such confusion, I propose to give each of the four offices a distinct English translation as follows: the Office of the Buddhist Registry (Senglu si 僧錄司), the Office of Buddhist Discipline (Senggang si 僧綱司), the Office of the Buddhist Rector (Sengzheng si 僧正司), and the Office of the Buddhist Assembly (Senghui si 僧會司).
31. Song 1976: 87.2193.
32. For a discussion on this office during the Qing, see Yang 2008:1–86.

33. The term Dusi 都司 is also known as Du sengtong si 都僧統司. For further discussion on this office, see Ji 1998: 634.
34. Typical Buddhist monastic officials in Dunhuang were known as "Du sengtong 都僧統" and "Du jiaoshou 都教授." For a detailed study on the development of the office overseeing religious affairs in Dunhuang, see Chikusa 1961.
35. See Zhang 2014: 218.
36. For an introduction on the two levels of regional offices, see Chen 2015:126–27.
37. Chen finds a reference to the appointment of the Buddhist monk Fazong 法宗 as district Buddhist Chief (Sengshou 僧首) in a historical account of the Luohan 羅漢 Cloisterin Nanhai County 南海 in Guangzhou 廣州. See Chen 2015: 127. For the original reference, see Yu, *Wenyuan ge siku quanshu ben*: *juan* 7, 8a.
38. Note that during the Tang, this same name was used to refer to the Central Buddhist Registry.
39. *Ming shilu*: 134.2289.
40. For a detailed discussion on these regional offices in the Qing and how officials were appointed to these offices, see Yang 2008: 37–64.
41. The edict is recorded in the *Expanded Collection on the Propagation and Clarification* (*Guang hongming ji* 廣弘明集), a work that the Buddhist monk Daoxuan 道宣 (596–667) had complied in 644 This was an expansion of an earlier *Collection on the Propagation and Clarification* (*Hongming ji* 弘明集) compiled by the Buddhist monk Sengyou 僧祐 (445–518). For the entire edict titled *Shatai sengtu zhao* 沙汰僧徒詔, see T2103: 272b8–b12.
42. For this reference, see T2145: 85c22.
43. See T2103: 298a24. The same paragraph is cited in T2126: 241b20–b25.
44. For the complete edict titled *Dili sengni zhi zhao* 帝立僧尼制詔, see T2103: 272b26–c05.
45. See Wei 1974: 3039.
46. Wei 1974: 3040. This edict is also recorded in T2126: 241b11–b15.
47. Wei 1974: 3040.
48. Wei 1974: 3044.
49. The position he held was described as Sengdu 僧都 and Guotong 國統. For a reference to this hybrid law in the *Continued Biographies of Eminent Monks*, see Daoxuan, T2060: 608a20–a21. For the entire biography of Huiguang, see Daoxuan, T2060: 607b18–608b29.
50. References to this text appear in multiple Buddhist catalogues and encyclopedias. See T2034: 48a16; T2034: 102b16; T2034: 107a18–108c29; T2060: 436b3–b6; T2149: 279c18–c29; T2122: 1023a16–a18; T2037: 809a25–a28. A fuller account of its compilation can be found in Fei Changfang, T2034: 108b24–b27. This account indicates that this law text was motivated by the need to adjudicate crimes committed by members of the Buddhist establishment. For a biography of Yanzong, see Daoxuan, T2060: 436b3–b6. For a study comparing the *Law and Ordinances from Various Scriptures* and the *Biographies of Eminent Monks*, see Zhang 2012: 165–66.
51. For a reference to this legal text in three catalogues, see T2034: 105a23–b15; T2149: 277c16–c24; T2122: 1022b26–b27.

52. This text is mentioned to consists of thirty scrolls in T2149: 277c17–c24.
53. For the biography of Lingyu on which the following account is based, see T2034: 105a23–b15, T2060: 495b5–498a22, 497c26. His biography in the latter provides the title of this text as being the *Rules for Monks*, but it does not specify its length.
54. For this edict titled *The Edict on the Purification of Ordained Buddhists and Daoists* (*Chu shatai fodao zhao* 出沙汰佛道詔), see T2103: 283c4–c5.
55. This edict is recorded in T2103: 329a21–b15 with the title "Emperor Taizong's Editor on the National Ordination of Buddhists" (*Tang taizong duseng yu tianxia zhao* 唐太宗度僧於天下詔), but this text did not provide a date of this edit. Because this edict caped the total number of Buddhists that can be ordained at three thousands and the biography of Mingjing 明淨 in the *Continued Biographies of Eminent Monks* (T2060: 594b19–11) also mentions an edict permitting the ordination of three thousand Buddhists in the third year of the Zhenguan era, Tang argued that this edict was issued in the third year (629) of the Zhenguan era. See Tang 1982: 15. The edict is also recorded in X1512: 163c21–164a10, where it was dated to the ninth year of the Zhenguan era (635). I thank Shao Yueyang for sharing Tang's dating of this edict.
56. Xuanwan's lay surname was Yang. He studied Buddhist monastic law with the Vinaya master Hong Zun 洪遵. Throughout his religious career in the court, he earned much trust from Emperor Li Shimin. He presided over the ceremony that conferred the Mahāyāna vows to the heir apparent. The emperor even built the Puguang 普光 Monastery for him to administer. When Xuanwan died at the Yanxin 延興 Monastery in 635, in the tenth month in the ninth year of the Zhenguan period, the emperor honored him with an imperial burial and thus began a tradition for the interment of eminent Buddhist monks. For a biography of Xuanwan, see T2060: 616a1–617c12.
57. This reference is found in a text that was composed in 1164; see X1512: 163c16–c20.
58. For the following negotiations between Xuanzang and Emperor Li Zhi, see Xuanzang's biography in T2053: 270a20–c23.
59. T2053: 270a2a-a22: "道士僧等犯罪。情難知者。可同俗法推勘。"
60. For Qi's memorial, see Song scholar Wang Pu's 王溥 (922–982) *Essential Documents and Regulations of the Tang*, which was completed in 961 and can be found in Wang 1955: vol. 50, 1b.
61. Zheng Xianwen argues that *Sengzhi* 僧制 became *Tiaozhi* 條制 in 636. Prior to 741, the *Daoge* 道格 and *Sengge* 僧格 were separate compilations. Later during the Tianbao era (742–756), the two documents were combined as the *Daoseng ge* 道僧格. See Zheng 2004b. Zhao Jing disagreed with this, arguing that the *Daoseng ge* was one of the legal texts included in a few regulations that were promulgated during the Zhenguan and Yonghui eras: *Zhenguan ge* 貞觀格, *Yonghui liubensi xingge* 永徽留本司行格, and *Yonghui liubensi xingge zhongben* 永徽留本司行格中本. He also argued that this *Daoseng ge* later became the *Cibu ge* 祠部格. See Zhao 2014: 147, 150.
62. For a comparative list of articles in the Japanese *Statutes for Monks and Nuns* and the reconstructed Chinese *Regulations for Daoists and Buddhists*, see Niida 1997: 996–1009. For a summary of the proposed reconstructions of articles in the Chinese

Regulations for Daoists and Buddhists by other Chinese and Japanese scholars, see Zhao 2014: 151–62.

63. In the Buddhist context, the five pungent spices refer to garlic, scallions, onions, chives, and leeks.
64. I adopted Wallace Johnson's translation of *kushi* 苦使 as the chastisement from article 23 of the *Tang Code*. See Johnson 1979: 146.
65. See Niida 1997: 1003.
66. Wei 1974: 3040.
67. In 1998, Dai Jianguo discovered and identified a Ming copy of this Song Statute in the Tianyi ge Library 天一閣. For an introduction to this discovery, see Dai 1999: 71–86. For an edited publication of this law, see Shi, Nie, and Bai 2000.
68. For this article, see Tianyi ge bowuguan 2006: vol. 1, 185. For a transcription of this article, see Tianyi ge bowuguan 2006: vol. 2, 342.
69. Niida 1997: 996.
70. Another notable change in the Song was the introduction of an article granting wrongly accused and punished Buddhist clerical offenders the right to appeal to the Ministry of Justice (Xingbu 刑部) via the Fiscal Commission (Zhuanyun si 轉運司). See Xie 2002: 50.690.
71. See the article on ordained Buddhists and Daoists in Dou 1918: *juan* 6, 19b.
72. See Xie 2002: 50.690.
73. Dong Chunlin argued that the Song state regulations on Buddhist offenders became more specific than those promulgated during the Tang. This change led some of the Tang articles to not be included in the Song legal code. See Dong 2010.
74. Song 1976: 19.418.
75. *Ming shilu*: 144.2263.
76. Article 5 on crimes committed by officials in the section on general principles in the section on precedents (*tiaolie* 條例) discusses the procedure for ordained Buddhist offenders. See *Da Ming lü jijie fuli* 1908: 1.15a–15b. The precedents are not translated in Jiang Yonglin's English translation of the *Great Ming Code*.
77. Tian and Zheng 1999: 84. For annotations on this article, see Ma and Yang 1992:198–99. Note that recent studies on the nineteenth century Baxian County Archives reveal that laypeople have also brought ordained Buddhists to the hybrid court with charges of sexual offenses. This is discussed in an anonymous article "The Hybrid Court at Work: The Local Practice of the Buddhist Office in Qing China" I have reviewed for the journal *Buddhism, Law & Society*.
78. During the Yuan, there were military officials (*guanjun guan* 管軍官) and civil officials (*guanmin guan* 管民官).
79. For this reference, see Hong 2016: 53.1760. In what follows, I translate all occurrences of this term (*heshang mei de toumu* 和尚每的頭目) as "the abbot of the monastery."
80. Song 1976: 102, 2620.
81. For this edict, see Hong 2016: 53.1780.
82. Hong 2016: 53.1780–81.
83. Song 1976: 19.418.
84. For record of this case, see Hong 2016: 39.1345.

85. Hong 2016: 39.1345.
86. For this reference, see Hong 2016: 20.439.
87. Song 1976: 20.439.
88. Hong 2016: 39.1346.
89. For this edict, see Hong 2016: 39.1347.
90. Hong 2016: 33.1128.
91. For this edict, see Hong 2016: 53.1758.
92. See Hong 2016: 33.1128–1130.
93. For these cases of leapfrog appeals, see Hong 2016: 33.1129–1130.
94. Hong 2016: 33.1130.
95. For this reference, see Hong 2016: 33.1134–1135.
96. The background of this proposal can be found in Hong 2016: 53.1760.
97. This edict has been preserved in Hong 2016: 33.1134–1135. The following summary is based on the full edict in Hong 2016: 33.1134–1135. The rules stated in this edict were formally incorporated into the Yuan legal system and were collected in the *Da yuan tongzhi tiaoge* 29.339–340. The rule prohibiting civil officials from intervening in internal disputes among ordained Buddhist monks was cited in a document issued in 1314. See Hong 2016: 53.1759.
98. Hong 2016: 33.1128–1130.
99. For this case, see Hong 2016: 53.1759.
100. Song 1976: 19.418.
101. Hong 2016: 33.1135.
102. For this case, see Hong 2016: 53.1760.
103. Hong 2016: 67.1892.
104. T2103: 125b3.
105. T2126: 241b20–b25.
106. The order to not beat ordained Buddhists in the state court is mentioned in Bai 1983: 89.35b. In an interlinear note, the Southern Song scholar Chao Zhongde 晁仲德 comments that this is cited from an edict issued by Tang Emperor Li Yu, ordering that all state courts be prohibited from beating and insulting ordained Buddhist monks and nuns. This edict is also recorded in X1512: 75.194a17–a18.
107. For this case, see Hong 2016: 49.1650.
108. For this case, see Hong 2016: 49.1650.
109. See articles 410–416 for rules on illicit sexual intercourse in the *Tang Code* in Johnson 1979: 473–79.
110. For this regulation, see the commentary on article 57 concerning Daoist priests and nuns in the *Tang Code*. For article 57 in Chinese, see Zhangsun 1983: 143–45; for its English translation, see Johnson 1979: 270–74.
111. See *Song xingtong* (6.19b) in the section on ordained Buddhists and Daoists having illicit sexual intercourse, which says that according to the miscellaneous codes, ordained Daoist priests and nuns who engaged in illicit sexual intercourse would receive a penalty two degrees heavier than ordinary lay offenders.
112. See article 57 in the *Tang Code* in Zhangsun 1983: 143–45. For its English translation, see Johnson 1979: 270–74.

113. See *Song xingtong*: 26.22b; *Great Ming Code*: art. 396; *Great Qing Code*: art. 372. For an English translation of article 396, see Jiang 2005: 217. For the English translation of article 372, see Jones 1994: 352. In the Ming, examples of these types of punishment for lay offenders ranged from a flogging of eighty blows with a heavy stick for having illicit sexual intercourse with consent (or adultery; see article 390) to as much as being strangled for having done so without consent (rape).
114. There is a detailed description of the following procedure in the section that discusses Yuan's legal system in the official *History of the Yuan*. See the chapter on *Criminal law* (*Xingfa zhi* 刑法志) in Song 1976: 104.2654.
115. Xie 2002: 50.690.
116. Xie 2002: 51.722–23.
117. *Da Yuan tongzhi tiaoge*: 29.336.
118. Song 1976: 100.2565; 101.2599.
119. Song 1976: 103.2639.
120. Hong 2016: 65.1830.
121. *Da Yuan tongzhi tiaoge*: 3.41.
122. See article 21 in *Statutes for Monks and Nuns* in Niida 1997: 1005; Niida 1997: 996.
123. See article 7 in Niida 1997: 1000.
124. See article 7 in Niida 1997: 1000.
125. Niida 1997: 1000. See also article 3 in Zhangsun 1983: 3.4.
126. See article 16 in Niida 1997: 1002.
127. *Song xingtong*: 26.22b.
128. Xie 2002: 50.690.
129. Xie 2002: 50.697.
130. For a study and translation of one set of these rules, see Yifa 2009.
131. Its abridged version, *Rules for the Chan School* (*Chanmen guishi* 禪門規式) survives in the eleventh century compilation of the *Record of the Transmission of the Lamplight Compiled during the Jingde Era* (*Jingde chuandeng lu* 景德傳燈錄). The verse version is the *Pure Rules of Baizhang in Standard Verse* (*Baizhang gui shengsong* 百丈規繩颂). For the three commentaries, see X1245 (Zongji); T2025; X1244.
132. See T2076: 251a23–a24; X1244: 550c10–c13.
133. See T2025.1121c6–c7; X1244: 373a16–c4.
134. See T2076: 251a24–a28; T2025: 1121c20–c22; X1244: 373a16–c4; X1245 (Baizhang Huaihai): 550c14–550a1.
135. For these rules, see Zhuhong 1983: vol. 8, 4866–67.
136. See Zhuhong 1983: vol. 8, 4866–67.
137. In his study on Tibetan Buddhist monks living in Beijing during the Ming, Du Changshun mentions the Tibetan monk Zhangyang shajia 章陽沙加, who was the head of the Phag mo grub pa sect in Tibet and was appointed as the Imperial Preceptor (Guoshi 國師) during the Hongwu period. See Du 2005: 62. Chen Qingying identifies this monk as the second Phag mo grub pa leader, Shakya rgyal mtshan (1340–1373), the nephew of Da'i situ Byang chub rgyal mtshan (1302–1364). See Chen 2017: 43. But this monk passed away long before 1456.
138. *Ming shilu*: 267.5675.

139. The following solution can be found in the Qing monk Yirun's commentary on the *Pure Rules of Baizhang*. He reported that the imagined questions and answers are from the Ming monk Zhuhong's *Anthology of Teachings at Yunqi* (*Yunqi fahui* 雲棲法匯), but the quoted questions and answers are absent there. See X1244: 373a16–c4.
140. T2025.1121c25–c26; X1244:420a23–c10.
141. See Zhuhong 1983: vol. 8, 5023.
142. A case recorded in the *Compendium of Statutes and Substatutes of the Yuan* reveals that ordained Buddhist monks took full advantage of the joint investigation option. In 1321, monk Zhai Deyuan 翟德淵 sued the district judge for adjudicating a case concerning a fight between a Buddhist monk Li Mingxiu 李明秀 and a layperson, in his absence, and for accepting a one-sided testimonial from the lay litigant as adequate to justify punishing the monk litigant with twenty-seven blows of flogging. For this case, see Hong 2016: 67.1909–1910.

Chapter 6

1. For the report, see Xianjia and Xianqi 2018.
2. For more on the rise of Longquan Monastery, see Hernádez 2016.
3. For a few examples, see Shi Zhaohui 2018; Associated Press 2018; Johnson 2018.
4. Other scholars have also discussed the relationship between the state and Buddhism from other perspectives. Timothy Brook observes three positions in the interaction between the state and Buddhism: patronage, prohibition, and regulation. See Brook 2009: 22–42. Focusing on the interaction between the state and the Buddhist institutions in the implementation of economic projects, Ji Zhe concludes that such interactions involve but are not limited to the monasteries' cooperation with the state. See Ji 2004: 1–13.
5. Ch'en 1973: 66; 124.
6. Yu 2005: 105.
7. Yu 2005: 133–34.
8. Yu 2005: 133.
9. Welch 1968: 137.
10. Welch 1968: 132.
11. Welch 1968: 135–36.
12. Welch 1968: 135.
13. In certain contexts, a monk who had sex could remain in the monastic community. For a detailed discussion on such examples in the Buddhist monastic law, see Clarke 2009a.
14. This term is *kalpikāraka* in Sanskrit or *jingren* 淨人 in Chinese.
15. Xianjia and Xianqi 2018: 62–86.
16. Xianjia and Xianqi 2018: 6.
17. Xianjia and Xianqi 2018:7.
18. Xianjia and Xianqi 2018: 7.
19. Xianjia and Xianqi 2018: 8.

20. Xianjia 2018.
21. For the official statement, see Longquan si 2018.
22. See Beijing shi renda changwei hui 2009.
23. See T1421: 80bc3–80c9. It is noteworthy that this advice is absent in the sections elaborating on the same probationary offense in all the other *Vinaya* texts. Therefore, the extent to which this passive attitude in the *Mahīśāsaka Vinaya* represents the Buddhist approach to handling cases of sexual assault remains uncertain.
24. For examples on the use of these other Vinaya texts in Dunhuang, see Liu 2020c.
25. For citations from the *Mahīśāsaka Vinaya*, see Xianjia and Xianqi 2018: 27. For studies on the resurgence of monastic discipline among Buddhists in modern and contemporary China, see Bianchi 2016; Bianchi 2017; Campo 2016; Campo 2017. More information on the revival of disciplining Buddhist monastics can be found at the website of the research project "Vinaya Revival in Twentieth Century China and Taiwan," www.vinayarevival.com.
26. My discussion below focuses on the negotiation over the jurisdiction of the Buddhist Association of China. For detailed studies on the history and development of the Buddhist Association of China and its charter, see Huang 2014; Ji 2015.
27. Welch 1968: 141.
28. Welch 1972: 17.
29. Welch 1968: 26.
30. See Welch 1968: 44.
31. For a detailed study of the establishment of this association in mainland China after 1949, see Li 2005.
32. For a detailed introduction of the founding of the Buddhist Association in China in 1953, see Li 2005.
33. See Zhongguo fojiao xiehui 1953. This charter has eleven articles.
34. The second national assembly passed this revision during meetings between March 26 and 31, 1957. See Zhongguo fojiao xiehui 1957.
35. The fourth national assembly passed this revision on December 23, 1980. This charter has seventeen articles. For the charter, see Zhongguo fojiao xiehui 1981.
36. The fifth national assembly of the Buddhist Association of China passed this version on March 1, 1987. It has seventeen articles. See Zhongguo fojiao xiehui 1987.
37. The sixth national assembly passed this version on October 19, 1993. It has seventeen articles and became effective on October 19, 1993. See Zhongguo fojiao xiehui 1993.
38. The seventh national assembly passed this revision on September 18, 2002. This charter has forty-four articles. It became effective fifteen days after the assembly passed it, with approval from the government. For the charter, see Zhongguo fojiao xiehui 2002b.
39. The eighth national assembly passed this revision on February 3, 2010. This charter has forty-nine articles. See Zhongguo fojiao xiehui 2010.
40. The ninth national assembly passed this revision on April 22, 2015. It became effective on the day the government officially approved it. This charter has forty-seven articles. For the charter, see Zhongguo fojiao xiehui 2015.

41. The tenth national assembly passed a revision of this charter on December 2, 2020. This revision has not yet been published in the association's official journal, *Fayin*, as of July 2021.
42. For examples of the lawsuits in which the association had been represented, see Xu 2013: 13–14.
43. See Zhonghua fojiao zonghui 1912.
44. For this draft, see Zhongguo fojiao zhonghui 1912. This charter had twenty-three articles and was approved on February 12, 1912.
45. See article 8d.
46. See article 8e; article 11a; article 11c.
47. See article 11c.
48. See article 8g.
49. See article 8. On April 1, 1912, Buddhists gathered at Liuyun 留雲 Monastery, in Shanghai, to prepare for the establishment of the General Buddhist Association of China (Zhonghua fojiao zonghui 中華佛教總會). Soon afterward, twenty-two provincial offices and over four hundred county offices were established for this association.
50. See article 11b.
51. See article 8.
52. See Neiwu bu 1912a.
53. See Zhonghua fojiao zonghui 1914.
54. See Neiwu bu 1912b.
55. See Zhonghua fojiao zonghui 1913.
56. See Article 11b Zhonghua fojiao zonghui 1913.
57. See Article 11j in Zhonghua fojiao zonghui 1913.
58. See Zhu 1914a.
59. See Zhu 1914b.
60. For a detailed study on the history of this association between 1912 and 1915, see Xu 2013.
61. For the reference to this petition by the Mongolian monk, see Neiwu bu 1917.
62. See Zhongguo fojiao hui 1919.
63. On May 5 and September 30, 1919, the governor of Jiangsu Province, Qi Yaolin, twice confirmed that the Ministry of the Interior had officially revoked this association in May 1919. See Qi 1919a; Qi 1919b.
64. See Zhongguo fojiao hui 1929.
65. See Zhongguo fojiao hui 1935b; Zhongguo fojiao hui 1935c. The version that passed had been built on an earlier draft that included twenty-nine articles. See Zhongguo fojiao hui 1935a.
66. The bylaws of the Buddhist community refer to the *Pure Rules* (*Qinggui* 清規), which contain disciplinary rules for residents of Chinese Buddhist monasteries and nunneries, established by the indigenous leaders of those communities.
67. In June 1936, the association's official journal published this draft charter along with its seventy articles. See Zhongguo fojiao hui 1936a. The same version was also published on August 1, 1936, in a Buddhist journal. The preface of the latter

reported director Zhang's consultation with the Buddhist monks in Shanghai. For the preface, see Zhongguo foijao hui 1936d. This draft version was published in Zhongguo fojiao hui 1936b.

68. See Zhongguo fojiao hui 1936a.
69. See Zhongguo fojiao hui 1936c.
70. These comments were published in two issues of the journal. See "Fulu."
71. See Guangwen 1936.
72. See Benseng 1936.
73. See Zhang 1936.
74. For an introductory note on this revision, see Zhongyang minxun bu 1936. This draft version was also published in two other Buddhist journals. See Zhongguo fojiao hui 1936a; 1936b.
75. Zhongguo fojiao hui 1936a: 66.
76. Zhongguo fojiao hui 1936a: 71.
77. The newly passed charter was published in the association's official journal in November 1936, but only had thirty-seven articles. See Zhongguo fojiao hui 1936e. The thirty-eight-article version was published in 1939. See Zhongguo fojiao hui 1939.
78. The charter for this association that the Jiangsu provincial government circulated on January 31, 1948, was identical to this 1936 version. For the 1948 charter, see Zhongguo fojiao hui 1948.
79. For a discussion on the history of this office and China's state policy on religion between 1949 and the present, see Yang 2011: 65–84.
80. Existing scholarship on the history of these government offices and legislation on the management of Buddhist affairs largely centers on the articles concerning the handling of Buddhist monastic property. See Welch 1968: 129–42. For a discussion on the 1913 and 1915 legislation on managing monasteries and temples during the Beiyang government, see Guo 2005: 23–27, 43. For a detailed discussion of the history and content of the legislation on managing monasteries and temples in the Republican era, see Chen 2008.
81. One unique feature of the legal governance of Buddhist establishments in China has been the differentiation of Chinese Buddhist monasteries from Tibetan Buddhist monasteries and those located on the frontiers of Tibet and Xinjiang. From 1929 to 1935, the Ministry of the Interior promulgated regulations for Chinese, Tibetan, and Mongolian Buddhists, respectively. In contemporary China, the differentiation between Chinese and non-Chinese Buddhist institutions has been retained. The Buddhist Association of China only oversees the Chinese Buddhist community, but the jurisdiction of the State Administration of Religious Affairs covers the Tibetan Buddhist community. For this differentiation, see Guomin zhengfu 1930; Guomin zhengfu 1931; Guomin zhengfu 1935; Guojia zongjiao shiwu ju 2010. Article 11 in the 1929 legislation explicitly states that this regulation did not apply to the Buddhist monasteries in central and eastern Tibet, Xinjiang, and Qinghai.
82. For these articles, see Neiwu bu 1913.

83. For the 1921 legislation, see Neiwu bu 1921. For the January 1929 legislation, see Guomin zhengfu 1929a.
84. See Neiwu bu 1915.
85. For an introduction to these criticisms by the Buddhist community, see Chen 2008: 56.
86. See Guomin zhengfu 1929a.
87. For the telegraphs, see Sichuan sheng fojiao hui 1929.
88. See Shoupei 1929: 2–3; Xingzheng yuan 1929a; Sichuan fojiao hui 1929; Honghu 1929: 51–65.
89. See Jishan et al. 1929. These ordained and lay Buddhists include Jishan 寂山, Taixu 太虛, Yuanying 圓瑛, Renshan 仁山, Huizong 惠宗, Xie Zhuchen 謝鑄陳, Wang Yiting 王一亭, Guan Jiongzhi 關炯之, and Zhong Kanghou 鍾康候.
90. See Sichuan fojiao hui 1929.
91. See Xingzheng yuan 1929a.
92. See Xingzheng yuan 1929b.
93. See Guomin zhengfu 1929c.
94. See Guomin zhengfu 1929d.
95. See Xingzheng yuan 1929c.
96. See Xingzheng yuan 1929d; Guomin zhengfu 1929c.
97. See Guomin zhengfu 1929b.
98. See Guomin zhengfu 1930.
99. See Neiwu bu 1915: 5–6.
100. See Neiwu bu 1921: 47.
101. Guomin zhengfu 1929a: 3.
102. See Zhonghua renmin gongheguo guowuyuan 1994.
103. See Zhonghua renmin gongheguo guowuyuan 2005.
104. For this revision, see Zhonghua renmin gongheguo guowuyuan 2018.
105. See Guojia zongjiao shiwuju 2018.
106. For a discussion of the offense of sexual intercourse in the Buddhist monastic law in the *Dharmaguptaka Vinaya*, which is predominant in China, see T1428: 568c7–572b5. Note that the *Dharmaguptaka Vinaya* does mention that monks should not use coarse and harsh language (*cu'e yu* 麁惡語) on women. See T1428: 582a14.
107. Johnson 2018 states that Xuecheng has been banished to a small temple in Fujian Province.
108. For this change, see the newly added article 14 in Zuigao renmin fayuan 2019.
109. For this case, see Chen, Zhang, Liu, and Dang 2011: vol. 3, 53.1759.
110. For examples of such privileges, see Welch 1968: 132.
111. See Neizheng bu 1932.
112. For the inquiry and reply, see Neizheng bu 1937.

Chapter 7

1. See Zuigao renmin fayuan 1994.

2. This is a right defined by article 9 in the *Law of Succession* that went into effect on October 1, 1985. See Quanguo renmin daibiao dahui 1985.
3. See article 14 in Zhongguo fojiao xiehui 2006.
4. See Yunnan sheng Yuxi zhongji renmin fayuan 2012.
5. See Yunnan sheng gaoji renmin fayuan 2012.
6. For this themed webpage, see https://fo.ifeng.com/special/sengrenyichan/.
7. I analyze fourteen of these cases in the present chapter. The only case I exclude is a 2015 lawsuit between the biological children of the monk Weiyuan 偉願 from Yufo Monastery, in Shanghai, and a lay disciple of this monk. In 1998, the monk had left a notarized last will and testament specifying that he would give two properties he had purchased to two of his lay disciples, on the condition that they use them to provide housing for vegetarian seniors who practiced Buddhism. When the monk passed away in 2000, the lay disciples inherited the said properties, and they began renting them out in May 2011. Because the beneficiaries had repurposed the two properties, the monk's three children sued them on May 20, 2013, and promised to turn these properties into housing for vegetarian Buddhist seniors, to fulfill their father's last wishes as declared in his will. On December 10, 2013, the Kunshan People's Court in Jiangsu Province ruled in favor of the deceased monk's children. The lay disciples unsuccessfully appealed twice, once in the Suzhou Intermediate People's Court in Jiangsu Province, and once in Jiangsu High People's Court. For the final judgment in this case, see Jiangsu sheng gaoji renmin fayuan 2015.
8. For the judgment of this case, see Jiangxi sheng nancheng xian renmin fayuan 2020.
9. See Jiangxi sheng nancheng xian renmin fayuan 2020.
10. The Buddhist Association of China offered this explanation in an editorial comment at the beginning of its official statement on the handling of deceased monks' bequests. For the editorial opinion, see Zhongguo fojiao xiehui 1999: 40.
11. This change was announced in the *Notice on the Registration of Legal Persons for Religious Organizations*. See Guojia zongjiao shiwuju and Minzheng bu 2019.
12. For earlier studies of various cases among the nine cases dated between 1984 and 2012, see Huang 2013; Li 2015; Shi 2013; Tang 2015; Wu Caiyu 2016; Wu Caiyu 2019; Wu Guoping 2016; Wu Zhaojun 2018; Yu 2012; Yu 2015; Zhang 2009.
13. See Human Rights Watch 1997.
14. For the report, see The Law Library of Congress 2018: 5. For Zhang's argument, see Zhang 2012: 242–43.
15. See Zhongguo fojiao xiehui 1999.
16. See Zhongguo fojiao xiehui 1999: 40.
17. For a summary of these demands from the three parties, see Fenghuang wang 2012a.
18. For the published statement, see Zhongguo fojiao xiehui 2002a.
19. The Buddhist Association of China did not specify the name of this text in its 1998 reply, but provided this info in the later 2002 reply, which I discuss below.
20. See Zhongguo fojiao xiehui 2002a: 35.
21. See T1483: 977c24.

22. See Zhongguo fojiao xiehui 1999: 40. For the original *Pure Rules of Baizhang* in Chinese, see T2025: 1109c17–1160b15. I am unable to find the phrase quoted in the statement from the Buddhist Association of China in this original text.
23. See T1808: 505c19–506a1.
24. See T1428: 859b20–c4.
25. See X730: 460b17–b21.
26. See T1458: 567c18–568c12.
27. See Quanguo renmin daibiao dahui 1985.
28. Cao 1985: 171.
29. See T2061: 801c23–24.
30. See Tang and Lu 1990: vol. 2, 150–52.
31. See Zhongguo fojiao xiehui 2006.
32. See Zhongguo fojiao xiehui 2006. At the Buddhist Association of China's ninth national assembly on July 24, 2019, another new article was added, but the article from the 2006 version dealing with deceased Buddhists' property remained unchanged. See Zhongguo fojiao xiehui 2019.
33. Article 10 in the *Law of Succession* designates the children of the deceased as legitimate heirs to the estates left by the deceased. For this article 10, see the 1985 *Law of Succession* at the following link: https://www.gqb.gov.cn/node2/node3/node5/node9/node101/userobject7ai1284.html.
34. Zhongguo fojiao xiehui 2002a: 34–35.
35. For the court's judgment in this case, see Lianyungang shi haizhou qu renmin fayuan 2018.
36. For the three judgments in this case, see Liaoning sheng Anshan shi qianshan qu renmin fayuan 2008a; Liaoning sheng Anshan shi qianshan qu renmin fayuan 2008b; Liaoning sheng gaoji renmin fayuan 2009. I was not able to obtain copies of the first two judgments. For access to the final judicial judgment, I thank Mr. Sun Shuning 孫樹寧, the legal representative of the plaintiffs in this case, who assisted me in locating a copy online. In analyzing this case, I also consulted the document listing the lay heirs' arguments against the monastery and the transcript of the lay heir's lawyer's defense in court. Mr. Sun had posted this document and the transcript on social media. For the lawyer's defense, see Yang 2008.
37. See Yang 2008.
38. See Liaoning sheng gaoji renmin fayuan 2016.
39. See Liaoning sheng gaoji renmin fayuan 2016.
40. For the defense of the legal representative posted online, see Yang 2008.
41. For this case, see Fenghuang wang 2012a.
42. See Jiangsu sheng Yangzhou shi zhongji renmin fayuan 2017.
43. See Guangdong sheng Wengyuan xian remin fayuan 2016.
44. For a summary of this case, see Fenghuang wang 2012b.
45. Shanghai shi gaoji renmin fayuan 2005: 108.
46. Monk Farong had been the treasurer of Xinglong Monastery. When he died suddenly in 1996, his stepson demanded to inherit his possessions, including furniture, cash,

antique coins, and a bank account balance. For a summary of this case, see Zheng 2001: 216.

47. For a report on this case, see Fenghuang wang 2012c.
48. The following introduction of this case is based on the judgment from the first trial. See Guangdong sheng Wengyuan xian renmin fayuan, 2016.
49. This will is included in the judgment. See Guangdong sheng Wengyuan xian renmin fayuan 2016.
50. See Guangdong sheng Wengyuan xian renmin fayuan 2016.
51. For a summary of this case, see Shi 2013.
52. See Zuigao renmin fayuan 2005.
53. See Zuigao renmin fayuan 1994.
54. See Zuigao renmin fayuan 2021.
55. See Zheng, Liu, and Wang 2021.

Epilogue

1. *Spotlight*, directed by Tom McCarthy (Los Angeles: Open Road Films, 2015).
2. For examples, see Vitello 2014; Johnson 2018; Dyson and Newland 2019; Barghout 2022.
3. See Phillips 2021.
4. For example, see revelations of sexual misconduct by the Tibetan Buddhist teacher Lama Norlha Rinpoche from the Kagyu Thubten Choling in New York, in Deveaux 2017and Miller 2018. For a case against a Chinese Buddhist leader, see the case of Xuecheng in Liu 2020a.
5. See *Janice Doe v. Sogyal Rinpoche et al.*, Superior Court of California, County of Santa Cruz, case no. CISCV129647. In Tibetan, his name is spelled Bsod rgyal.
6. For a pretrial judgement on this lawsuit by Master Elwood, see Han v Dorje, No. E191921, 2021 BCSC 939. This court document is also available online at the following link: https://www.bccourts.ca/jdb-txt/sc/21/09/2021BCSC0939.htm.
7. In Tibetan, his name is spelled O rgyan 'phrin las rdo rje.
8. See Han v. Dorje, No. E191921, 2021 BCSC 939.
9. For a report on this update, see Agsar 2022.
10. On February 20, 2002, Middlesex Superior Court Judge Sandra Hamlin convicted John Geoghan of fondling a ten-year-old boy in a Waltham swimming pool in 1991 and sentenced him to a nine- to ten-year prison term. For a report on this conviction, see Ranalli 2002. On March 7, 2002, however, Superior Court of Massachusetts Judge Margaret R. Hinkle approved John Geoghan's motion to dismiss two earlier convictions of sexual abuse of young children on the grounds that the statute of limitations had expired. For this dismissal, see Commonwealth v. John Geoghan, Nos. 99-11434, 001-001, Mass. S. Ct., March 7, 2002. Although Geoghan was not the first priest to be convicted in a state court, his conviction had a far more profound impact on how clerical offenders could be held to state law. The earliest publicized clerical offender was Gilbert Gauthe, a Catholic priest who was convicted in 1985. For reports

on Gauthe's case, see Berry 1985. The report is also accessible online at https://www.bishop-accountability.org/news/1985_05_23_Berry_TheTragedy.htm. For further discussions on clerical sexual abuse and clerical immunity, see Lupu and Tuttle 2004.

11. See Miller 2018.
12. See *Nihongi*: chapter 22, 1330–31.
13. See *South Korean Monk Gets Six Years in Prison for* Stealing Japanese Religious Items.
14. For more information on this Buddhist monk killer, see the entry on Ryuun Daimai at the following link: https://www.madisons.jp/murder/text_japan/ryuun.html.
15. See "Monk Gets Suspended Jail Term over Threat to Japanese Envoy."
16. See "76 sui heshang he nüzi zai chansi youhui qi zhengzhi."
17. See "Buddhist Baptized on Eve of Execution."
18. See Wickrama 2012.
19. See "Jet-Set Monk Gets a Further 16 Years for Rape of Minor."
20. See "Sister of Pregnant Woman Killed by Monk Demands Apology."
21. See "Buddhist Monk Arrested after Fatal Stabbing of Muslim Teenager."
22. The Supreme Council of Abbots is also known as the State Sanghmahayanayaka Committee (SCC). See Ashin and Crosby 2017: 200. I thank Kate Crosby and Christian Lammarts for the email exchanges that helped me better understand the situation in Myanmar.
23. In 2018, Thailand passed the *Sangha Act*, a law that enables the king to appoint or remove a monk from the Sangha Supreme Council, an agency that is responsible for establishing and running the Buddhist monastic courts, where "disputes between monks that cannot be handled at the local level may be dealt with." See Schonthal 2020: 209. For further discussion on this agency, see Borchert and Darlington 2017: 18.
24. See Ashin and Crosby 2017.
25. This is also known as the Sanghamahanayaka Committee (SSC).
26. The summary below is based on a detailed introduction on the Buddhist judicial system in Sri Lanka. See Schonthal 2020.
27. Schonthal 2020: 210.
28. Schonthal 2020: 210.
29. Examining a fifth-century letter from Bishop Leo of Bourges in southern France, Charles West observed that the church forbid clerics from initiating lawsuits in the state court. But if a layperson were to have sued a cleric, as a defendant, the cleric, with approval from the bishop, could have contested the plaintiff's accusations in the state court. These policies are similar to what we see in Buddhism, as discussed in Chapter 1 on the litigation panic. For an analysis of the letter, see West 2021.
30. Cross 1917: 551–57.
31. It is important to note that in Buddhism, the equivalent of the Christian ordained minister is absent. In Christianity, a Christian practitioner could be a monk or nun living in celibacy in a monastery or nunnery, an ordained minister who can lead religious services but lives a lay life, or an ordinary lay Christian. In Buddhism, Buddhist practitioners are either ordained monastics or lay householders. The category of an ordained minister living a lay life did not exist in early Buddhism. Noteworthy

exceptions can be found in some Japanese Buddhist communities, where an individual can be ordained as a minister who can lead religious services but need not live in celibacy.

32. Cross 1917: 552. It is important to note that in the Christian context, an ordained clerk could be either a layperson or a monk, but in the Buddhist tradition, an ordained Buddhist was always referred to as a monastic but never a layperson.
33. Cross 1917: 552. This ordinance is usually cited as 25 Edw. III., stat. 6, c. 4. It refers to item 4 of statute 6 issued by King Edward III during the twenty-fifth year of his reign. For the ordinance, see House of Commons of Great Britain 1965: vol. 1, 325.
34. Cross 1917: 552–53.
35. Cross 1917: 555. This statute is usually cited as 6 Anne, c. 9, s. 4. It refers to statute 4 in chapter 9 of the statutes issued by Queen Anne in 1707. For the original statute, see The House of Commons of Great Britain, 1965: vol. 8, 563.
36. For a discussion on the English courts during the Anglo-Saxon era, see Zinkeisen 1895.
37. Cross 1917: 545–49.
38. Glenn contended that the Buddha had "other than things legal in mind" and refuted those who claimed that the Buddha's teachings have legal implications. See Glenn 2014: 320, 330–33.

Bibliography

Primary Texts from the Buddhist Canon

T99 *Za ahan jing* 雜阿含經. T99: 1a1–373b18.
T192 *Fo suoxing zan* 佛所行讚. T192: 1a1–54c10.
T271 *Foshuo pusaxing fangbian jingjie shentong bianhua jing* 佛説菩薩行方便境界神通變化經. T271: 300b9–316b15.
T272 *Da sazhe niqianzi suoshuo jing* 大薩遮尼乾子所説經. T272: 317a2–365c20.
T287 *Foshuo shidi jing* 佛説十地經. T287: 535a22–574c16.
T383 *Moye furen jing* 摩耶夫人經. T383: 1005a2–1015a16.
T397a *Yuezang fen* 月藏分. In *Da fangdeng daji jing* 大方等大集經. T397: 298a3–381c12.
T397b *Xumizang fen* 須彌藏分. In *Da fangdeng daji jing* 大方等大集經. T397: 381c16–394a27.
T410 *Da fangguang shilun jing* 大方廣十輪經. T410: 681a2–720a14.
T411 *Dacheng daji dizang shilun jing* 大乘大集地藏十輪經. T411: 721a3–777c4.
T998 *Foshuo huixianglun jing* 佛説迴向輪經. T998: 577a19–578a28.
T1421 *Wufen lü* 五分律. T1421: 1a4–194b28.
T1422 *Mishasai wufen jieben* 彌沙塞五分戒本. T1422: 194c4–206b19.
T1423 *Wufen biqiuni jieben* 五分比丘尼戒本. T1423: 206b24–214a13.
T1425 *Mohe sengqi lü* 摩訶僧祇律. T1425: 227a4–549a3.
T1426 *Mohe sengqi lü dabiqiu jieben* 摩訶僧祇律大比丘戒本. T1426: 549a8–556a19.
T1427 *Mohe sengqi biqiuni jieben* 摩訶僧祇比丘尼戒本. T1427: 556a24–566c6.
T1428 *Sifen lü* 四分律. T1428: 567a1–1014b20.
T1429 *Sifen lü biqiu jieben* 四分律比丘戒本. T1429: 1015a4–1023a11.
T1431 *Sifen biqiuni jieben* 四分比丘尼戒本. T1431: 1030c15–1041a18.
T1435 *Shisong lü* 十誦律. T1435: 1a5–470b20.
T1436 *Shisong biqiu boluotimucha jieben* 十誦比丘波羅提木叉戒本. T1436: 470b25–479a6.
T1437 *Shisong biqiuni boluotimucha jieben* 十誦比丘尼波羅提木叉戒本. T1437: 479a11–488b21.
T1440 *Sapuoduo pini piposha* 薩婆多毘尼毘婆沙. T1440: 503c16–564c19.
T1442 *Genben shuoyiqieyou bu pinaiye* 根本説一切有部毘奈耶. T1442: 627a4–905a7.
T1443 *Genben shuoyiqieyou bu biqiuni pinaiye* 根本説一切有部苾芻尼毘奈耶. T1443: 907a2–1020b10.
T1446 *Genben shuoyiqieyou bu pinaiye suiyi shi* 根本説一切有部毘奈耶隨意事. T1446: 1044c11–1048b23.
T1451 *Genben shuoyiqieyou bu pinaiye zashi* 根本説一切有部毘奈耶雜事. T1451: 207a4–414b19.
T1454 *Genben shuoyiqieyou bu jiejing* 根本説一切有部戒經. T1454: 500b17–508a14.

T1455 *Genben shuoyiqieyou bu biqiuni jiejing* 根本說一切有部苾芻尼戒經. T1455: 508a19–517b23.
T1458 *Genben sapoduo bu lüshe* 根本薩婆多部律攝. T1458: 525a4–617a26.
T1462 *Shanjianlü piposha* 善見律毘婆沙. T1462: 673b4–800c12.
T1463 *Pinimu jing* 毘尼母經. T1463: 801a4–850c26.
T1483 *Foshuo Mulian wen jielü zhong wubai qingzhong shi* 佛說目連問戒律中五百輕重事. T1483: 972b14–995c11.
T1545 *Api damo da piposha lun* 阿毘達磨大毘婆沙論. T1545: 247a3–1004:a9.
T1808 Daoxuan 道宣. *Sifen lü shanbu suiji jiemo* 四分律刪補隨機羯磨. T1808: 492a3–511b1.
T2025 Dehui 德輝. *Chixiu Baizhang qinggui* 勅修百丈清規. T2025.48: 1109c18–1160b15.
T2028 *Jiading biqiu shuo danglaibian jing* 迦丁比丘說當來變經. T2028: 7a22–9c14.
T2029 *Foshi biqiu jiatanyan shuofamojing jie bai ershi zhang* 佛使比丘迦旃延說法沒盡偈 百二十章. T2029: 9c20–12c2.
T2034 Fei Changfang 費長房. *Lidai sanbao ji* 歷代三寶記. T2034: 22c27–127c18.
T2037 Jue'an 覺岸, comp. *Shishi jigu lüe* 釋氏稽古略. T2037: 737a4–902c6.
T2042 *Ayu wang zhuan* 阿育王傳. T2042: 99a13–131a24.
T2053 Huili 慧立. *Da Tang Daci'en si sanzang fashi zhuan* 大唐大慈恩寺三藏法師傳. T2053: 220c7–280a6.
T2060 Daoxuan 道宣. *Xu gaoseng zhuan* 續高僧傳. T2060: 425a1–707a27.
T2061 Zaining 贊寧. *Song gaoseng zhuan* 宋高僧傳. T2061: 709a4–900a11.
T2076 Baizhang Huaihai 百丈懷海. *Chanmen guishi* 禪門規式. In *Jingde chuandeng lu* 景德傳燈錄. T2076: 250c27–251b3.
T2087 Xuanzang 玄奘. *Da Tang xiyu ji* 大唐西域記. T2087: 867b14–947c1.
T2092 Yang Xuanzhi 楊衒之. *Louyang qielan ji*洛陽伽藍記. T2092: 999a4–1022b18.
T2103 Daoxuan 道宣. *Guang hongming ji* 廣弘明集. T2103: 52.125b3.
T2122 Daoshi 道世. *Fayuan zhulin* 法苑珠林. T2122: 269a2–1030a24.
T2126 Zanning 贊寧. *Da Song sengshi lüe* 大宋僧史略. T2126: 54.241b20–b25.
T2145 Sengyou 僧祐. *Chu sanzang ji ji* 出三藏記集. T2145: 1a3–114a23.
T2149 Daoxuan 道宣. *Da Tang neidian lu* 大唐內典錄. T2149: 219a3–342a18.
T2788 *Lüjie benshu* 律戒本疏. T2788: 616c14–644c12.
X730 *Pini zuochi xushi* 毗尼作持續釋. X730: 347b13–522b21.
X1244 Yirun 儀潤. *Baizhang conglin qinggui zhengyi ji* 百丈叢林清規證義記. X1244: 373a3–521c22.
X1245 Zongji 宗賾. *Chanyuan qinggui* 禪苑清規. X1245: 522a6–556a14.
X1245 Baizhang Huaihai 百丈懷海. *Baizhang gui shengsong* 百丈規繩誦. X1245: 63.550a16–553b19.
X1512 Zu Xiu 祖琇. *Longxing biannian tonglun* 隆興編年通論. X1512: 116a3–254a6.

Dge slong ma'i 'dul ba rnam par 'byed pa. In *Bka' 'gyur*. Dpe bsdur ma. Vol. 9, *ta*. 72–897.
'Dul ba phran tshegs kyi gzhi. In *Bka' 'gyur*. Dpe bsdur ma. Vol. 10, *tha*, 3–877; vol. 11, *da*, 3–979.
Dul ba rnam par 'byed pa. In *Bka' 'gyur*. Dpe bsdur ma. Vol. 5, ca, 62–vol. 8, 734.
'Dus pa chen po las sa'i snying po 'khor lo bcu pa zhes bya ba theg pa chen po'i mdo. In *Bka' 'gyur*. Dpe bsdur ma. Vol. 65, *zha*. 251–624.
Las brgya tham pa (Karmaśataka). In *Bka' 'gyur*. Dpe bsdur ma. Vol. 73, *ha*. 3–838.

'Phags pa byang chub sems dpa'i spyod yul gyi thabs kyi yul la rnam par 'phrul pa bstan pa. In *Bka' 'gyur*. Dpe bsdur ma. Vol. 57, *pa*. 220–376.

' Phags pa zla ba'i snying pos zhus pa'i mdo las sangs rgyas kyi bstan pa gnas pa dang 'jig pa'i tshul lung bstan pa (Candragarbha Sūtra). In *Bka' 'gyur*. Dpe bsdur ma. Vol. 76, *ā*. 617–33.

Sangs rgyas kyi spyod pa zhes bya ba'i snyan dngags chen po. In *Bstan 'gyur*. Dpe bsdur ma. Vol. 96, *ge*, 3–275.

Ting nge 'dzin gyi mi mthun pa'i phyogs rnam par gzhag pa. In *Bstan 'gyur*. Dpe bsdur ma. Vol. 64, *ki*. 365–371.

Primary Sources

Da Ming lü jijie fuli 大明律集解附例. Beijing: Xiuding falüguan cang, 1908.

Da Yuan tongzhi tiaoge 大元通制條格. Taibei: Huawen shuju, 1968.

Ming shilu 明實錄. 133 vols. Nangang: Zhongyang yanjiuyuan lishi yuyan yanjiusuo, 1962–1966. This edition is a facsimile reproduction of the manuscript copy in the fomer Library of Congress in Beiping (Guoli Beiping tushuguan 國立北平圖書館).

Nihongi: Chronicles of Japan from the Earliest Times to A.D. 697. Translated by William George Aston. 2 vols. London: Published for the Japan Society, 1896.

Song xingtong 宋刑統. Edited by Xue Meiqing 薛梅卿. Beijing: Falü chubanshe, 1999.

Bai Juyi 白居易. *Baikong liutie* 白孔六帖. 100 vols. Taipei: Taiwan shangwu yinshuguan, 1983.

Beijing shi renda changwei hui 北京市人大常委會. "Beijingshi shishi Zhonghua renmin gongheguo funü quanyi baozhangfa banfa xiuding cao'an 北京市實施《中華人民共和國婦女權益保障法》辦法 (修訂草案)." Standing Committee of Beijing Municipal People's Congress. May 4, 2009. http://www.bjrd.gov.cn/zdgz/lfgz/lfgs/201212/t20121207_102561.html. Accessed September 21, 2018.

Benseng 本僧. "Xiuding fojiaohui zhangcheng zhi shangque 修訂佛教會章程草案之商榷." *Haichao yin* 海潮音 17.8 (1936): 108–10.

Chen Gaohua 陳高華, Zhang Fan 張帆, Liu Xiao 劉曉, and Dang Baohai 黨寶海, eds. *Yuan dianzhang* 元典章. 4 vols. Beijing: Zhonghua shuju, 2011.

Dou Yi 竇儀. *Song Jianlong chong xiangding xingtong* 宋建隆重詳訂刑統. Guowuyuan fazhiju chongjiao Tianyige ben, 1918.

Fenghuang wang 鳳凰網. "Guangzhou Guangxiao si Shi Youjin fashi caichan jicheng jiufen an 廣州光孝寺釋有錦法師財產繼承糾紛案." Ifeng.com. October 11, 2012a. https://fo.ifeng.com/special/sengrenyichan/pandian/detail_2012_10/11/18183747_0.shtml. Accessed July 7, 2021.

Fenghuang wang 鳳凰網. "Juzan fashi yichan jiufen an 巨贊法師遺產糾紛案." Ifeng.com. October 11, 2012b. https://fo.ifeng.com/special/sengrenyichan/pandian/detail_2012_10/11/18183476_0.shtml. Accessed July 7, 2021.

Fenghuang wang 鳳凰網. "Wutaishan Longquan si Shi Hanjing fashi caichan jicheng jiufen an 五台山龍泉寺釋含淨法師財產繼承糾紛案." Ifeng.com. October 11, 2012c. https://fo.ifeng.com/special/sengrenyichan/pandian/detail_2012_10/11/18183847_0.shtml. Accessed July 7, 2021.

Guangdong sheng Wengyuan xian renmin fayuan 廣東省翁源縣人民法院. *Wengyuan xian Donghua si yu Zhongguo jianshe yinhang gufen youxian gongsi Wengyuan zhihang suoyouquan queren jiufen yishen minshi panjueshu* 翁源縣東華寺與中國建設銀行

股份有限公司翁源支行所有權確認糾紛一審民事判決書. 2016 yue 0229 min chu 137 hao 2016 粵0229民初137號.

Guangwen 廣文. "Du Zhongyang minxun bu xiuding Zhongguo fojiao hui zhangcheng cao'an yihou 讀中央民訓部修訂中國佛教會章程草案以後." *Haichao yin* 海潮音 17.7 (1936): 96–100.

Guojia zongjiao shiwu ju 國家宗教事務局. "Zangchuan fojiao simiao guanli banfa藏传佛教寺庙管理办法." Sara.gov.cn. Effective November 1, 2010. http://www.sara.gov.cn/zcfg/fg/xzfgjbmgz20170904204343165711/5085.htm. Accessed October 1, 2018.

Guojia zongjiao shiwuju 國家宗教事務局. "Guanyu dui jubao Xuecheng he Beijing Longquan si youguan wenti de diaocha heshi qingkuang关于对举报学诚和北京龙泉寺有关问题的调查核实情况." Sara.gov.cn. August 23, 2018. http://www.sara.gov.cn/xwfb/xwjj20170905093618359691/583630.htm. Published on August 23, 2018. Accessed February 19, 2019.

Guojia zongjiao shiwuju 國家宗教事務局 and Minzheng bu 民政部. *Guanyu zongjiao huodong changsuo banli faren dengji shixiang de tongzhi* 關於宗教活動場所辦理法人登記事項的通知. Effective April 1, 2019. http://big5.www.gov.cn/gate/big5/www.gov.cn/gongbao/content/2019/content_5395498.htm. Acessed October 27, 2023.

Guomin zhengfu 國民政府. "Simiao guanli tiaoli 寺廟管理條例." *Sifa gongbao* 司法公報 4 (1929a): 1–3. Effective January 25, 1929. 21 articles.

Guomin zhengfu 國民政府. "Jiandu simiao tiaoli cao'an 監督寺廟條例草案." *Zhengfu gongbao* 政府公報 41 (1929b): 127–28. 13 articles.

Guomin zhengfu 國民政府. "Ling Lifa yuan: Chi jiang simiao guanli tiaoli xunji heyi jufu you 令立法院: 飭將寺廟管理條例迅即核議具復由." *Guomin zhengfu gongbao* 國民政府公報 315 (1929c): 1.

Guomin zhengfu 國民政府. "Ling Lifa yuan: Wei ju xingzhengyuan zhuan ju neizhengbu chengzhun simiao guanli tiaoli zheng weijing xiuzheng gongbu yiqian zanhuan shixing yang chazhao shenhe jufu you 令立法院: 爲據行政院轉據內政部呈准寺廟管理條例征未經修正公布以前暫緩施行仰查照審核具覆由." *Sifa gongbao* 司法公報 22 (1929d): 38.

Guomin zhengfu 國民政府. "Jiandu simiao tiaoli監督寺廟條例." *Neizheng bu gongbao* 內政部公報 2.12 (1930): 67–68. Effective December 7, 1929. 13 articles.

Guomin zhengfu 國民政府. "Menggu lama simiao jiandu tiaoli蒙古喇嘛寺廟監督條例." *Xingzhengyuan gongbao* 行政院公報 263(1931): 6–7. Effective June 15, 1931. 18 articles.

Guomin zhengfu 國民政府. "Guanli lama simiao tiaoli管理喇嘛寺廟條例." *Guomin zhengfu gongbao* 國民政府公報 1917 (1935): 4. Effective December 9, 1935. 8 articles.

Honghu 宏護. "Fojiao tuanqi qingqiu gaiding xinban simiao guanli tiaoli zhi dianwen 佛教团体请求改订新颁寺廟管理條例之电文." *Dayun foxueshe yuekan* 大雲佛學社月刊 26.92 (1929): 51–65.

Hong Jinfu 洪金富. *Yuan dianzhang*元典章. 4 vols. Taipei: Zhongyang yanjiuyuan lishi yuyan yanjiusuo, 2016.

Human Rights Watch. *China: State Control of Religion*. (Washington, DC: Human Rights Watch, 1997). https://www.hrw.org/reports/1997/china1/. Accessed March 21, 2021.

Jiangsu sheng gaoji renmin fayuan 江蘇省高級人民法院. *Lu Moujia deng yu Mei Mou deng jicheng jiufen zaishen fucha yu shenpan jiandu minshi caidingshu* 盧某甲等與梅某等繼承糾紛再審複查與審判監督民事裁定書. 2015 Su shen er min zi di 00008 hao 2015蘇審二民字第00008號.

Jiangsu sheng Yangzhou shi zhongji renmin fayuan 江蘇省揚州市中級人民法院. *Yangzhou Wenfeng si yu Jiaotong yinhang gufen youxian gongsi hehua zhihang suoyouquan jiufen ershen minshi caidingshu* 揚州文峰寺與交通銀行股份有限公司揚州荷花支行所有權確認糾紛二審民事裁定書. 2017 Su 10 min zhong 396 hao 2017 蘇10民終396號.

Jiangxi sheng nancheng xian renmin fayuan 江西省南城縣人民法院. *Fuzhou shi linchuan qu fojiao xiehui yu fuzhou shi linquan qu fangwu zhengshou yu buchang bangongshi xingzheng peichang caidingshu* 撫州市臨川區佛教協會與撫州市臨川區房屋徵收與補償辦公室行政賠償裁定書. 2020 Gan 1021 xing pei chu 8 hao 2020贛1021行賠初8號.

Jishan 寂山, Taixu 太虛, Yuanying 圓瑛, Renshan 仁山, Huizong 惠宗, Xie Zhuchen 謝鑄陳, Wang Yiting 王一亭, Guan Jiongzhi 關炯之, and Zhong Kanghou 鍾康候. "Zhi Lifayuan Yuanzhang qing caina gefang yijian xiuzheng simiao guanli tiaoli bing congzhong yuanzhu bing qingshi fuhan 致立法院院长请采纳各方意见修正寺廟管理條例从中援助并请示复函." *Zhongguo fojiaohui yuekan* 中國佛教會月刊 4 (1929): 1.

The Law Library of Congress. *China: Religion and Chinese Law*. 2018. Online publication published on www.justice.gove, accessed on March 21, 2021, but the page is not found on October 27, 2023.

Lianyungang shi haizhou qu renmin fayuan 連雲港市海州區人民法院. *Haizhou Bixia si yu Li Mou1 Li Mou2 deng jicheng jiufen yishen minshi panjueshu* 海州碧霞寺與李某1 李某2等繼承糾紛一審民事判決書. 2018 蘇 0706 民初 555 號. Available on the China Judgements Online 中国判决文书网database at https://wenshu.court.gov.cn/. Accessed June 28, 2021.

Liaoning sheng Anshan shi qianshan qu renmin fayuan 遼寧省鞍山市千山區人民法院. 2008 An qian chuzi di 846 hao 2008 鞍千初字第 846 號. 2008a.

Liaoning shengAnshan shi zhongji renmin fayuan 遼寧省鞍山市中级人民法院. 2008 An min er zhong zi di 603 hao 2008 鞍民二终字第 603 号. 2008b.

Liaoningsheng gaoji renmin fayuan 遼寧省高級人民法院. *Yang Shubo Yang Shuze Yang Shumin Anshan Shi Qianshan Xiangyan si jicheng jiufen yi'an* 楊樹波楊樹則楊樹敏鞍山市千山香岩寺繼承糾紛一案 . 2009 Liao li san minshen zi di 484 hao 2009 遼立三民申字第 484 號.

Liaoning sheng gaoji renmin fayuan 遼寧省高級人民法院. *Shangsu ren Zhao Zhuo yin yu bei shangsu ren Jianping xian Mituo si caichan sunhai peichang jiufen ershen minshi panjueshu* 上訴人趙卓因與被上訴人建平縣彌陀寺財產損害賠償糾紛二審民事判決書. 2016 Liao min zhong 17 hao 2016 遼民終 147 號.

Longquan si 龍泉寺. "Yanzheng shengming 嚴正聲明." Ifeng.com. https://fo.ifeng.com/a/20180802/45097173_0.shtml. Accessed September 21, 2018.

Menon, Nivedita. "Ayodhya for Buddhists: All India Confederation of SC/ST Organisations." *Kafila* (blog). January 8, 2011. https://kafila.online/2011/01/08/ayodhya-for-buddhistsall-india-confederation-of-scst-organizations/. Accessed April 8, 2022.

Multiple Authors. "Fulu: Benhui shencha zhangcheng cao'an zhi yijian 附錄:本會審查章程草案之意見." Pts. 1 and 2. *Zhongguo fojiaohui bao* 中國佛教會報 7 (1936): 57–86; 8 (1936): 32–68.

Neiwu bu 內務部. "Neiwu bu zifu Hunan dudu zhonghua fojiao zonghui zhangcheng getiao junxu xiuzheng qingchi zunzhao benbu tongxing chongding huizhang chengbu shending yi ming jiexian wen 內務部咨覆湖南都督中華佛教總會章程各條均須修

正請飭遵照本部通行重訂會章呈部審定以明界限文." *Zhengfu gongbao* 政府公報 115 (1912a): 8–9.

Neiwu bu 內務部. "Neiwu bu fu Guowu yuan Fojiao zonghui zhangcheng yingjia xiugai han 內務部覆國務院佛教總會章程應加修改函. *Zhengfu gongbao* 政府公報 212 (1912b): 12–13. Published on December 8, 1912.

Neiwu bu內務部. "Siyuan guanli zanxing guize 寺院管理暫行規則." *Zhengfu gongbao* 政府公報 403 (1913): 307–8. Effective June 20, 1913.

Neiwu bu 內務部. "Guanli simiao tiaoli 管理寺廟條例." *Jiangsu sheng gongbao* 江蘇省公報 690 (1915): 2–6. Effective October 29, 1915. 31 articles.

Neiwu bu內務部. "Yuan jucheng ren Zhonghua fojiao huizhang Zhangjia deng: cheng yijian wei zunpi shangai huizhang qingli anyou 原具呈人中華佛教會會長章嘉等：呈一件爲遵批删改會章請立案由 . *Zhengfu gongbao* 政府公報 215 (1917): 8. The document was dated May 3, 1917. It was published on May 12, 1917.

Neiwu bu 內務部. "Xiuzheng guanli simiao tiaoli 修正管理寺庙条例." *Shanghai lüshi gonghui baogao shu* 上海律師公會報告書 2 (1921): 44–47. Effective May 20, 1921.

Neizheng bu 內政部. "Wei sifayuan jieshi gonggong chusuo ji simiao anguan yingfou bianru lülin ji sengdao yingfou renwei jumin ji gongmin yi'an you 為司法院解釋公共處所及寺廟庵觀應否編入閭鄰及僧道應否認為居民及公民一案由." *Neizheng gongbao* 內政公報 5.24 (1932): 16–17.

Neizheng bu 內政部. "Zhun zi wei sengni xishi yapian yingfou yi bushou qinggui lun wu bei xuanwei simiao zhuchi zhi zige 准咨為僧尼吸食鴉片應否以不守清規論無被選為寺廟主持之資格." *Neizheng gongbao* 內政公報 10.6 (1937): 272–73.

Qi Yaolin 齊耀林. "Neiwu bu zixing banli jiaoyu sengtu ji chanyang jiaoyi deng ying jizhao tiaoli banli bude zaiyong fojiao hui mingyi內務部咨行辦理教育僧徒及闡揚教義等應即照條例辦理不得再用佛教會名義." *Jiangsu sheng gongbao* 江蘇省公報 1942 (1919a): 2–3.

Qi Yaolin 齊耀林. "Neiwu bu zi jieshi zhonghuoa fojiao buneng cunzai 內務部咨解釋中華佛教不能存在." *Jiangsu sheng gongbao* 江蘇省公報 2077 (1919b): 2–3.

Quanguo renmin daibiao dahui 全國人民代表大會. *Zhonghua renmin gongheguo jicheng fa* 中華人民共和國繼承法. Effective October 1, 1985. https://www.gov.cn/gongbao/shuju/1985/gwyb198512.pdf. Accessed on October 27, 2023.

Shanghai shi gaoji renmin fayuan 上海市高級人民法院. "Shanghai shi gaoji renmin fayuan guanyu Qian Bochun nengfou jicheng heshang Qian Anding yichan de qingshi baogao 上海市高級人民法院關於錢伯春能否繼承和尚錢安定遺產的請示報告." In *Zuigao renmin fayuan sifa jieshi yu qingshi dafu quanshu* 最高人民法院司法解釋與請示答復全書, edited by Zuigao renmin fayuan 最高人民法院， 108. Beijing: Zhongguo fazhi chubanshe,2005. Inquiry dated September 4, 1986.

Shen Wendi 沈文迪. "Qiantao 16 nian cheng simiao zhuchi: yiming sharen yifan de shuangmian rensheng 潛逃16年成寺廟主持: 一名殺人疑犯的雙面人生." *The Paper* 澎湃, February 6, 2018. https://www.thepaper.cn/newsDetail_forward_1980028. Accessed April 15, 2022.

Shoupei 守培. "Shoupei fashi wei simiao guanli tiaoli shang neizhengbu han 守培法師為寺廟管理條例上內政部函." *Haichao yin*海潮音 10.3 (1929): 2–3.

Shi Nai'an 施耐庵 and Luo Guanzhong 羅貫中. *Shuihu zhuan* 水浒传. Beijing: Renmin wenxue chubanshe, 2005.

Sichuan fojiaohui 四川佛教會. "Sichuan fojiaohui wei xinban simiao guanli tiaoli shang guofu dian 四川佛教会为新颁寺廟管理条例上国府电." *Hongfa shekan* 弘法社刊 9 (1929): 53–55.

Sichuan sheng fojiao hui 四川省佛教會. "Chengqing xiuzheng simiao guanli tiaoli daidian yi 呈请修正寺廟管理條例代电一." *Shijie fojiao jushili linkan* 世界佛教居士林林刊 23 (1929): 1–9.

Song Lian 宋濂. *Yuanshi* 元史. 15 vols. Beijing: Zhonghua shuju, 1976.

Supreme Court of India. *Vineet Kumar Muarya vs. Union of India & ORS*, Writ Petition (Civil) No. 294/2018, Item No. 38, Court No. 10, Section X. Issued on July 3, 2018a. Judges Hon'ble Mr. Justice Rohinton Fali Nariman and Hon'ble Ms. Justice Indu Malhotra.

Supreme Court of India. *Vineet Kumar Muarya vs. Union of India & ORS*. Writ Petition (Civil) No. 294/2018, Item No. 17, Court No. 2, Section X. Issued on July 23, 2018b. Judges Hon'ble Mr. Justice Ranjan Gogoi and Hon.ble Mrs. Justice R. Banumathi.

Supreme Court of India. *M Siddiq (D) Thr Lrs vs. Mahant Suresh Das &Ors*. Civil Appeal Nos. 10866–10867 of 2010. Issued on November 9, 2019.

Supreme Court of India. *Buddha Education Foundation and Anrs vs. Sri Gopal Singh Vasharad*. Diary No. 466/2011. Filed in the Supreme Court of India on March 1, 2011.

Tian Tao 田濤 and Zheng Qin 鄭秦, eds. *Da Qing lüli* 大清律例. 47 vols. Beijing: Falü chubanshe, 1999.

Tianyi ge bowuguan 天一閣博物館 and Zhongguo shehui kexue yanjiu suo 中國社會科學研究所. *Tianyi ge cang Ming chaoben Tiansheng ling jiaozheng* 天一閣藏明鈔本天聖令校正. 2 vols. Beijing: Zhonghua shuju, 2006.

Wang Pu 王溥. *Tang huiyao* 唐會要. Beijing: Zhonghua shuju, 1955. Reprinted from the Qing Wuyingdian juzhenban congshu ben, 1990.

Wei Shou 魏收. *Wei shu* 魏書 . 130 vols. Beijing: Zhonghua shuju, 1974.

Xianjia 賢佳. "Yixie jiaoliu taolun一些交流討論." Mzhy.org. August 2, 2018. http://www.mzhy.org/20180802-2/. Accessed July 9, 2021.

Xianjia 賢佳 and Xianqi 賢啟. "Zhongda qingkuang huibao 重大情況匯報." www.imedao.com. August 1, 2018. http://xqdoc.imedao.com/164f59c8b1799c43fe3a7953.pdf. Accessed September 20, 2018.

Xie Shenfu 謝深甫, ed. *Qingyuan tiaofa shilei* 慶元條法事類. Ha'erbin: Heilongjiang renmin chubanshe, 2002.

Xingzheng yuan 行政院. "Ling Neizheng bu: Ling fa Jiangzhe fojiao lianhehui suocheng simiao guanli tiaoli xiugai ziju yifen yang heyi jufu you 令內政部:令發江浙佛教聯合會所呈寺廟管理條例修改字句一份仰核議具覆由." *Xingzhengyuan gongbao* 行政院公報 35 (1929a): 9–10.

Xingzheng yuan 行政院. "Ling Neizheng bu: Ling fa Sichuan fojiaohui qing shanding xinban simiao guanli tiaoli shuotie yijian yangbing anhe fuyou 令內政部: 令發四川佛教會請刪定新頒寺廟管理條例說帖一件仰併案核覆由." *Xingzhengyuan gongbao* 行政院公報 36 (1929b): 22. Dated on April 3, 1929.

Xingzheng yuan 行政院. " Ling Neizheng bu: Cheng simiao guanli tiaoli qing zhuanchi lifayuan congsu shending gongbu you 令內政部: 呈寺廟管理條例請轉飭立法院從速審定公布由." *Xingzheng yuan gongbao* 行政院公報 79 (1929c): 24.

Xingzheng yuan 行政院. " Ling Neizheng bu: Wei qianqing congsu shending simiao guanli tiaoli jing chengjiao lifayuan 令內政部: 爲前請從速審定寺廟管理條例經呈交立法院." *Xingzheng yuan gongbao* 行政院公报 82 (1929d): 11.

Xuanzang 玄奘. *Da Tang xiyu ji* 大唐西域記. Beijing: Zhonghua shuju, 1985.

Yang Yunhua 楊蘊華. "Benyuan yichan fading jicheng an beigao Yang shubo daili ci 本願遺產法定繼承案被告楊樹波代理詞." Sina.com.cn. August 6, 2008. http://blog.sina.com.cn/s/blog_59b60b910100afl8.html. Accessed July 7, 2021.

Yu Jing 余靖. *Wuxi ji* 武溪集. Wenyuan ge Siku quanshu ben 文淵閣四庫全書本.

Yunnan sheng Yuxi zhongji renmin fayuan 雲南省玉溪中級人民法院. *Yu zhong xing chuzi di 116 hao xingshi fudai mingshi panjueshu* 玉中刑初字第116號刑事附帶民事判決書. 2012.

Yunnan sheng gaoji renmin fayuan 雲南省高級人民法院. *Yun gao xing zhong zi di 1484 hao xingshi panjueshu* 雲高刑終字第1484號刑事判決書. 2012.

Zhangsun Wuji 長孫無忌. *Tanglü shuyi* 唐律疏議. Beijing: Zhonghua shuju, 1983.

Zhang Tinghao 張廷灝. "Dui zhangcheng cao'an zhong sidian shiyi 對章程草案中四點釋疑." *Haichao yin* 海潮音 17.9 (1936): 113–114.

Zhongguo fojiao hui 中國佛教會. "Fojiao hui zhangcheng 佛教會章程." *Jueshe congshu* 覺社叢書 4 (1919): 45–49. Published July 1919.

Zhongguo fojiao hui 中國佛教會. "Zhongguo fojiao hui huizhang 中國佛教會會章." *Shijie fojiao jushilin linkan* 世界佛教居士林林刊. 23 (1929): 4–5.

Zhongguo fojiao hui 中國佛教會. "Xiuzheng zhongguo fojiao hui zhangcheng cao'an 修正中國佛教會章程草案." *Haichao yin* 海潮音 16.5 (1935a): 118–19.

Zhongguo fojiao hui 中國佛教會. "Xiuzheng zhongguo fojiao hui zhangcheng 修正中國佛教會章程." Pts. 1 and 2. *Foxue banyuekan* 佛學半月刊 112 (1935b): 26–27; 113(1935c): 23.

Zhongguo fojiao hui 中國佛教會. "Zhongguo fojiao hui zhangcheng cao'an 中國佛教會章程草案." *Zhongguo fojiao huibao* 中國佛教會報 6 (1936a): 65–79.

Zhongguo fojiao hui 中國佛教會. "Zhongguo fojiao hui zhangcheng cao'an 中國佛教會章程草案." *Foxue banyuekan* 佛學半月刊 132 (1936b): 13–20.

Zhongguo fojiao hui 中國佛教會. "Jiyao shengming 急要聲明." *Zhongguo fojiao hui huibao* 中國佛教會會報 8(1936c): 32.

Zhongguo fojiao hui 中國佛教會. "Zhongyang minxun bu xiuding fojiao hui zhangcheng cao'an 中央民訓部修訂佛教會章程草案. " *Renhaideng yuekan* 人海燈月刊 3.8 (1936d): 308–321.

Zhongguo fojiao hui 中國佛教會. "Dahui tongguo zhi xiuzheng zhongguo fojiao hui zhangcheng 大會通過之修正中國佛教會章程. " *Zhongguo fojiao hui huibao* 中國佛教會會報 11(1936e): 27–34.

Zhongguo fojiao hui 中國佛教會. "Xiuding zhongguo fojiao hui zhangcheng 修訂中國佛教會章程." *Anhui zhengzhi* 安徽政治 2.27 (1939): 18–21. This version is also published in *Neizheng gongbao* 內政公報 12.7–9 (1939): 60–65.

Zhongguo fojiao hui 中國佛教會. "Zhongguo fojiao hui zhangcheng 中國佛教會章程." *Jiangsu sheng zhengfu gongbao* 江蘇省政府公報 3.4 (1948): 19–22.

Zhongguo fojiao hui 中國佛教會. "Zhongguo fojiao hui zhangcheng 中國佛教會章程." *Xiandai foxue* 现代佛学 6 (1953): 16. Reprinted in *Xiandai foxue* 现代佛学. Vol. 3. Tianjin: Tianjin guji chubanshe, 1995. 177.

Zhongguo fojiao xiehui 中国佛教协会. "Zhongguo fojiao xiehui zhangcheng 中国佛教协会章程." *Xiandai foxue* 现代佛学 5 (1957): 26. Reprinted in *Xiandai foxue* 现代佛学. Vol. 6. Tianjin: Tianji guji chubanshe, 1995. 165.

Zhongguo fojiao xiehui 中國佛教协會. "Zhongguo fojiao xiehui zhangcheng中国佛教协会章程. " *Fayin* 法音 1 (1981): 12. Effective December 23, 1980.

Zhongguo fojiao xiehui 中國佛教协會. "Zhongguo fojiao xiehui zhangcheng中国佛教协会章程." *Fayin* 法音 3 (1987): 30. Effective March 1, 1987. 17 articles.

Zhongguo fojiao xiehui 中國佛教協會. *Quanguo hanchuan fojiao siyuan gongzhu guiyue tongze* 全國漢傳佛教寺院共住規約通則. Promulgated and effective October 21,

1993. https://www.chinabuddhism.com.cn/js/hb/2012-03-15/492.html. Accessed on October 27, 2023.

Zhongguo fojiao xiehui 中國佛教協會. "Zhongguo fojiao xiehui guanyu sengren yichan chuli wenti de fuhan 中國佛教協會關於僧人遺產處理問題的復函." *Fayin* 法音 3 (1999): 40–41.

Zhongguo fojiao xiehui 中國佛教協會. "Zhongguo fojiao xiehui guanyu siyuan yichan wenti de fuhan 中國佛教協會關於寺院遺產問題的復函." *Fayin* 法音 9 (2002a): 34–36.

Zhongguo fojiao xiehui 中国佛教協會. "Zhongguo fojiao xiehui zhangcheng 中国佛教协会章程." *Fayin* 法音 10 (2002b): 25–28.

Zhongguo fojiao xiehui 中國佛教協會. *Quanguo hanchuan fojiao siyuan gongzhu guiyue tongze* 全國漢傳佛教寺院共住規約通則 . Revised and passed February 25, 2006. Posted on www.tydscs.com. http://www.tydscs.com/juanzengshixiang/2018-08-03/da8ca68d91d359ae797dbeab7badd245.html. Accessed on October 27, 2023.

Zhongguo fojiao xiehui 中国佛教協會. "Zhongguo fojiao xiehui zhangcheng 中国佛教协会章程." Passed on February 3, 2010, at the Association's National Assembly. Posted on www.Qqhrzslh.com. http://www.qqhrzslh.com/zhengce_view.Asp?id=75. Accessed on July 25, 2021.

Zhongguo fojiao xiehui 中国佛教協會. "Zhongguo fojiao xiehui zhangcheng 中国佛教协会章程." www.sara.gov.cn. April 21, 2015. http://www.sara.gov.cn/zjttzd/337899.jhtml. Accessed on July 25, 2021.

Zhongguo fojiao xiehui 中國佛教協會. *Quanguo hanchuan fojiao siyuan gongzhu guiyue tongze* 全國漢傳佛教寺院共住規約通則. Revised and passed on July 24, 2019. Posted on www.qqhrzslh.com. http://www.qqhrzslh.com/zhengce_view.Asp?id=71. Acessed on October 27, 2023.

Zhonghua fojiaojiao zonghui 中華佛教總會. "Zhonghua fojiao zonghui zhangcheng中華佛教總會章程." *Foxue congbao* 佛學叢報 1 (1912): 1–10. Effective February 12, 1912.

Zhonghua fojiao zonghui 中華佛教總會. "Zhonghua fojiao zonghui zhangcheng中華佛教總會章程. Pts. 1 and 2. *Fojiao yubao* 佛教月報 1 (1913): 1–10; 2 (1913): 1–6. 27 articles.

Zhonghua fojiao zonghui 中華佛教總會. "Zhonghua fojiao zonghui chengqing da zongtong baohu fojiao bing song zhangcheng wen 中華佛教總會呈請大總統保護佛教並送章程文." *Foxue congbao* 佛學叢報 12 (1914): 1–2.

Zhongyang minxun bu 中央民訓部. "Zhongyang minxunbu xiuding fojiaohui zhangcheng cao'an 中央民訓部修訂佛教會章程草案." *Renhaideng yuekan* 人海燈月刊 3.8 (1936): 308–21.

Zhonghua renmin gongheguo guowuyuan 中華人民共和國國務院. *Zongjiao huodong changsuo guanli tiaoli* 宗教活動場所管理條例. Effective January 31, 1994. https://www.gd.gov.cn/zwgk/gongbao/1994/8/content/post_3357107.html. Accessed on October 27, 2023.

Zhongguo renmin gongheguo guowuyuan 中華人民共和國國務院. "Zongjiao shiwu tiaoli 宗教事務條例." Gov.cn. Effective March 1, 2005. http://www.gov.cn/gongbao/content/2005/content_63293.htm. Accessed on July 12, 2021.

Zhonghua renmin gongheguo guowuyuan 中華人民共和國國務院. *Zongjiao shiwu tiaoli* 宗教事務條例. Effective February 1, 2018. Posted on www.gov. cn. http://www.gov.cn/zhengce/content/2017-09/07/content_5223282.htm. Accessed on July 12, 2021.

Zhu Qiling 朱啟鈐. "Neiwu zhang Zhu Qiling cheng Zhonghua fojiao zonghui zhangcheng qingchi xiuzheng yidu liubi wen bing piling 內務總長朱啟鈐呈中華佛教總會章程請飭修正以杜流弊文並批令." *Zhengfu gongbao* 政府公報 754 (1914a): 59–60.

Zhu Qiling 朱啟鈐. "Wei chi zhishi ju Zhonghua fojiao zonghui chengcheng fengchi xiugai zhangcheng ying zhaoji sengzhong kaihui taolun nijiang huiqi zhanzhi yangli jiuyue 為飭知事據中華佛教總會呈稱奉飭修改章程應召集僧眾開會討論擬將會期展至陽曆九月." *Zhengfu gongbao* 政府公報 794 (1914b): 83. Dated July 18, 1914.

Zhuhong 袾宏. *Lianchi dashi quanji* 蓮池大師全集. Taipei: Zhonghua fojiao wenhuaguan, 1983.

Zuigao renmin fayuan 最高人民法院. "Zuigao renmin fayuan minshi shenpan ting guanyu Qian Bochun nengfo jicheng heshang Qian Anding yichan de dianhua dafu 最高人民法院民事審判庭關於錢伯春能否繼承和尚錢安定遺產的電話答覆." In *Zuigao renmin fayuan sifa jieshi yu qingshi dafu quanshu* 最高人民法院司法解釋與請示答覆全書 edited by Zuigao renmin fayuan 最高人民法院, 108. Beijing: Zhongguo fazhi chubanshe, 2005. Effective October 16, 1987.

Zuigao renmin gaoyuan 最高人民法院. "*Zuigao renmin fayuan dui Guowuyuan zongjiao shiwu ju yisi guanyu sengren yichan chuli yijian de fuhan* 最高人民法院對國務院宗教事務局一司關於僧人遺產處理意見的復函." Effective October 13, 1994. http://www.npcxj.com/index.php/Mobile/Lew/info/type1/sifajieshijiwenjian/id/6705.html. Accessed on March 19, 2021.

Zuigao renmin fayuan 最高人民法院. *Zuigao renmin fayuan guanyu xiugai guanyu minshi susong zhengju de ruogan guiding de jueding* 最高人民法院关于修改《关于民事诉讼证据的若干规定》的决定. Effective October 14, 2019. http://gongbao.court.gov.cn/Details/0c15319f2bdbabb8e398035f775385.html. Accessed on October 27, 2023.

Zuigao renmin fayuan 最高人民法院. *Zuigao renmin fayuan guanyu feizhi bufen sifa jieshi ji xiangguan guifanxing wenjian de jueding* 最高人民法院關於廢止部分司法解釋及相關規範性文件的決定. Passed December 23, 2020, published December 29, 2020, and effective January 1, 2021. http://gongbao.court.gov.cn/Details/ae5b93285eab867ce0346bee77be26.html. Accessed on October 27, 2023.

Secondary Sources

"Buddhist Baptized on Eve of Execution." *The Times* (London), July 5, 1962.

"Buddhist Monk Arrested after Fatal Stabbing of Muslim Teenager." *Myanmar Mix*, June 23, 2020.

"Jet-Set Monk Gets a Further 16 Years for Rape of Minor." *Asia Times*, October 18, 2018.

"Monk Gets Suspended Jail Term over Threat to Japanese Envoy." *The Korea Times*, September 19, 2010.

Sgra bye brag tu rtogs byed chen mo skad bzhi shan sbyar ma 翻译名义集：藏梵英汉对照词典 *Tibetan-Sanskrit-English-Chinese Dictionary of Buddhism: An Edition and Translation of the Mahavyutpatti*. Lhasa: Bod ljongs mi dmangs dpe skrun khang, 2015.

"Sister of Pregnant Woman Killed by Monk Demands Apology." *The National Thailand*, June 16, 2020.

"South Korean Monk Gets Six Years in Prison for Stealing Japanese Religious Items." *The Japan Times*, August 13, 2015.

The Range of the Bodhisattva, A Mahāyāna Sūtra: The Teachings of the Nirgrantha Satyaka. Translated by Lozang Jamspal. New York: Tibet House, 2010.

"76 sui heshang he nüzi zai chansi youhui qi zhengzhi jiang qingren shishou wusi jiashu huopei 90 wan 76 岁和尚和女子在禅寺幽会起争执将情人失手捂死家属获赔90万." *Sohu.com*. October 13, 2021. https://www.sohu.com/a/494748469_121123818. Accessed on October 27, 2023.

Agsar, Wendy Biddlecombe. "Karmapa Case Discontinued." *Tricycle*. November 18, 2022.

Ashin, Janaka and Kate Crosby. "Heresy and Monastic Malpractice in the Buddhist Court Cases (Vinicchaya) of Modern Burma (Myanmar)." *Contemporary Buddhism* 18.1 (2017): 199–261.

Associated Press in Beijing. "Senior Chinese Monk Resigns amid Sexual Misconduct Claims." *The Guardian*, August 15, 2018.

Baker, John H. *An Introduction to English Legal History*. 3rd ed. London: Butterworths, 1990. First edition published 1971.

Bai Wengu 白文固. "Tangdai sengji guanli zhidu 唐代僧籍管理制度." *Pumen xuebao* 普門學報 15 (2003): 233–65.

Barghout, Caroline. "Winnipeg Buddhist Monk Sentenced to 11 Years for Sexual Abuse of Two Girls." *CBC News*. October 24, 2022.

Barrett, T. H. "Buddhism and Law in China: The Emergence of Distinctive Patterns in Chinese History." In *Buddhism and Law: An Introduction*, edited by Rebecca Redwood French and Mark A. Nathan, 207–15. Cambridge: Cambridge University Press, 2014.

Beal, Samuel. *Buddhist Records of the Western World*. London: Trübner & Co., 1884.

Berry, Jason. "The Tragedy of Gilbert Gauthe." *The Times of Acadiana*. May 23, 1985.

Bianchi, Ester. "Dangdai zhongguo fojiao de jielü fuxing yu sengtuan zaisheng 当代中国佛教的戒律复兴与僧团再生." In *Ershi shijie zhongguo fojiao de liangci fuxing* 二十世纪中国佛教的两次复兴, edited by Ji Zhe 汲喆, Daniela Campo, and Wang Qiyuan, 153–63. Shanghai: Fudan daxue chubanshe, 2016.

Bianchi, Ester. "Yijie weishi 以戒为师: Theory and Practice of Monastic Discipline in Modern and Contemporary Chinese Buddhism." *Studies in Chinese Religions* 3.2 (2017): 111–41.

Borchert, Thomas & Susan M. Darlington. "Political Disrobing in Thailand." *Buddhism, Law & Society* 3 (2017–18): 113–56.

Brook, Timothy. "The Politics of Religion: Late Imperial Origins of Regulatory State." In *Making Religion, Making the State: The Politics of Religion in Modern China*, edited by Yoshiko Ashiwa and David L. Wank, 22–42. Stanford: Stanford University Press, 2009.

Bsod nams rgyal mtshan. *The Mirror Illuminating the Royal Genealogies*. Translated by Per K. Sørensen. Weisbaden: Otto Harrassowitz, 1994.

Bsod nams rgyal mtshan. *The Clear Mirror: A Traditional Account of Tibet's Golden Age*. Translated by McComas Taylor and Lama Choedak Yuthok. Ithaca: Snow Lion Publications, 1996.

Bühler, Georg. *The Sacred Laws of the Āryas: As Taught in the Schools of Āpastamba, Gautama, Vasiṣṭha, and Baudhāyana*. New York: Christian Literature Co., 1898.

Buswell, Robert and Donald Lopez. *The Princeton Dictionary of Buddhism*. Princeton: Princeton University Press, 2014.

Campbell, Gerald. "Clerical Immunities in France During the Reign of Philip III." *Speculum* 39.3 (1964): 404–24.

Campo, Daniela. "Minguo shiqi de jielü fuxing chutan 民国时期的戒律复兴初探." In *Ershi shiji zhongguo fojiao de liangci fuxing* 二十世纪中国佛教的两次复兴, edited by Ji Zhe 汲喆, Daniela Campo, and Wang Qiyuan, 133–48. Shanghai: Fudan daxue chubanshe, 2016.

Campo, Daniela. "A Different Buddhist Revival: The Promotion of Vinaya (*jielü* 戒律) in Republican China." *Journal of Global Buddhism* 18 (2017): 129–54.

Cao Shibang 曹仕邦. "Cong zongjiao yu wenhua beijing lun siyuan jingyi yu sengni siyou caichan zaihua fazhan de yuanyin 從宗教與文化背景論寺院經濟與僧尼私有財產在華發展的原因." *Huagang foxue xuebao* 華崗佛學學報 8 (1985): 159–84.

Chen Dengwu 陳登武. "Cong neilü dao wangfa: Tangdai sengren de falü guifan 從內律到王法: 唐代僧人的法律规范." *Zhengda faxue pinglun* 政大法學評論, no. 111 (2009): 1–79.

Chen, Gilbert. "Monastic Mobility, Social Embeddedness, and Kinship Networks: Buddhist Clerical Sexuality in Late-Qing Sichuan." *Late Imperial China* 43.1 (2022): 85–126.

Chen, Gilbert. *Living in This World: A Social History of Buddhist Monks and Nuns in Nineteenth-Century Western China*. PhD diss., Washington University in St. Louis, 2019.

Chen Jinlong 陳金龍. "Minguo simiao guanli tiaoli de banbu yu feizhi 民國寺廟管理條例的頒布與廢止." *Fayin* 法音 4 (2008): 54–59.

Chen Qingying 陳慶英. *Xizang lishi* 西藏歷史. Beijing: Wuzhou chuanbo chubanshe, 2017.

Chen Yihe 陳義和. *Fojiao yu Songdai falü* 佛教與宋代法律. Beijing: Zhongguo zhengfa daxue chubanshe, 2015.

Ch'en, Kenneth. *Chinese Transformation of Buddhism*. Princeton: Princeton University Press, 1973.

Cheney, Christopher R. "The Punishment of Felonious Clerks." *The English Historical Review* 51.202 (1936): 215–36.

Chikusa Masaaki 竺沙雅章. "Tonkō no sōkan seido 敦煌の僧官制度." *Tōhō gakuhō* 東方學報 31 (1961): 117–98.

Chinchilla, Norma Stoltz, Nora Hamilton, and James Loucky. "The Sanctuary Movement and Central American Activism in Los Angeles." *Latin American Perspectives* 36.6 (2009): 101–26.

Clarke, Shayne. "One Rule for All? Saṃghāvaśeṣa Indemnity for the Sarvāstivādin Monastic Hierarchy." In *Buddhist and Indian Studies in Honour of Professor Sodo Mori*, edited by Publication Committee, 387–98. Hamamatsu: Kokusai Bukkyoto Kyokai, 2002.

Clarke, Shayne. "Monks Who Have Sex: Parajika Penance in Indian Buddhist Monasticism." *Journal of Indian Philosophy* 37.1 (2009a): 1–43.

Clarke, Shayne. "Locating Humour in Indian Buddhist Monastic Law Codes: A Comparative Approach." *Journal of Indian Philosophy* 37.4 (2009b): 311–30.

Clarke, Shayne. *Family Matters in Indian Buddhist Monasticisms*. Honolulu: University of Hawai'i Press, 2014a.

Clarke, Shayne (ed.). *Vinaya Texts. Gilgit Manuscripts in the National Archives of India: Facsimile Edition*. Vol. 1. New Delhi: The National Archives of India; Tokyo: International Research Institute for Advanced Buddhology, Soka University, 2014b.

Clarke, Shayne. "On Some Curious Cases Where the Buddha Did Not Make a Rule: Palliative Care, Assisted Suicide, and Abortion in an Indian Buddhist Monastic Law Code." *International Journal of Buddhist Thought & Culture* 31.1 (2021): 13–113.

Cross, Arthur Lyon. "The English Criminal Law and Benefit of Clergy during the Eighteenth and Early Nineteenth Century." *The American Historical Review* 22.3 (1917): 544–65.

Dai Jianguo 戴建國. "Tianyi ge cang Ming chaoben Guanpin ling kao 天一閣藏明抄本官品令考." *Lishi yanjiu* 歷史研究 3 (1999): 71–86.

Dalzell, George W. *Benefit of Clergy in America & Related Matters*. Winston-Salem: J. F. Blair, 1955.

Deveaux, Tynette. "Kagyu Thubten Choling addresses sangha about Lama Norlha Rinpoche's sexual misconduct with students." *Lion's Roar*, July 15, 2017. https://www.lionsroar.com/kagyu-thubten-choling-addresses-sangha-about-lama-norhla-rinpoches-sexual-misconduct-with-students/. Accessed on October 27, 2023.

Dong Chunlin 董春林. "Lun Tang Song sengdao fa zhi yanbian 論唐宋僧道法之演變." *Jiangxi shehui kexue* 江西社會科學 10 (2010): 138–43.

Downs, John Emmanuel. "The Concept of Clerical Immunity." PhD diss., Catholic University of America, 1941.

Du Changshun 杜常順. "Mingdai liuzhu jingshi de zangchuan fojiao sengren 明代留住京師的藏傳佛教僧人." *Zhongguo zangxue* 中國藏學 2 (2005): 62.

Duggan, Anne J. "Henry II, the English Church and the Papacy, 1154–1176." In *Henry II: New Interpretations*, edited by Christopher Harper-Bill and Nicholas Vincent, 154–83. Woodbridge: Boydell Press, 2007.

Dunggan, Charles. "The Becket Dispute and the Criminous Clerks." *Bulletin of the Institute of Historical Research* 35.91 (1962): 1–28.

Dyson, Damcho and Tahlia Newland. "This is Abuse." *Tricycle*, July 15, 2019.

French, Rebecca Redwood and Mark A. Nathan, eds. *Buddhism and Law: An Introduction*. Cambridge: Cambridge University Press, 2014.

Fraher, Richard M. "The Becket Dispute and Two Decretist Traditions: The Bolognese Masters Revisited and Some New Anglo-Norman Texts." *Journal of Medieval History* 4.4 (1978): 347–368.

Gabel, Leona C. *Benefit of Clergy in England in the Later Middle Age*. New York: Octagon Books, 1969. Originally completed as a PhD thesis in 1929.

Garner, Bryan (ed.). *Black's Law Dictionary*. 11th ed. St. Paul: Thomson Reuters, 2019.

Ginsburgh, Tom and Benjamin Schonthal. *Buddhism and Comparative Constitutional Law*. Cambridge: Cambridge University Press, 2022.

Glenn, Patrick. *Legal Traditions of the World: Sustainable Diversity in Law*. Oxford: Oxford University Press, 2014. First edition published 2000.

González, Sergio. "The Sanctuary Movement." *Oxford Research Encyclopedia of American History*. June 30, 2020.

Granoff, Phyllis. "Justice and Anxiety: False Accusations in Indian Literature." *Rivista degli studi orientali* 83.1/4 (2010): 377–98.

Granoff, Phyllis. "The Not-So-Long Arm of the Law." In *Texts and Transformations: Essays in Honor of the 75th Birthday of Victor H. Mair*, edited by Haun Saussy, 289–310. Amherst: Cambria Press, 2018.

Guo Huaqing. "Beiyang zhengfu de simiao guanli zhengce pinxi 北洋政府的寺廟管理政策評析." *Guangzhou daxue xuebao* 廣州大學學報 1 (2005): 23–27; 43.

He Guangzhong 賀光中. "Lidai sengguan zhidu kao 歷代僧官制度考." *Dongfang xuebao* 東方學報 1.2 (1958): 187–225.

Heirman, Ann. *Regulations for Nuns according to the Dharmaguptakavinaya*. Delhi: Motilal Banarsidass Publishers, 2002.

Heirman, Ann. "Where Is the Probationer in the Chinese Buddhist Nunneries?" *Zeitschrift der Deutschen Morgenländischen Gesellschaft* 158.1 (2008): 105–37.

Helmholz, Richard. *The Canon Law and the Ecclesiastical Jurisdiction from 597 to the 1640s*. Oxford: Oxford University Press, 2004.

Hernádez, Javier C. "China's Tech-Savvy, Burned-Out and Spiritually Adrift, Turn to Buddhism." *The New York Times*, September 7, 2016.

Hirakawa Akira. *Monastic Discipline for the Buddhist Nuns: An English Translation of the Chinese Text of the Mahāsāṃghika Bhikṣuṇī-Vinaya*. Patna: Kashi Prasad Jayaswal Research Institute, 1982.

Horner, I. B. *The Book of the Discipline*. Vol. 1. London: The Pali Text Society, 1938.

Horner, I. B. *The Book of the Discipline*. Vol. 2. London: The Pali Text Society, 1940.

Horner, I. B. *The Book of the Discipline*. Vol. 3. Oxford: The Pali Text Society, 1942.

Horner, I. B. *The Book of the Discipline*. Vol. 4. London: The Pali Text Society, 1951.

Horner, I. B. *The Book of the Discipline*. Vol. 5. London: The Pali Text Society, 1952.

Horner, I. B. *The Book of the Discipline*. Vol. 6. London: The Pali Text Society, 1966.

Huang Xianian 黃夏年. "Zhonghua fojiao zonghui de chengli jiqi zhangcheng yanjiu 中華佛教總會的成立及其章程研究." In *Xingyun dashi renjian fojiao lilun shijian yanjiu* 星雲大師人間佛教理論實踐研究, edited by Foguangshan renjian foxue yanjiuyuan 佛光山人間佛學研究院 and etc., 100–123. Taibei: Foguangshan renjian fojiao yanjiuyuan, 2014.

Huang Xiaolin 黄晓林. "Sengren yichan jiufen Zhong de shenceng falü wenti jiexi: Zongjiao tuanji zizhi yu sifa shencha 僧人遗产纠纷中的深层法律问题解析-宗教团体自治与司法审查." *Fazhi yanjiu* 法治研究 8 (2013): 68–73.

Hucker, Charles. *A Dictionary of Official Titles in Imperial China*. Stanford: Stanford University Press, 1985.

Hultzsch, Eugen. "The Date of Asoka." *The Journal of the Royal Asiatic Society of Great Britain and Ireland*, October 1914: 943–51.

Hultzsch, Eugen, ed. *Inscriptions of Asoka*. Oxford: Clarendon Press, 1925.

Jansen, Berthe. *The Monastery Rules: Buddhist Monastic Organization in Pre-Modern Tibet*. Oakland: University of California Press, 2018.

Ji Xianlin 季羡林. *Dunhuang xue da cidian* 敦煌學大辭典.Shanghai: Shanghai cishu chubanshe, 1998.

Ji Zhe. "Buddhism and the State: The New Relationship." *China Perspectives* 55 (2004): 1–13.

Ji Zhe 汲喆. "Buddhist Institutional Innovations." In *Modern Chinese Religion II: 1850–2015*, edited by Jan Kiely, Vincent Goossaert, and John Lagerwey, 748–56. Leiden: Brill, 2015.

Jiang, Yonglin. *The Great Ming Code: Da Ming Lu*. Seattle: University of Washington Press, 2005.

Johnson, Ian. "#MeToo in the Monastery: A Chinese Abbot's Fall Stirs Questions on Buddhism's Path." *New York Times*, September 15, 2018.

Johnson, Wallace. *The T'ang Code, Volume 1: General Principles*. Princeton: Princeton University Press, 2019. Originally published 1979.

Jones, William C. *The Great Qing Code*. Oxford: Clarendon Press, 1994.

Jolly, Julius. *The Minor Law Books*. Vol. 33 of *Sacred Books of the East*. London: Clarendon Press, 1889.

Karma Lekshe Tsomo. *Sisters in Solitude: Two Traditions of Buddhist Monastic Ethics for Women: A Comparative Analysis of the Chinese Dharmaguptaka and the Tibetan*

Mūlasarvāstivāda Bhikṣuṇī Prātimokṣa Sūtra. Albany: State University of New York Press, 1996.

Lammerts, D. Christin. *Buddhist Law in Burma: A History of Dhammasattha Texts and Jurisprudence, 1250–1850*. Honolulu: University of Hawai'i Press, 2018.

Lee, Luke T. and Whalen W. Lai. "The Chinese Conceptions of Law: Confucian, Legalist, and Buddhist." *The Hastings Law Journal* 29.6 (1978): 1307–29.

Li Gang 李刚. "Zhongguo fojiao xiehui chengli jingguo kaolüe 中國佛教協會成立經過考略." *Dangdai zhongguo shi yanjiu* 當代中國史研究 12.2 (2005): 110–14.

Li Yanli 李艳莉. "Zongjiao caichan quan zhidu yanjiu 宗教财产权制度研究." MA thesis, Xinan zhengfa daxue, 2015.

Liu, Cuilan. "Noble or Evil: The Ṣaḍvārgika Monks Reconsidered." *Acta Orientalia* 66.2 (2013): 179–95.

Liu, Cuilan. "Hybrid Courts and Hybrid Laws: The Legal Governance of Buddhism in Imperial China." *Journal of Chinese Religions* 47.2 (2019): 152–92.

Liu, Cuilan. "The Fall of a Chinese Buddhist Monk: Law and State Governance of Buddhism in Post-Imperial China." *Journal of Law and Religion* 35.3 (2020a): 432–49.

Liu, Cuilan. "Buddhism in Court: Clerical Privileges and the Jurisdiction of the Buddhist Clergy in Indian Buddhism." *History of Religions* 60.2 (2020b): 103–31.

Liu, Cuilan. "Legally Buddhist: Monks, Nuns, and Legal Texts in Dunhuang." *Studies in Chinese Religions* 6.4 (2020c): 407–42.

Liu, Cuilan and Susan Andrews. "Introduction." In *Rules of Engagement: Medieval Traditions of Buddhist Monastic Regulation*, edited by Susan Andrews, Jinhua Chen, and Cuilan Liu, 1–16. Bochum: Projek Verlag, 2014.

Liu Liyan 柳立言. *Songdai de zongjiao shenfen yu sifa* 宋代的宗教、身分與司法. Beijing: Zhonghua shuju, 2012.

Lupu, Ira C. and Robert W. Tuttle. "Sexual Misconduct and Ecclesiastical Immunity." *BYU Law Review* 2004.5 (2004): 1789–1896.

Ma Jianshi 馬建石 and Yang Yutang 楊育堂. *Da Qing lüli tongkao jiaozhu* 大清律例通考校注. Beijing: Zhongguo zhengfa daxue chubanshe, 1992.

Matters, Michael D. "The Sanctuary Movement 1980–1988: An Organizational Analysis of Structures and Cultures." PhD diss., University of Illinois at Chicago, 1994.

McClish, Mark. "From Law to Dharma: State Law and Scared Duty in Ancient India." *Journal of Law and Religion* 34.3 (2019): 284–309.

Miller, Lama Willa B. "Breaking the Silence on Sexual Misconduct." *Lion's Roar*, May 19, 2018. https://www.lionsroar.com/breaking-the-silence-on-sexual-misconduct/. Accessed on October 27, 2023.

Mingfu 明復. *Zhongguo sengguan zhidu yanjiu* 中國僧官制度研究. Taipei: Mingwen shuju, 1981.

Nattier, Jan. *Once Upon a Future Time: Studies in a Buddhist Prophecy of Decline*. Berkeley: University of California Press, 1991.

Nattier, Jan. "The Heart Sūtra: A Chinese Apocryphal Text?" *The Journal of the International Association of Buddhist Studies* 15.2 (1992): 153–223.

Ng, Zhiru. *The Making of a Savior Bodhisattva: Dizang in Medieval China*. Honolulu: University of Hawai'i Press, 2007.

Niida Noboru 仁井田陞. *Tōrei shūi ho: tsuketari Tō-Nichi ryorei taishō ichiran* 唐令拾遺補: 附唐日両令対照一覧. Tokyo: Tōkyō Daigaku Shuppankai, 1997.

Olivelle, Patrick. *Dharmasutras: The Law Codes of Āpastamba, Gautama, Baudhāyana, and Vasiṣṭha*. Oxford: Oxford University Press, 1999.

Olivelle, Patrick. *Dharmasūtras: The Law Codes of Āpastamba, Gautama, Baudhāyana, and Vaiṣṭha*. Delhi: Motilal Banarsidass Publishers, 2000.

Olivelle, Patrick. *Manu's Code of Law: A Critical Edition and Translation of the Mānava-Dharmaśāstra*. New York: Oxford University Press, 2004.

Olivelle, Patrick. *Life of the Buddha by Aśvaghoṣa*. New York: New York University Press, 2008.

Olivelle, Patrick. "Dharmaśāstra: A Textual History." In *Hinduism and Law*, edited by Timothy Lubin, Donald R. Davis, and Jayanth K. Krishnan, 28–57. Cambridge: Cambridge University Press, 2010.

Olivelle, Patrick. "Penance and Punishment: Marking the Body in Criminal Law and Social Ideology of Ancient India." *Journal of Hindu Studies* 4.1 (2011): 1–19.

Olivelle, Patrick. *King, Governance, and Law in Ancient India: Kauṭilya's Arthaśāstra*. Oxford: Oxford University Press, 2013.

Olivelle, Patrick. "Judges and Courts in Ancient India: On Dharmastha and Prāḍvivāka." In *Sahasram Ati Srajas: Indo-Iranian and Indo-European Studies in Honor of Stephanie W. Jamison*, edited by Dieter Gunkel, Joshua Timothy Katz, Brent Harmon Vine, and Michael L Weiss, 305–13. Ann Arbor: Beech Stave Press, 2016.

Olivelle, Patrick. *A Dharma Reader: Classical Indian Law*. New York: Columbia University Press, 2017.

Olivelle, Patrick and Mark McClish. "The Four Feet of Legal Procedure and the Origins of Jurisprudence in Ancient India." *Journal of the American Oriental Society* 135.1 (2015): 33–47.

Oldenberg, Hermann. *The Vinaya Piṭakaṃ: One of the Principal Buddhist Holy Scriptures in the Pāli Language*. Vol. 3. London: Williams and Norgate, 1881.

Oldenberg, Hermann. *The Vinaya Piṭakaṃ: One of the Principal Buddhist Holy Scriptures in the Pāli Language*. Vol. 4. London: Williams and Norgate, 1882.

Pharr, Clyde, Theresa Sherrer Davidson, and Mary Brown Pharr. *The Theodosian Code and Novels: And the Sirmondian Constitutions*. Princeton: Princeton University Press, 1952.

Phillips, Kimberley. "A Culture of Clerical Immunity in Myanmar Is Putting Children at Risk of Abuse." *Time*, December 6, 2018. https://time.com/5470903/clerical-sexual-abuse-children-buddhist-monks-myanmar/. Acessed on October 27, 2023.

Poole, A. Lane. "Outlawry as a Punishment of Criminous Clerks." In *Historical Essays in Honour of James Tait*, edited by John Goronwy Edwards, 239–46. Manchester: Manchester University Press, 1933.

Prebish, Charles. *Buddhist Monastic Discipline: The Sanskrit Prātimokṣa Sutra of the Mahāsāṃghikas and Mūlasarvāstivādins*. University Park: Pennsylvania State University Press, 1975.

Prebish, Charles. *A Survey of Vinaya Literature*. London: Routlege, 1996.

Rabben, Linda. *Sanctuary and Asylum*. Seattle: University of Washington Press, 2016.

Ranalli, Ralph. "History of Case May Have Influenced Severity of Term." *The Boston Globe*, February 21, 2002.

Rhaldi, Sherab. "Ye shes sde: Tibetan Scholar and Saint." *Bulletin of Tibetology* 38.1 (2002): 2–36.

Roth, Gustav. *Bhikṣuṇīivinaya: Manual of Discipline for Buddhist Nuns*. Patna: K. P. Jayaswal Research Institute, 1970.

Ruskola, Teemu. *Legal Orientalism: China, the United States, and Modern Law*. Cambridge: Harvard University Press, 2013.

Schonthal, Benjamin. *Buddhism, Politics and the Limits of Law: The Pyrrhic Constitutionalism of Sri Lanka*. Cambridge: Cambridge University Press, 2016.

Schonthal, Benjamin. "Judging in the Buddha's Court: A Buddhist Judicial System in Contemporary Asia." *Asian Journal of Law and Society* 8.2 (2020): 206–25.

Schonthal, Benjamin. "Buddhist Law Beyond the Vinaya: Monastic Constitution (katikavata-s) and Their Transformations in Colonial Sri Lanka." *History of Religions* 60.4 (2021): 287–324.

Schonthal, Benjamin. "Buddhist Rules about Rules: Procedure and Process in the (Theravada)Buddhist Legal System." *Amerian Journal of Comparative Law* 69.3 (2022): 539–573.

Schopen, Gregory. *Bones, Stones, and Buddhist Monks: Collected Papers on the Archaeology, Epigraphy, and Text of Monastic Buddhism in India*. Honolulu: University of Hawai'i Press, 1997.

Schopen, Gregory. "The Good Monks and His Money in a Buddhist Monasticism of 'the Mahāyāna Period.'" *The Eastern Buddhist* 32.1 (2000): 85–105.

Schopen, Gregory. *Buddhist Monks and Business Matters: Still More Papers on Monastic Buddhism in India*. Honolulu: University of Hawai'i Press, 2004.

Schopen, Gregory. *Figments and Fragments of Mahayana Buddhism in India: More Collected Papers*. Honolulu: University of Hawai'i Press, 2005.

Schopen, Gregory. "The Buddhist Nun as an Urban Landlord and a "Legal Person" in Early India." In *Devadattīyam, Johannes Bronkhorst Felicitation Volume*, edited by F. Voegeli et al., 595–609. Bern: Peter Lang, 2012.

Schopen, Gregory. *Buddhist Nuns, Monks, and Other Worldly Matters: Recent Papers on Monastic Buddhism in India*. Honolulu: University of Hawai'i Press, 2014.

Shi Jinbo 史金波, Nie Hongying 聶鴻音, and Bai Bin 白濱. *Tiansheng gaijiu xinding lüling* 天聖改舊新定律令. Beijing: Falü chubanshe, 2000.

Shi Junyi 施君怡. "Sengren yichan de jicheng wenti yanjiu 僧人遗产的继承问题研究." *Shangqing* 商情 47 (2013): 281–82.

Shi Zhaohui 釋昭慧. "Tongding sitong: Jiexi fomen zhong de jiegouxing zui'e 痛定思痛: 解析佛門中的結構性罪惡." *Duan chuanmei* 端傳媒, August 16, 2018.

Silk, Jonathan. *Managing Monks: Administrators and Administrative Roles in Indian Buddhist Monasticism*. New York: Oxford University Press, 2008.

Sirks, Adriaan Johan Boudewijn. "The *episcopalis audientia* in Late Antiquity." *Droit et Cultures* 65.1 (2013): 79–88.

Soothill, William Edward and Lewis Hodous, comps. *A Dictionary of Chinese Buddhist Terms: With Sanskrit and English Equivalents and a Sanskrit-Pali Index*. Delhi: Motilal Banarsidass, 1937. Reprinted 1977.

Stewart, Tracy N. "Creating Ecclesiastical Immunity: How the Supreme Court of North Carolina Stripped Civil Protections from Religious Bodies in *Harris v. Matthews*." *North Carolina Law Review* 86.6 (2008): 1743–61.

Stubbs, William (ed.). *Radulfi de Diceto Decani Lundoniensis opera historica, or the Historical Works of Master Ralph de Diceto, Dean of London*. Vol. 1. London: Longman and Co., 1876.

Sullivan, Winnifred Fallers and Robert A. Yelle. "Law and Religion: An Overview." In *Encyclopedia of Religion*, 2nd ed., edited by Lindsay Jones, 5325–32. Detroit: Macmillan Reference, 2005.

Tang Geng'ou 唐耕耦 and Lu Hongji 陸宏基. *Dunhuang shehui jingji wenxian zhenji shilu* 敦煌社會經濟文獻真跡釋錄. Vol. 2. Beijing: Shumu wenxian chubanshe, 1990.

Tang Hui 唐卉. "Sengren yichan jicheng wenti yanjiu僧人遗产继承问题研究." MA thesis, Xinan zhengfa daxue 西南政法大学, 2015.

Tang Yongtong 湯用彤. *Suitang fojiao shigao* 隋唐佛教史稿. Beijing: Zhonghua shuju, 1982.

The House of Commons of Great Britain. *The Statutes of the Realm*. Vols. 1–11. London: Dawsons of Fall Mall, 1965.

Vitello, Paul. "Joshu Sasaki, 107, Tainted Zen Master." *The New York Times*, August 4, 2014.

Vogel, Howard J. "A Survey and Commentary on the New Literature in Law and Religion." *Journal of Law and Religion* 1.1 (1983): 79–169.

Wang Long 王龙. "Xixia wen Shilun jing kaolun 西夏文《十轮经》考论." *Xixia yanjiu* 西夏研究 2 (2017): 16–24.

Wang, Pachow. *A Comparative Study of the Prātimokṣa: On the Basis of Its Chinese, Tibetan, Sanskrit and Pāli Versions*. Delhi: Motilal Banarsidass Publishers, 2007.

Wallace, Vesna. *Buddhism in Mongolian History, Culture, and Society*. Oxford: Oxford University Press, 2015.

Weinstein, Stanley. *Buddhism under the T'ang*. New York: Cambridge University Press, 1987.

Welch, Holmes. *The Buddhist Revival in China*. Cambridge: Harvard University Press, 1968.

Welch, Holmes. *Buddhism under Mao*. Cambridge: Harvard University Press, 1972.

West, Charles. "Pope Leo of Bourges, Clerical Immunity and the Early Medieval Secular." *Early Medieval Europe* 29.1 (2021): 86–108.

Wickrama, Jayaraj P. "Buddhist Monk Sentenced to Death." *Ceylon Today*, February 22, 2012.

Witte, John. "The Study of Law and Religion in the United States: An Interim Report." *Ecclesiastical Law Journal* 14 (2012): 327–54.

Wu Caiyu 吴才毓. "*Senglü yichan wenti de minfa lichang* 僧侣遗产问题的民法立场." *Fashang yanjiu* 法商研究 5 (2016): 18–28.

Wu Caiyu 吴才毓. "Zaifang senglü yichan de falü wenti 再访僧侣遗产的法律问题." *Dongnan daxue xuebao* 东南大学学报 21.4 (2019): 93–100.

Wu Guoping 吴国平. "Sengren yichan jicheng falü wenti tanjiu 僧人遗产继承法律问题探究." *Fujian Jiangxia xueyuan xuebao* 福建江夏学院学报 1 (2016): 51–61.

Wu Zhaojun 吴昭军. "Sengni yichan chuli de minfa lujing yu caipan yiju 僧尼遗产处理的民法路径与裁判依据." *Zhongguo budongchan fa yanjiu* 中国不动产法研究 2 (2018): 45–58.

Xie Chongguang 謝重光 and Bai Wengu 白文固. *Zhongguo sengguan zhidushi* 中國僧官制度史. Xining: Qinghai renmin chubanshe, 1990.

Xie Chongguang 謝重光. *Zhonggu fojiao sengguan zhidu he shehui shenghuo* 中古佛教僧官制度和社會生活. Beijing: Shangwu yinshuguan, 2009.

Xu Xiaozheng 許效正. "Zhonghua fojiao zonghui (1912–1915) shuping 中華佛教總會(1912–1915) 述評." *Fayin luntan* 法音論壇 4 (2013): 10–15.

Yamazaki Hiroshi 山崎宏. *Shina chūsei bukkyō no tenkai* 支那中世佛教の展開.Tokyo: Shimizu shoten, 1942.

Yan Yaozhong 嚴耀中. *Fojiao jielü yu Zhongguo shehui* 佛教戒律與中國社會. Shanghai: Shanghai guji chubanshe, 2007.

Yang, C. K. *Religion in Chinese Society: A Study of Contemporary Social Functions of Religion and Some of Their Historical Factors*. Berkeley: University of California Press, 1967. First published 1961.

Yang Fenggang. *Religion in China: Survival and Revival under Communist Rule*. Oxford: Oxford University Press, 2011.

Yang Jian 楊健. *Qing wangchao fojiao shiwu guanli* 清王朝佛教事務管理. Beijing: Shehui kexue wenxian chubanshe, 2008.

Yifa. *The Origins of Buddhist Monastic Codes in China: An Annotated Translation and Study of the Chanyuan qinggui*. Honolulu: University of Hawai'i Press, 2009.

Yu, Anthony C. *State and Religion in China: Historic and Textual Perspectives*. Chicago: Open Court, 2005.

Yu Fei 俞飞. "Guofa vs. Fofa 国法 vs 佛法." *Reinmin fayuan bao* 人民法院报, July 23, 2012.

Yu Miao 于淼. "Fangzhang yichan nengfou you qinshu jicheng? Yunnan Yuxi Lingzhao si fangzhang Shi Yongxiu yichan jiufen anli jiexi 方丈遺產能否由親屬繼承？雲南玉溪靈照寺釋永修遺產糾紛案例解析." *Zhongguo zongjiao* 中國宗教 8 (2015): 48–49.

Zhang Haifeng 張海峰. *Tangdai falü yu fojiao* 唐代法律與佛教. Shanghai: Shanghai renmin chubanshe, 2014.

Zhang Jianwen 張建文. "Hanchuan fojiao sengren de yichan jicheng wenti 漢傳佛教僧人的遺產繼承問題." Fojiao wenhua 佛教文化 3 (2009): 85–89.

Zhang Jingzhen 張徑真. "Zhongjing fashi yu Daoseng ge shuwei Zhongguo diyibu zongjiao fadian kaozheng 眾經法式與道僧格孰為中國第一部宗教法典考證." *Fazhi yu jingji* 法制與經濟 1 (2012): 165–66.

Zhang Jingzhen 張徑真. *Falü shijiao xia de Sui Tang fojiao guanli yanjiu* 法律視角下的隋唐佛教管理研究. Beijing: Zhongguo shehui kexue chubanshe, 2018.

Zhang, Qianfan. *The Constitution of China: A Contextual Analysis*. Oxford: Hart Publishing, 2012.

Zhang Yisun 張怡孫. *Zang han da cidian* 藏漢大辭典. 2 vols. Beijing: Minzu chubanshe, 2004.

Zhao Jing 趙晶. *Tiansheng ling yu Tang Song fashi kaolun* 天聖令與唐宋法制考論. Shanghai: Shanghai guji chubanshe, 2014.

Zheng Dong 郑东 (ed.). *Hunyin jiating falü wenti dayi yu anli dianping* 婚姻家庭法律問題與案例點評. Beijing: Gongshang chubanshe, 2001.

Zheng Xianwen 鄭顯文. *Tangdai lüling zhidu yanjiu* 唐代律令制度研究. Beijing: Beijing daxue chubanshe, 2004a.

Zheng Xianwen 鄭顯文. "Tangdai daoseng ge jiqi fuyuan yanjiu 唐代道僧格及其復原研究." *Pumen xuebao* 普門學報 20 (2004b): 137–78.

Zheng Xuelin 鄭學林, Liu Min 劉敏, and Wang Dan 王丹. "Guanyu shiyong Minfa dian jicheng bian de jieshi (1): Ruogan zhongdian wenti de lijie yu shiyong 關於適用民法典繼承編的解釋（一): 若干重點問題的理解與適用." *Renmin sifa* 人民司法 16 (2021): 25–31.

Zinkeisen, Franke. "The Anglo-Saxon Courts of Law." *Political Science Quarterly* 10.1 (1895): 132–44.

Zhou Bozhan 周伯戡. "Bei Wei sengcao zhidu: Jianlun Zhongguo sengguan de qiyuan 北魏僧曹制度考-兼論中國僧官的起源." *Taida lishi xuebao* 台大歷史學報 67 (2021): 183–277.

Zürcher, Erik. *The Buddhist Conquest of China: The Spread and Adaptation of Buddhism n Early Medieval China*. Leiden: Brill, 2007. First edition published 1959.

Index

For the benefit of digital users, indexed terms that span two pages (e.g., 52–53) may, on occasion, appear on only one of those pages.